MR. SCOOTLES™

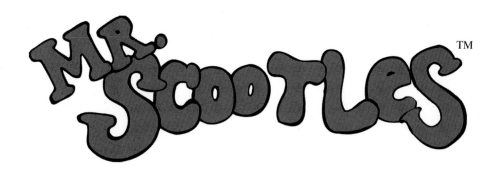

BY

H.C.NOEL

ALTERNA COMICS
WWW.ALTERNACOMICS.COM

PETER SIMETI
PRESIDENT AND PUBLISHER
PUBLISHER@ALTERNACOMICS.COM

ERIN KOHUT
EDITOR-IN-CHIEF
EDITOR_IN_WONDERLAND@YAHOO.COM

ADVERTISING
ADVERTISING@ALTERNACOMICS.COM

READER LETTERS
LETTERS@ALTERNACOMICS.COM

**LICENSING FOR FILM
OR MERCHANDISING**
LICENSING@ALTERNACOMICS.COM
-OR- CONTACT A SPECIFIC CREATOR

ISBN: 978-1-934985-03-8

MR. SCOOTLES
VOLUME 1
ORIGINALLY PUBLISHED IN MR. SCOOTLES ISSUES 1-5
2008 FIRST PRINTING
PUBLISHED BY ALTERNA COMICS, INC. OFFICE OF PUBLICATION: 23 TRUMPET LANE, LEVITTOWN, NY 11756.
ALTERNA COMICS AND ITS LOGOS ARE ™ AND © 2007-2008 ALTERNA COMICS, INC. ALL RIGHTS RESERVED.
MR. SCOOTLES AND ALL RELATED CHARACTERS ARE ™ AND © 2003-2008 H.C. NOEL. ALL RIGHTS RESERVED.
THE STORY PRESENTED IN THIS PUBLICATION IS FICTIONAL. ANY SIMILARITIES TO EVENTS OR PERSONS LIVING
OR DEAD IS PURELY COINCIDENTAL. WITH THE EXCEPTION OF ARTWORK USED FOR REVIEW PURPOSES, NO
PORTION OF THIS PUBLICATION MAY BE REPRODUCED BY ANY MEANS WITHOUT THE EXPRESSED WRITTEN
CONSENT OF THE COPYRIGHT HOLDER.
PRINTED IN USA.

INTRODUCTION

One of the most enjoyable things about being a comic reader is when you discover something new. Something no one has ever done before and you have the thrill of not knowing where the story is going. Its originality sets it apart from other books and you're eager to tell people about the treasure you've found.

If you're reading this, then you've found that kind of comic.

Mr. Scootles takes you on a roller coaster ride and doesn't let you off until you're about to soil your pants. Howie Noeldechen has created a truly unique world for Mr. Scootles and his cast. It's a funny, dark and twisted world, much like it's creator.

I had the pleasure of meeting Howie at the MOCCA Comic Con in NYC a few years back. He was there doing free sketches of Mr. Scootles for anyone who purchased his book and complaining about the lack of air conditioning (Howie doesn't like to sweat apparently). I was new to the world of self-publishing and it was nice to meet a fellow publisher and talk shop. After chatting for a bit, I bought copies of Mr. Scootles #1 and 2. I wasn't sure what to expect from the book, but I had an idea it would be different. Right from the start I was impressed. Howie had managed to take an animated cartoon character and bring him into the real world in a way that was neither cute nor stupid. He did what only Howie would think of; he connected him to Hell. Somehow a 1930's animated film had become a portal to Hell and in watching it, college students Jason and Kelly, had opened the portal and released Mr. Scootles from his cartoon limbo and sent him to Hell. That was just the first issue.

From there it's all down hill for the cigar smoking Scootles and the two poor college students. They end up having to deal with the psycho Professor Sentalanqua, the Gatekeeper from Hell and Victor, the Angel of War and we're left trying to figure out what the heck "The Curse of Weston Lang, Jr." (Mr. Scootles' creator) is and how this all fits together.

And then there's Howie's styling artwork. Not many writers are able to express themselves visually and there are even fewer who can pull it off. But just as Dave Sim was to Cerebus and Jeff Smith was to Bone, I don't think any other artist could do Mr. Scootles justice but Howie. It's the perfect mix of animation and realistic comic art that just feels right. Who else could illustrate the Pig Beast, the Web of Bones, Mr. Scootles and still make a sexy Gatekeeper from Hell? Only Howie I tell you and he's not even paying me to say that. (Though his wife, Shelley, offered me free beer and said she'd let me win next time we played pool.)

As with any great story, Mr. Scootles leaves you wanting more and hopefully this first trade collection is just the first of many adventures. I'm eager to see where Howie takes Mr. Scootles and all the characters in his universe and I believe anyone reading this will too.

Now quit reading this and enjoy the book!

—**Rich Bernatovech**

Rich Bernatovech is the creator and writer of the comic book series Sentinels. He is currently working on many more amazing projects including Neverminds.

Mr. Scootles
otherwise known as
Mr. Scootles vs. The Inferno
sometimes referred to as
Weston Lang, Jr: A Biography
and known in England as
Sir Scootles The First

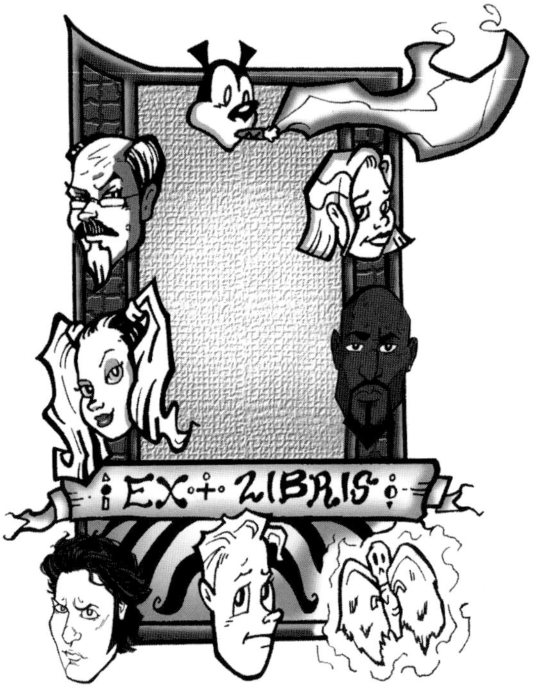
EX + LIBRIS

This book is for my family and my friends.

Acknowledgements:

Thank you to Shelley Noeldechen.
Without you, this tale would not have been completed. I love you.

Thank you to my friends who modeled and provided inspiration:
Shelley Noeldechen, Howard and Jean Noeldechen, Victor Guest, Chad Sartori, and Chuck Gemelli.

For more information visit www.hcnoel.com and write to info@hcnoel.com.

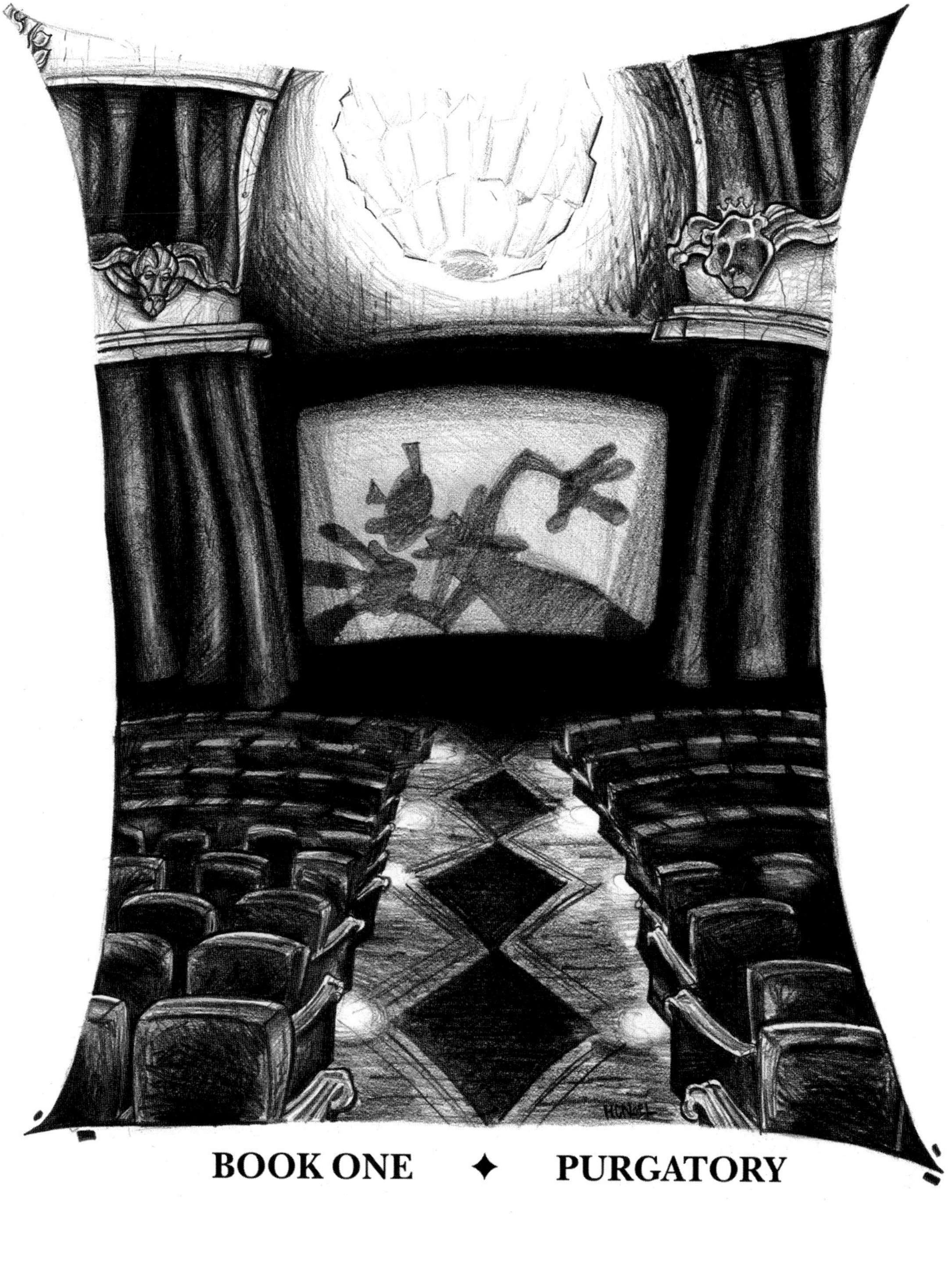

BOOK ONE ✦ PURGATORY

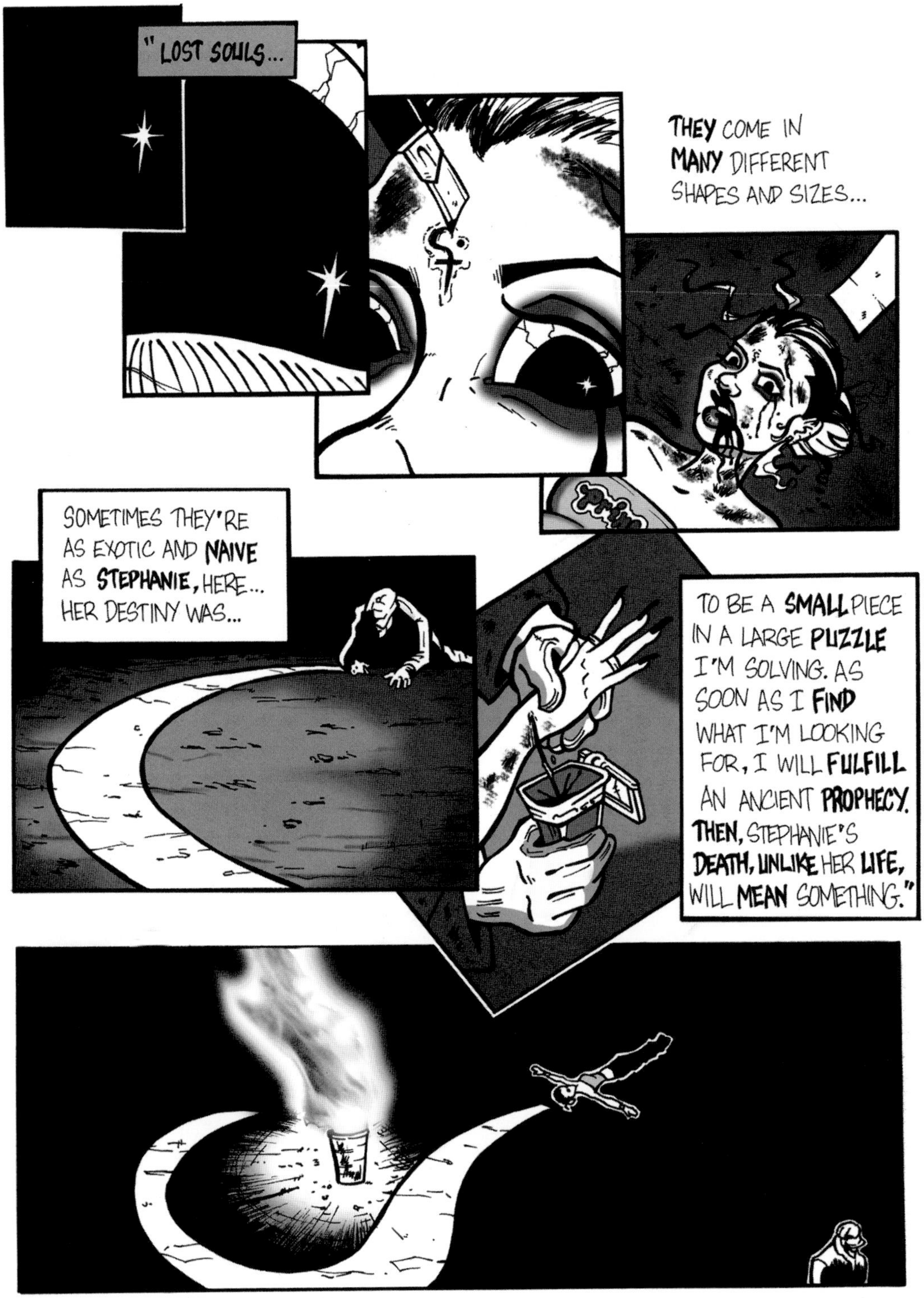
"LOST SOULS...
THEY COME IN MANY DIFFERENT SHAPES AND SIZES...
SOMETIMES THEY'RE AS EXOTIC AND NAIVE AS STEPHANIE, HERE... HER DESTINY WAS...
TO BE A SMALL PIECE IN A LARGE PUZZLE I'M SOLVING. AS SOON AS I FIND WHAT I'M LOOKING FOR, I WILL FULFILL AN ANCIENT PROPHECY. THEN, STEPHANIE'S DEATH, UNLIKE HER LIFE, WILL MEAN SOMETHING."

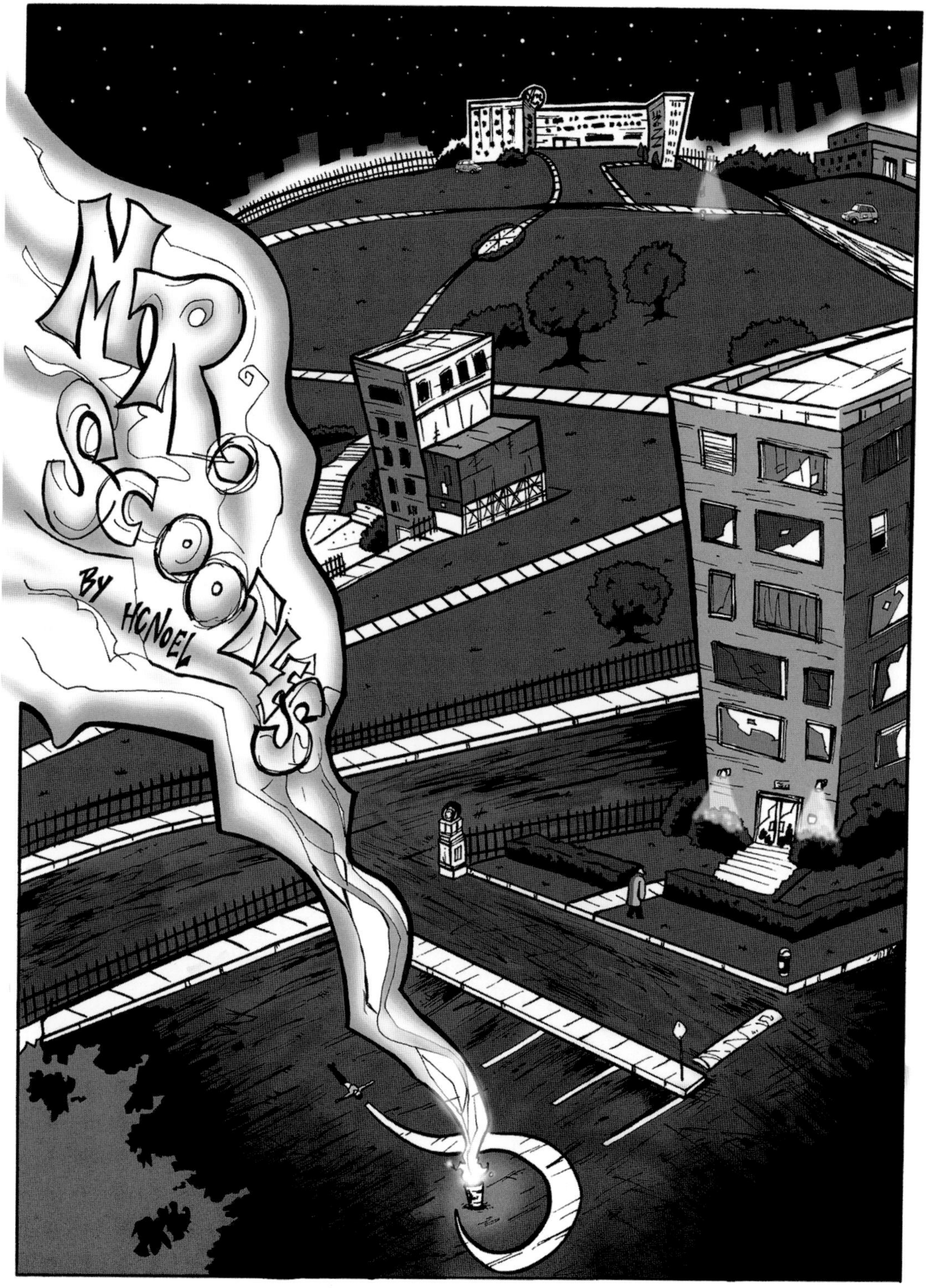
MR SCOONES
BY HCNOEL

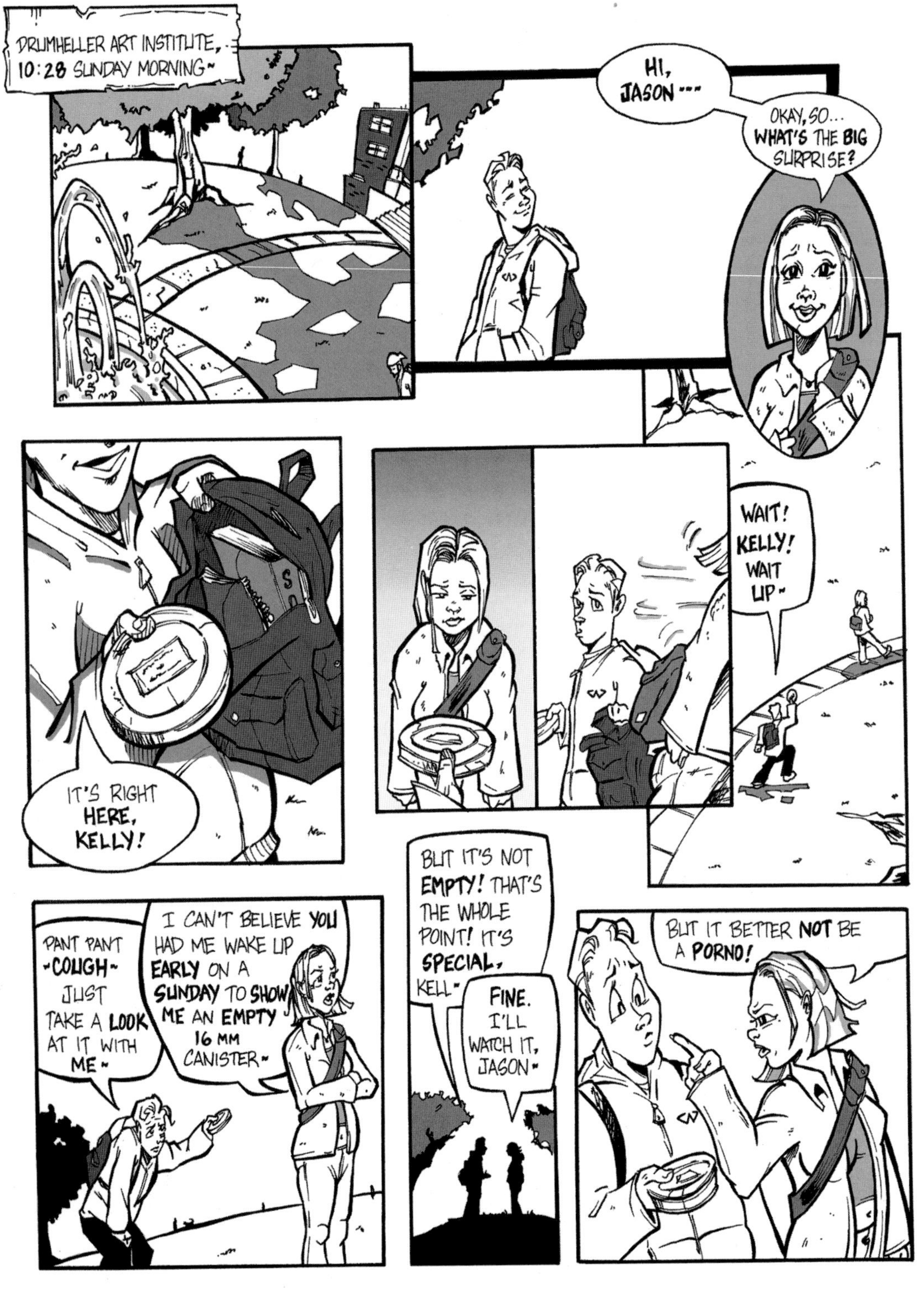
DRUMHELLER ART INSTITUTE, 10:28 SUNDAY MORNING~
HI, JASON~~~
OKAY, SO... WHAT'S THE BIG SURPRISE?
IT'S RIGHT HERE, KELLY!
WAIT! KELLY! WAIT UP~
PANT PANT ~COUGH~ JUST TAKE A LOOK AT IT WITH ME~
I CAN'T BELIEVE YOU HAD ME WAKE UP EARLY ON A SUNDAY TO SHOW ME AN EMPTY 16 MM CANISTER~
BUT IT'S NOT EMPTY! THAT'S THE WHOLE POINT! IT'S SPECIAL, KELL~
FINE. I'LL WATCH IT, JASON~
BUT IT BETTER NOT BE A PORNO!

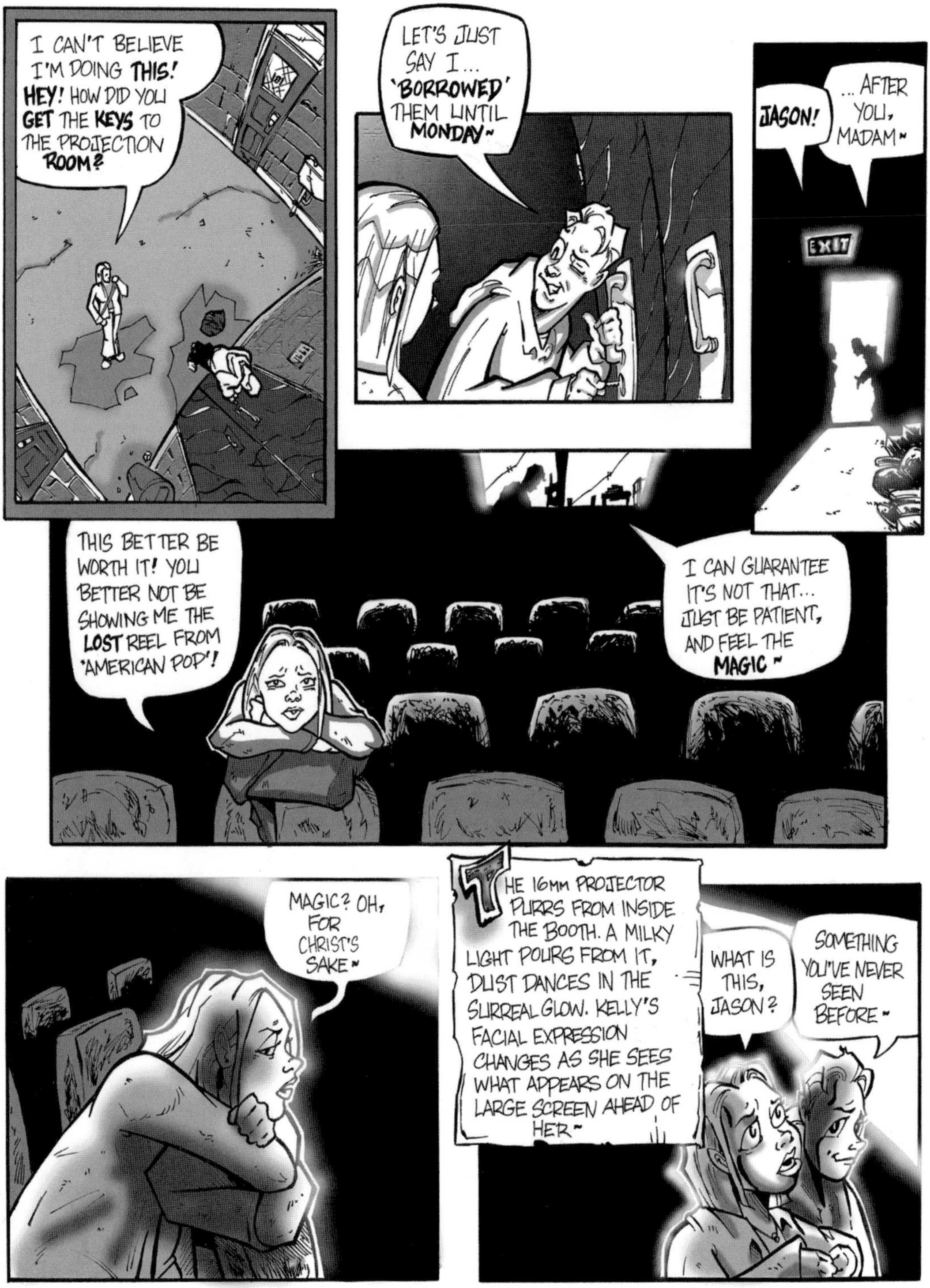
I CAN'T BELIEVE I'M DOING THIS! HEY! HOW DID YOU GET THE KEYS TO THE PROJECTION ROOM?
LET'S JUST SAY I... 'BORROWED' THEM UNTIL MONDAY~
JASON!
... AFTER YOU, MADAM~
EXIT
THIS BETTER BE WORTH IT! YOU BETTER NOT BE SHOWING ME THE LOST REEL FROM 'AMERICAN POP'!
I CAN GUARANTEE IT'S NOT THAT... JUST BE PATIENT, AND FEEL THE MAGIC~
MAGIC? OH, FOR CHRIST'S SAKE~
THE 16MM PROJECTOR PURRS FROM INSIDE THE BOOTH. A MILKY LIGHT POURS FROM IT, DUST DANCES IN THE SURREAL GLOW. KELLY'S FACIAL EXPRESSION CHANGES AS SHE SEES WHAT APPEARS ON THE LARGE SCREEN AHEAD OF HER~
WHAT IS THIS, JASON?
SOMETHING YOU'VE NEVER SEEN BEFORE~

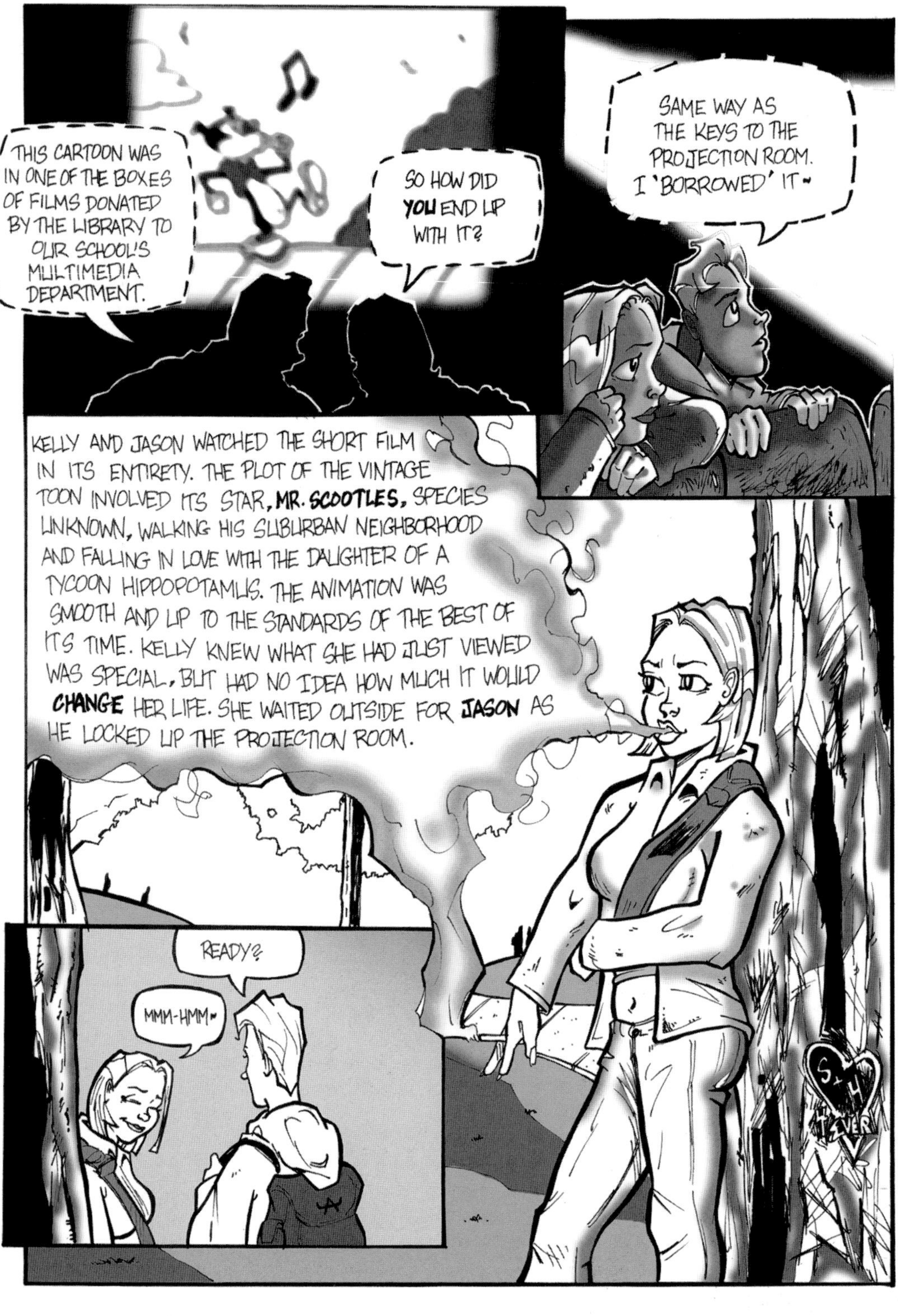
THIS CARTOON WAS IN ONE OF THE BOXES OF FILMS DONATED BY THE LIBRARY TO OUR SCHOOL'S MULTIMEDIA DEPARTMENT.
SO HOW DID YOU END UP WITH IT?
SAME WAY AS THE KEYS TO THE PROJECTION ROOM. I 'BORROWED' IT…
KELLY AND JASON WATCHED THE SHORT FILM IN ITS ENTIRETY. THE PLOT OF THE VINTAGE TOON INVOLVED ITS STAR, MR. SCOOTLES, SPECIES UNKNOWN, WALKING HIS SUBURBAN NEIGHBORHOOD AND FALLING IN LOVE WITH THE DAUGHTER OF A TYCOON HIPPOPOTAMUS. THE ANIMATION WAS SMOOTH AND UP TO THE STANDARDS OF THE BEST OF ITS TIME. KELLY KNEW WHAT SHE HAD JUST VIEWED WAS SPECIAL, BUT HAD NO IDEA HOW MUCH IT WOULD CHANGE HER LIFE. SHE WAITED OUTSIDE FOR JASON AS HE LOCKED UP THE PROJECTION ROOM.
READY?
MMM-HMM…
S + H
4EVER

CAMPUS LIBRARY~

"JASON?"

"YES, KELLY?"

WHAT'S SO SPECIAL ABOUT MR. SCOOTLES?

WELL, MY FELLOW ANIMATION MAJOR, THAT'S WHAT WE'RE ABOUT TO FIND OUT...

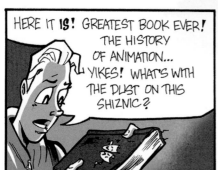

HERE IT **IS**! GREATEST BOOK EVER! THE HISTORY OF ANIMATION... YIKES! WHAT'S WITH THE DUST ON THIS SHIZNIC?

HELLO?!? WE DO GO TO ART SCHOOL... I BET HALF THE CAMPUS DOESN'T EVEN KNOW WE HAVE A **LIBRARY!**

HEY! THERE'S OUR GUY~

CHECK THIS OUT, KELL... "MR. SCOOTLES WAS ONE OF THE MOST POPULAR CHARACTERS OF THE EARLY 1930'S. HOWEVER HE COMPLETELY DISAPPEARED FROM ANIMATION FOLLOWING THE SUICIDE OF HIS CREATOR, WESTON LANG, JR." HMMM... DOESN'T SAY ANYTHING ELSE...

THERE'S NOTHING MUCH AFTER SUICIDE, JASON... EXCEPT FOR THE DECOMPOSING~

YOU THINK OLD FORGOTTEN CREATIONS LIKE SCOOTLES HAVE AN AFTERLIFE?

"MAYBE THEY GET REINCARNATED AS GREETING CARD ILLUSTRATIONS~"

"GOD, I HOPE NOT, THAT SOUNDS LIKE HELL TO ME..."

WELL, AS LONG AS WE REMEMBER MR. SCOOTLES, HE'LL ALWAYS BE ALIVE... ESPECIALLY WITH THE FILM REEL YOU HAVE...

YEAH, I BET WESTON LANG, JR. WOULD BE PROUD~

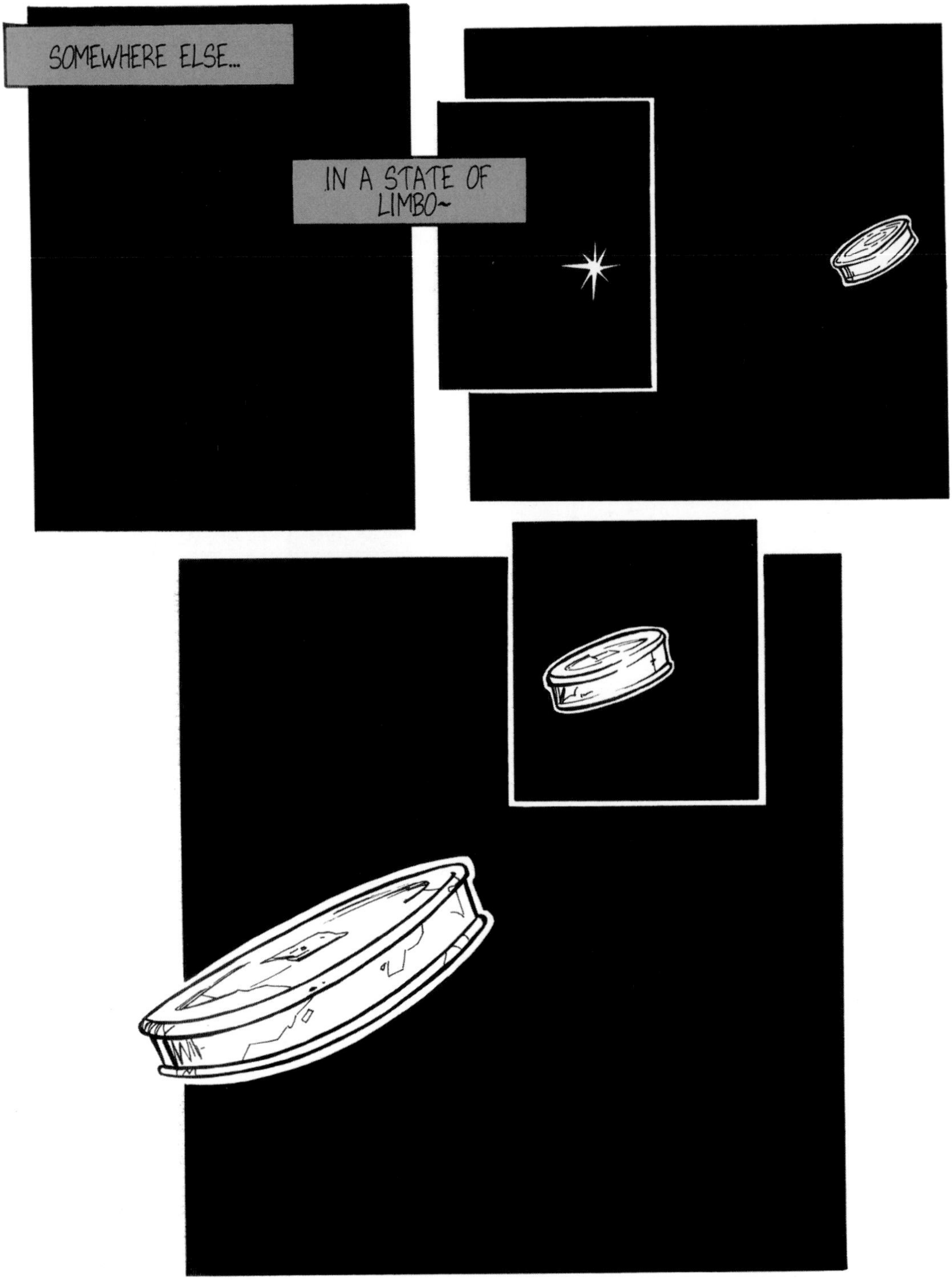
SOMEWHERE ELSE...
IN A STATE OF LIMBO~

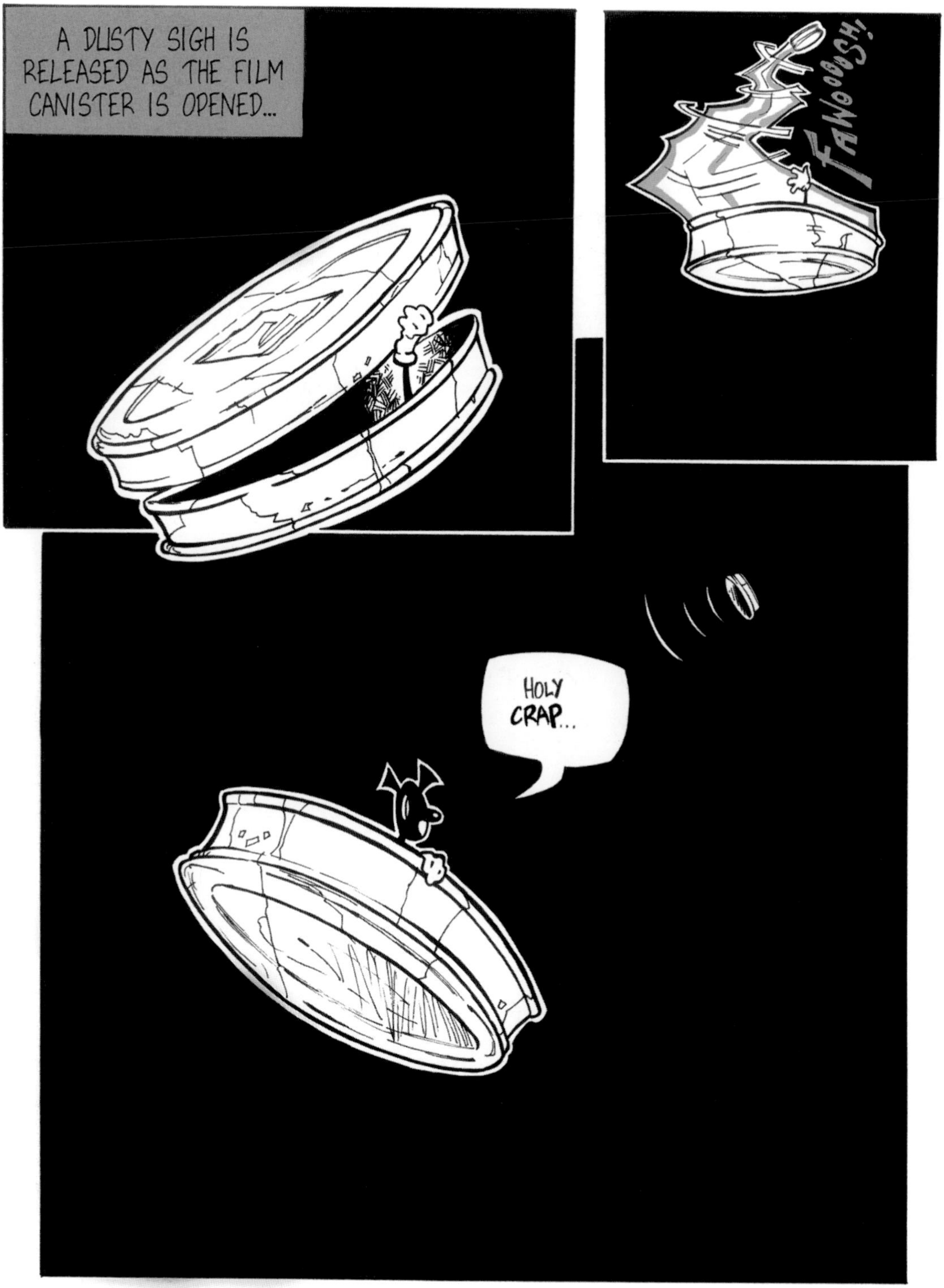
A DUSTY SIGH IS RELEASED AS THE FILM CANISTER IS OPENED...
FAWOOOOSH!
HOLY CRAP...

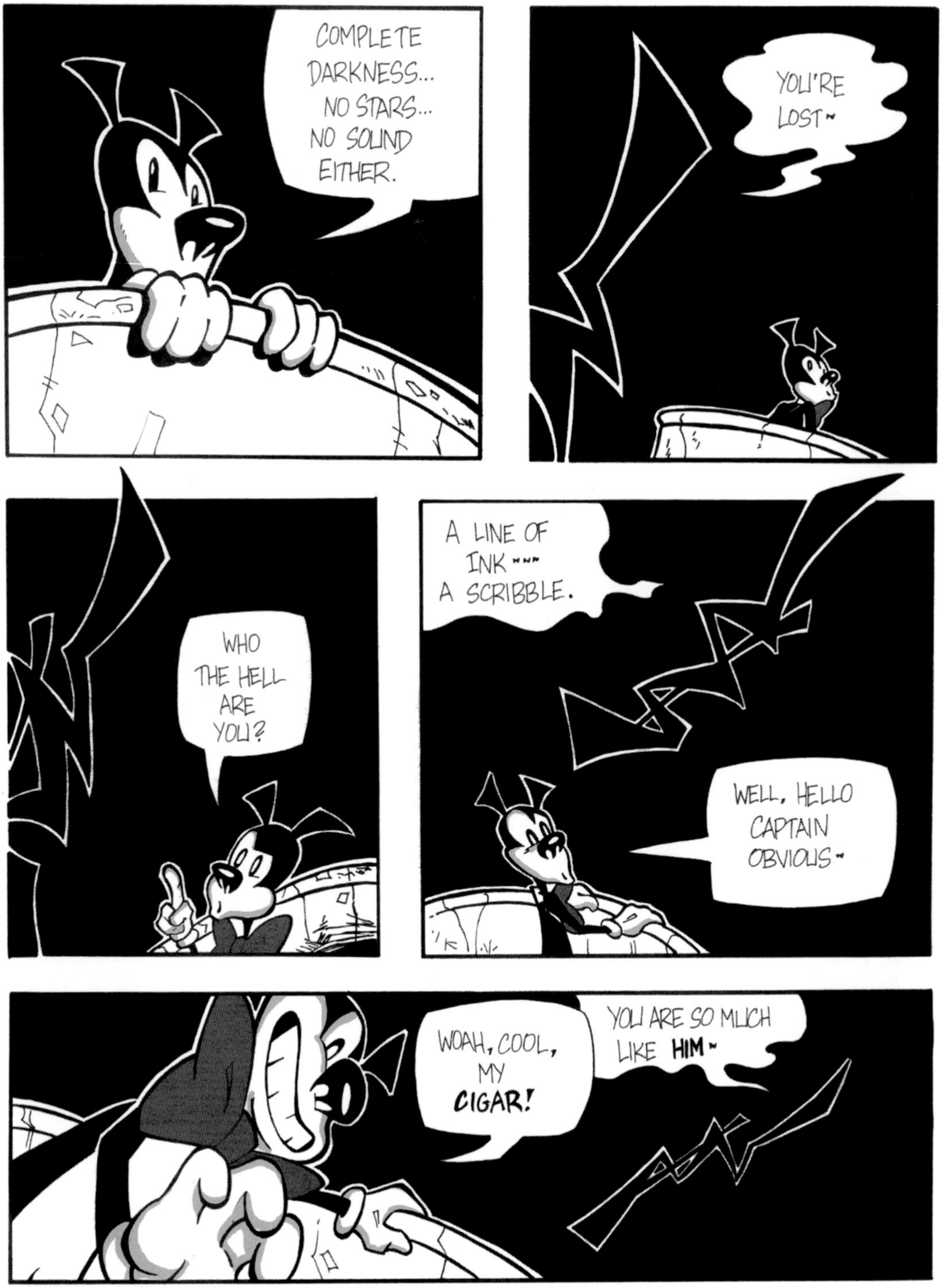
COMPLETE DARKNESS... NO STARS... NO SOUND EITHER.
YOU'RE LOST~
WHO THE HELL ARE YOU?
A LINE OF INK~~~ A SCRIBBLE.
WELL, HELLO CAPTAIN OBVIOUS~
WOAH, COOL, MY CIGAR!
YOU ARE SO MUCH LIKE HIM~

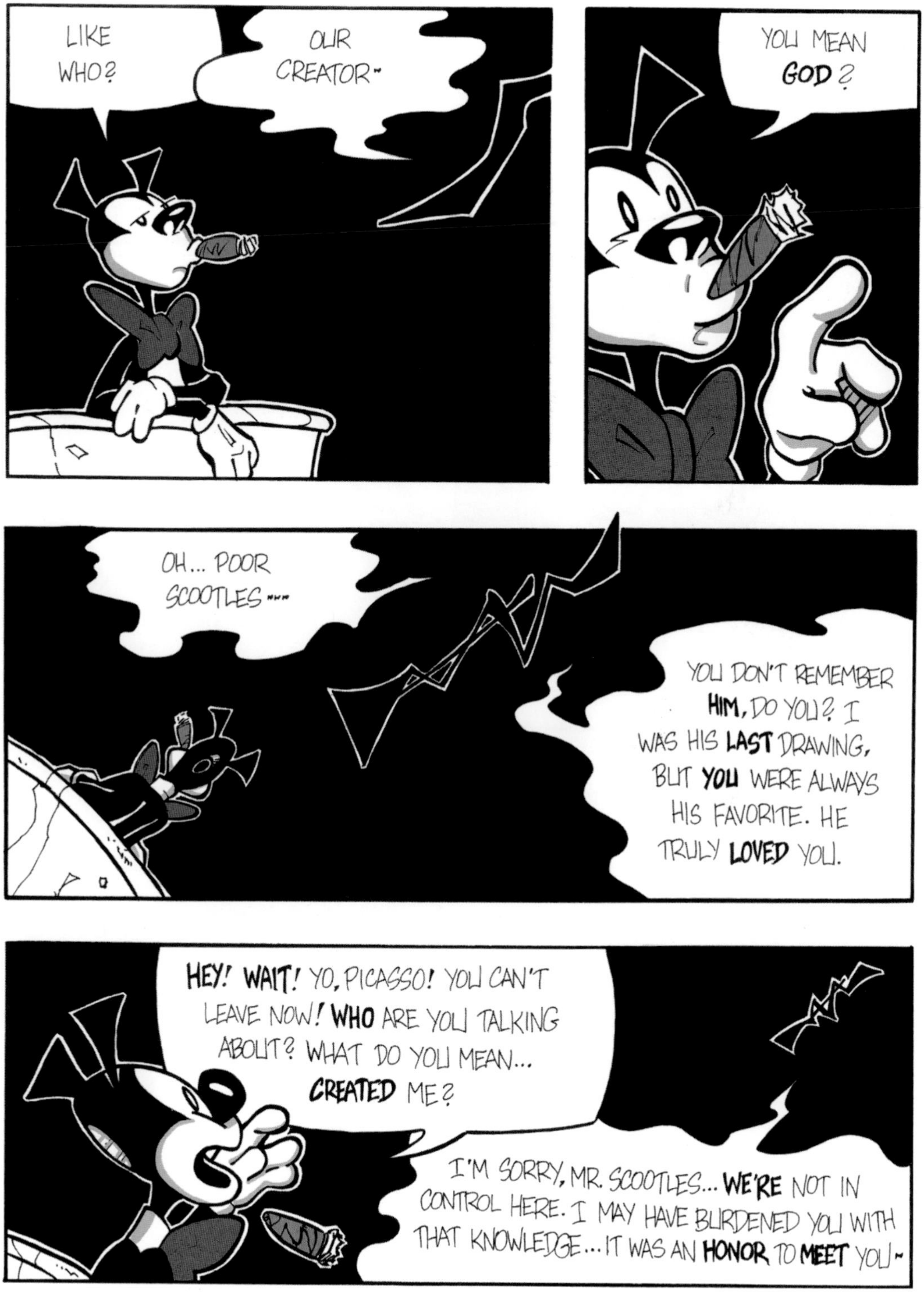

LIKE WHO?
OUR CREATOR~
YOU MEAN GOD?
OH... POOR SCOOTLES~~~
YOU DON'T REMEMBER HIM, DO YOU? I WAS HIS LAST DRAWING, BUT YOU WERE ALWAYS HIS FAVORITE. HE TRULY LOVED YOU.
HEY! WAIT! YO, PICASSO! YOU CAN'T LEAVE NOW! WHO ARE YOU TALKING ABOUT? WHAT DO YOU MEAN... CREATED ME?
I'M SORRY, MR. SCOOTLES... WE'RE NOT IN CONTROL HERE. I MAY HAVE BURDENED YOU WITH THAT KNOWLEDGE... IT WAS AN HONOR TO MEET YOU~

PICASSO?
RUMBLE
WHAT THE~
CCCRAK!
AAAAAIIIGHH!

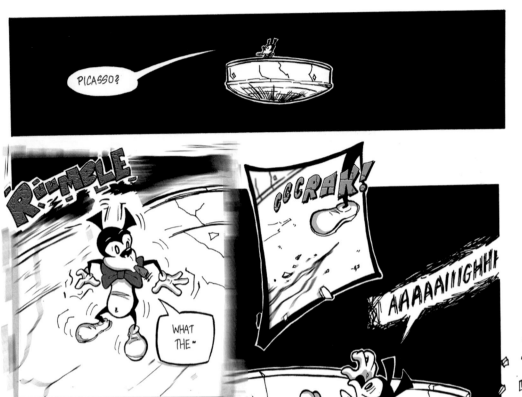

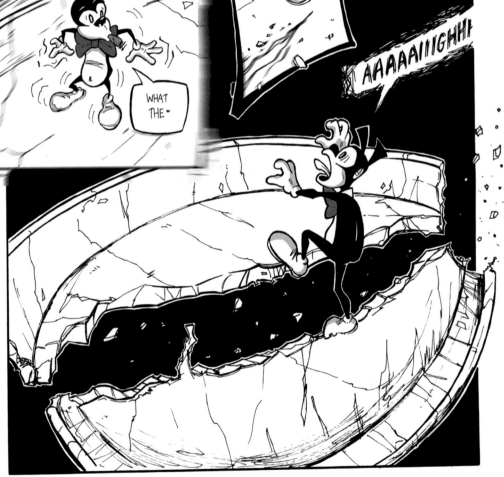

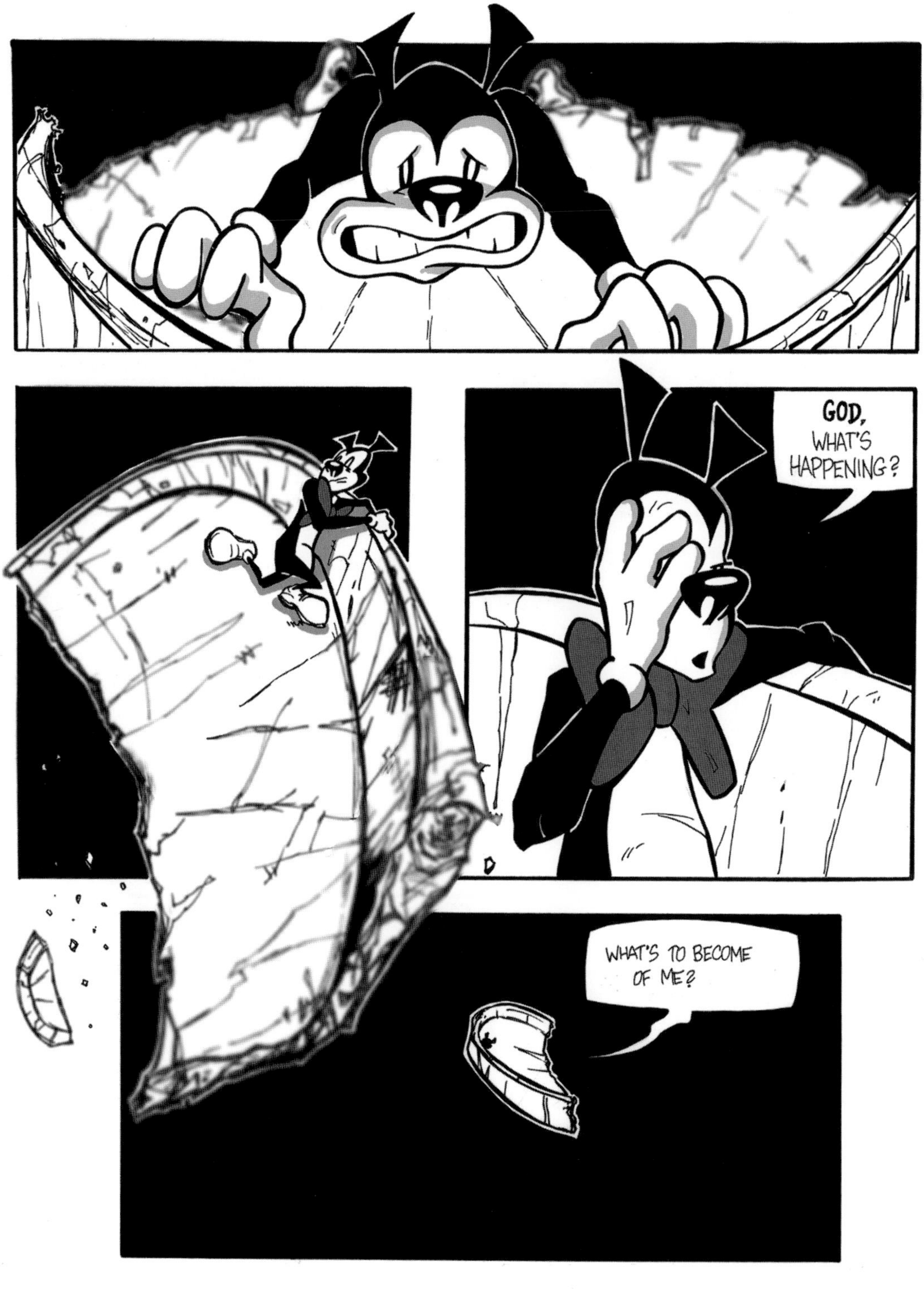
GOD, WHAT'S HAPPENING?
WHAT'S TO BECOME OF ME?

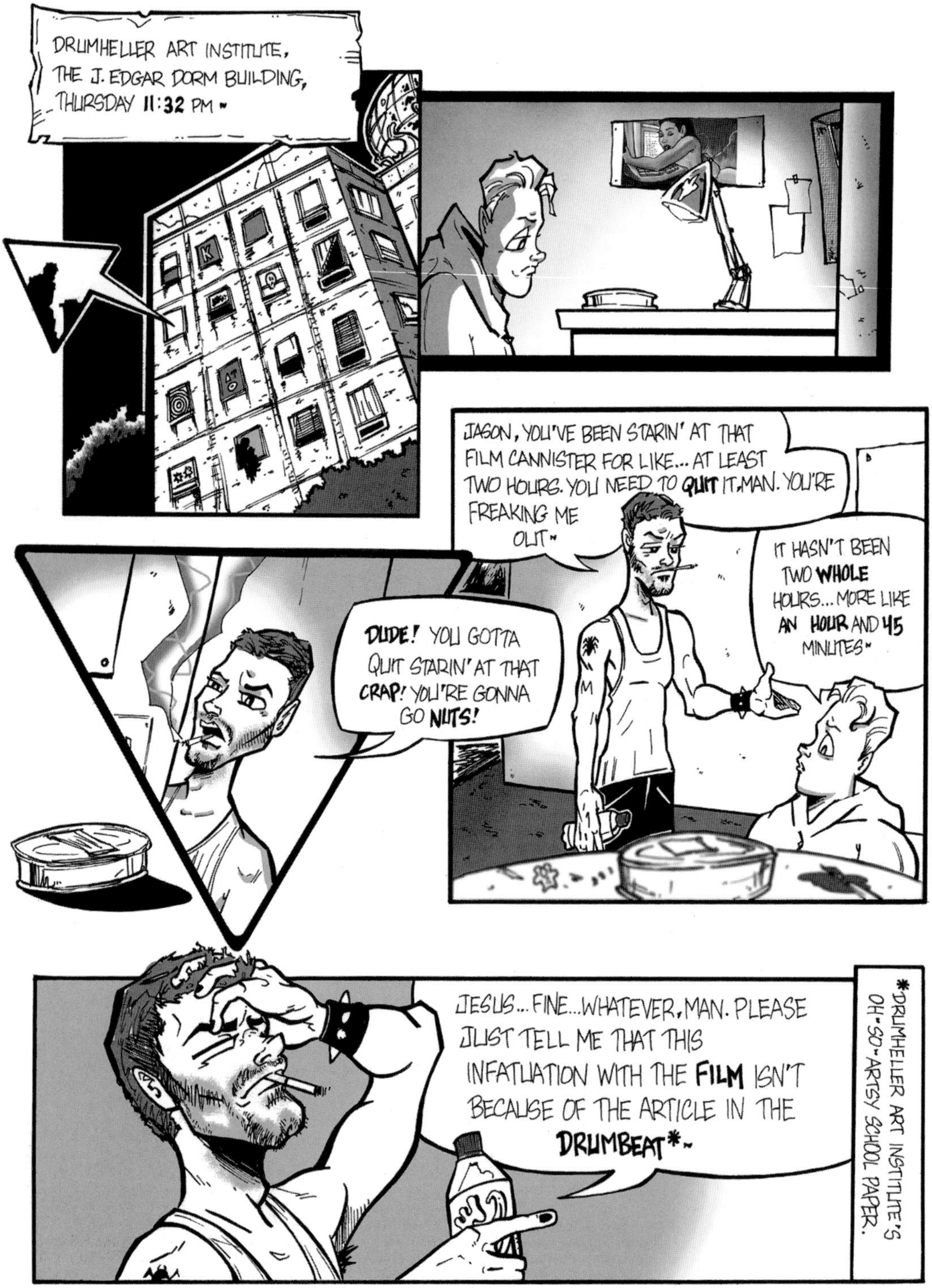
DRUMHELLER ART INSTITUTE, THE J. EDGAR DORM BUILDING, THURSDAY 11:32 PM~
JASON, YOU'VE BEEN STARIN' AT THAT FILM CANNISTER FOR LIKE... AT LEAST TWO HOURS. YOU NEED TO QUIT IT, MAN. YOU'RE FREAKING ME OUT~
IT HASN'T BEEN TWO WHOLE HOURS... MORE LIKE AN HOUR AND 45 MINUTES~
DUDE! YOU GOTTA QUIT STARIN' AT THAT CRAP! YOU'RE GONNA GO NUTS!
JESUS... FINE... WHATEVER, MAN. PLEASE JUST TELL ME THAT THIS INFATUATION WITH THE FILM ISN'T BECAUSE OF THE ARTICLE IN THE DRUMBEAT*~
*DRUMHELLER ART INSTITUTE'S OH-SO-ARTSY SCHOOL PAPER.

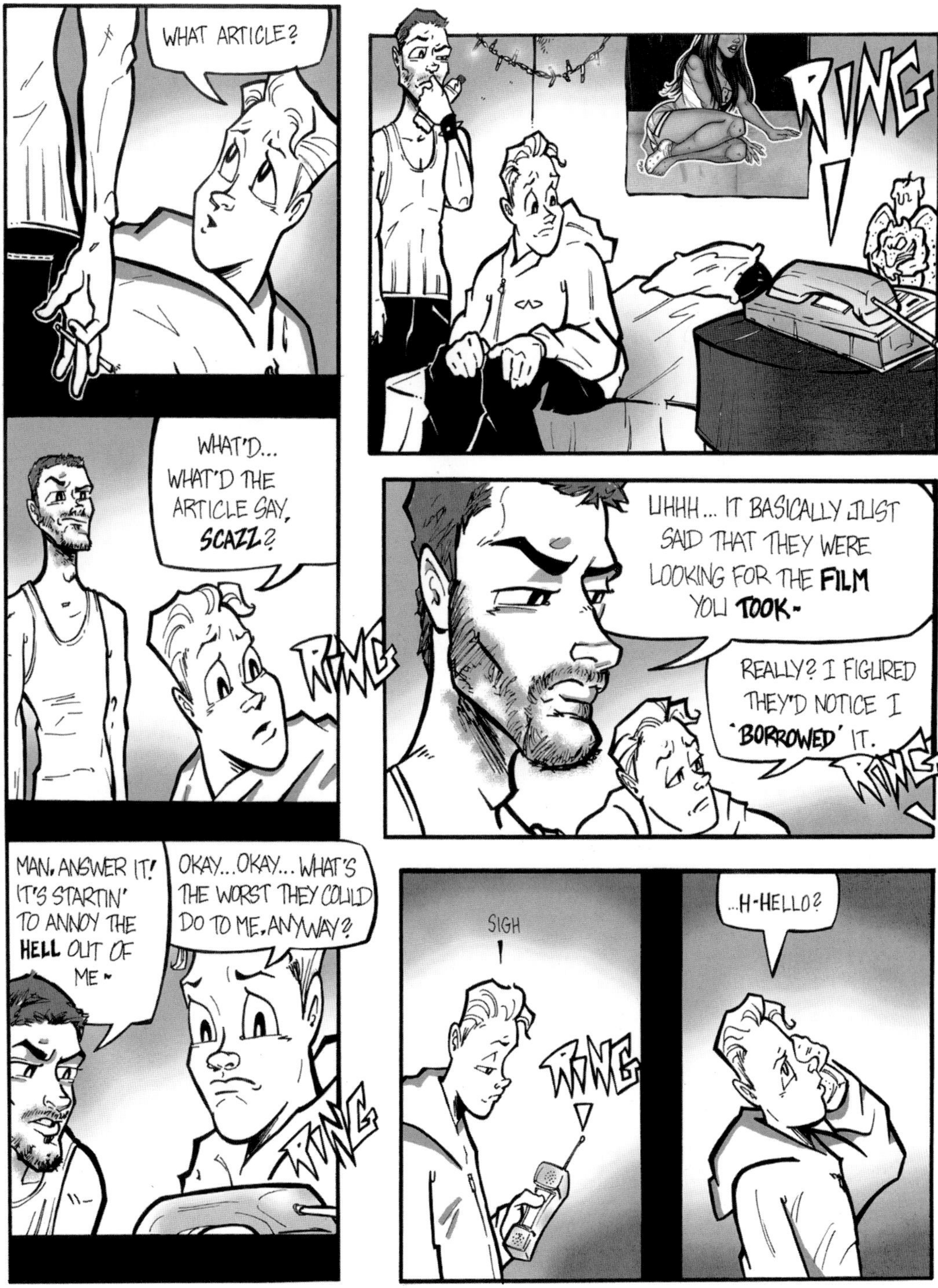
WHAT ARTICLE?
RING!
WHAT'D... WHAT'D THE ARTICLE SAY, SCAZZ?
RING
UHHH... IT BASICALLY JUST SAID THAT THEY WERE LOOKING FOR THE FILM YOU TOOK-
REALLY? I FIGURED THEY'D NOTICE I 'BORROWED' IT.
RING
MAN, ANSWER IT! IT'S STARTIN' TO ANNOY THE HELL OUT OF ME-
OKAY... OKAY... WHAT'S THE WORST THEY COULD DO TO ME, ANYWAY?
RING
SIGH
RING!
...H-HELLO?

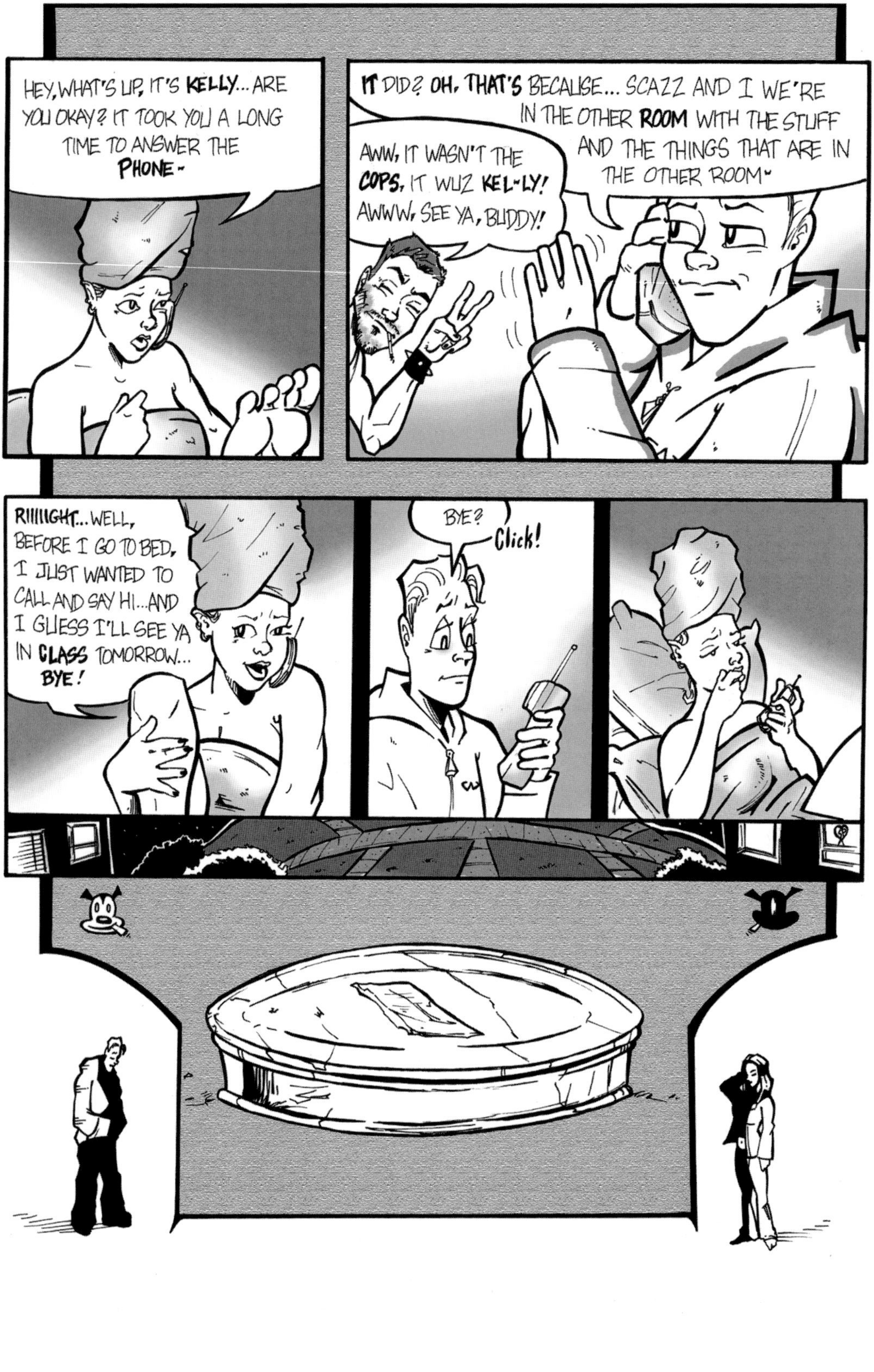

HEY, WHAT'S UP, IT'S KELLY... ARE YOU OKAY? IT TOOK YOU A LONG TIME TO ANSWER THE PHONE~
IT DID? OH, THAT'S BECAUSE... SCAZZ AND I WE'RE IN THE OTHER ROOM WITH THE STUFF AND THE THINGS THAT ARE IN THE OTHER ROOM~
AWW, IT WASN'T THE COPS, IT WUZ KEL~LY! AWWW, SEE YA, BUDDY!
RIIIIGHT... WELL, BEFORE I GO TO BED, I JUST WANTED TO CALL AND SAY HI... AND I GUESS I'LL SEE YA IN CLASS TOMORROW... BYE!
BYE?
Click!

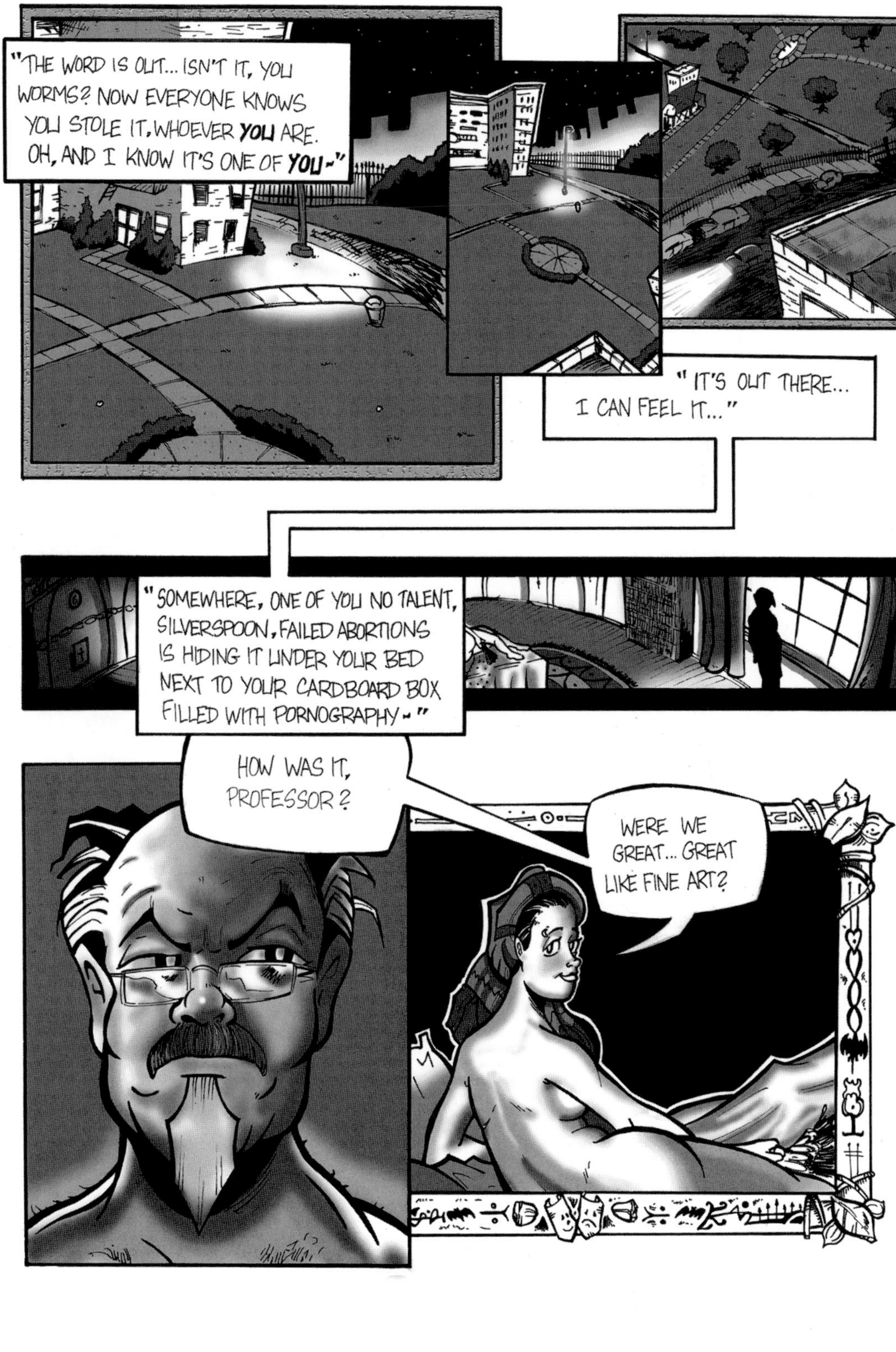
"THE WORD IS OUT... ISN'T IT, YOU WORMS? NOW EVERYONE KNOWS YOU STOLE IT, WHOEVER **YOU** ARE. OH, AND I KNOW IT'S ONE OF **YOU**."
"IT'S OUT THERE... I CAN FEEL IT..."
"SOMEWHERE, ONE OF YOU NO TALENT, SILVERSPOON, FAILED ABORTIONS IS HIDING IT UNDER YOUR BED NEXT TO YOUR CARDBOARD BOX FILLED WITH PORNOGRAPHY."
HOW WAS IT, PROFESSOR?
WERE WE GREAT... GREAT LIKE FINE ART?

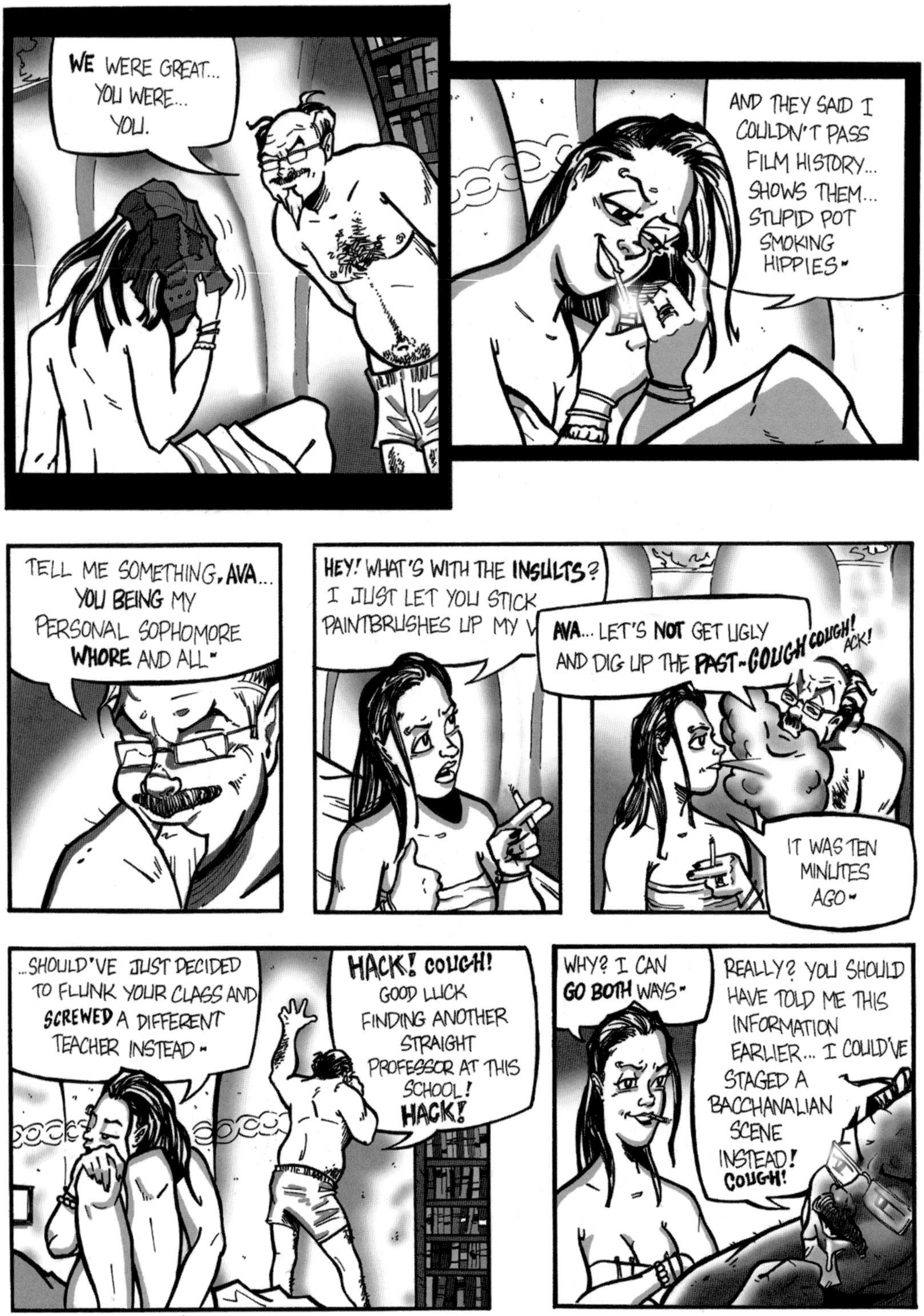
WE WERE GREAT... YOU WERE... YOU.
AND THEY SAID I COULDN'T PASS FILM HISTORY... SHOWS THEM... STUPID POT SMOKING HIPPIES—
TELL ME SOMETHING, AVA... YOU BEING MY PERSONAL SOPHOMORE WHORE AND ALL—
HEY! WHAT'S WITH THE INSULTS? I JUST LET YOU STICK PAINTBRUSHES UP MY V
AVA... LET'S NOT GET UGLY AND DIG UP THE PAST—COUGH COUGH! ACK!
IT WAS TEN MINUTES AGO—
...SHOULD'VE JUST DECIDED TO FLUNK YOUR CLASS AND SCREWED A DIFFERENT TEACHER INSTEAD—
HACK! COUGH! GOOD LUCK FINDING ANOTHER STRAIGHT PROFESSOR AT THIS SCHOOL! HACK!
WHY? I CAN GO BOTH WAYS—
REALLY? YOU SHOULD HAVE TOLD ME THIS INFORMATION EARLIER... I COULD'VE STAGED A BACCHANALIAN SCENE INSTEAD! COUGH!

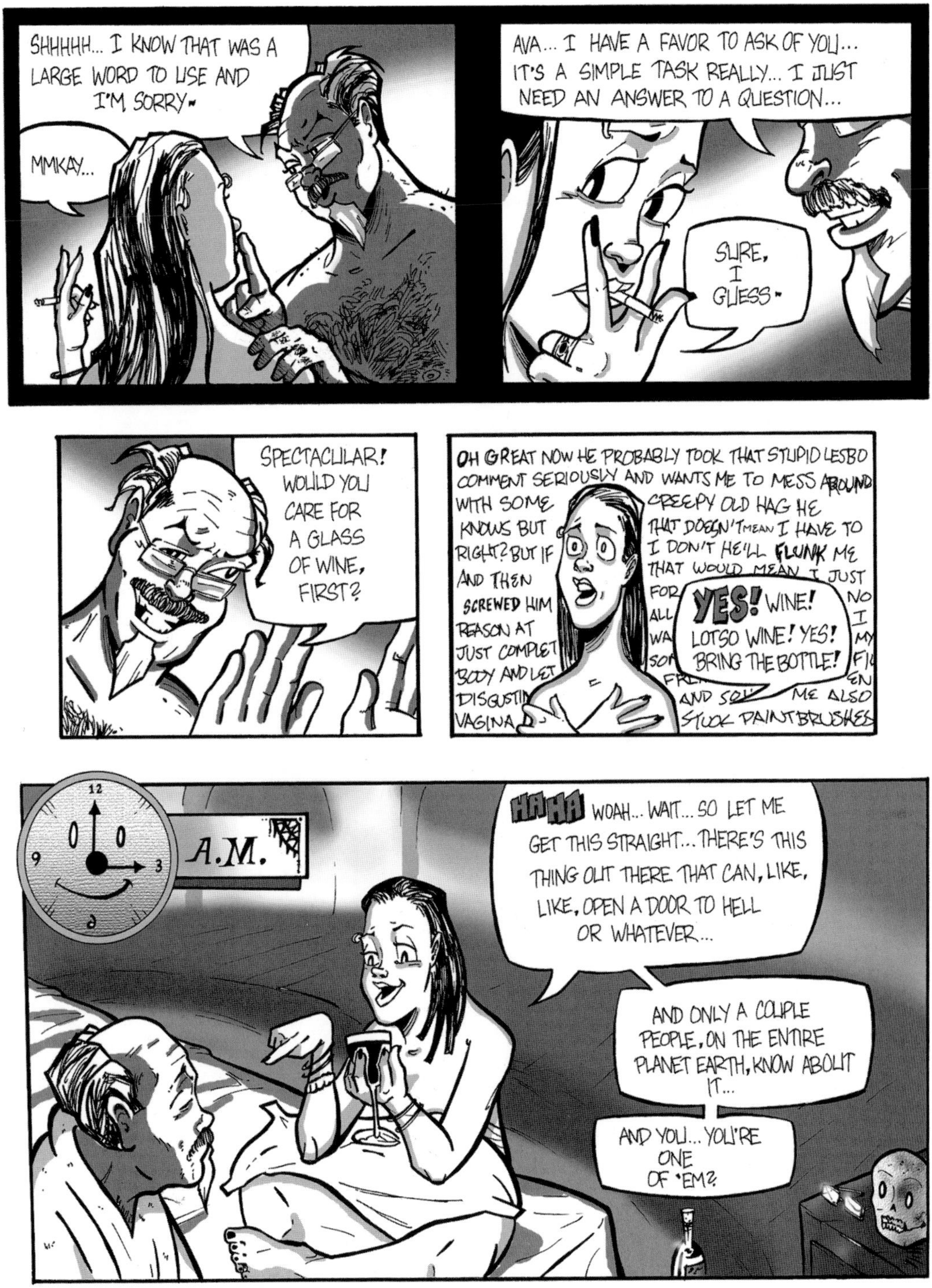

SHHHHH... I KNOW THAT WAS A LARGE WORD TO USE AND I'M SORRY...
MMKAY...
AVA... I HAVE A FAVOR TO ASK OF YOU... IT'S A SIMPLE TASK REALLY... I JUST NEED AN ANSWER TO A QUESTION...
SURE, I GUESS...
SPECTACULAR! WOULD YOU CARE FOR A GLASS OF WINE, FIRST?
OH GREAT NOW HE PROBABLY TOOK THAT STUPID LESBO COMMENT SERIOUSLY AND WANTS ME TO MESS AROUND
WITH SOME
CREEPY OLD HAG HE
KNOWS BUT
THAT DOESN'T MEAN I HAVE TO
RIGHT? BUT IF
I DON'T HE'LL FLUNK ME
AND THEN
THAT WOULD MEAN I JUST
SCREWED HIM
REASON AT
BODY AND LET
VAGINA
ME ALSO
STUCK PAINTBRUSHES
YES! WINE! LOTSO WINE! YES! BRING THE BOTTLE!
A.M.
HA HA WOAH... WAIT... SO LET ME GET THIS STRAIGHT... THERE'S THIS THING OUT THERE THAT CAN, LIKE, LIKE, OPEN A DOOR TO HELL OR WHATEVER...
AND ONLY A COUPLE PEOPLE, ON THE ENTIRE PLANET EARTH, KNOW ABOUT IT...
AND YOU... YOU'RE ONE OF 'EM?

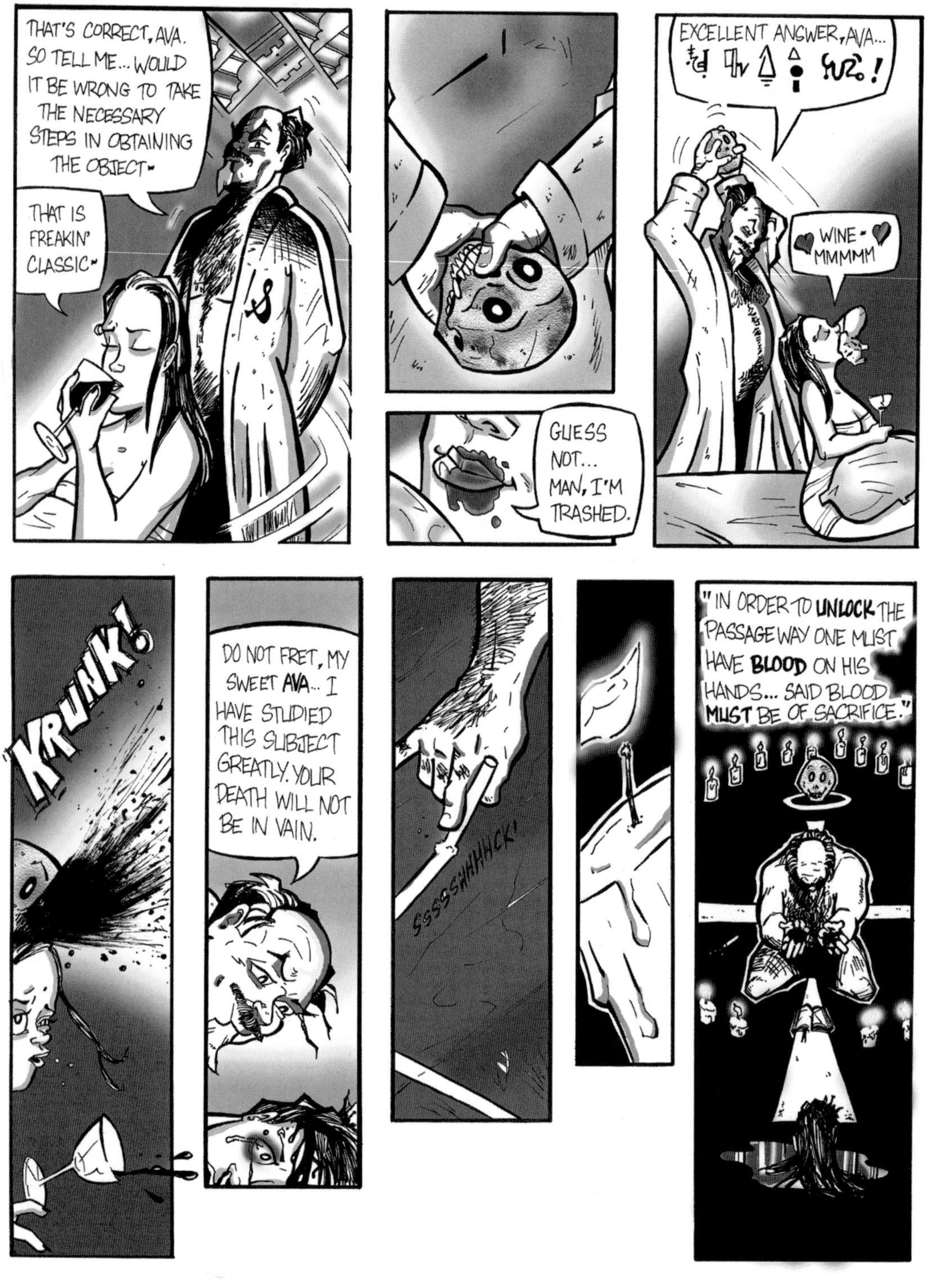
THAT'S CORRECT, AVA. SO TELL ME... WOULD IT BE WRONG TO TAKE THE NECESSARY STEPS IN OBTAINING THE OBJECT…
THAT IS FREAKIN' CLASSIC…
GUESS NOT... MAN, I'M TRASHED.
EXCELLENT ANSWER, AVA...
WINE-MMMMM
KRUNK!
DO NOT FRET, MY SWEET AVA... I HAVE STUDIED THIS SUBJECT GREATLY. YOUR DEATH WILL NOT BE IN VAIN.
SSSSSWHHHCK!
"IN ORDER TO UNLOCK THE PASSAGE WAY ONE MUST HAVE BLOOD ON HIS HANDS... SAID BLOOD MUST BE OF SACRIFICE."

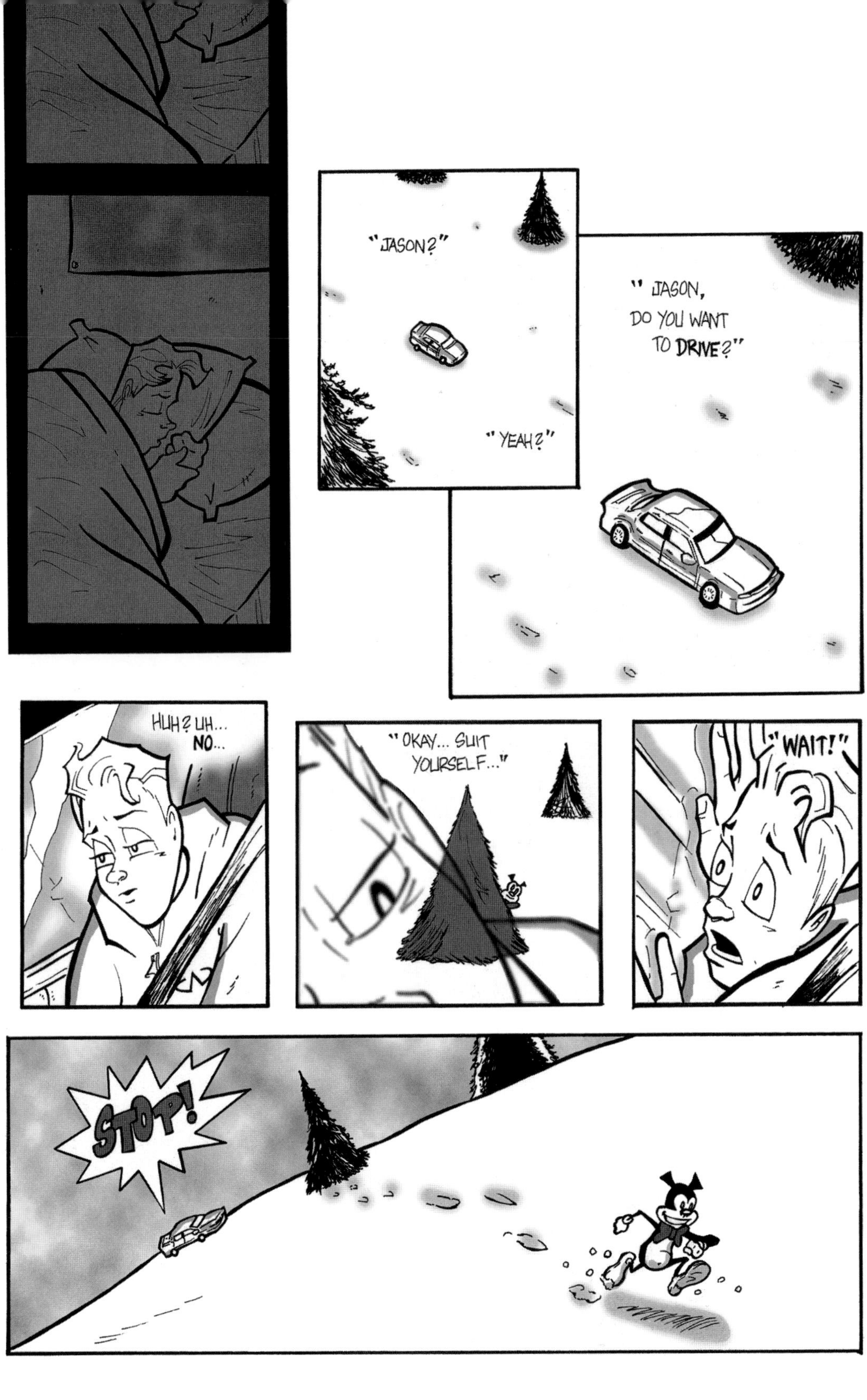
"JASON?"
"YEAH?"
"JASON, DO YOU WANT TO DRIVE?"
HUH? UH... NO...
"OKAY... SUIT YOURSELF..."
"WAIT!"
STOP!

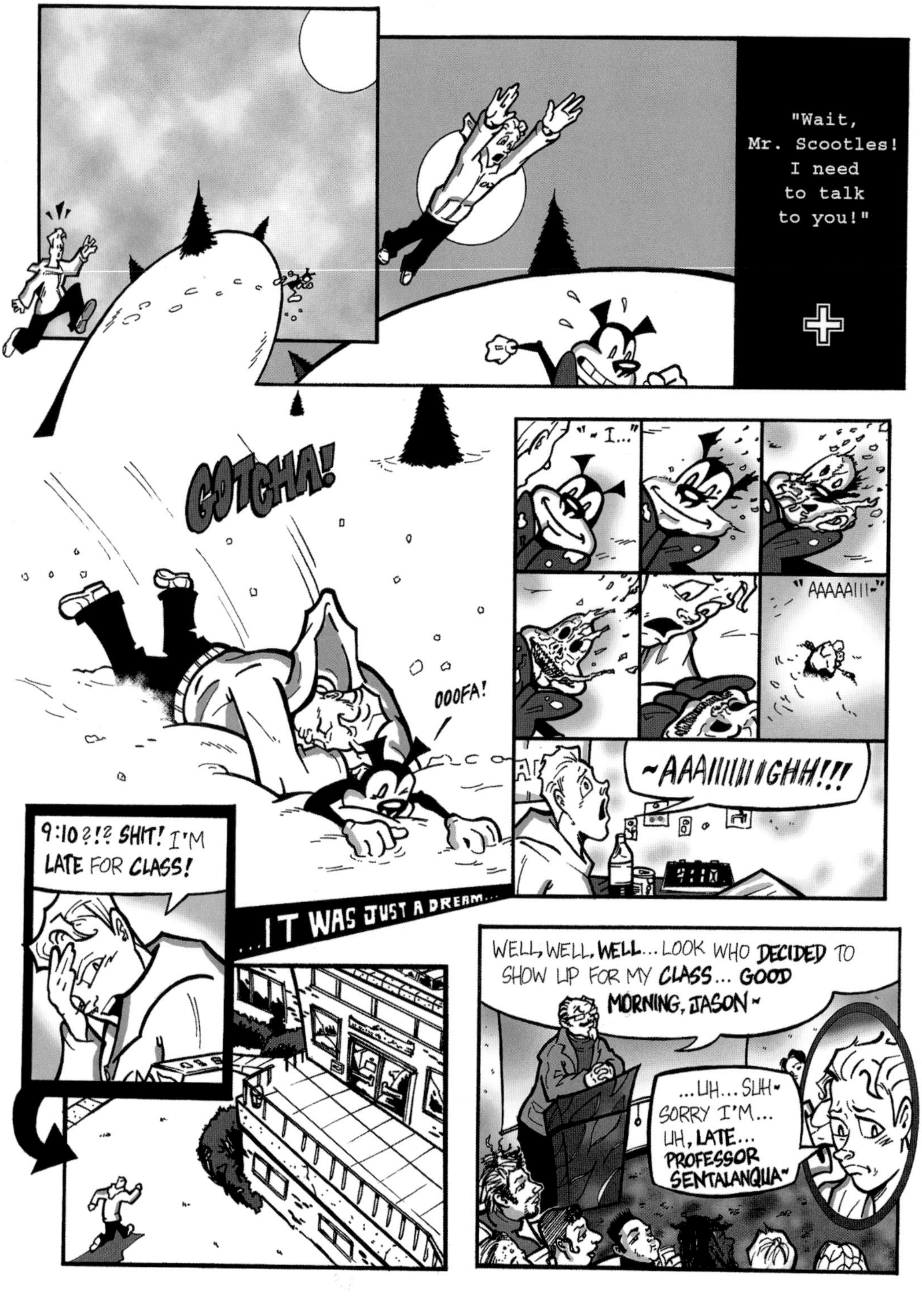
"Wait, Mr. Scootles! I need to talk to you!"
GOTCHA!
OOOFA!
"I..."
"AAAAAIII-"
~AAAIIIIIIIGHH!!!
9:10?!? SHIT! I'M LATE FOR CLASS!
...IT WAS JUST A DREAM...
WELL, WELL, WELL... LOOK WHO DECIDED TO SHOW UP FOR MY CLASS... GOOD MORNING, JASON~
...UH... SUH~ SORRY I'M... UH, LATE... PROFESSOR SENTALANQUA~

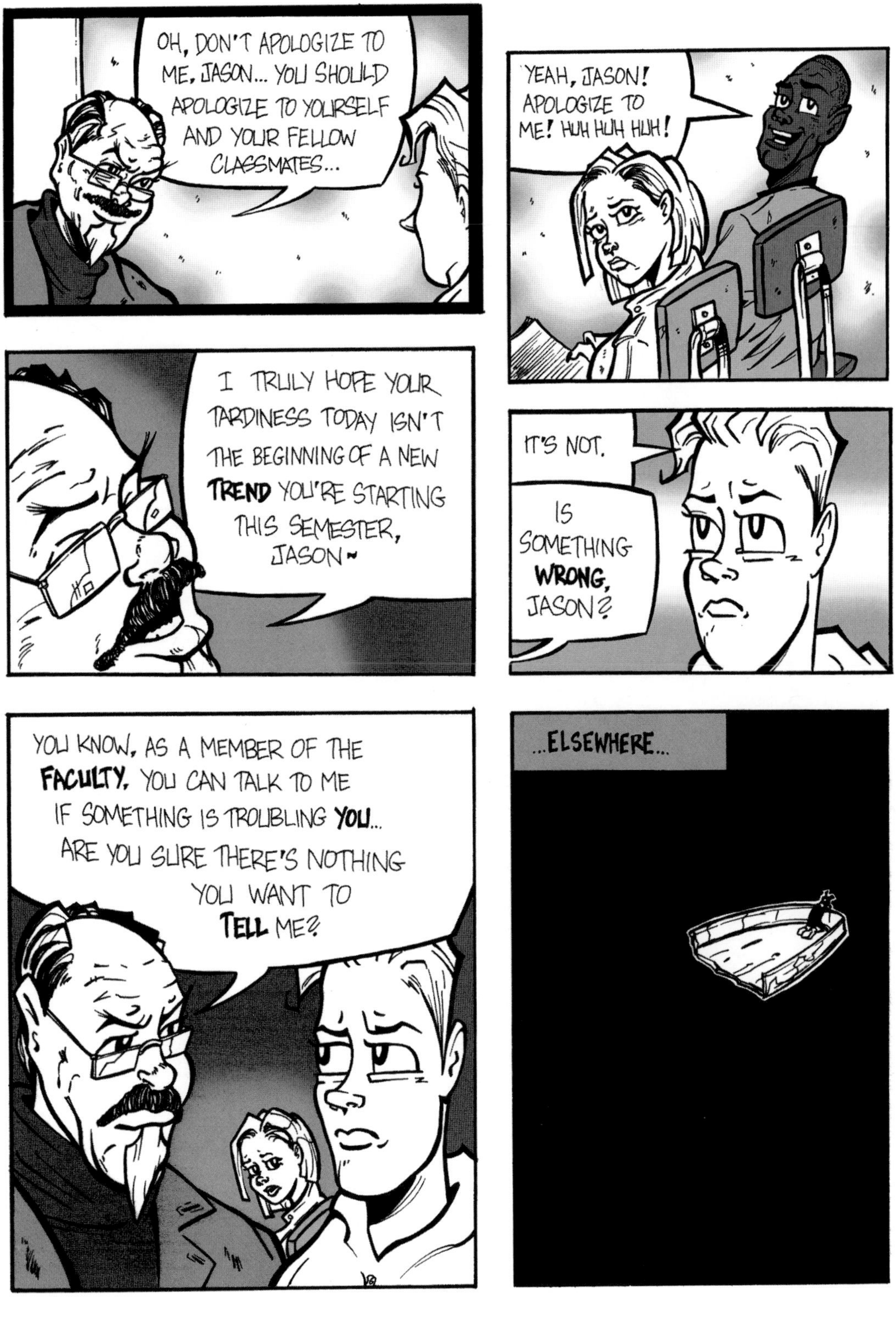
OH, DON'T APOLOGIZE TO ME, JASON... YOU SHOULD APOLOGIZE TO YOURSELF AND YOUR FELLOW CLASSMATES...
YEAH, JASON! APOLOGIZE TO ME! HUH HUH HUH!
I TRULY HOPE YOUR TARDINESS TODAY ISN'T THE BEGINNING OF A NEW TREND YOU'RE STARTING THIS SEMESTER, JASON~
IT'S NOT.
IS SOMETHING WRONG, JASON?
YOU KNOW, AS A MEMBER OF THE FACULTY, YOU CAN TALK TO ME IF SOMETHING IS TROUBLING YOU... ARE YOU SURE THERE'S NOTHING YOU WANT TO TELL ME?
...ELSEWHERE...

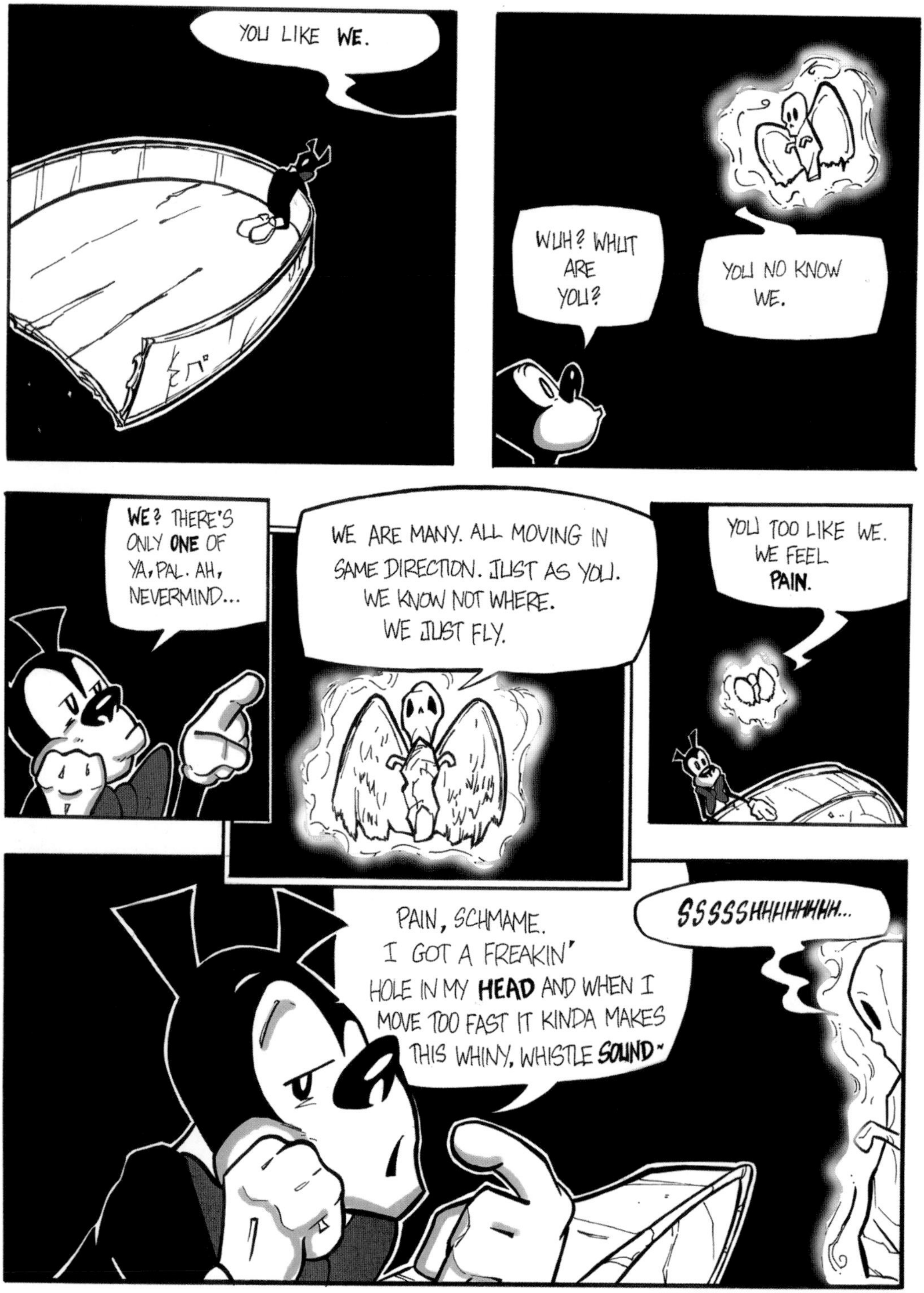

YOU LIKE WE.
WUH? WHUT ARE YOU?
YOU NO KNOW WE.
WE? THERE'S ONLY ONE OF YA, PAL. AH, NEVERMIND...
WE ARE MANY. ALL MOVING IN SAME DIRECTION. JUST AS YOU. WE KNOW NOT WHERE. WE JUST FLY.
YOU TOO LIKE WE. WE FEEL PAIN.
PAIN, SCHMAME. I GOT A FREAKIN' HOLE IN MY HEAD AND WHEN I MOVE TOO FAST IT KINDA MAKES THIS WHINY, WHISTLE SOUND~
SSSSSHHHHHHH...

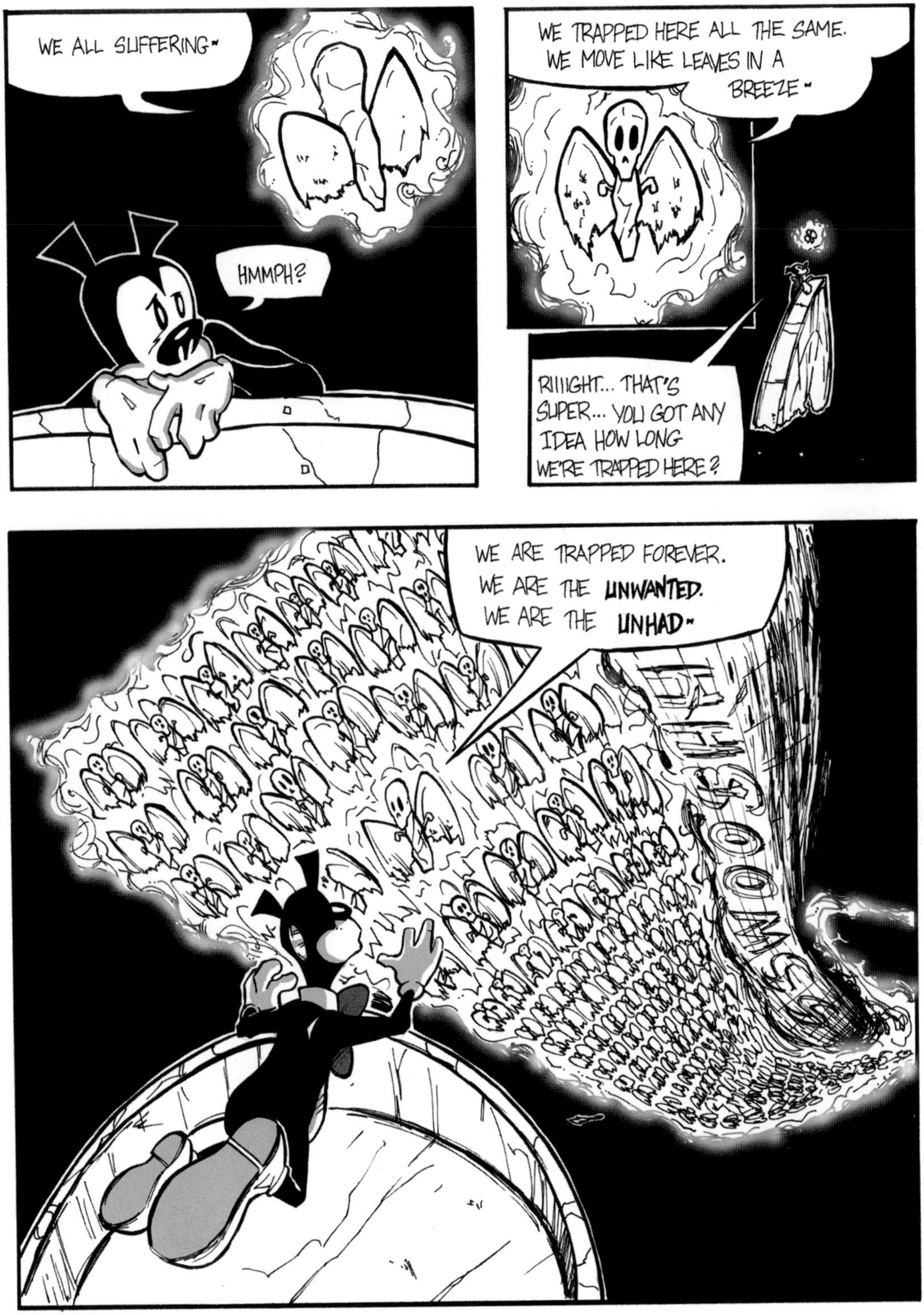
WE ALL SUFFERING~
HMMPH?
WE TRAPPED HERE ALL THE SAME. WE MOVE LIKE LEAVES IN A BREEZE~
RIIIIGHT... THAT'S SUPER... YOU GOT ANY IDEA HOW LONG WE'RE TRAPPED HERE?
WE ARE TRAPPED FOREVER. WE ARE THE UNWANTED. WE ARE THE UNHAD~

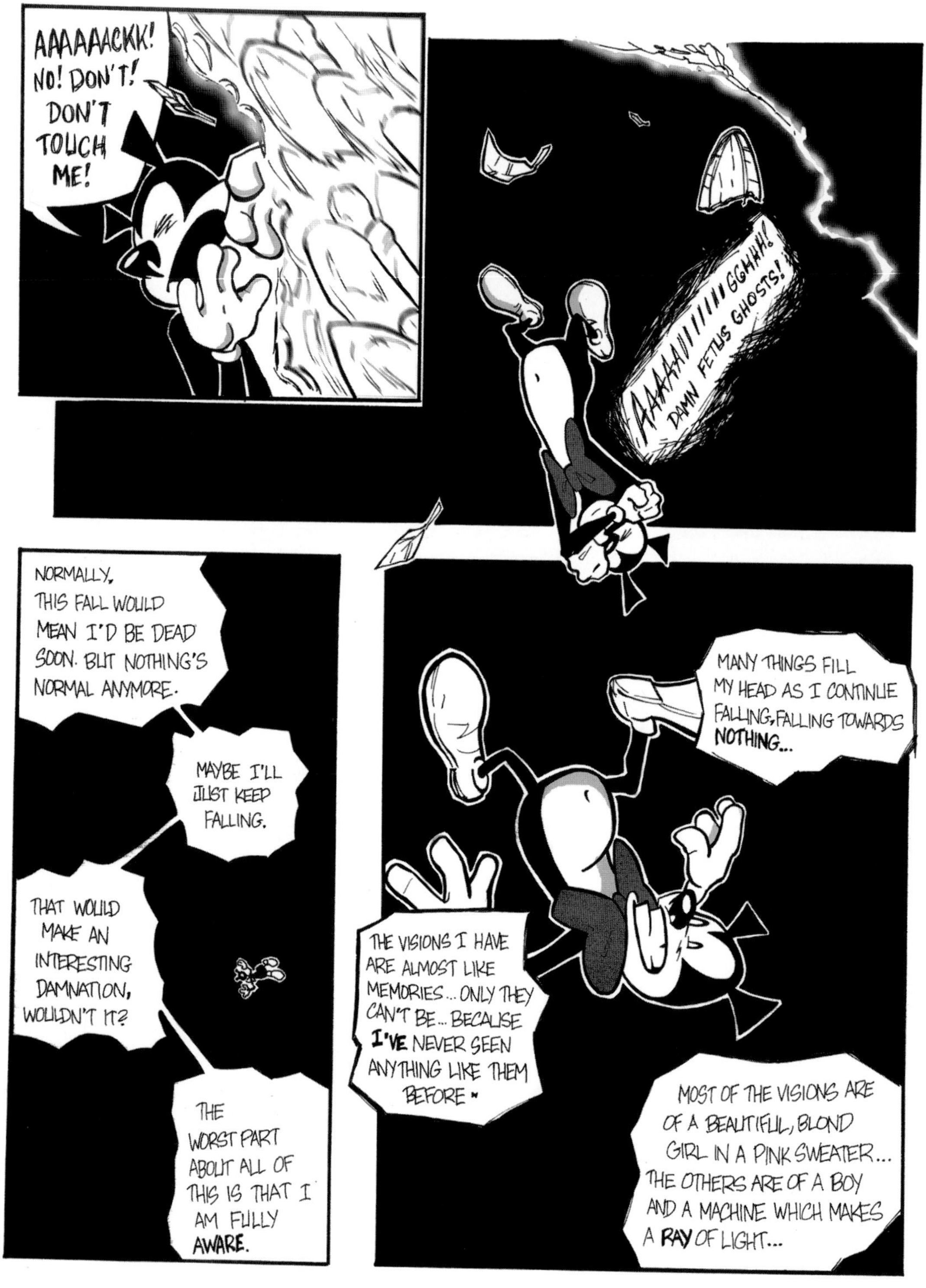

AAAAAACKK! NO! DON'T! DON'T TOUCH ME!
AAAAAAH!!!!!!GGHHH! DAMN FETUS GHOSTS!
NORMALLY, THIS FALL WOULD MEAN I'D BE DEAD SOON. BUT NOTHING'S NORMAL ANYMORE.
MAYBE I'LL JUST KEEP FALLING.
THAT WOULD MAKE AN INTERESTING DAMNATION, WOULDN'T IT?
THE WORST PART ABOUT ALL OF THIS IS THAT I AM FULLY **AWARE**.
MANY THINGS FILL MY HEAD AS I CONTINUE FALLING, FALLING TOWARDS **NOTHING**...
THE VISIONS I HAVE ARE ALMOST LIKE MEMORIES... ONLY THEY CAN'T BE... BECAUSE **I'VE** NEVER SEEN ANYTHING LIKE THEM BEFORE
MOST OF THE VISIONS ARE OF A BEAUTIFUL, BLOND GIRL IN A PINK SWEATER... THE OTHERS ARE OF A BOY AND A MACHINE WHICH MAKES A **RAY** OF LIGHT...

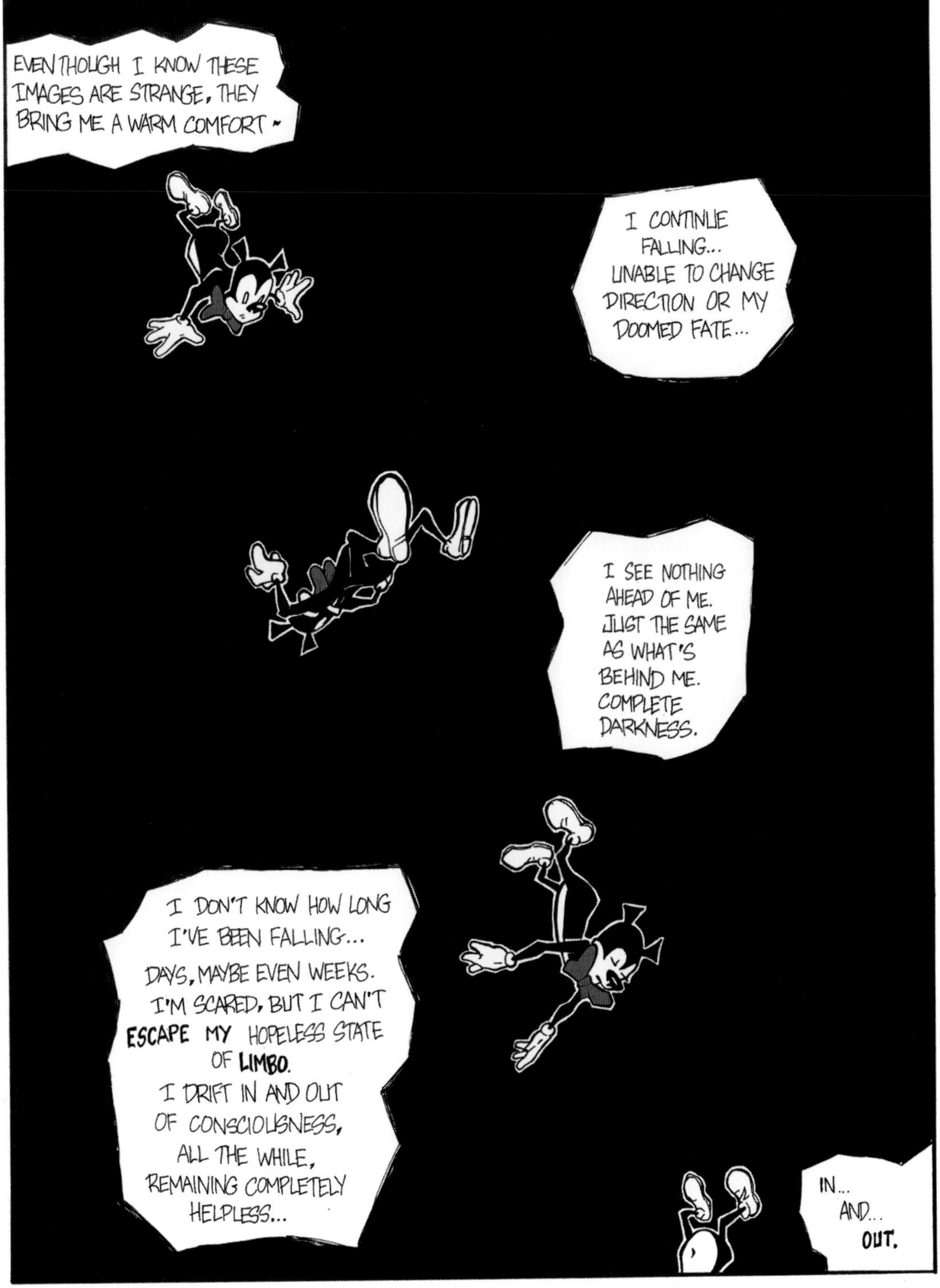
EVEN THOUGH I KNOW THESE IMAGES ARE STRANGE, THEY BRING ME A WARM COMFORT ~
I CONTINUE FALLING... UNABLE TO CHANGE DIRECTION OR MY DOOMED FATE...
I SEE NOTHING AHEAD OF ME. JUST THE SAME AS WHAT'S BEHIND ME. COMPLETE DARKNESS.
I DON'T KNOW HOW LONG I'VE BEEN FALLING... DAYS, MAYBE EVEN WEEKS. I'M SCARED, BUT I CAN'T ESCAPE MY HOPELESS STATE OF LIMBO. I DRIFT IN AND OUT OF CONSCIOUSNESS, ALL THE WHILE, REMAINING COMPLETELY HELPLESS...
IN... AND... OUT.

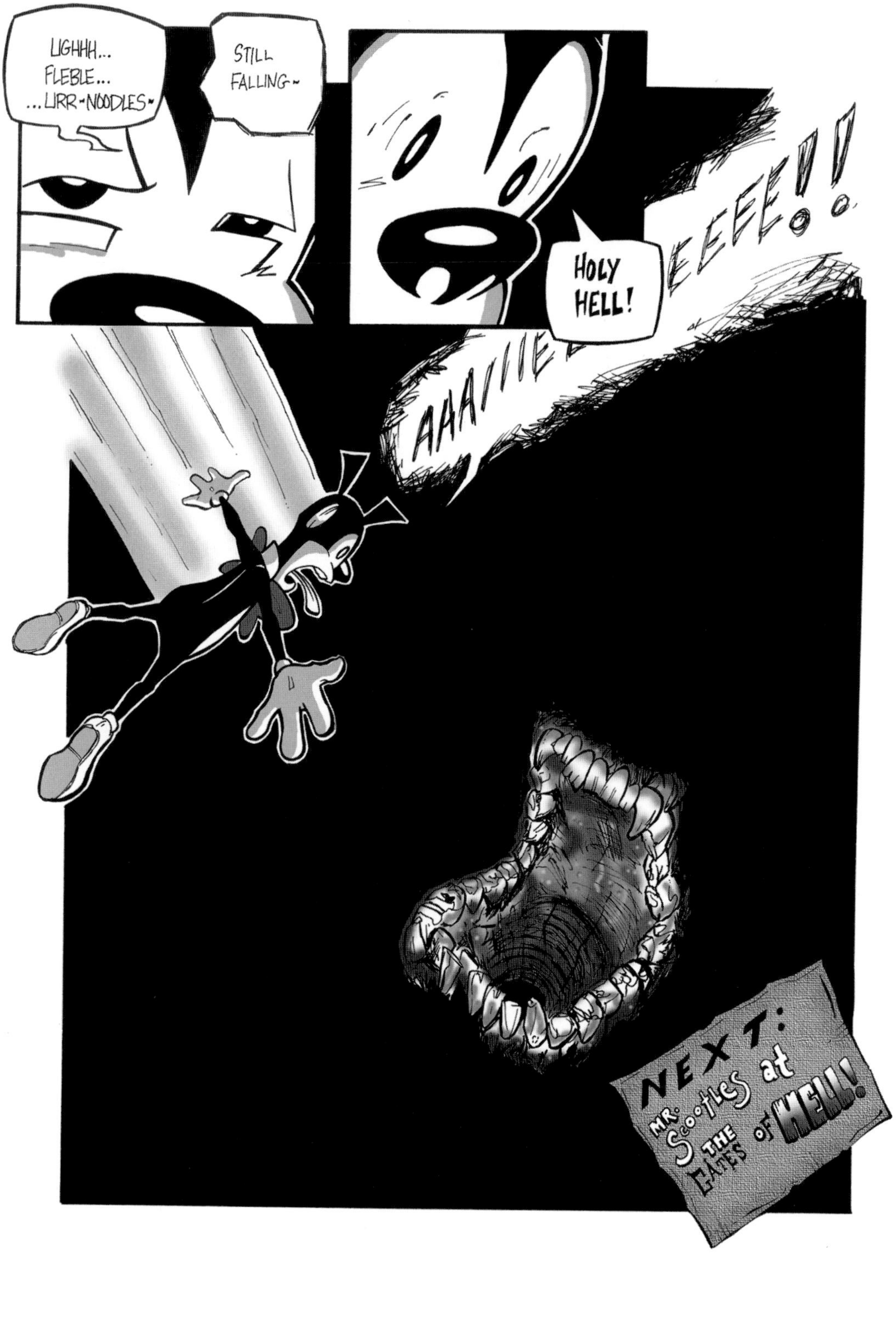
UGHHH...
FLEBLE...
...URR~NOODLES~
STILL
FALLING~
HOLY
HELL!
AAAIIIEEEEEEEE!!
NEXT:
MR. Scootles at THE GATES of HELL!

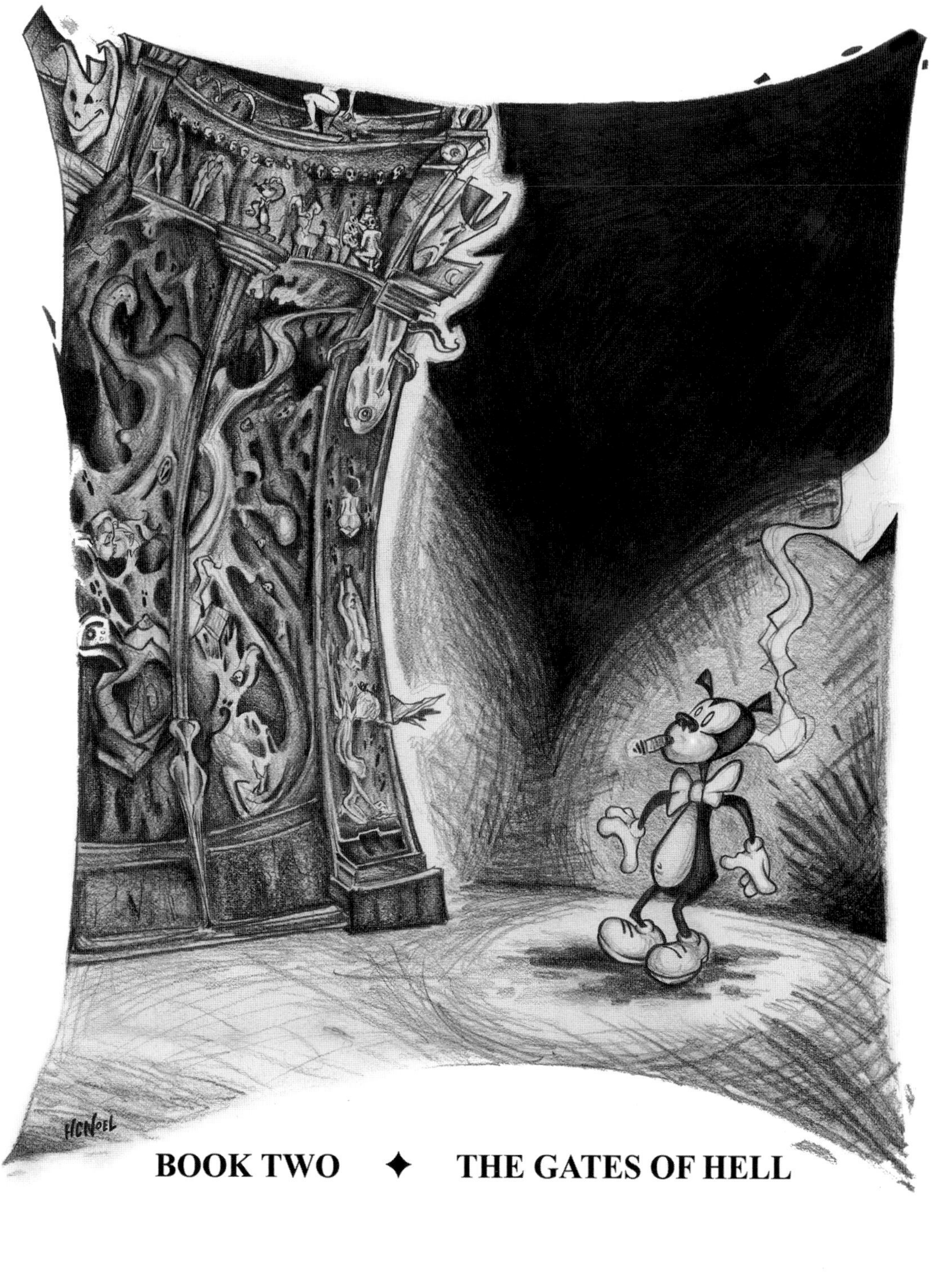
HCNOEL

BOOK TWO ✦ THE GATES OF HELL

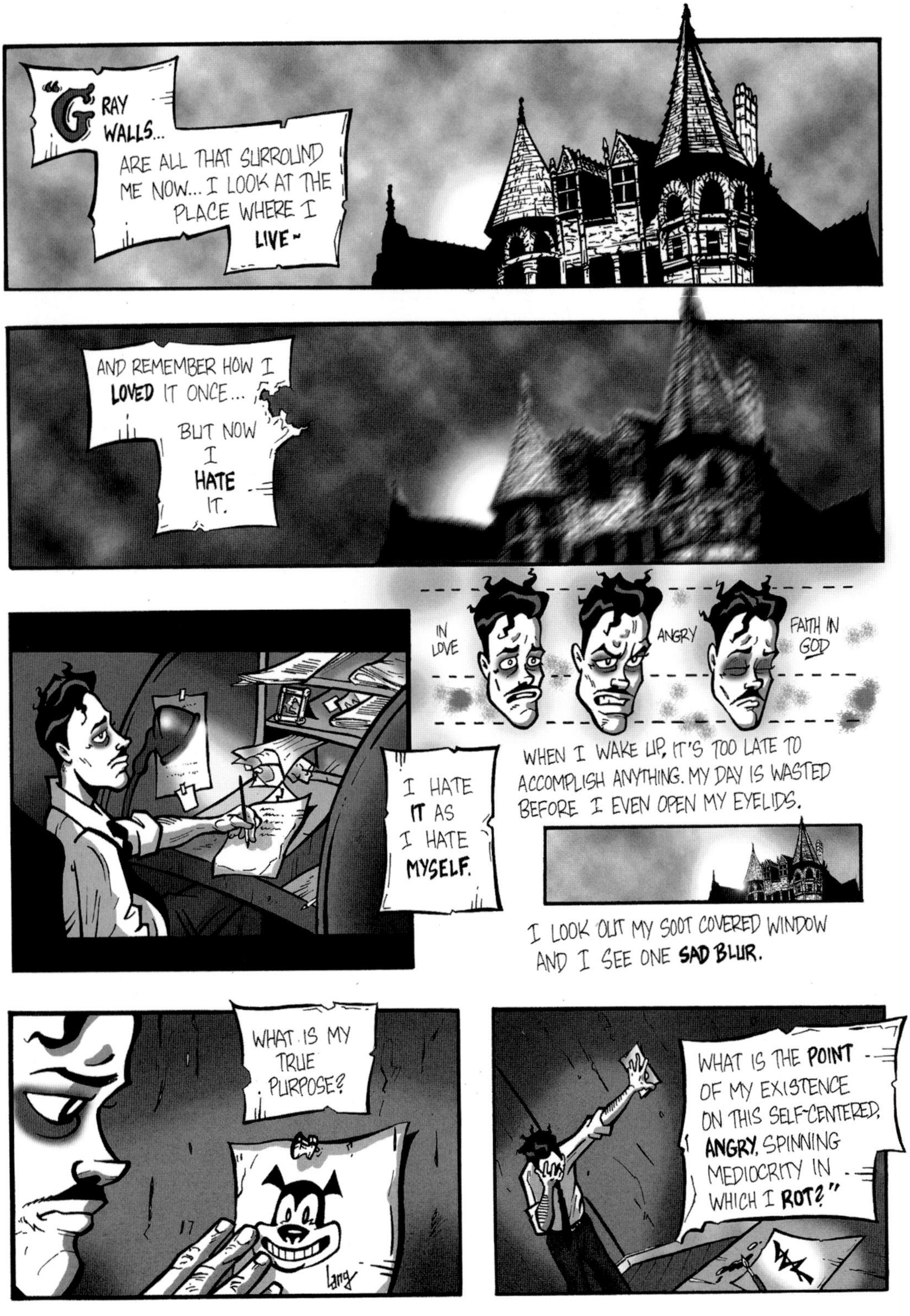
"GRAY WALLS...
ARE ALL THAT SURROUND ME NOW... I LOOK AT THE PLACE WHERE I LIVE~
AND REMEMBER HOW I LOVED IT ONCE...
BUT NOW I HATE IT.
IN LOVE
ANGRY
FAITH IN GOD
I HATE IT AS I HATE MYSELF.
WHEN I WAKE UP, IT'S TOO LATE TO ACCOMPLISH ANYTHING. MY DAY IS WASTED BEFORE I EVEN OPEN MY EYELIDS.
I LOOK OUT MY SOOT COVERED WINDOW AND I SEE ONE SAD BLUR.
WHAT IS MY TRUE PURPOSE?
WHAT IS THE POINT OF MY EXISTENCE ON THIS SELF-CENTERED, ANGRY, SPINNING MEDIOCRITY IN WHICH I ROT?"

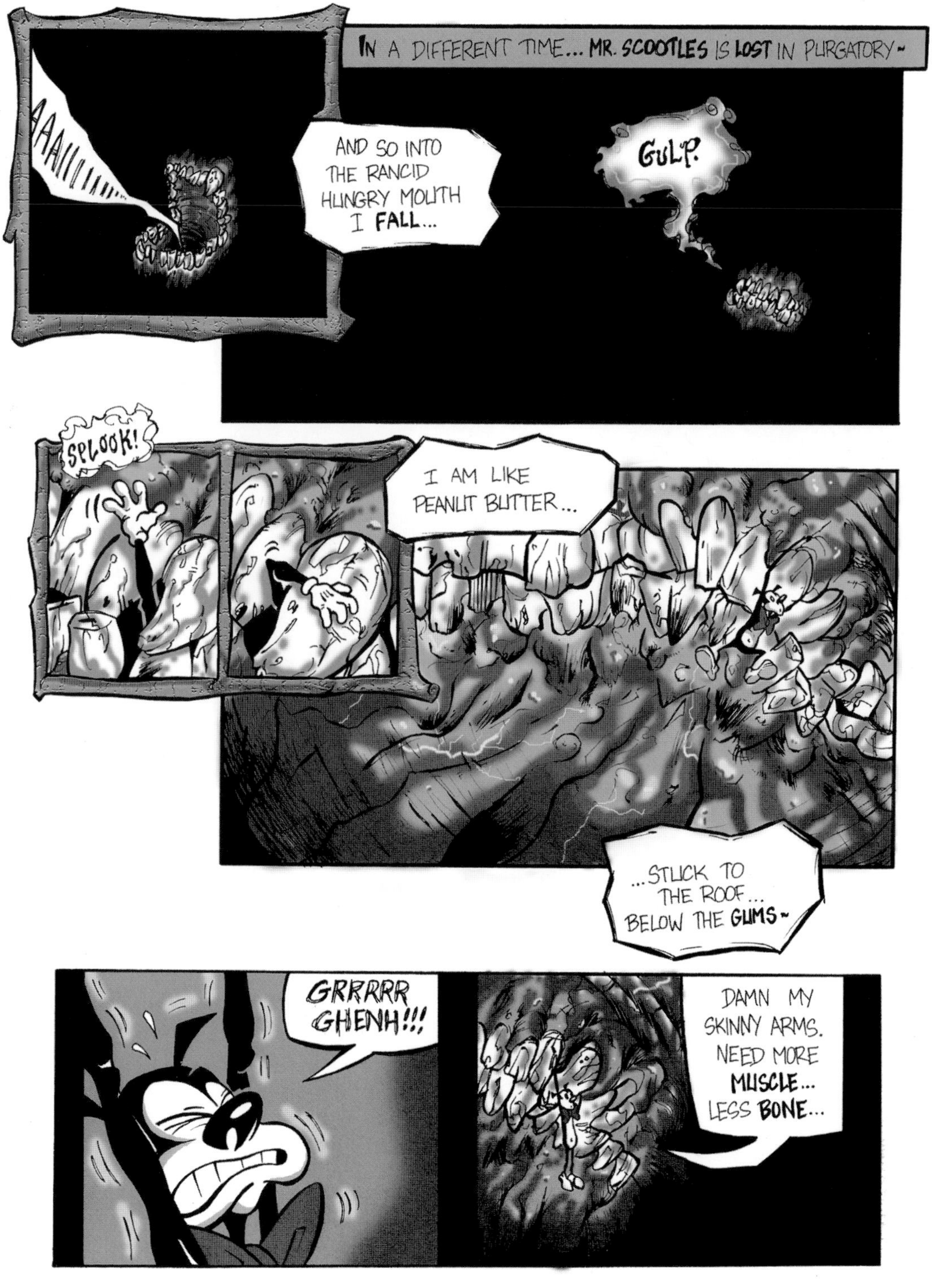

IN A DIFFERENT TIME... MR. SCOOTLES IS LOST IN PURGATORY~
AAAII...
AND SO INTO THE RANCID HUNGRY MOUTH I FALL...
GULP.
SPLOOK!
I AM LIKE PEANUT BUTTER...
...STUCK TO THE ROOF... BELOW THE GUMS~
GRRRRR GHENH!!!
DAMN MY SKINNY ARMS. NEED MORE MUSCLE... LESS BONE...

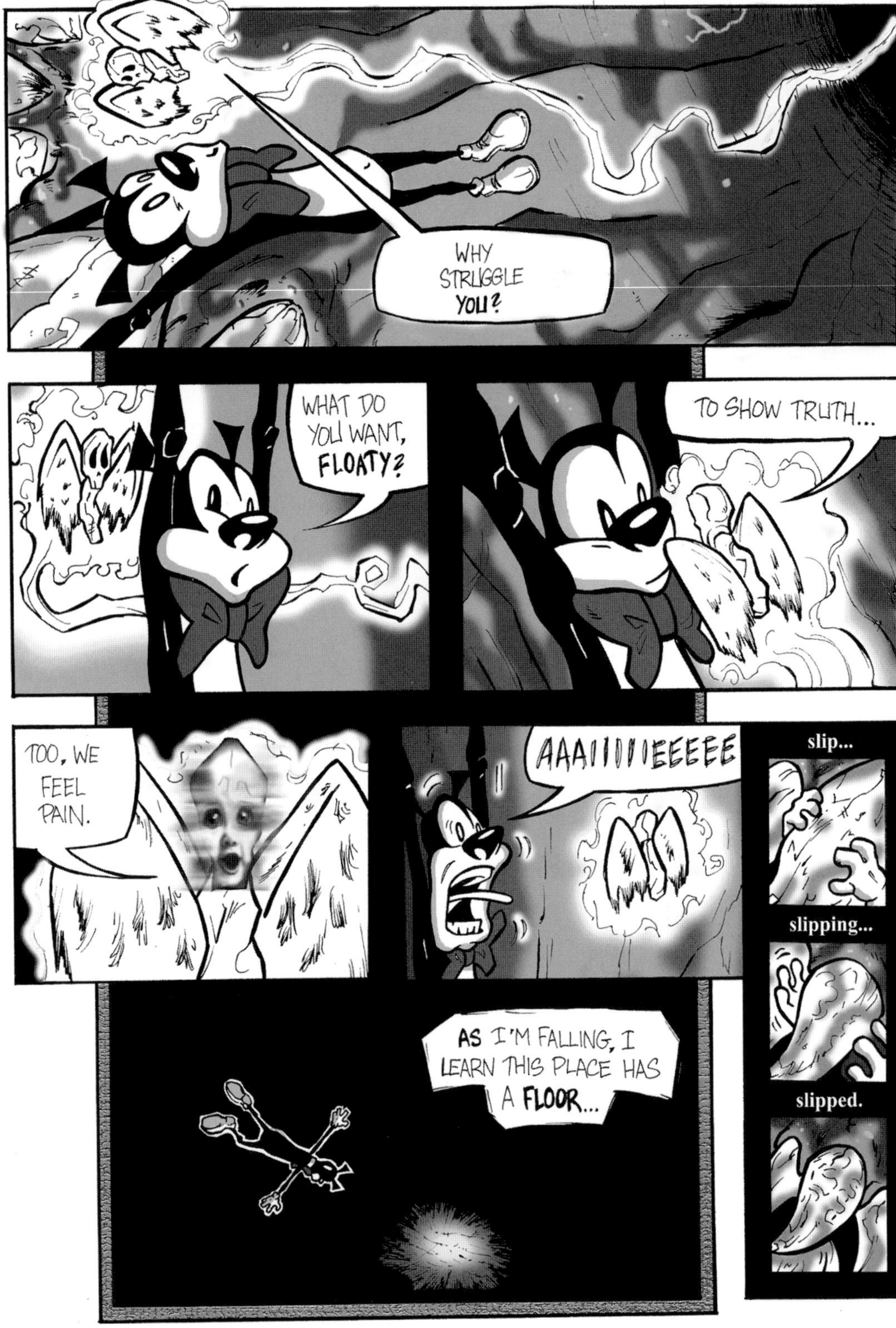

WHY STRUGGLE YOU?
WHAT DO YOU WANT, FLOATY?
TO SHOW TRUTH...
TOO, WE FEEL PAIN.
AAAIIIIIEEEEE
slip...
slipping...
slipped.
AS I'M FALLING, I LEARN THIS PLACE HAS A FLOOR...

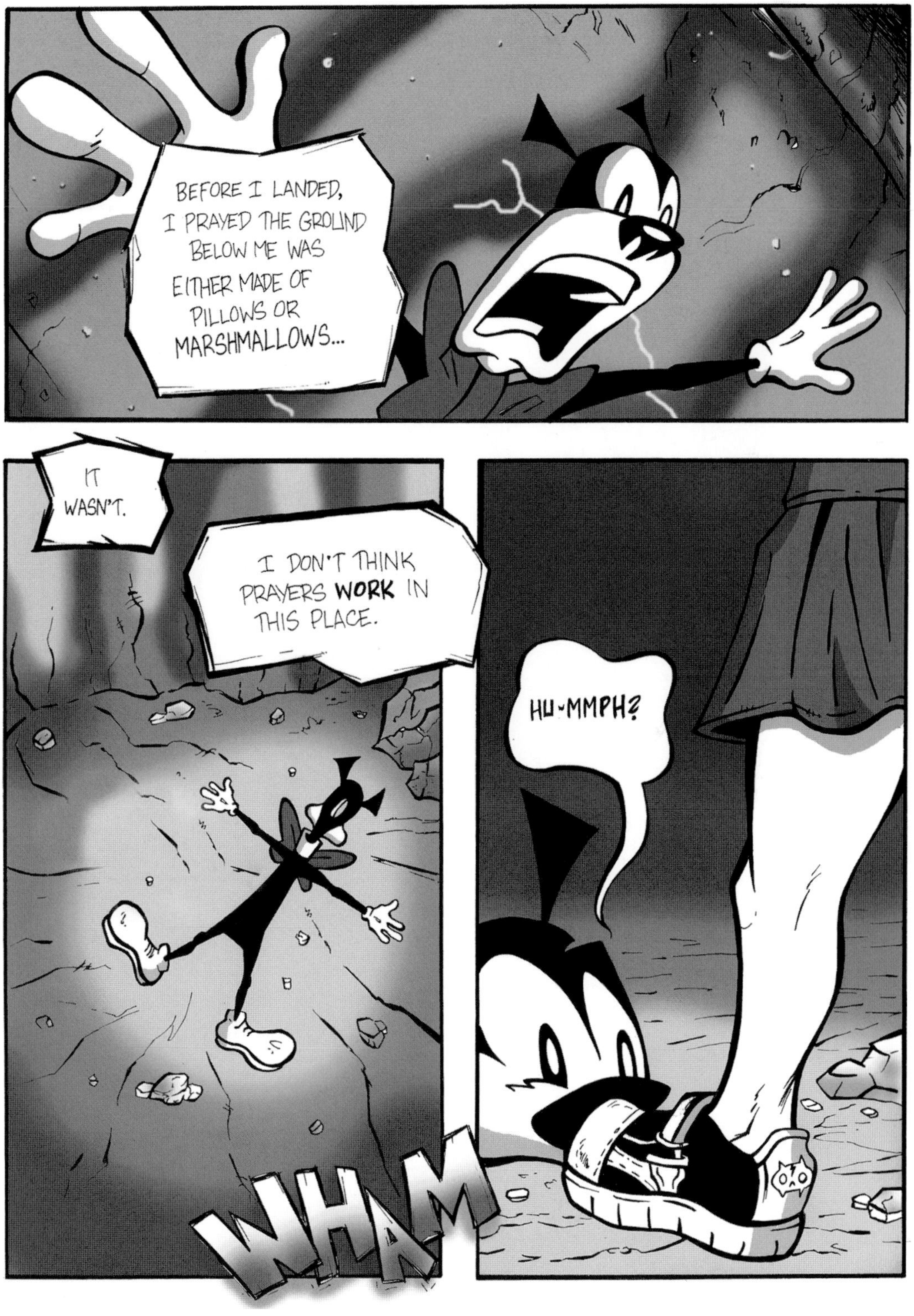
BEFORE I LANDED, I PRAYED THE GROUND BELOW ME WAS EITHER MADE OF PILLOWS OR MARSHMALLOWS...
IT WASN'T.
I DON'T THINK PRAYERS **WORK** IN THIS PLACE.
WHAM
HU-MMPH?

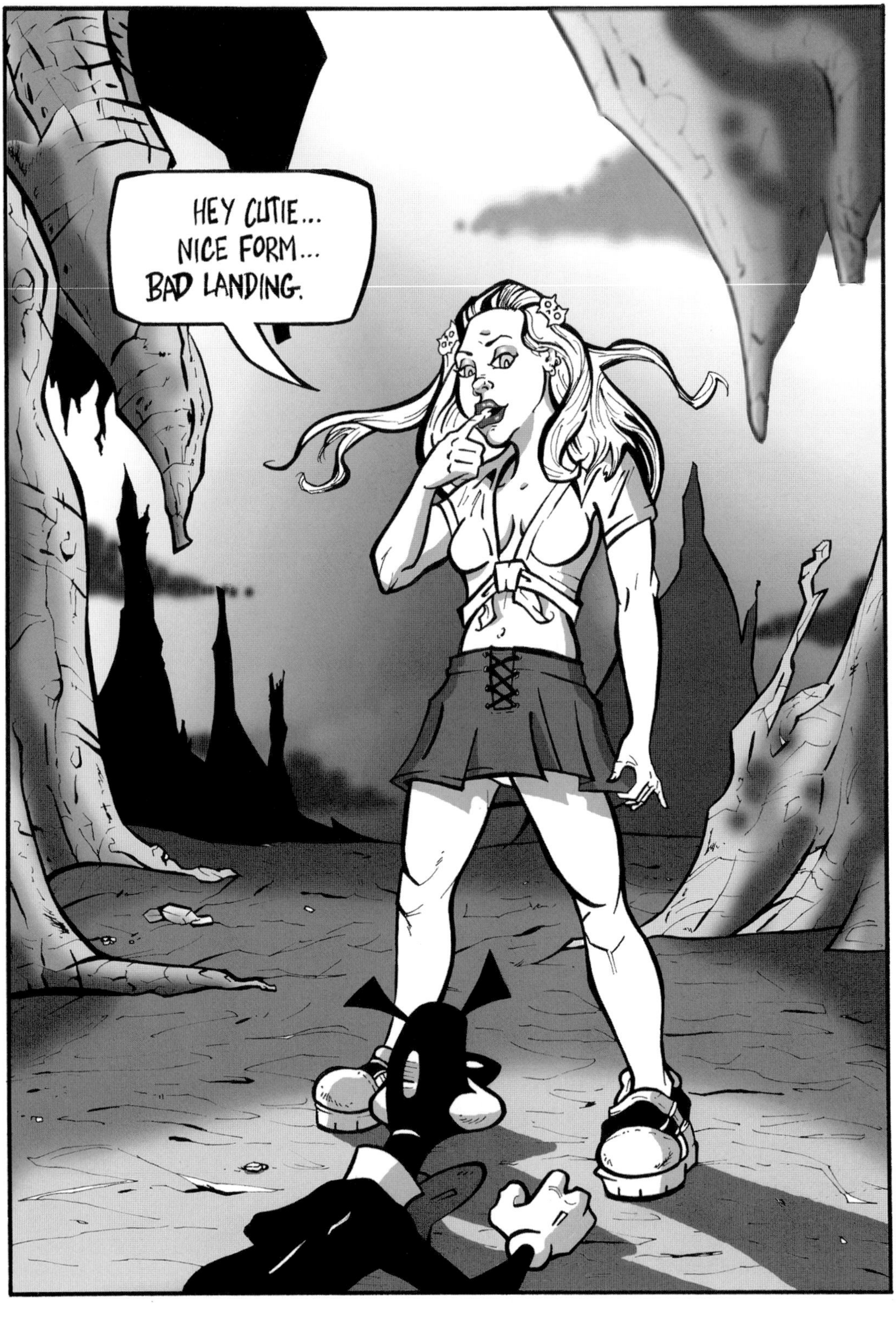
HEY CUTIE... NICE FORM... BAD LANDING.

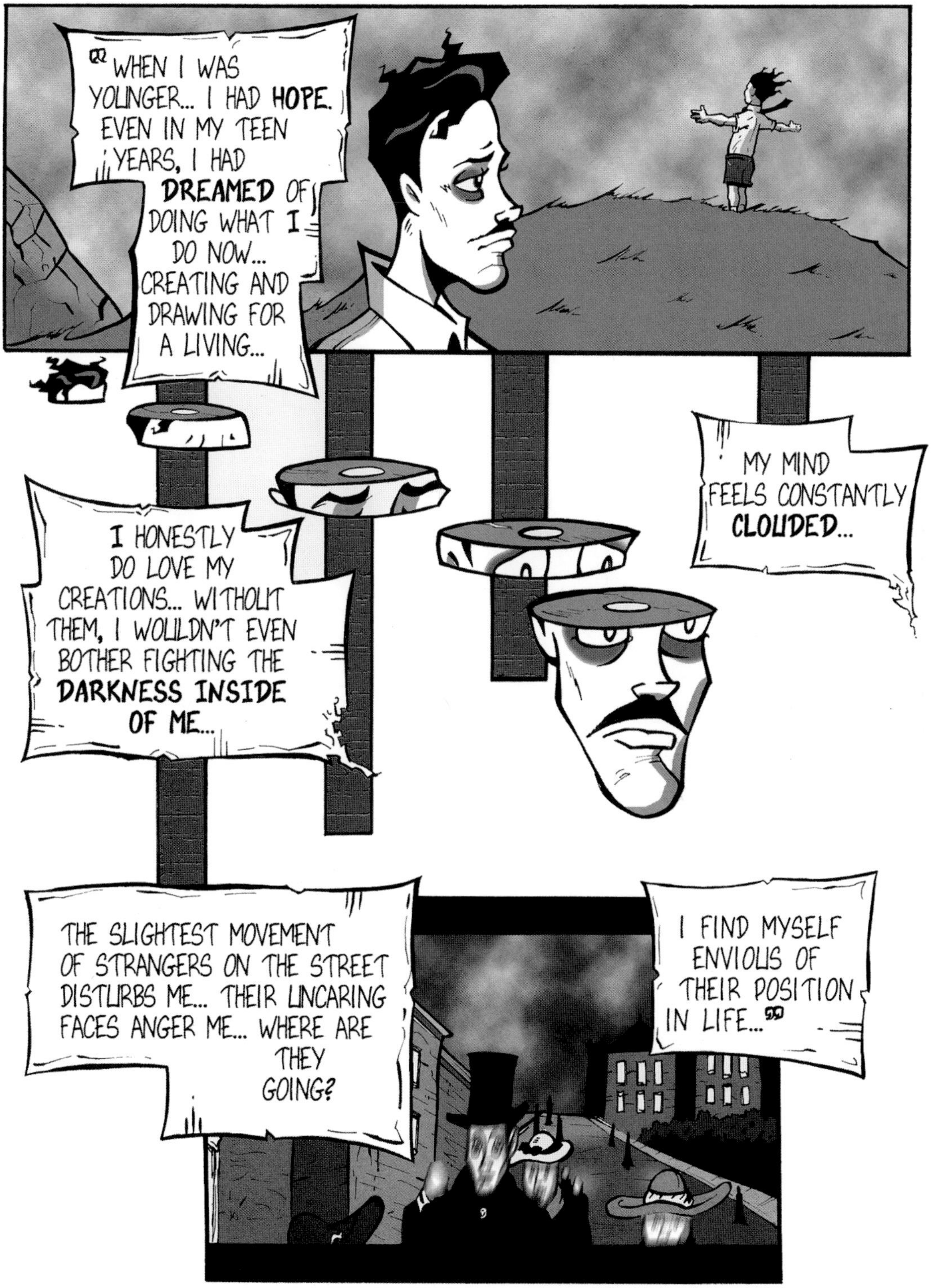
"WHEN I WAS YOUNGER... I HAD HOPE. EVEN IN MY TEEN YEARS, I HAD DREAMED OF DOING WHAT I DO NOW... CREATING AND DRAWING FOR A LIVING...
MY MIND FEELS CONSTANTLY CLOUDED...
I HONESTLY DO LOVE MY CREATIONS... WITHOUT THEM, I WOULDN'T EVEN BOTHER FIGHTING THE DARKNESS INSIDE OF ME...
THE SLIGHTEST MOVEMENT OF STRANGERS ON THE STREET DISTURBS ME... THEIR UNCARING FACES ANGER ME... WHERE ARE THEY GOING?
I FIND MYSELF ENVIOUS OF THEIR POSITION IN LIFE..."

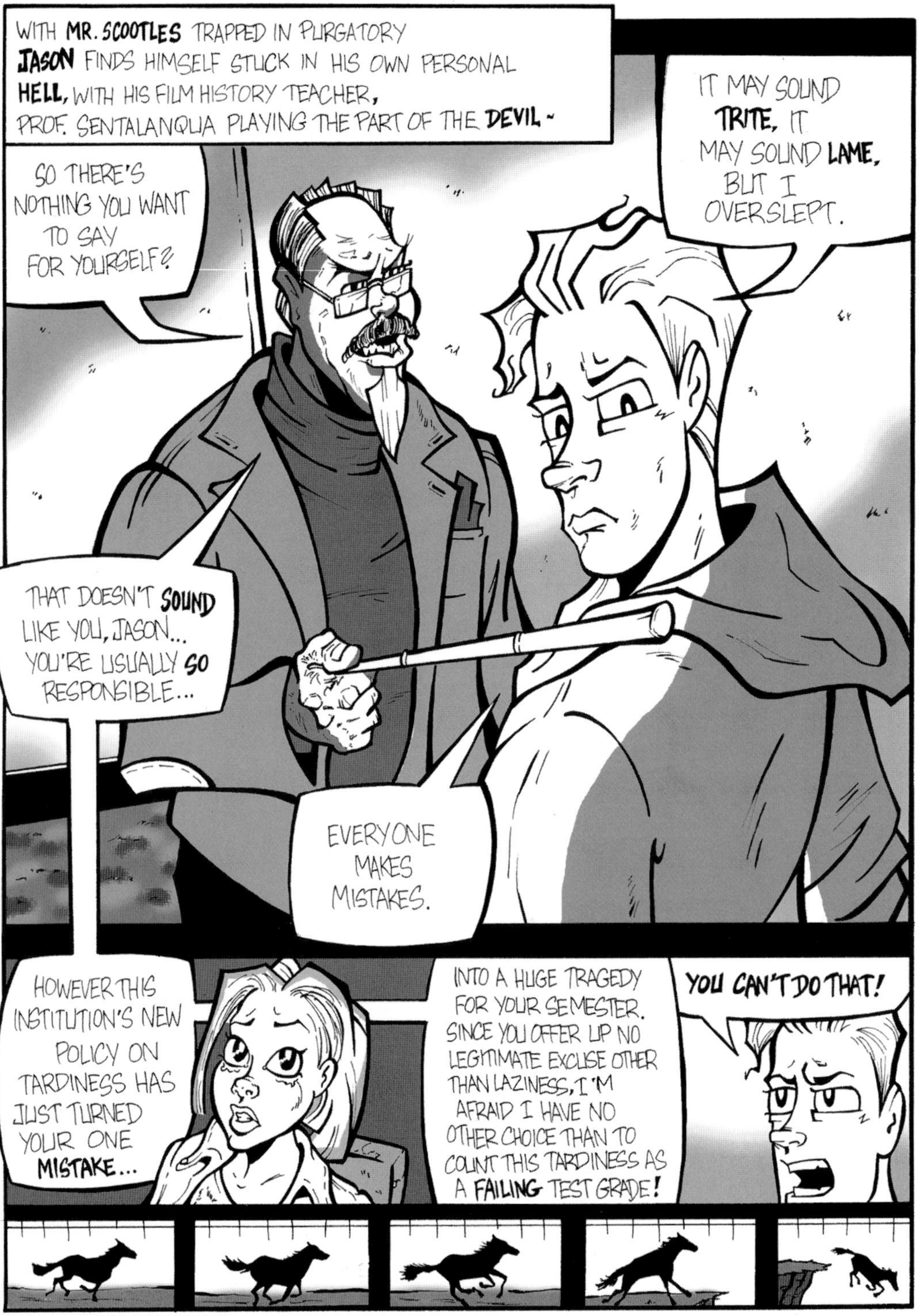
WITH MR. SCOOTLES TRAPPED IN PURGATORY
JASON FINDS HIMSELF STUCK IN HIS OWN PERSONAL
HELL, WITH HIS FILM HISTORY TEACHER,
PROF. SENTALANQUA PLAYING THE PART OF THE DEVIL~
SO THERE'S NOTHING YOU WANT TO SAY FOR YOURSELF?
IT MAY SOUND TRITE, IT MAY SOUND LAME, BUT I OVERSLEPT.
THAT DOESN'T SOUND LIKE YOU, JASON... YOU'RE USUALLY SO RESPONSIBLE...
EVERYONE MAKES MISTAKES.
HOWEVER THIS INSTITUTION'S NEW POLICY ON TARDINESS HAS JUST TURNED YOUR ONE MISTAKE...
INTO A HUGE TRAGEDY FOR YOUR SEMESTER. SINCE YOU OFFER UP NO LEGITIMATE EXCUSE OTHER THAN LAZINESS, I'M AFRAID I HAVE NO OTHER CHOICE THAN TO COUNT THIS TARDINESS AS A FAILING TEST GRADE!
YOU CAN'T DO THAT!

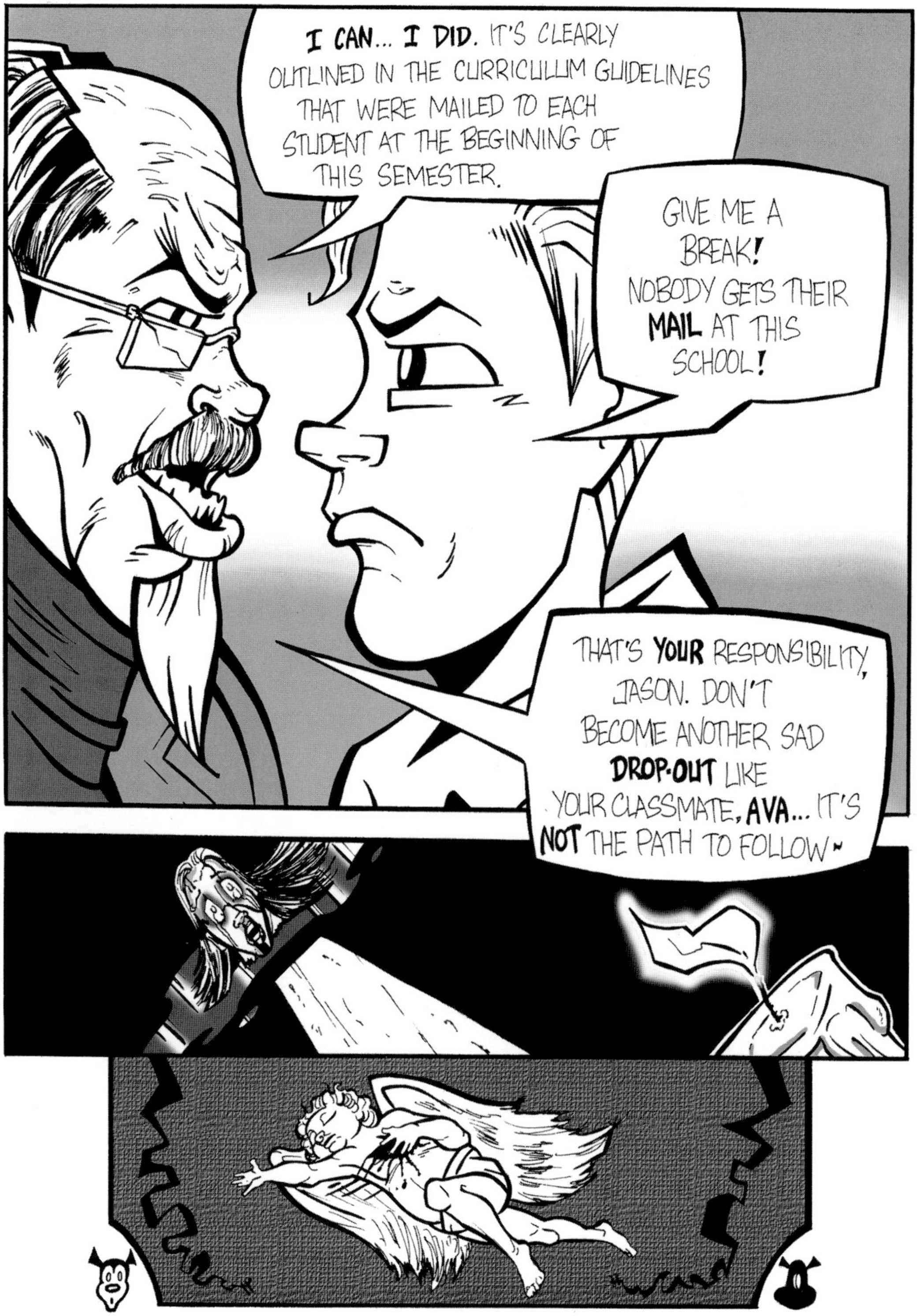
I CAN... I DID. IT'S CLEARLY OUTLINED IN THE CURRICULUM GUIDELINES THAT WERE MAILED TO EACH STUDENT AT THE BEGINNING OF THIS SEMESTER.
GIVE ME A BREAK! NOBODY GETS THEIR MAIL AT THIS SCHOOL!
THAT'S YOUR RESPONSIBILITY, JASON. DON'T BECOME ANOTHER SAD DROP-OUT LIKE YOUR CLASSMATE, AVA... IT'S NOT THE PATH TO FOLLOW~

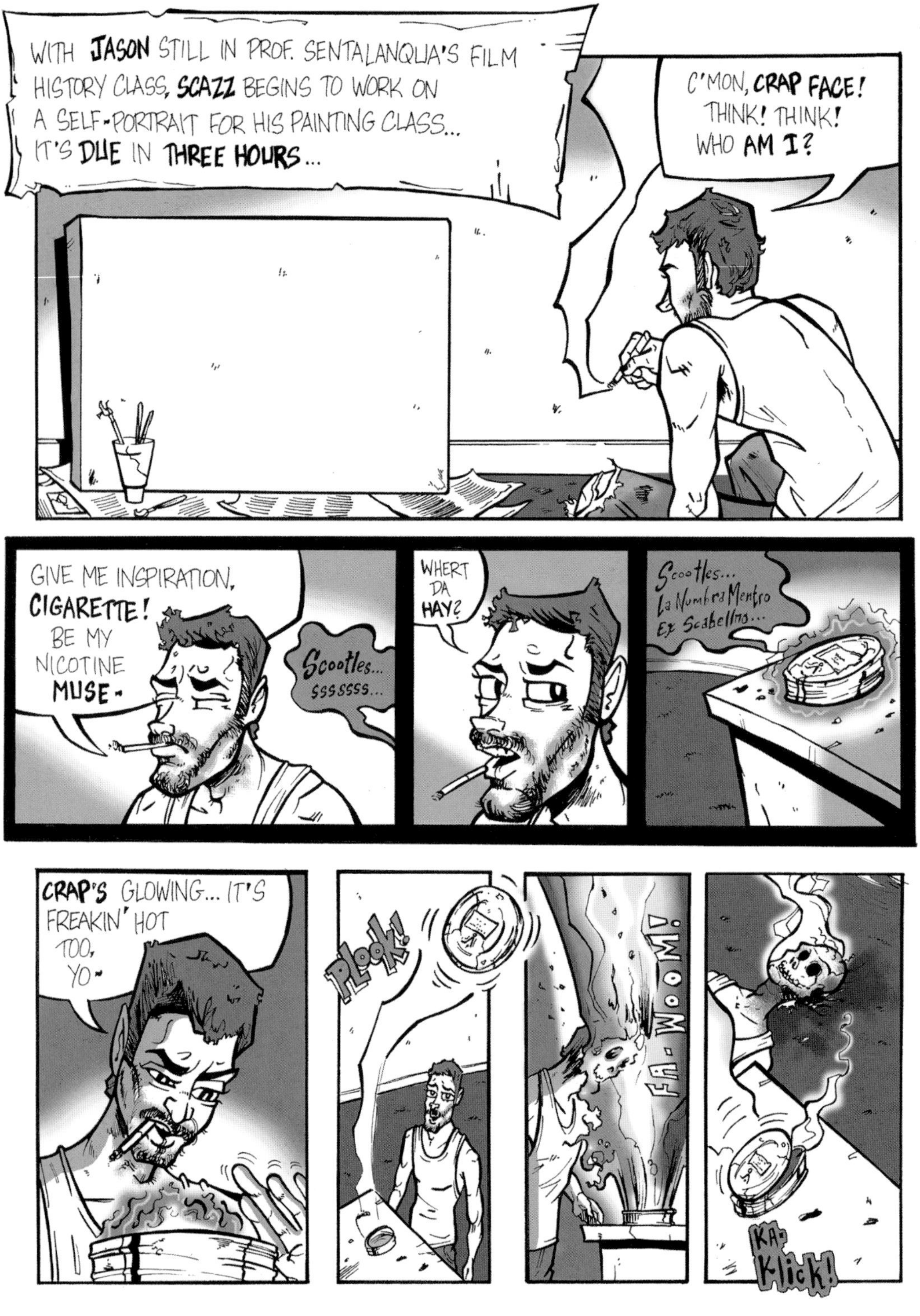
WITH JASON STILL IN PROF. SENTALANQUA'S FILM HISTORY CLASS, SCAZZ BEGINS TO WORK ON A SELF-PORTRAIT FOR HIS PAINTING CLASS... IT'S DUE IN THREE HOURS...
C'MON, CRAP FACE! THINK! THINK! WHO AM I?
GIVE ME INSPIRATION, CIGARETTE! BE MY NICOTINE MUSE-
Scootles... sssssss...
WHERT DA HAY?
Scootles... La Numbra Mentro Ex Scabellmo...
CRAP'S GLOWING... IT'S FREAKIN' HOT TOO, YO-
PLOOK!
FA-WOOM!
KA-KLICK!

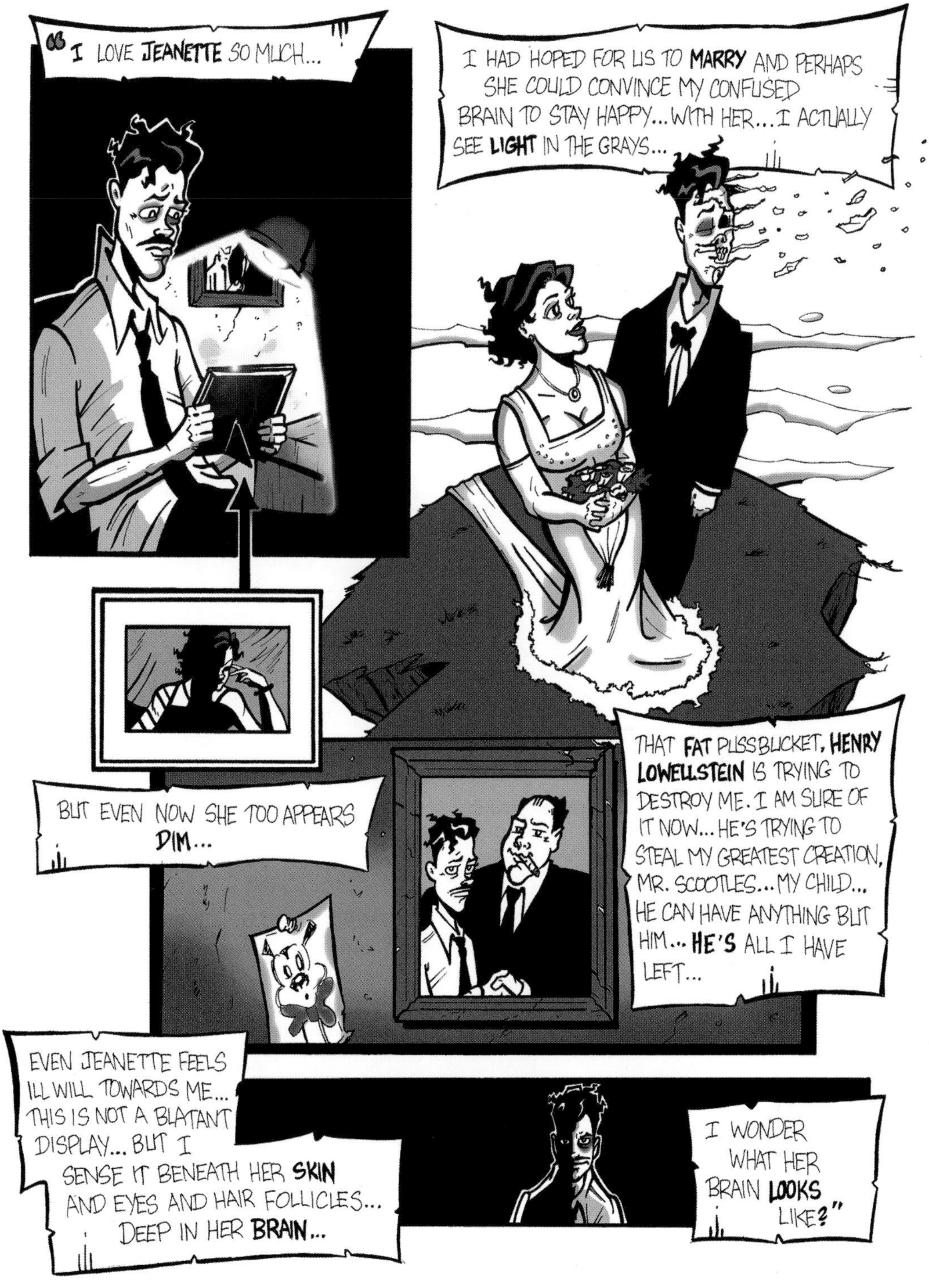
"I LOVE JEANETTE SO MUCH...
I HAD HOPED FOR US TO MARRY AND PERHAPS SHE COULD CONVINCE MY CONFUSED BRAIN TO STAY HAPPY... WITH HER... I ACTUALLY SEE LIGHT IN THE GRAYS...
BUT EVEN NOW SHE TOO APPEARS DIM...
THAT FAT PUSSBUCKET, HENRY LOWELLSTEIN IS TRYING TO DESTROY ME. I AM SURE OF IT NOW... HE'S TRYING TO STEAL MY GREATEST CREATION, MR. SCOOTLES... MY CHILD... HE CAN HAVE ANYTHING BUT HIM... HE'S ALL I HAVE LEFT...
EVEN JEANETTE FEELS ILL WILL TOWARDS ME... THIS IS NOT A BLATANT DISPLAY... BUT I SENSE IT BENEATH HER SKIN AND EYES AND HAIR FOLLICLES... DEEP IN HER BRAIN...
I WONDER WHAT HER BRAIN LOOKS LIKE?"

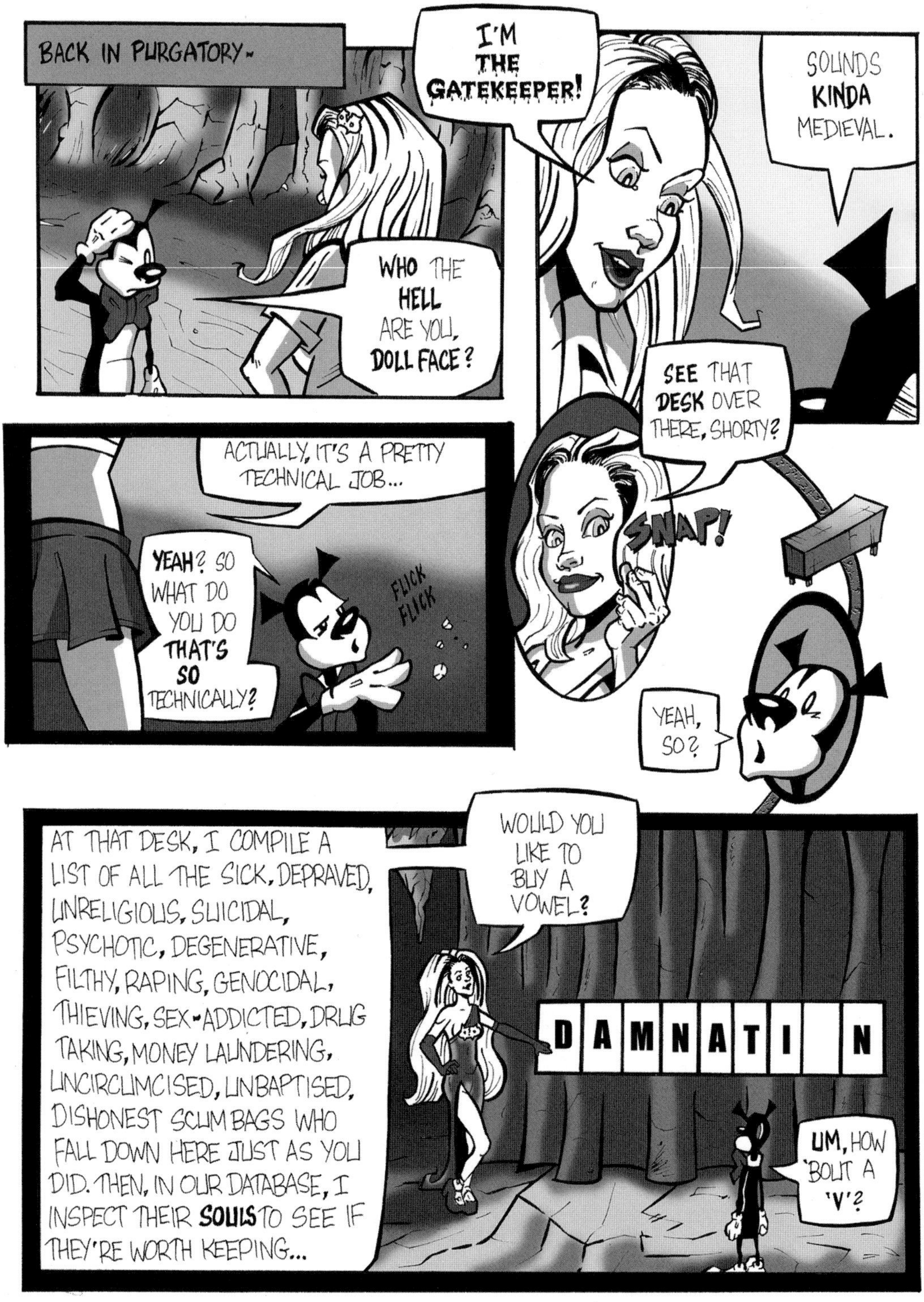

BACK IN PURGATORY...
WHO THE HELL ARE YOU, DOLL FACE?
I'M THE GATEKEEPER!
SOUNDS KINDA MEDIEVAL.
ACTUALLY, IT'S A PRETTY TECHNICAL JOB...
YEAH? SO WHAT DO YOU DO THAT'S SO TECHNICALLY?
FLICK FLICK
SEE THAT DESK OVER THERE, SHORTY?
SNAP!
YEAH, SO?
AT THAT DESK, I COMPILE A LIST OF ALL THE SICK, DEPRAVED, UNRELIGIOUS, SUICIDAL, PSYCHOTIC, DEGENERATIVE, FILTHY, RAPING, GENOCIDAL, THIEVING, SEX-ADDICTED, DRUG TAKING, MONEY LAUNDERING, UNCIRCUMCISED, UNBAPTISED, DISHONEST SCUM BAGS WHO FALL DOWN HERE JUST AS YOU DID. THEN, IN OUR DATABASE, I INSPECT THEIR SOULS TO SEE IF THEY'RE WORTH KEEPING...
WOULD YOU LIKE TO BUY A VOWEL?
D A M N A T I N
UM, HOW 'BOUT A 'V'?

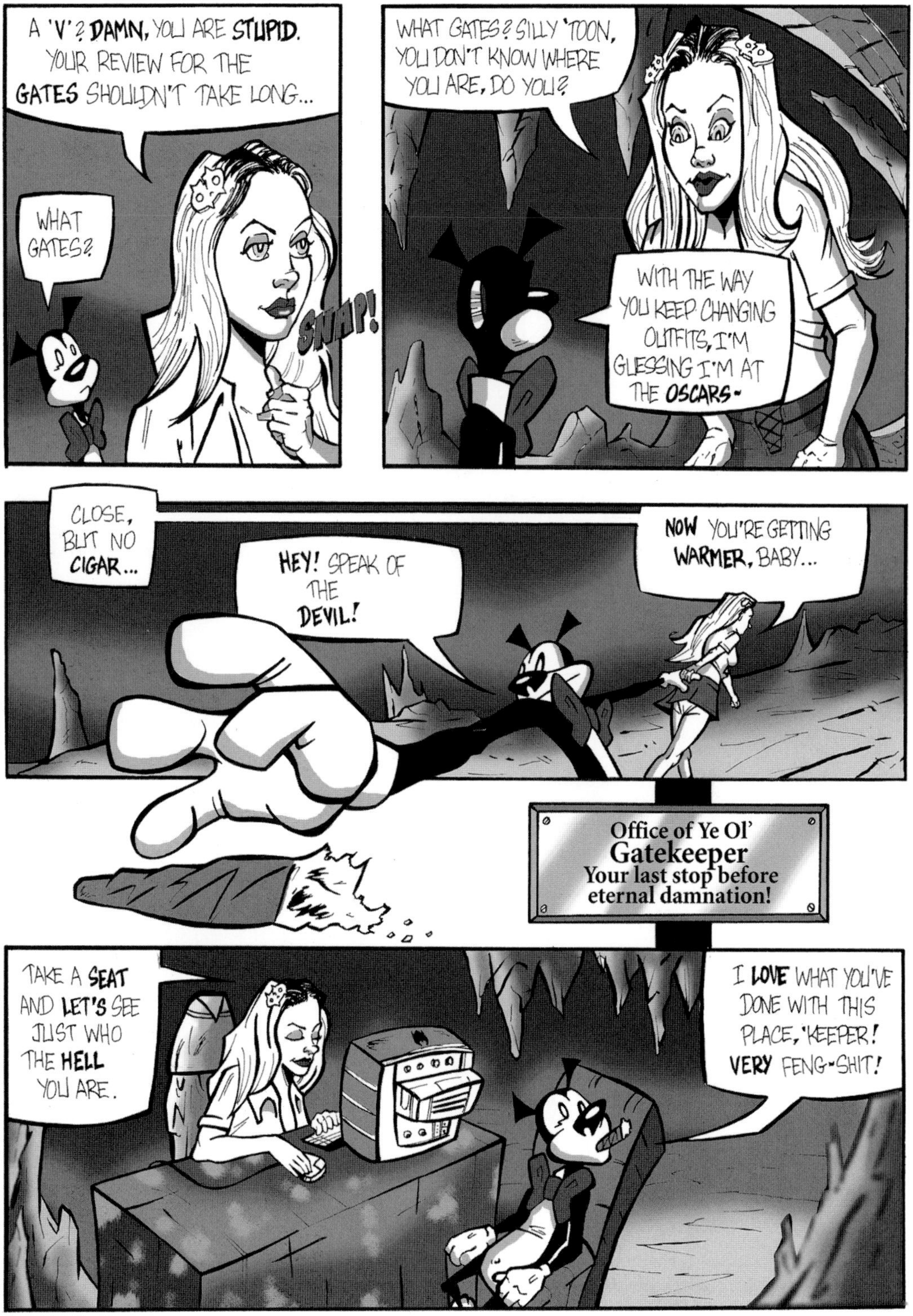

A 'V'? DAMN, YOU ARE STUPID. YOUR REVIEW FOR THE GATES SHOULDN'T TAKE LONG...
WHAT GATES?
SNAP!
WHAT GATES? SILLY 'TOON, YOU DON'T KNOW WHERE YOU ARE, DO YOU?
WITH THE WAY YOU KEEP CHANGING OUTFITS, I'M GUESSING I'M AT THE OSCARS~
CLOSE, BUT NO CIGAR...
HEY! SPEAK OF THE DEVIL!
NOW YOU'RE GETTING WARMER, BABY...
Office of Ye Ol' Gatekeeper Your last stop before eternal damnation!
TAKE A SEAT AND LET'S SEE JUST WHO THE HELL YOU ARE.
I LOVE WHAT YOU'VE DONE WITH THIS PLACE, 'KEEPER! VERY FENG-SHIT!

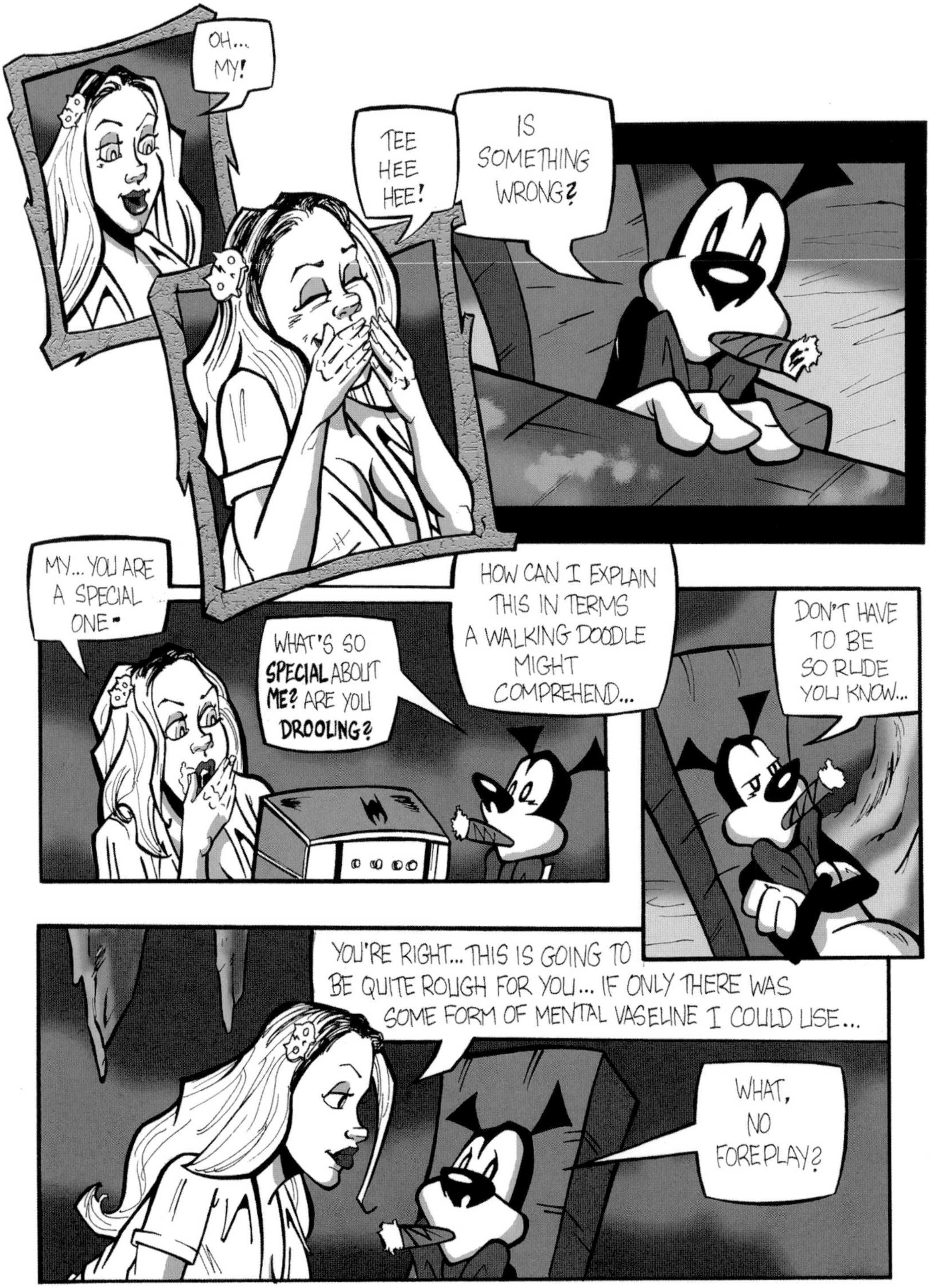
OH... MY!
TEE HEE HEE!
IS SOMETHING WRONG?
MY... YOU ARE A SPECIAL ONE...
WHAT'S SO SPECIAL ABOUT ME? ARE YOU DROOLING?
HOW CAN I EXPLAIN THIS IN TERMS A WALKING DOODLE MIGHT COMPREHEND...
DON'T HAVE TO BE SO RUDE YOU KNOW...
YOU'RE RIGHT... THIS IS GOING TO BE QUITE ROUGH FOR YOU... IF ONLY THERE WAS SOME FORM OF MENTAL VASELINE I COULD USE...
WHAT, NO FOREPLAY?

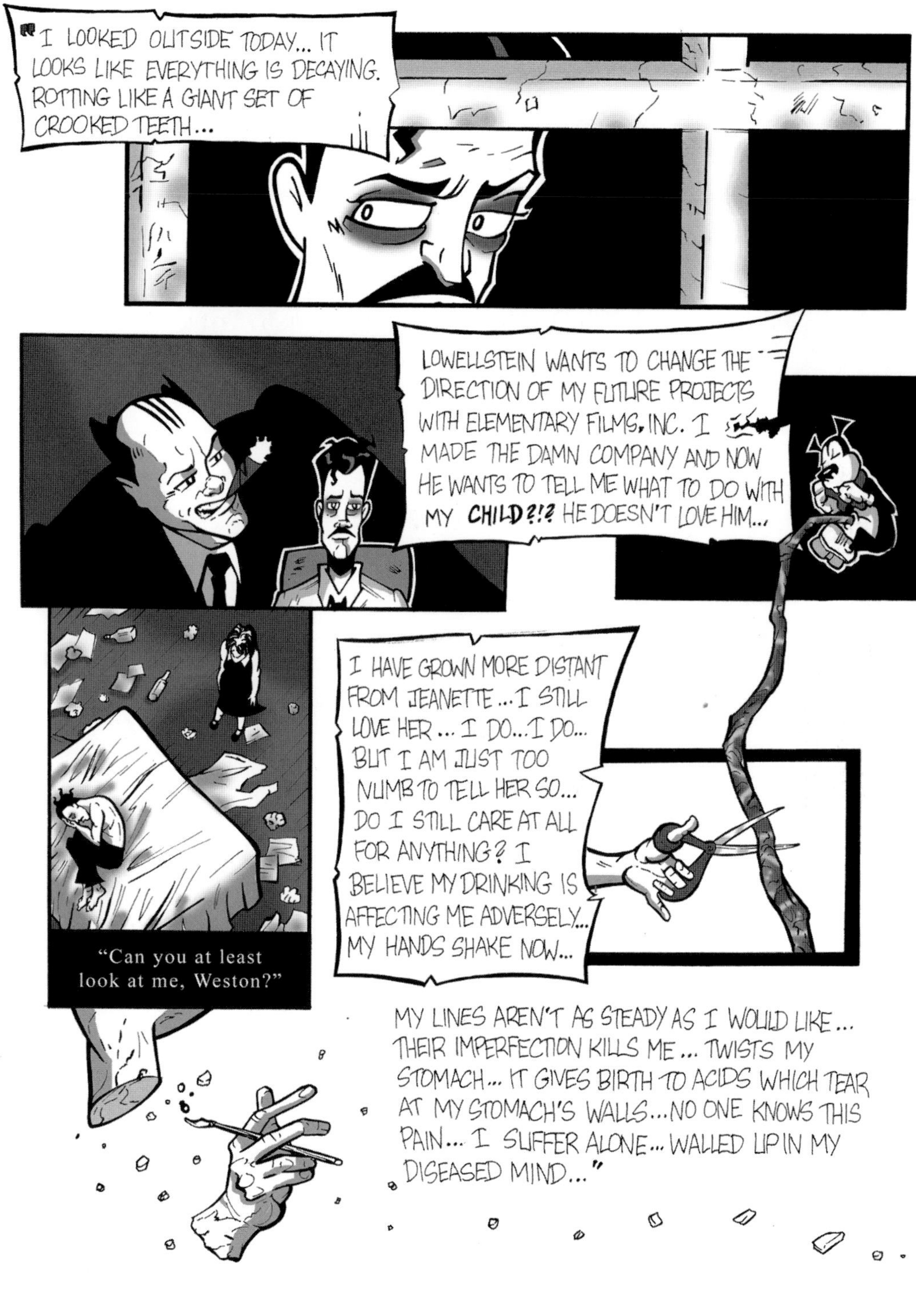
"I LOOKED OUTSIDE TODAY... IT LOOKS LIKE EVERYTHING IS DECAYING. ROTTING LIKE A GIANT SET OF CROOKED TEETH...
LOWELLSTEIN WANTS TO CHANGE THE DIRECTION OF MY FUTURE PROJECTS WITH ELEMENTARY FILMS, INC. I MADE THE DAMN COMPANY AND NOW HE WANTS TO TELL ME WHAT TO DO WITH MY CHILD?!? HE DOESN'T LOVE HIM...
I HAVE GROWN MORE DISTANT FROM JEANETTE... I STILL LOVE HER... I DO... I DO... BUT I AM JUST TOO NUMB TO TELL HER SO... DO I STILL CARE AT ALL FOR ANYTHING? I BELIEVE MY DRINKING IS AFFECTING ME ADVERSELY... MY HANDS SHAKE NOW...
"Can you at least look at me, Weston?"
MY LINES AREN'T AS STEADY AS I WOULD LIKE... THEIR IMPERFECTION KILLS ME... TWISTS MY STOMACH... IT GIVES BIRTH TO ACIDS WHICH TEAR AT MY STOMACH'S WALLS... NO ONE KNOWS THIS PAIN... I SUFFER ALONE... WALLED UP IN MY DISEASED MIND..."

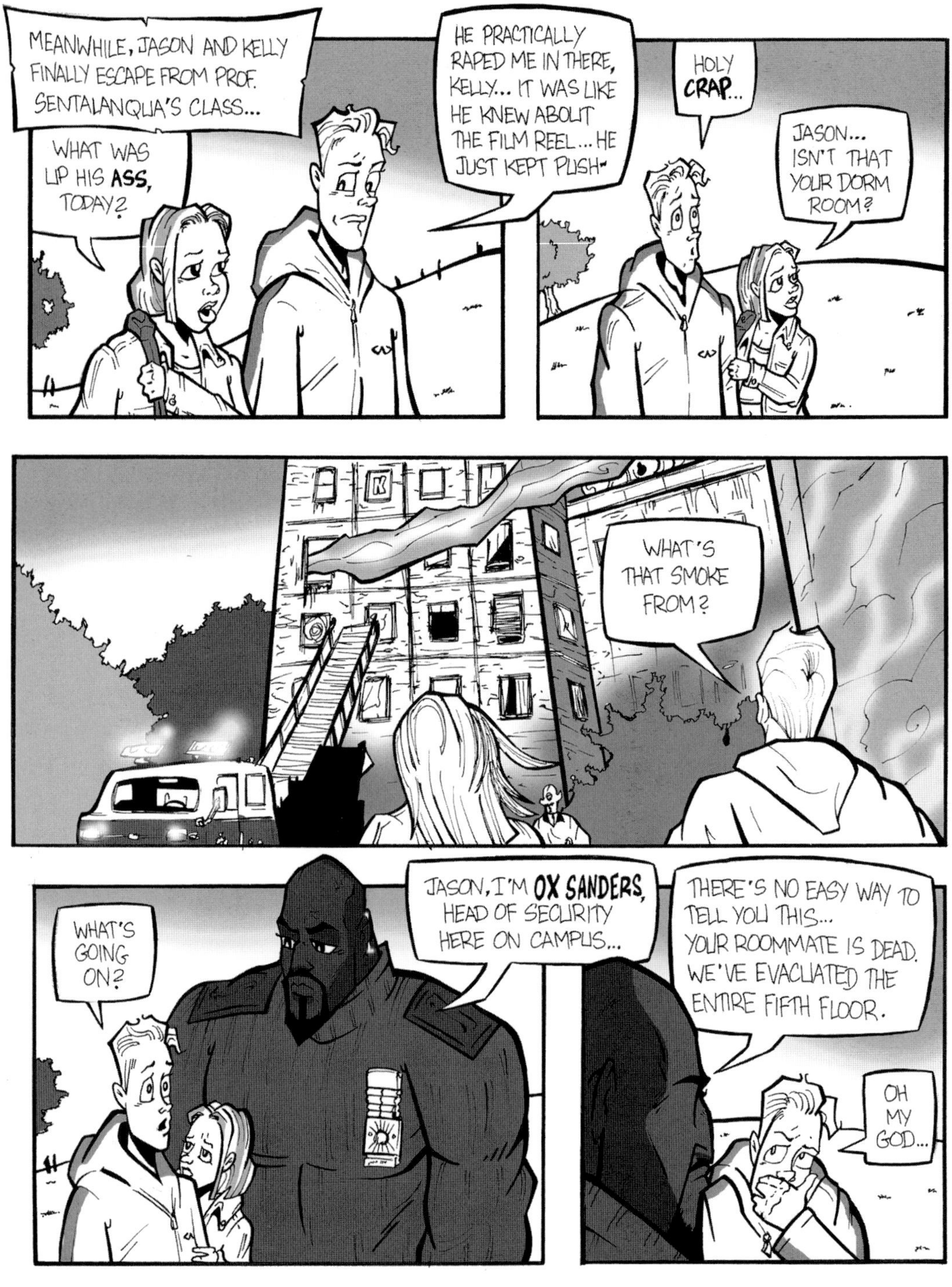
MEANWHILE, JASON AND KELLY FINALLY ESCAPE FROM PROF. SENTALANQUA'S CLASS...
WHAT WAS UP HIS ASS, TODAY?
HE PRACTICALLY RAPED ME IN THERE, KELLY... IT WAS LIKE HE KNEW ABOUT THE FILM REEL... HE JUST KEPT PUSH-
HOLY CRAP...
JASON... ISN'T THAT YOUR DORM ROOM?
WHAT'S THAT SMOKE FROM?
WHAT'S GOING ON?
JASON, I'M OX SANDERS, HEAD OF SECURITY HERE ON CAMPUS...
THERE'S NO EASY WAY TO TELL YOU THIS... YOUR ROOMMATE IS DEAD. WE'VE EVACUATED THE ENTIRE FIFTH FLOOR.
OH MY GOD...

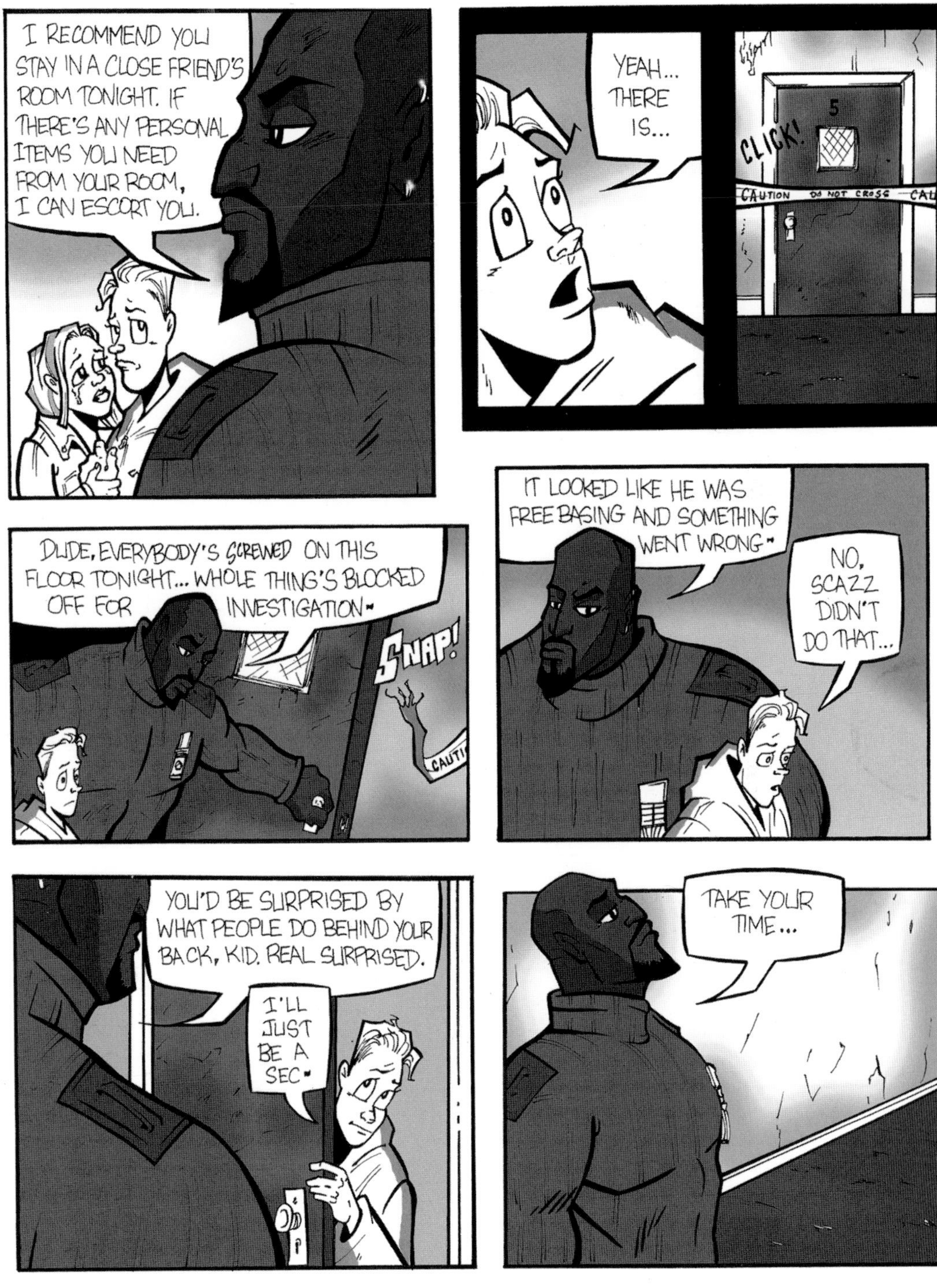
I RECOMMEND YOU STAY IN A CLOSE FRIEND'S ROOM TONIGHT. IF THERE'S ANY PERSONAL ITEMS YOU NEED FROM YOUR ROOM, I CAN ESCORT YOU.
YEAH... THERE IS...
5
CLICK!
CAUTION DO NOT CROSS
DUDE, EVERYBODY'S SCREWED ON THIS FLOOR TONIGHT... WHOLE THING'S BLOCKED OFF FOR INVESTIGATION.
SNAP!
CAUTI
IT LOOKED LIKE HE WAS FREE BASING AND SOMETHING WENT WRONG.
NO, SCAZZ DIDN'T DO THAT...
YOU'D BE SURPRISED BY WHAT PEOPLE DO BEHIND YOUR BACK, KID. REAL SURPRISED.
I'LL JUST BE A SEC.
TAKE YOUR TIME...

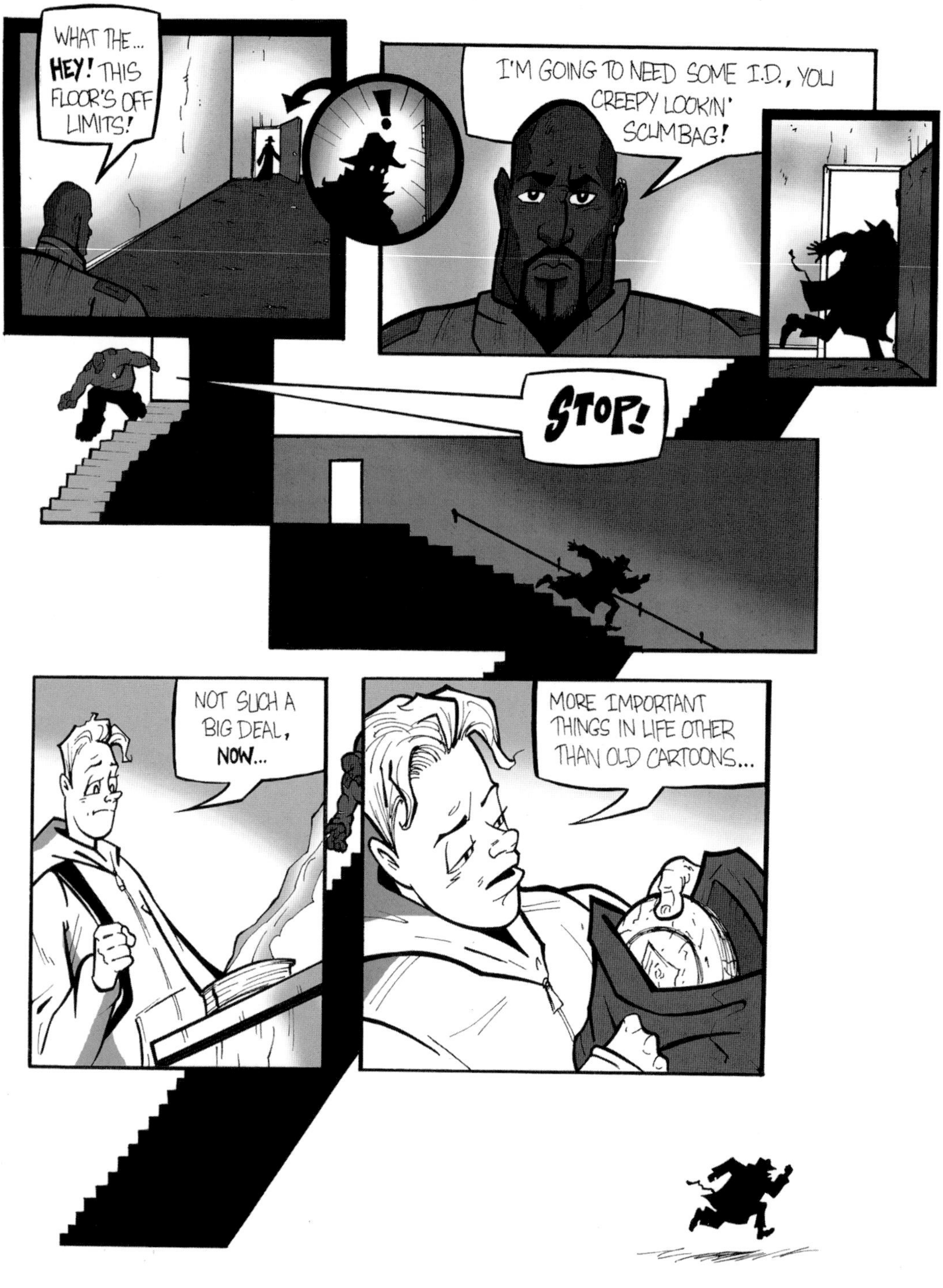
WHAT THE... **HEY!** THIS FLOOR'S OFF LIMITS!
I'M GOING TO NEED SOME I.D., YOU CREEPY LOOKIN' SCUMBAG!
STOP!
NOT SUCH A BIG DEAL, **NOW**...
MORE IMPORTANT THINGS IN LIFE OTHER THAN OLD CARTOONS...

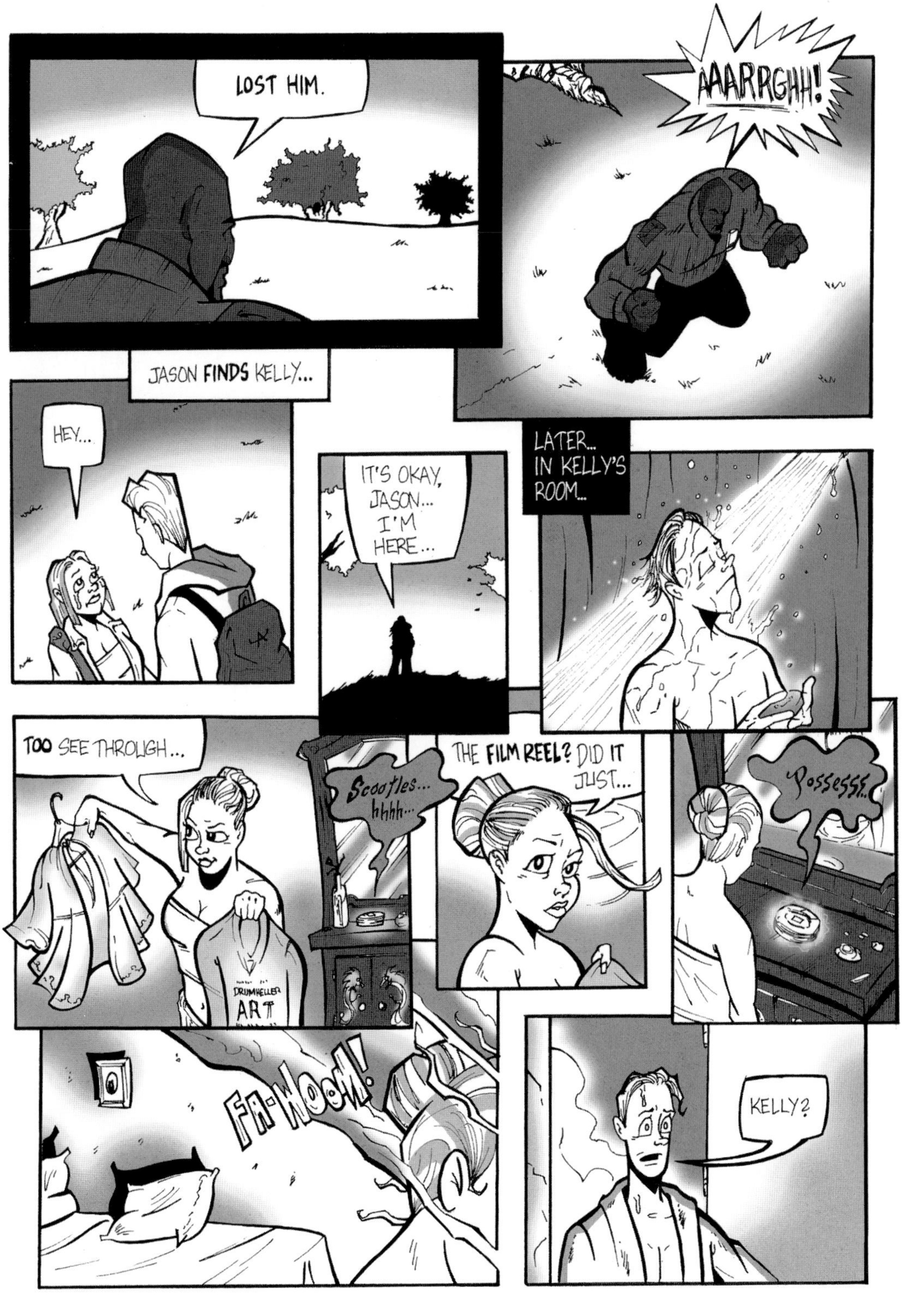
LOST HIM.
AAARRGHH!
JASON FINDS KELLY...
HEY...
IT'S OKAY, JASON... I'M HERE...
LATER... IN KELLY'S ROOM...
TOO SEE THROUGH...
DRUMHELLER ART
Scootles... hhhh...
THE FILM REEL? DID IT JUST...
Possesss...
FA-WOOM!
KELLY?

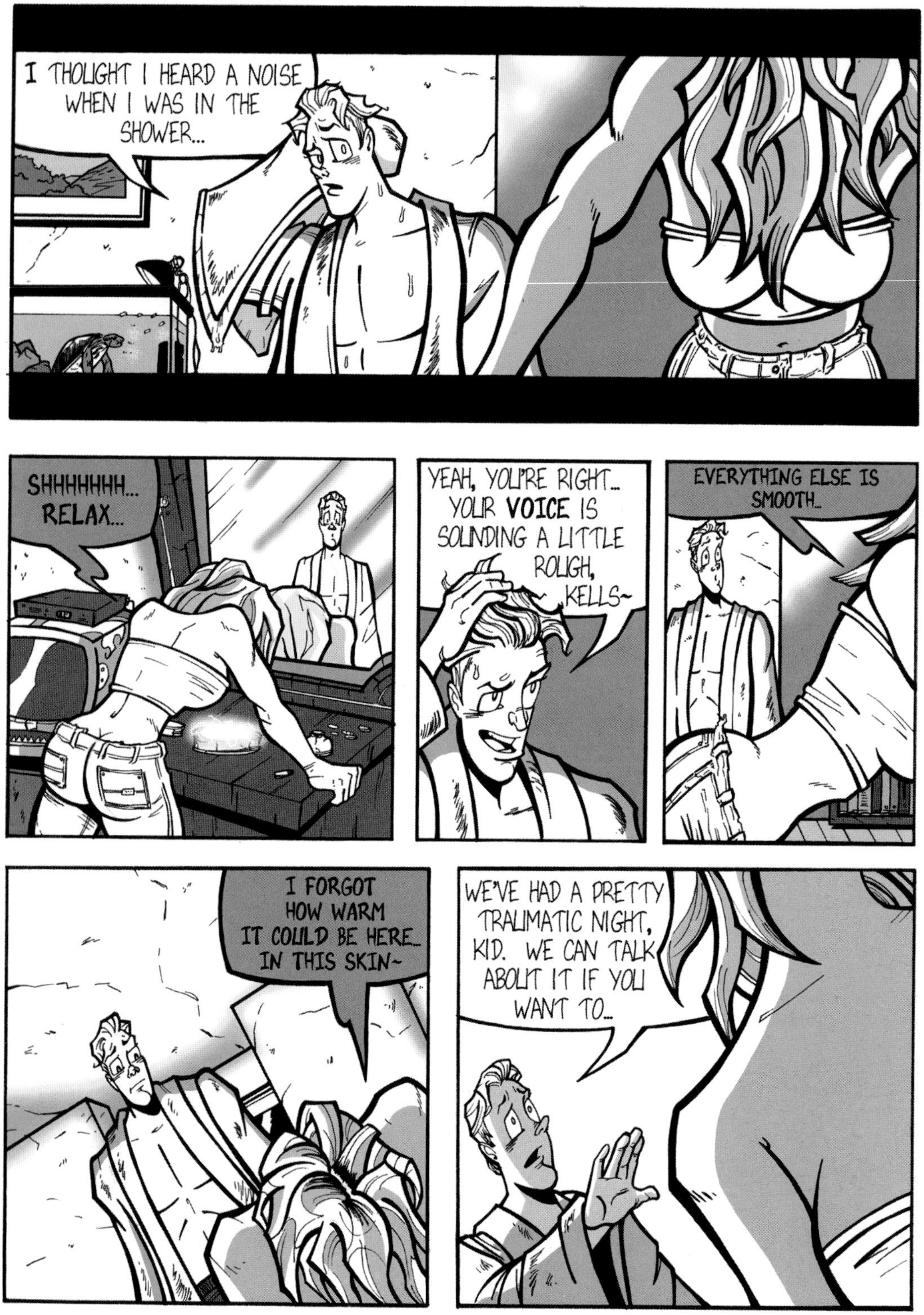
I THOUGHT I HEARD A NOISE WHEN I WAS IN THE SHOWER...
SHHHHHHH... RELAX...
YEAH, YOU'RE RIGHT... YOUR VOICE IS SOUNDING A LITTLE ROUGH, KELLS~
EVERYTHING ELSE IS SMOOTH...
I FORGOT HOW WARM IT COULD BE HERE... IN THIS SKIN~
WE'VE HAD A PRETTY TRAUMATIC NIGHT, KID. WE CAN TALK ABOUT IT IF YOU WANT TO...

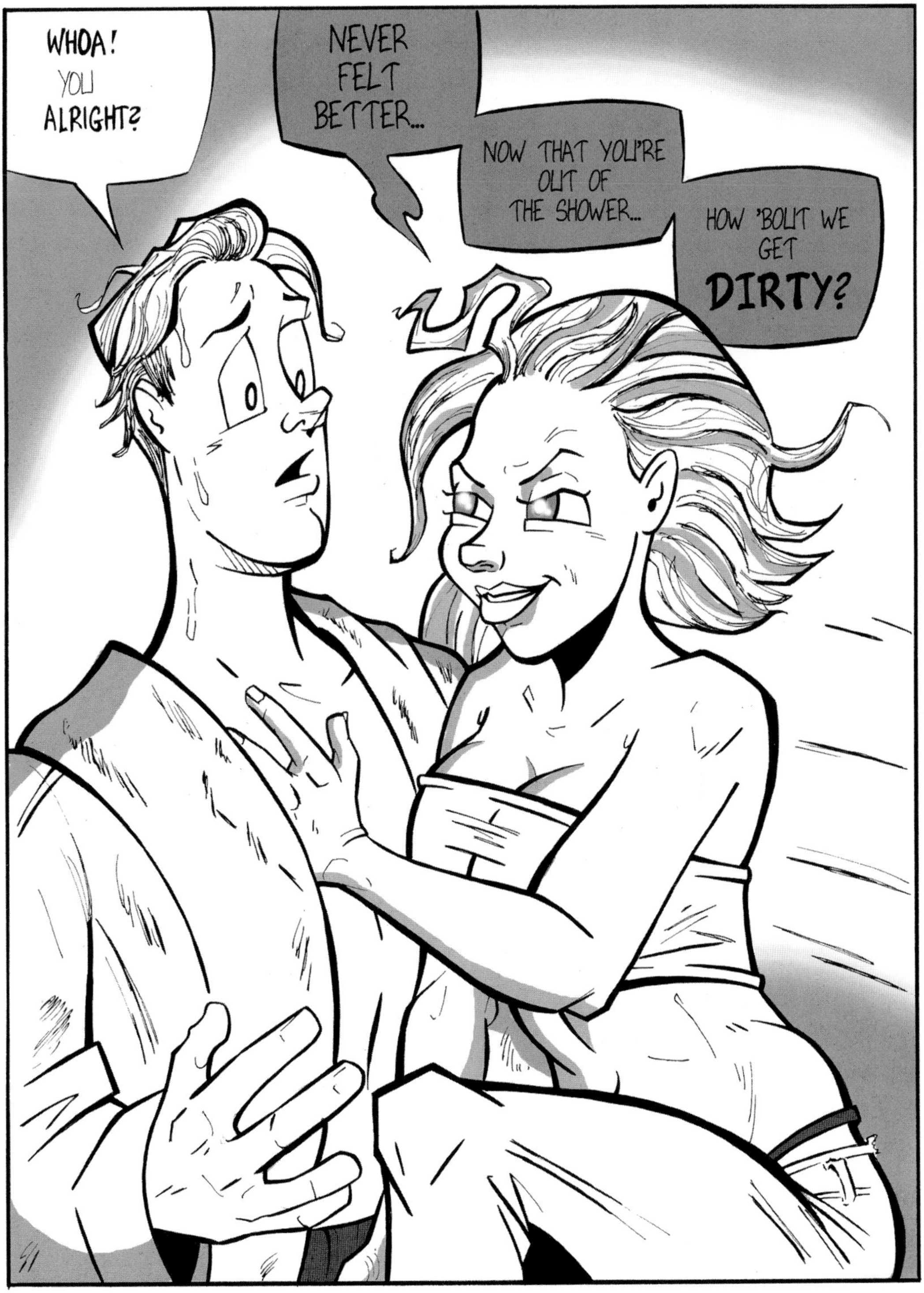
WHOA! YOU ALRIGHT?
NEVER FELT BETTER...
NOW THAT YOU'RE OUT OF THE SHOWER...
HOW 'BOUT WE GET DIRTY?

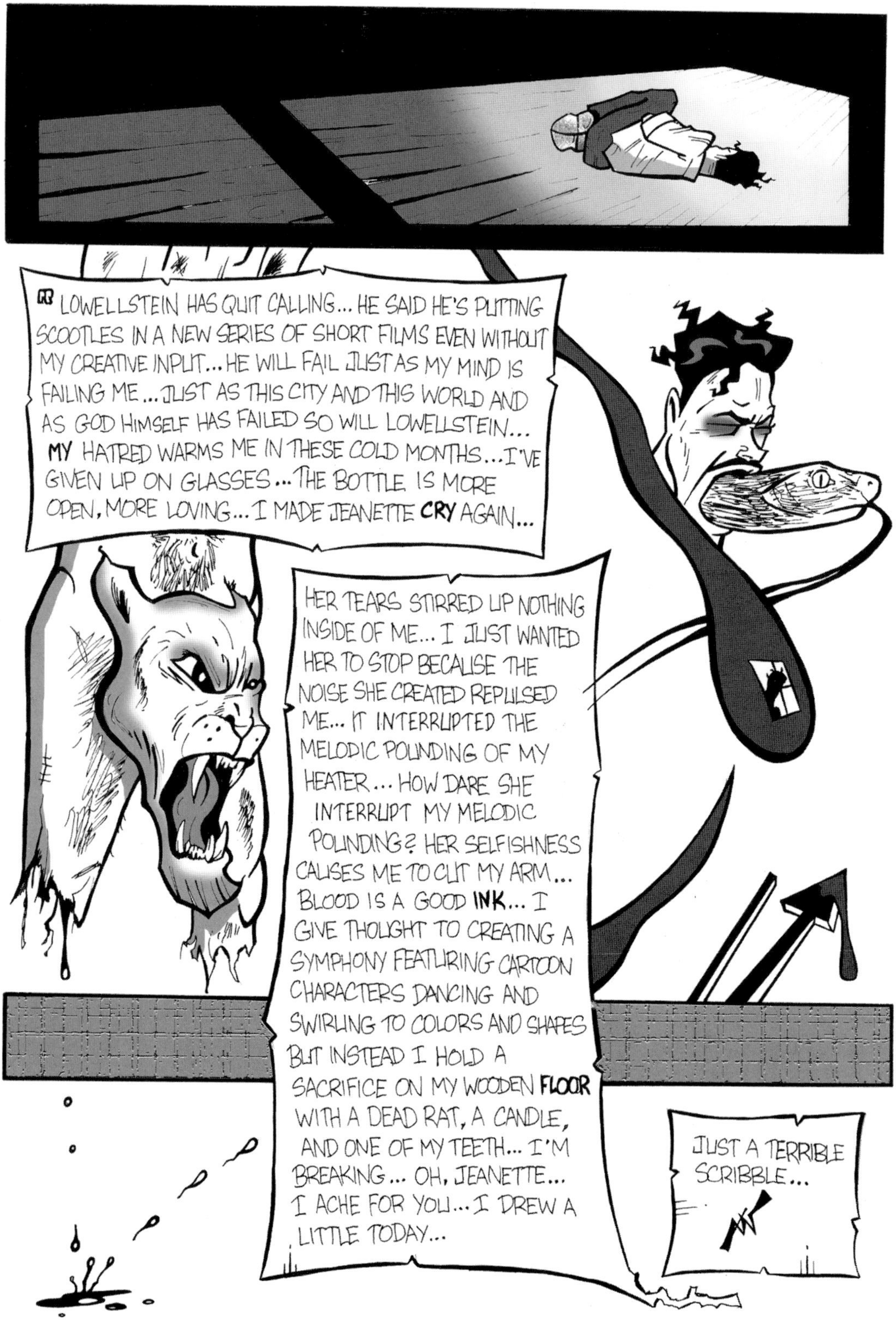
LOWELLSTEIN HAS QUIT CALLING... HE SAID HE'S PUTTING SCOOTLES IN A NEW SERIES OF SHORT FILMS EVEN WITHOUT MY CREATIVE INPUT... HE WILL FAIL JUST AS MY MIND IS FAILING ME... JUST AS THIS CITY AND THIS WORLD AND AS GOD HIMSELF HAS FAILED SO WILL LOWELLSTEIN... MY HATRED WARMS ME IN THESE COLD MONTHS... I'VE GIVEN UP ON GLASSES... THE BOTTLE IS MORE OPEN, MORE LOVING... I MADE JEANETTE CRY AGAIN...
HER TEARS STIRRED UP NOTHING INSIDE OF ME... I JUST WANTED HER TO STOP BECAUSE THE NOISE SHE CREATED REPULSED ME... IT INTERRUPTED THE MELODIC POUNDING OF MY HEATER... HOW DARE SHE INTERRUPT MY MELODIC POUNDING? HER SELFISHNESS CAUSES ME TO CUT MY ARM... BLOOD IS A GOOD INK... I GIVE THOUGHT TO CREATING A SYMPHONY FEATURING CARTOON CHARACTERS DANCING AND SWIRLING TO COLORS AND SHAPES BUT INSTEAD I HOLD A SACRIFICE ON MY WOODEN FLOOR WITH A DEAD RAT, A CANDLE, AND ONE OF MY TEETH... I'M BREAKING... OH, JEANETTE... I ACHE FOR YOU... I DREW A LITTLE TODAY...
JUST A TERRIBLE SCRIBBLE...

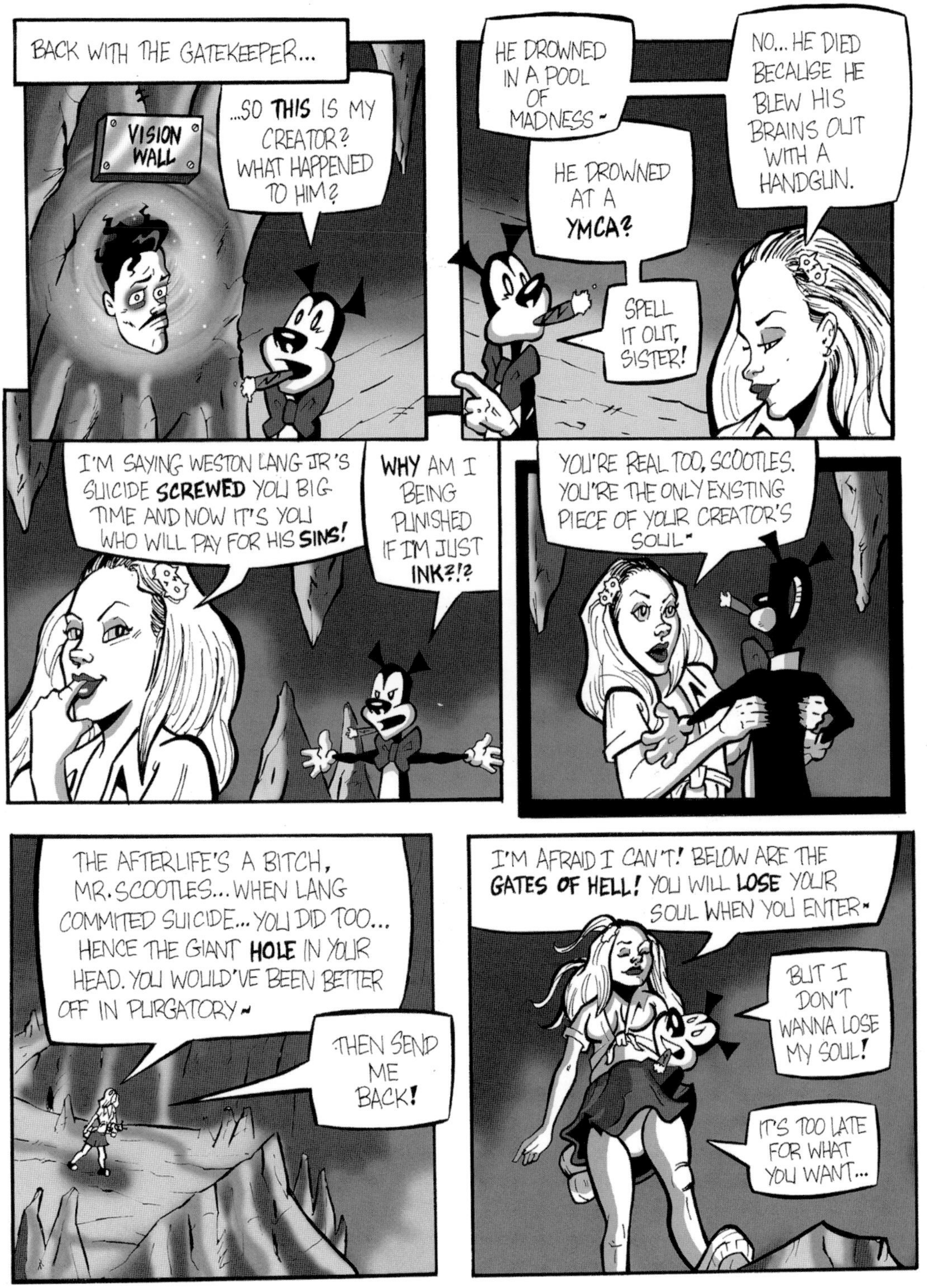
BACK WITH THE GATEKEEPER...
VISION WALL
...SO THIS IS MY CREATOR? WHAT HAPPENED TO HIM?
HE DROWNED IN A POOL OF MADNESS~
HE DROWNED AT A YMCA?
SPELL IT OUT, SISTER!
NO... HE DIED BECAUSE HE BLEW HIS BRAINS OUT WITH A HANDGUN.
I'M SAYING WESTON LANG JR'S SUICIDE SCREWED YOU BIG TIME AND NOW IT'S YOU WHO WILL PAY FOR HIS SINS!
WHY AM I BEING PUNISHED IF I'M JUST INK?!?
YOU'RE REAL TOO, SCOOTLES. YOU'RE THE ONLY EXISTING PIECE OF YOUR CREATOR'S SOUL~
THE AFTERLIFE'S A BITCH, MR. SCOOTLES... WHEN LANG COMMITED SUICIDE... YOU DID TOO... HENCE THE GIANT HOLE IN YOUR HEAD. YOU WOULD'VE BEEN BETTER OFF IN PURGATORY~
THEN SEND ME BACK!
I'M AFRAID I CAN'T! BELOW ARE THE GATES OF HELL! YOU WILL LOSE YOUR SOUL WHEN YOU ENTER~
BUT I DON'T WANNA LOSE MY SOUL!
IT'S TOO LATE FOR WHAT YOU WANT...

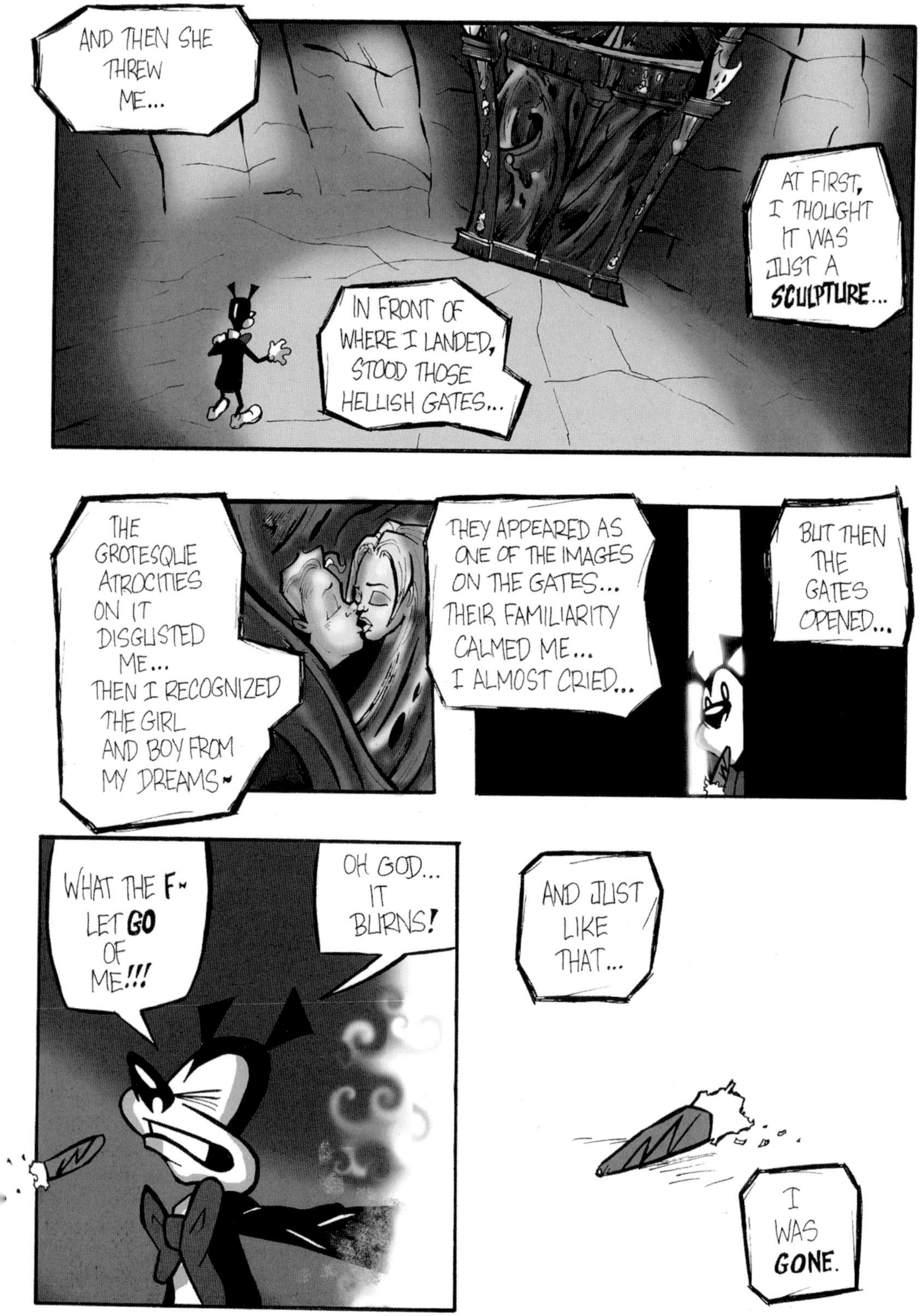
AND THEN SHE THREW ME...
AT FIRST, I THOUGHT IT WAS JUST A SCULPTURE...
IN FRONT OF WHERE I LANDED, STOOD THOSE HELLISH GATES...
THE GROTESQUE ATROCITIES ON IT DISGUSTED ME... THEN I RECOGNIZED THE GIRL AND BOY FROM MY DREAMS~
THEY APPEARED AS ONE OF THE IMAGES ON THE GATES... THEIR FAMILIARITY CALMED ME... I ALMOST CRIED...
BUT THEN THE GATES OPENED...
WHAT THE F~ LET GO OF ME!!!
OH GOD... IT BURNS!
AND JUST LIKE THAT...
I WAS GONE.

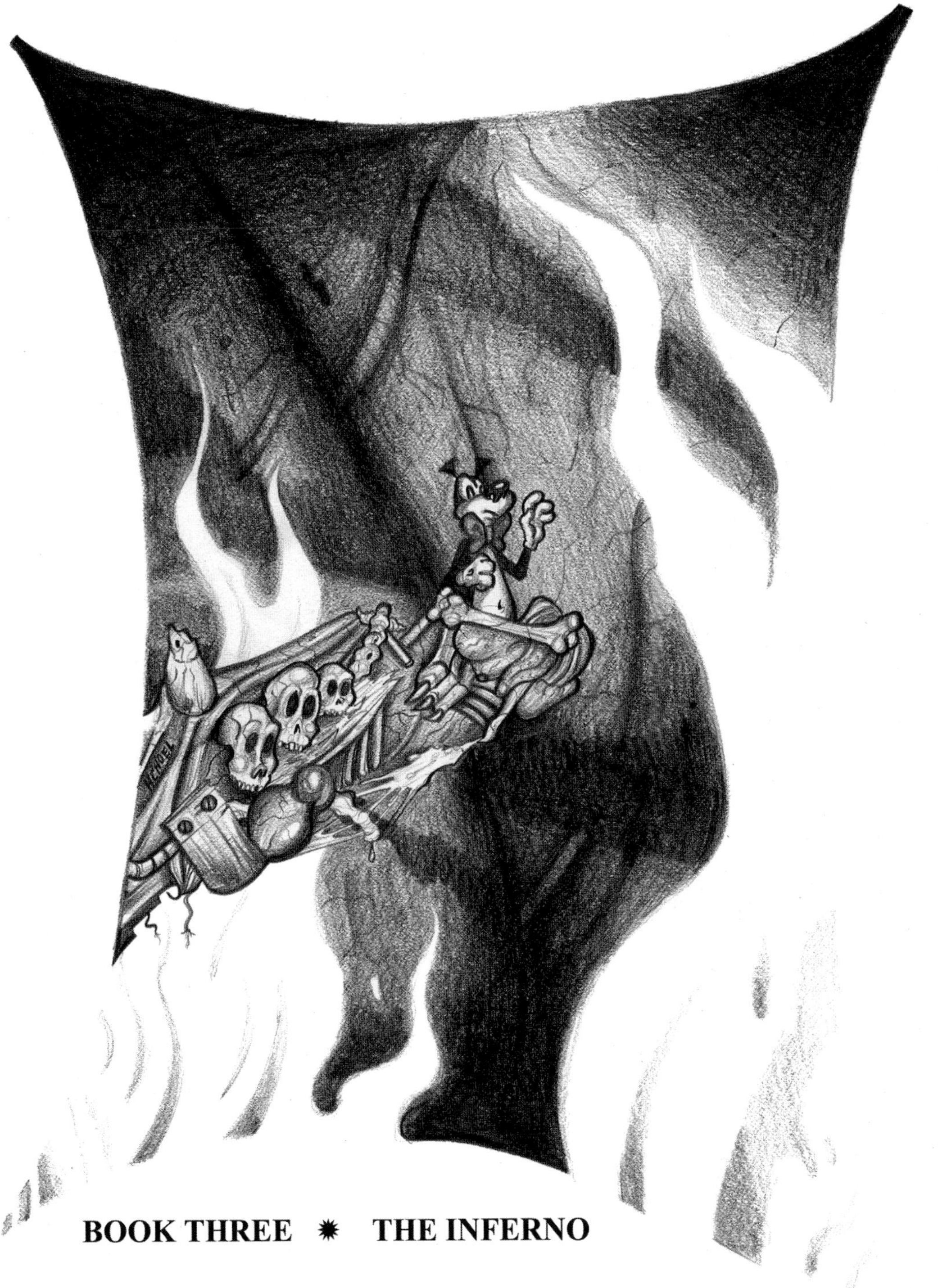

BOOK THREE ✷ THE INFERNO

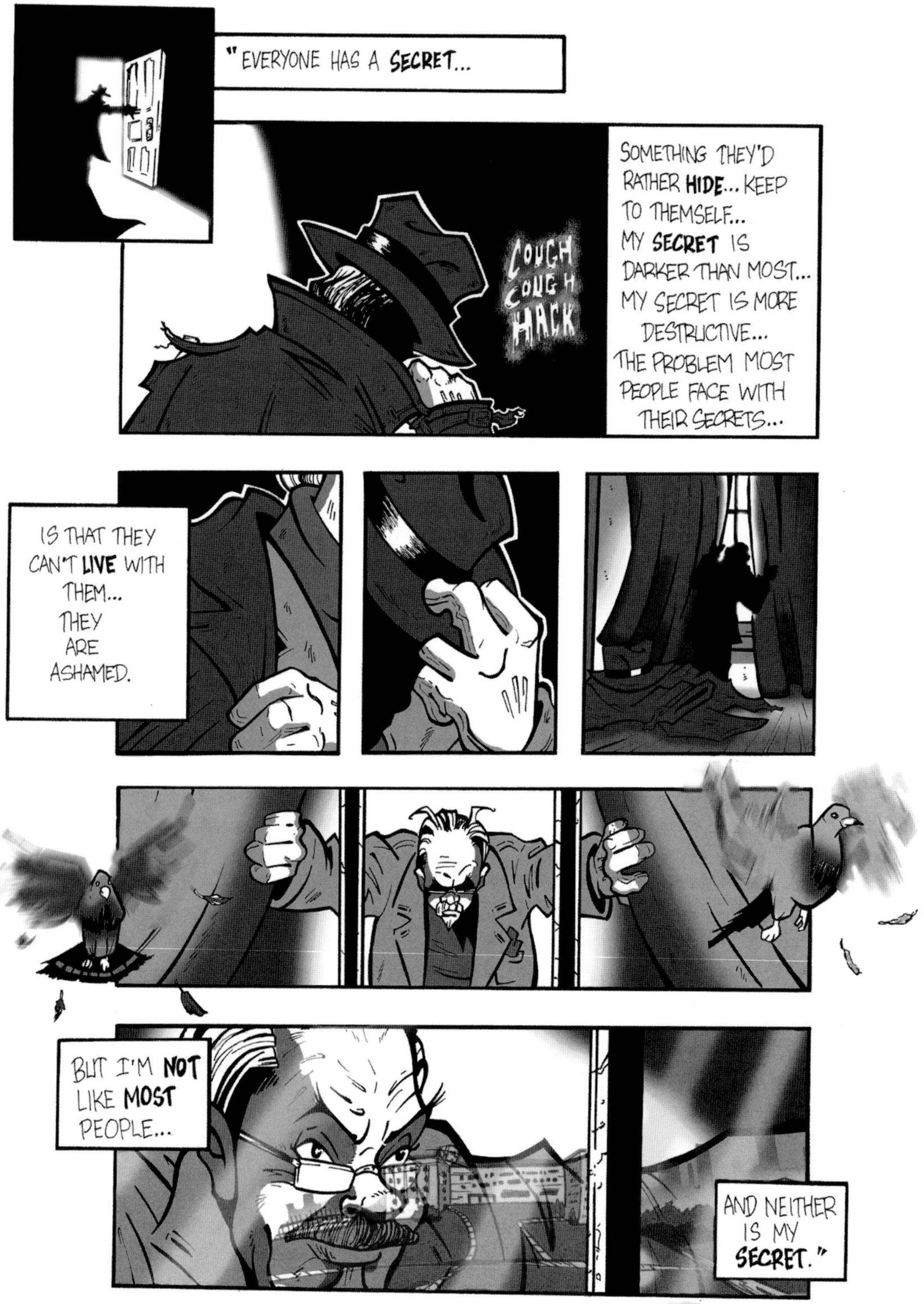
"EVERYONE HAS A SECRET...
SOMETHING THEY'D RATHER HIDE... KEEP TO THEMSELF... MY SECRET IS DARKER THAN MOST... MY SECRET IS MORE DESTRUCTIVE... THE PROBLEM MOST PEOPLE FACE WITH THEIR SECRETS...
COUGH COUGH HACK
IS THAT THEY CAN'T LIVE WITH THEM... THEY ARE ASHAMED.
BUT I'M NOT LIKE MOST PEOPLE...
AND NEITHER IS MY SECRET."

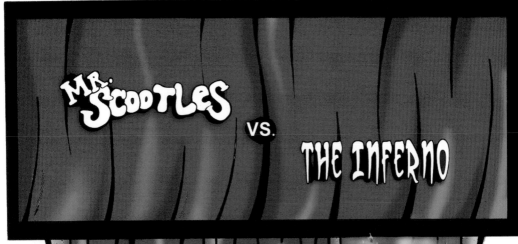

MR. SCOOTLES
VS.
THE INFERNO

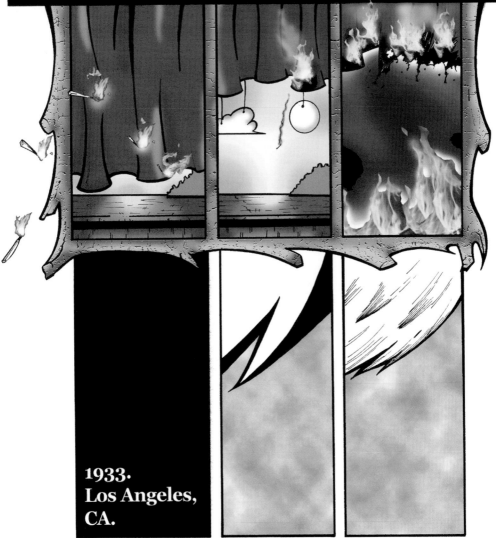

1933.
Los Angeles,
CA.

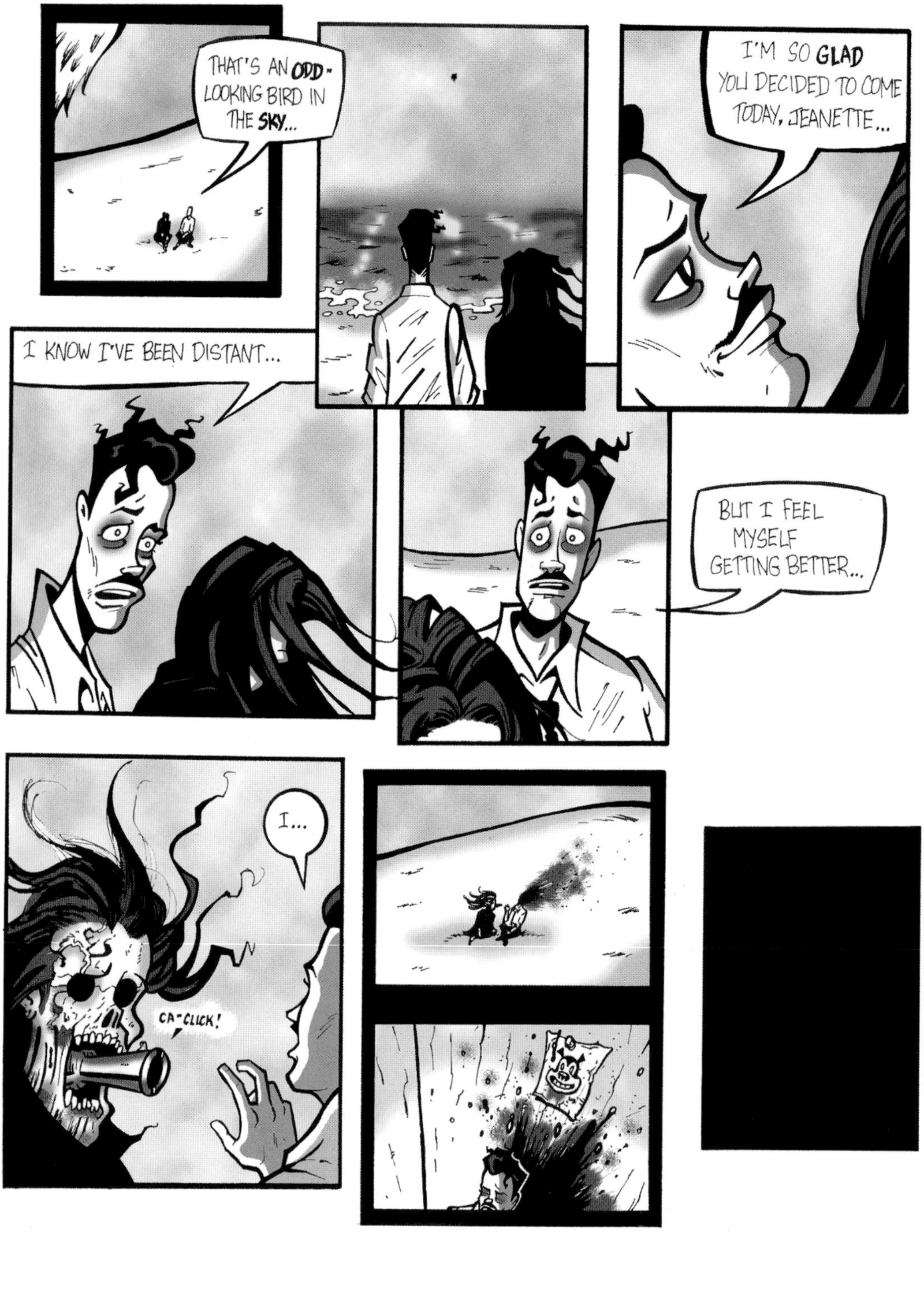
THAT'S AN ODD-LOOKING BIRD IN THE SKY...
I'M SO GLAD YOU DECIDED TO COME TODAY, JEANETTE...
I KNOW I'VE BEEN DISTANT...
BUT I FEEL MYSELF GETTING BETTER...
I...
CA-CLICK!

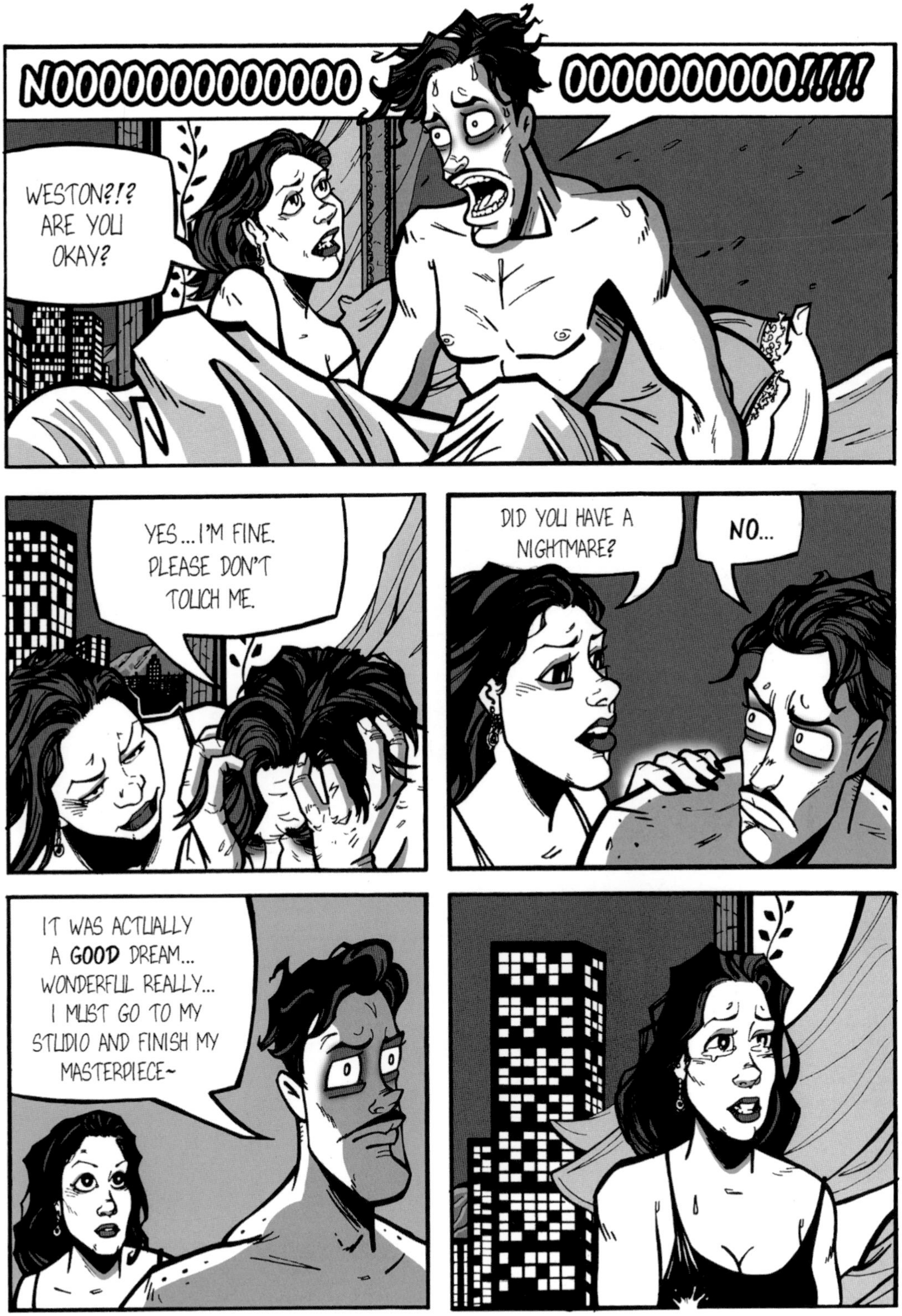
NOOOOOOOOOOOOOO
OOOOOOOOOOO!!!!!
WESTON?!? ARE YOU OKAY?
YES...I'M FINE. PLEASE DON'T TOUCH ME.
DID YOU HAVE A NIGHTMARE?
NO...
IT WAS ACTUALLY A GOOD DREAM... WONDERFUL REALLY... I MUST GO TO MY STUDIO AND FINISH MY MASTERPIECE~

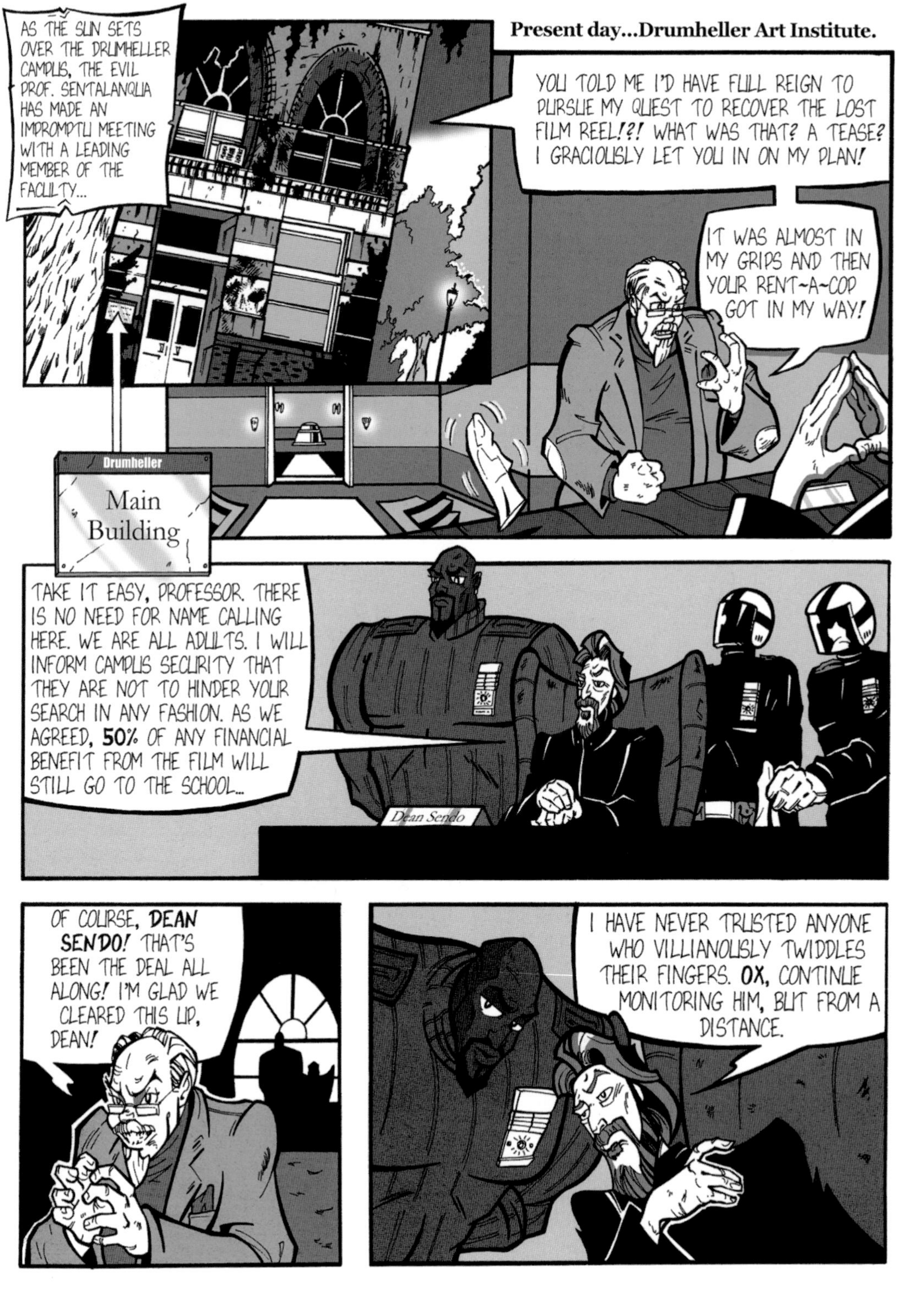
AS THE SUN SETS OVER THE DRUMHELLER CAMPUS, THE EVIL PROF. SENTALANQUA HAS MADE AN IMPROMPTU MEETING WITH A LEADING MEMBER OF THE FACULTY...
Present day...Drumheller Art Institute.
Drumheller
Main Building
YOU TOLD ME I'D HAVE FULL REIGN TO PURSUE MY QUEST TO RECOVER THE LOST FILM REEL!?! WHAT WAS THAT? A TEASE? I GRACIOUSLY LET YOU IN ON MY PLAN!
IT WAS ALMOST IN MY GRIPS AND THEN YOUR RENT~A~COP GOT IN MY WAY!
TAKE IT EASY, PROFESSOR. THERE IS NO NEED FOR NAME CALLING HERE. WE ARE ALL ADULTS. I WILL INFORM CAMPUS SECURITY THAT THEY ARE NOT TO HINDER YOUR SEARCH IN ANY FASHION. AS WE AGREED, 50% OF ANY FINANCIAL BENEFIT FROM THE FILM WILL STILL GO TO THE SCHOOL...
Dean Sendo
OF COURSE, DEAN SENDO! THAT'S BEEN THE DEAL ALL ALONG! I'M GLAD WE CLEARED THIS UP, DEAN!
I HAVE NEVER TRUSTED ANYONE WHO VILLIANOUSLY TWIDDLES THEIR FINGERS. OX, CONTINUE MONITORING HIM, BUT FROM A DISTANCE.

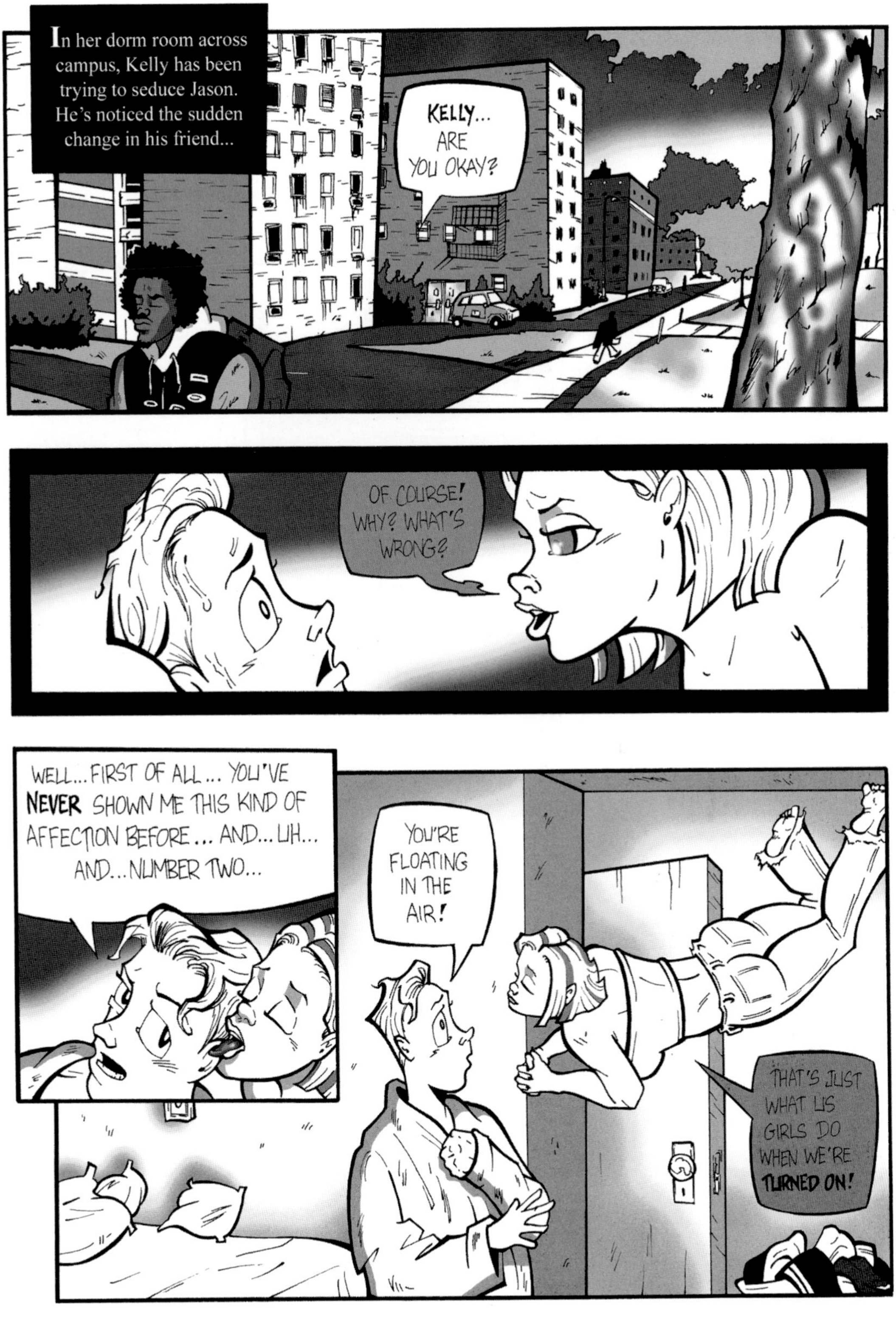
In her dorm room across campus, Kelly has been trying to seduce Jason. He's noticed the sudden change in his friend...
KELLY... ARE YOU OKAY?
OF COURSE! WHY? WHAT'S WRONG?
WELL... FIRST OF ALL... YOU'VE NEVER SHOWN ME THIS KIND OF AFFECTION BEFORE... AND... UH... AND... NUMBER TWO...
YOU'RE FLOATING IN THE AIR!
THAT'S JUST WHAT US GIRLS DO WHEN WE'RE TURNED ON!

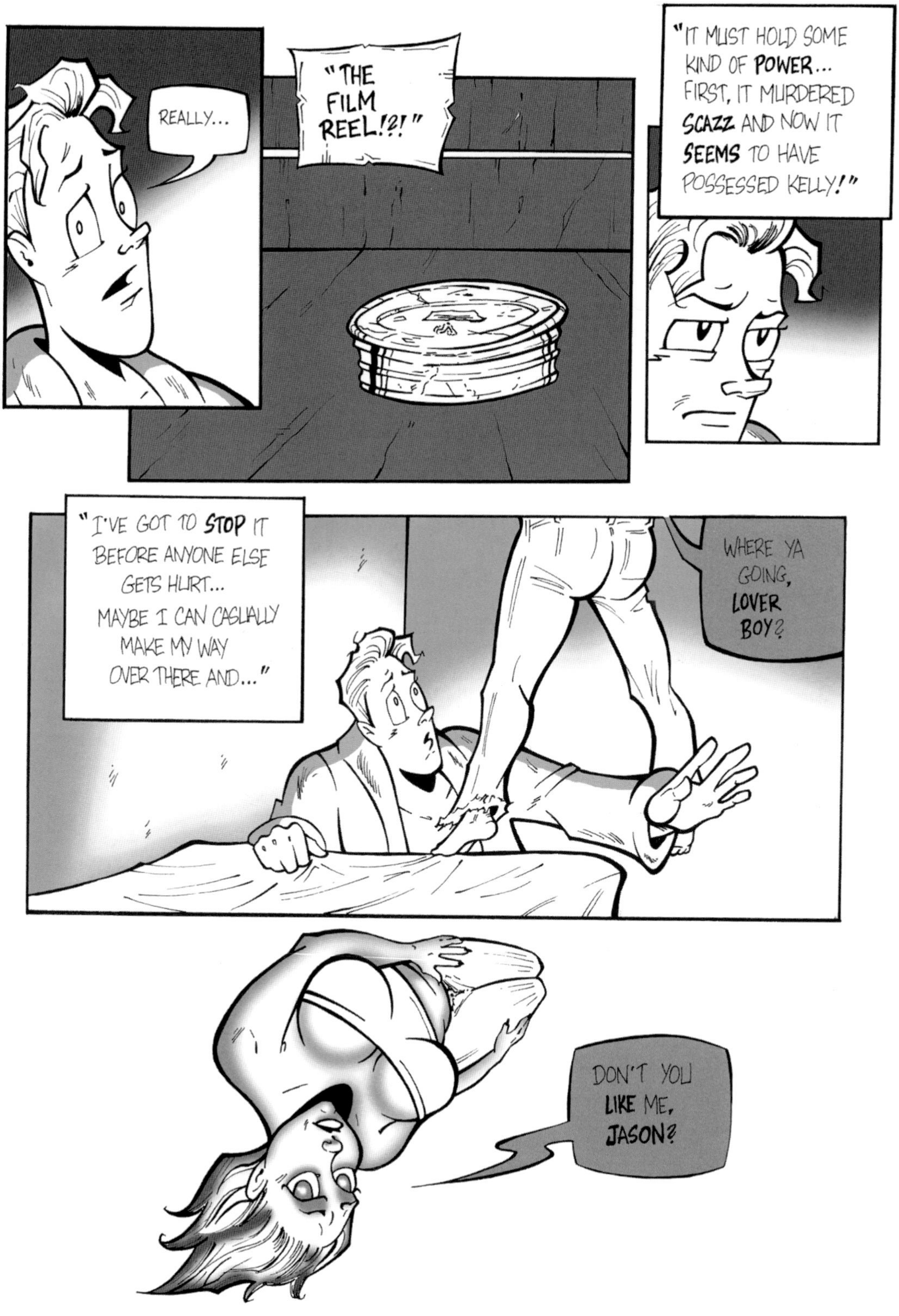
REALLY...
"THE FILM REEL!?!"
"IT MUST HOLD SOME KIND OF POWER... FIRST, IT MURDERED SCAZZ AND NOW IT SEEMS TO HAVE POSSESSED KELLY!"
"I'VE GOT TO STOP IT BEFORE ANYONE ELSE GETS HURT... MAYBE I CAN CASUALLY MAKE MY WAY OVER THERE AND..."
WHERE YA GOING, LOVER BOY?
DON'T YOU LIKE ME, JASON?

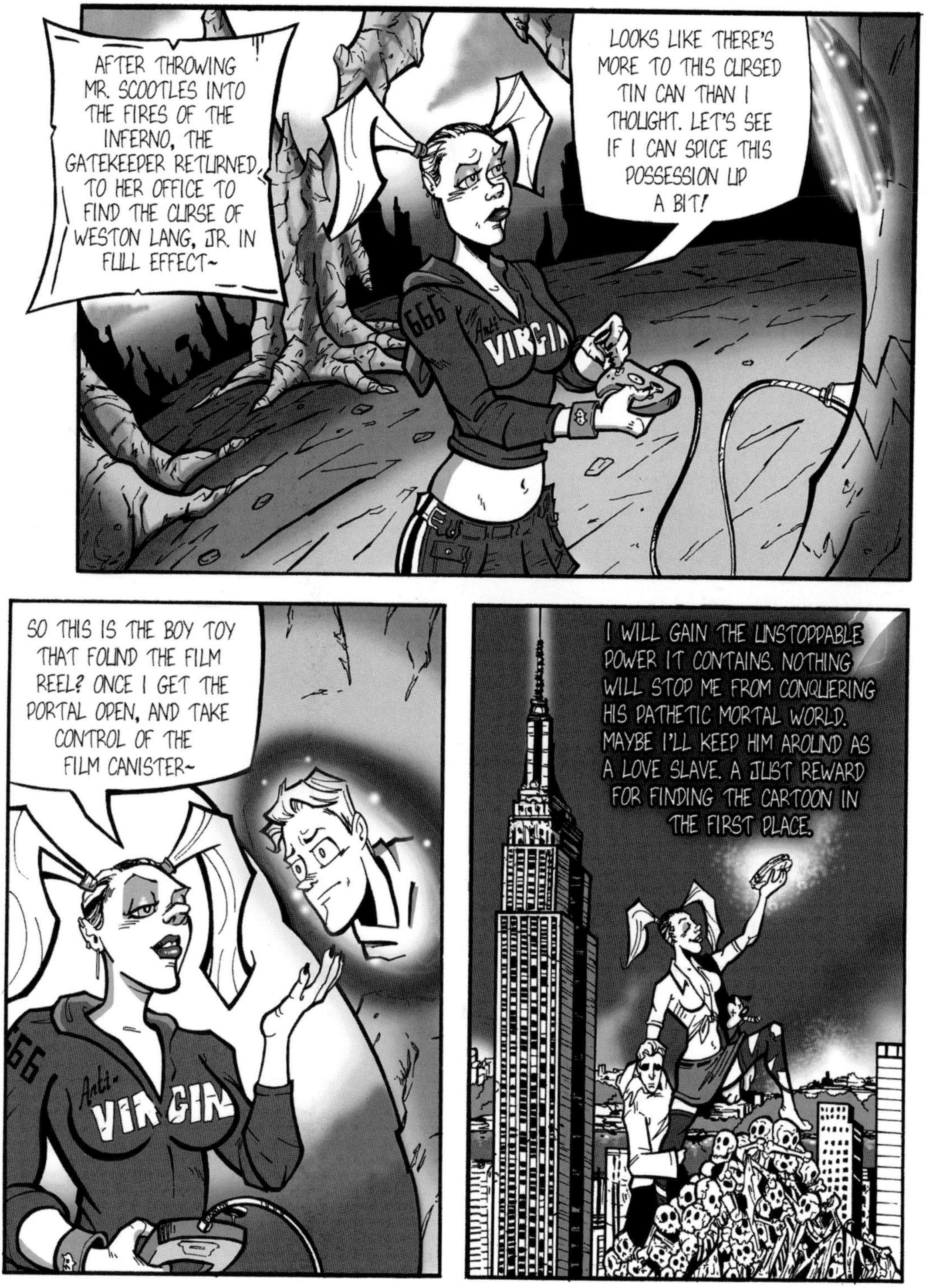
AFTER THROWING MR. SCOOTLES INTO THE FIRES OF THE INFERNO, THE GATEKEEPER RETURNED TO HER OFFICE TO FIND THE CURSE OF WESTON LANG, JR. IN FULL EFFECT~
LOOKS LIKE THERE'S MORE TO THIS CURSED TIN CAN THAN I THOUGHT. LET'S SEE IF I CAN SPICE THIS POSSESSION UP A BIT!
666
Anti-
VIRGIN
SO THIS IS THE BOY TOY THAT FOUND THE FILM REEL? ONCE I GET THE PORTAL OPEN, AND TAKE CONTROL OF THE FILM CANISTER~
I WILL GAIN THE UNSTOPPABLE POWER IT CONTAINS. NOTHING WILL STOP ME FROM CONQUERING HIS PATHETIC MORTAL WORLD. MAYBE I'LL KEEP HIM AROUND AS A LOVE SLAVE. A JUST REWARD FOR FINDING THE CARTOON IN THE FIRST PLACE.

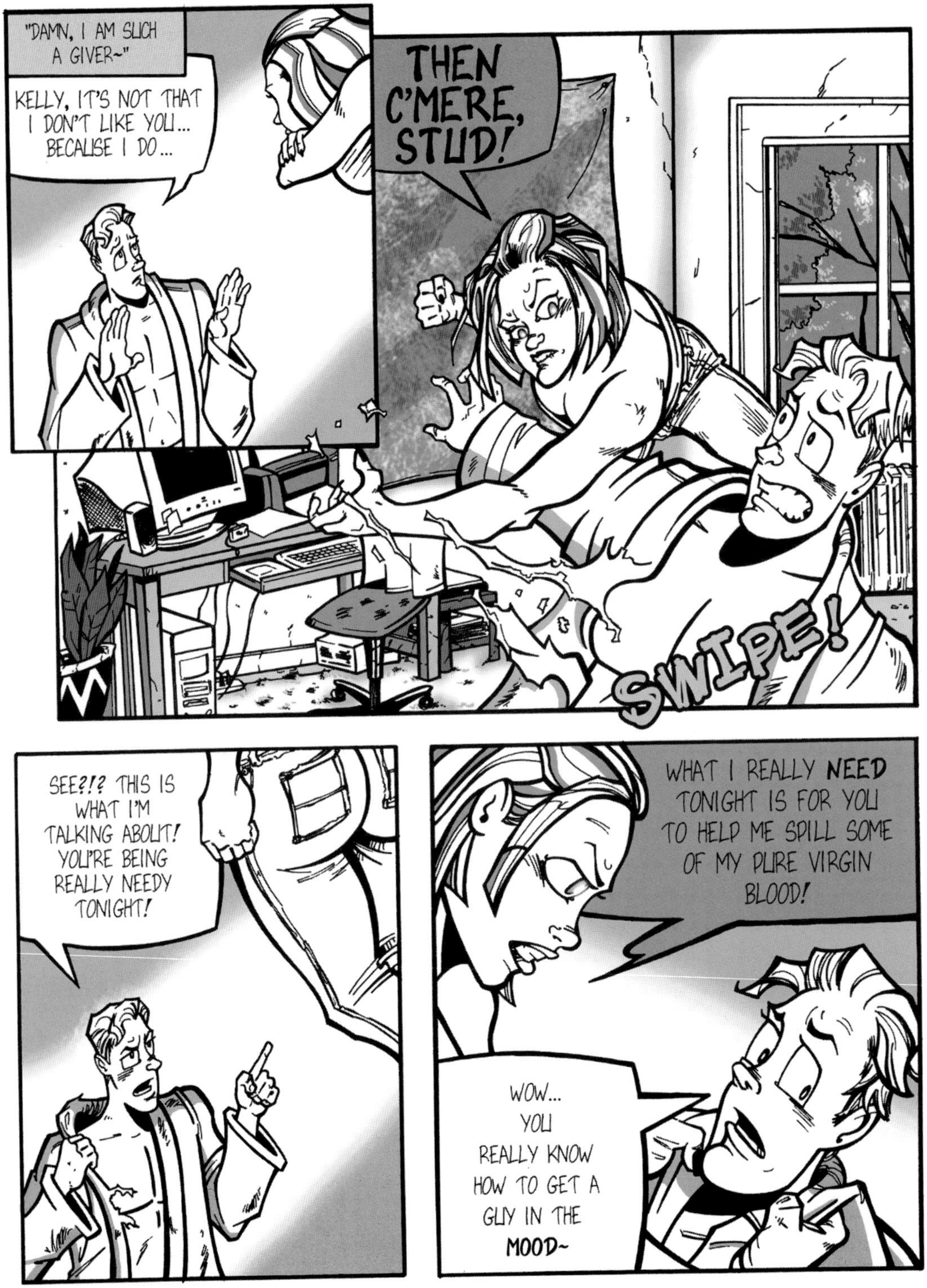
"DAMN, I AM SUCH A GIVER~"
KELLY, IT'S NOT THAT I DON'T LIKE YOU... BECAUSE I DO...
THEN C'MERE, STUD!
SWIPE!
SEE?!? THIS IS WHAT I'M TALKING ABOUT! YOU'RE BEING REALLY NEEDY TONIGHT!
WHAT I REALLY **NEED** TONIGHT IS FOR YOU TO HELP ME SPILL SOME OF MY PURE VIRGIN BLOOD!
WOW... YOU REALLY KNOW HOW TO GET A GUY IN THE **MOOD**~

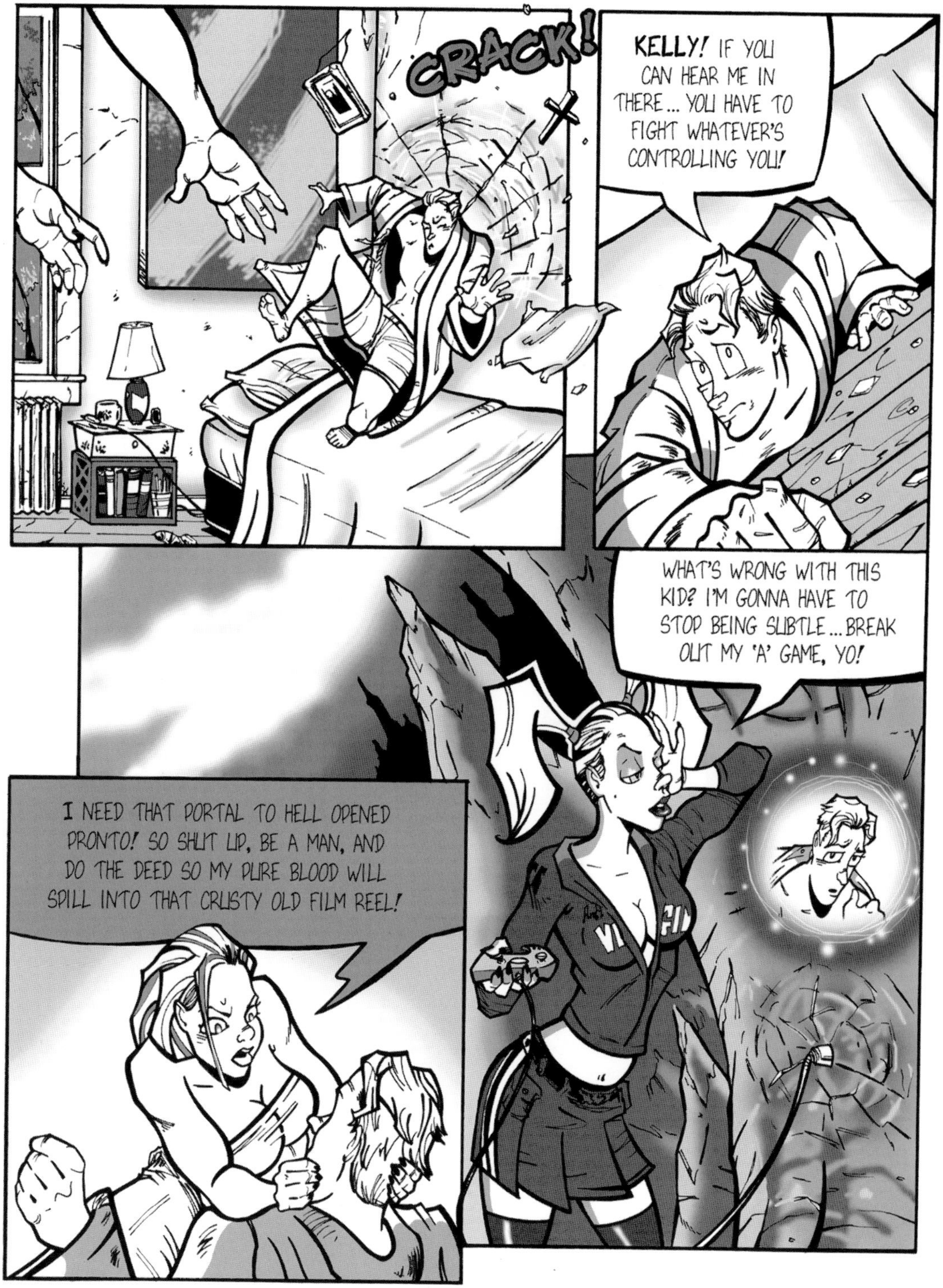
CRACK!
KELLY! IF YOU CAN HEAR ME IN THERE... YOU HAVE TO FIGHT WHATEVER'S CONTROLLING YOU!
WHAT'S WRONG WITH THIS KID? I'M GONNA HAVE TO STOP BEING SUBTLE... BREAK OUT MY 'A' GAME, YO!
I NEED THAT PORTAL TO HELL OPENED PRONTO! SO SHUT UP, BE A MAN, AND DO THE DEED SO MY PURE BLOOD WILL SPILL INTO THAT CRUSTY OLD FILM REEL!

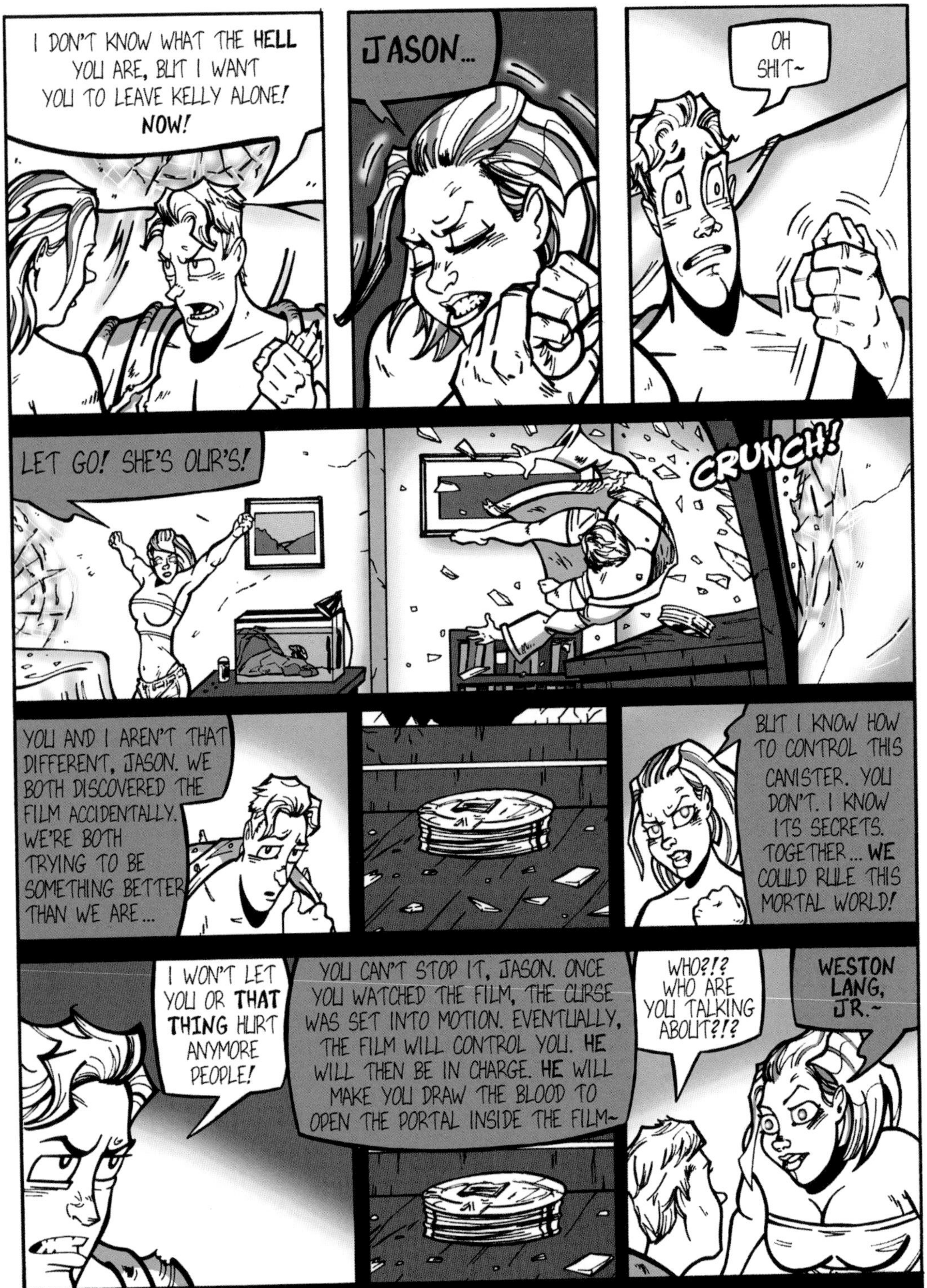
I DON'T KNOW WHAT THE **HELL** YOU ARE, BUT I WANT YOU TO LEAVE KELLY ALONE! **NOW!**
JASON...
OH SHIT~
LET GO! SHE'S OUR'S!
CRUNCH!
YOU AND I AREN'T THAT DIFFERENT, JASON. WE BOTH DISCOVERED THE FILM ACCIDENTALLY. WE'RE BOTH TRYING TO BE SOMETHING BETTER THAN WE ARE...
BUT I KNOW HOW TO CONTROL THIS CANISTER. YOU DON'T. I KNOW ITS SECRETS. TOGETHER... **WE** COULD RULE THIS MORTAL WORLD!
I WON'T LET YOU OR **THAT THING** HURT ANYMORE PEOPLE!
YOU CAN'T STOP IT, JASON. ONCE YOU WATCHED THE FILM, THE CURSE WAS SET INTO MOTION. EVENTUALLY, THE FILM WILL CONTROL YOU. **HE** WILL THEN BE IN CHARGE. **HE** WILL MAKE YOU DRAW THE BLOOD TO OPEN THE PORTAL INSIDE THE FILM~
WHO?!? WHO ARE YOU TALKING ABOUT?!?
WESTON LANG, JR.~

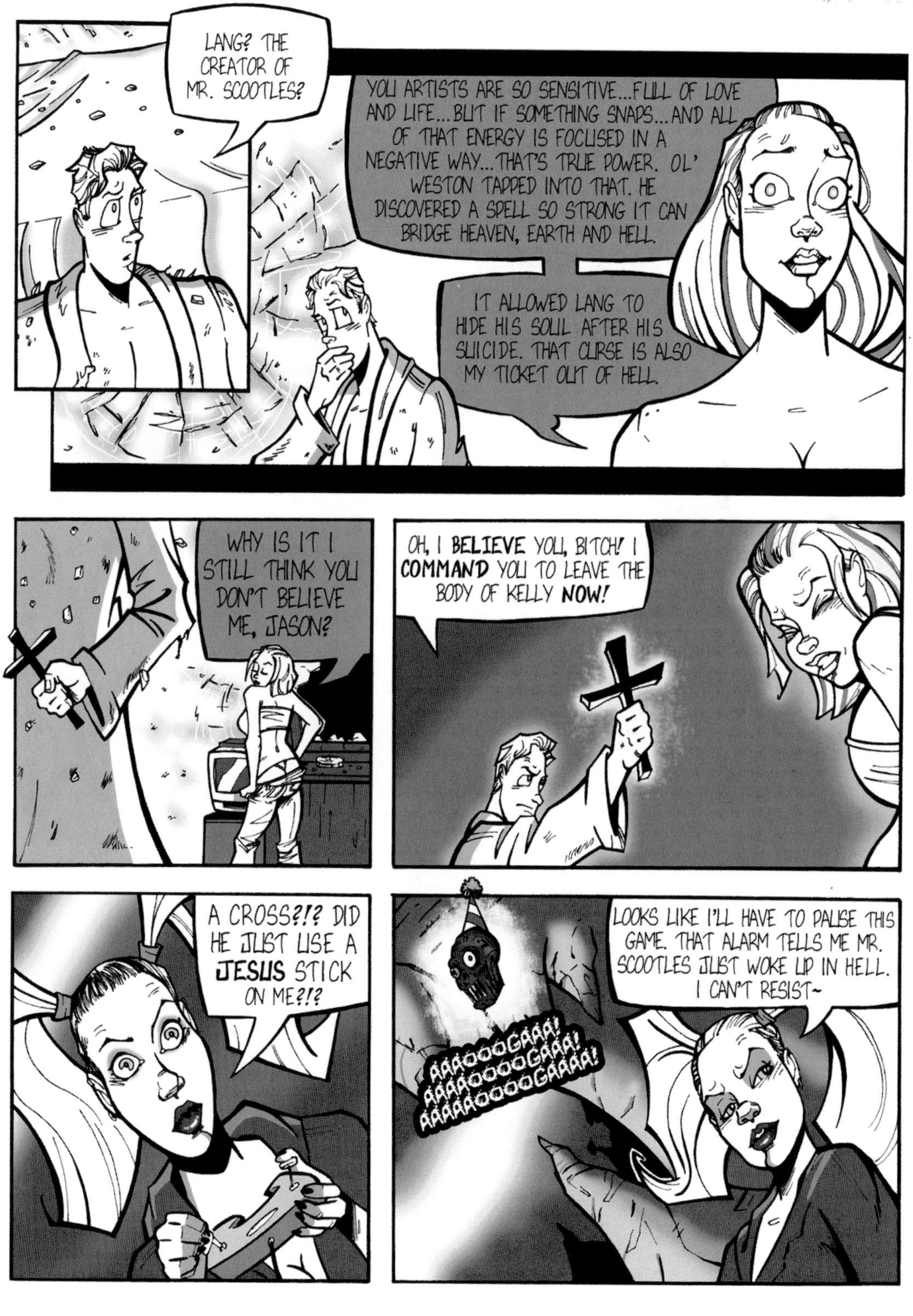
LANG? THE CREATOR OF MR. SCOOTLES?
YOU ARTISTS ARE SO SENSITIVE...FULL OF LOVE AND LIFE...BUT IF SOMETHING SNAPS...AND ALL OF THAT ENERGY IS FOCUSED IN A NEGATIVE WAY...THAT'S TRUE POWER. OL' WESTON TAPPED INTO THAT. HE DISCOVERED A SPELL SO STRONG IT CAN BRIDGE HEAVEN, EARTH AND HELL.
IT ALLOWED LANG TO HIDE HIS SOUL AFTER HIS SUICIDE. THAT CURSE IS ALSO MY TICKET OUT OF HELL.
WHY IS IT I STILL THINK YOU DON'T BELIEVE ME, JASON?
OH, I BELIEVE YOU, BITCH! I COMMAND YOU TO LEAVE THE BODY OF KELLY NOW!
A CROSS?!? DID HE JUST USE A JESUS STICK ON ME?!?
AAAOOOOGAAA! AAAAOOOOGAAA! AAAAAOOOOGAAAA!
LOOKS LIKE I'LL HAVE TO PAUSE THIS GAME. THAT ALARM TELLS ME MR. SCOOTLES JUST WOKE UP IN HELL. I CAN'T RESIST~

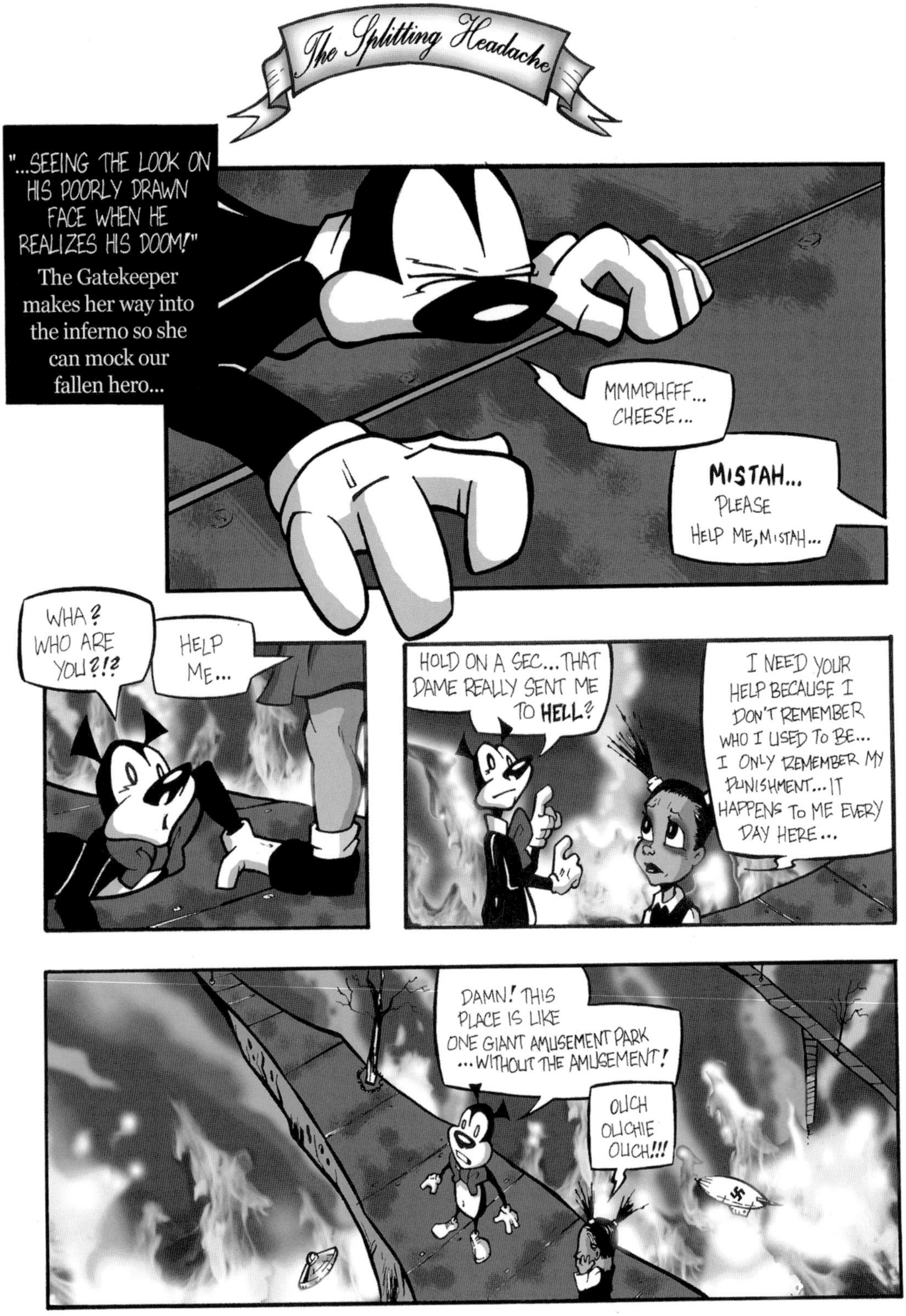
The Splitting Headache
"...SEEING THE LOOK ON HIS POORLY DRAWN FACE WHEN HE REALIZES HIS DOOM!" The Gatekeeper makes her way into the inferno so she can mock our fallen hero...
MMMPHFFF... CHEESE...
MISTAH... PLEASE HELP ME, MISTAH...
WHA? WHO ARE YOU?!?
HELP ME...
HOLD ON A SEC... THAT DAME REALLY SENT ME TO HELL?
I NEED YOUR HELP BECAUSE I DON'T REMEMBER WHO I USED TO BE... I ONLY REMEMBER MY PUNISHMENT... IT HAPPENS TO ME EVERY DAY HERE...
DAMN! THIS PLACE IS LIKE ONE GIANT AMUSEMENT PARK ...WITHOUT THE AMUSEMENT!
OUCH OUCHIE OUCH!!!

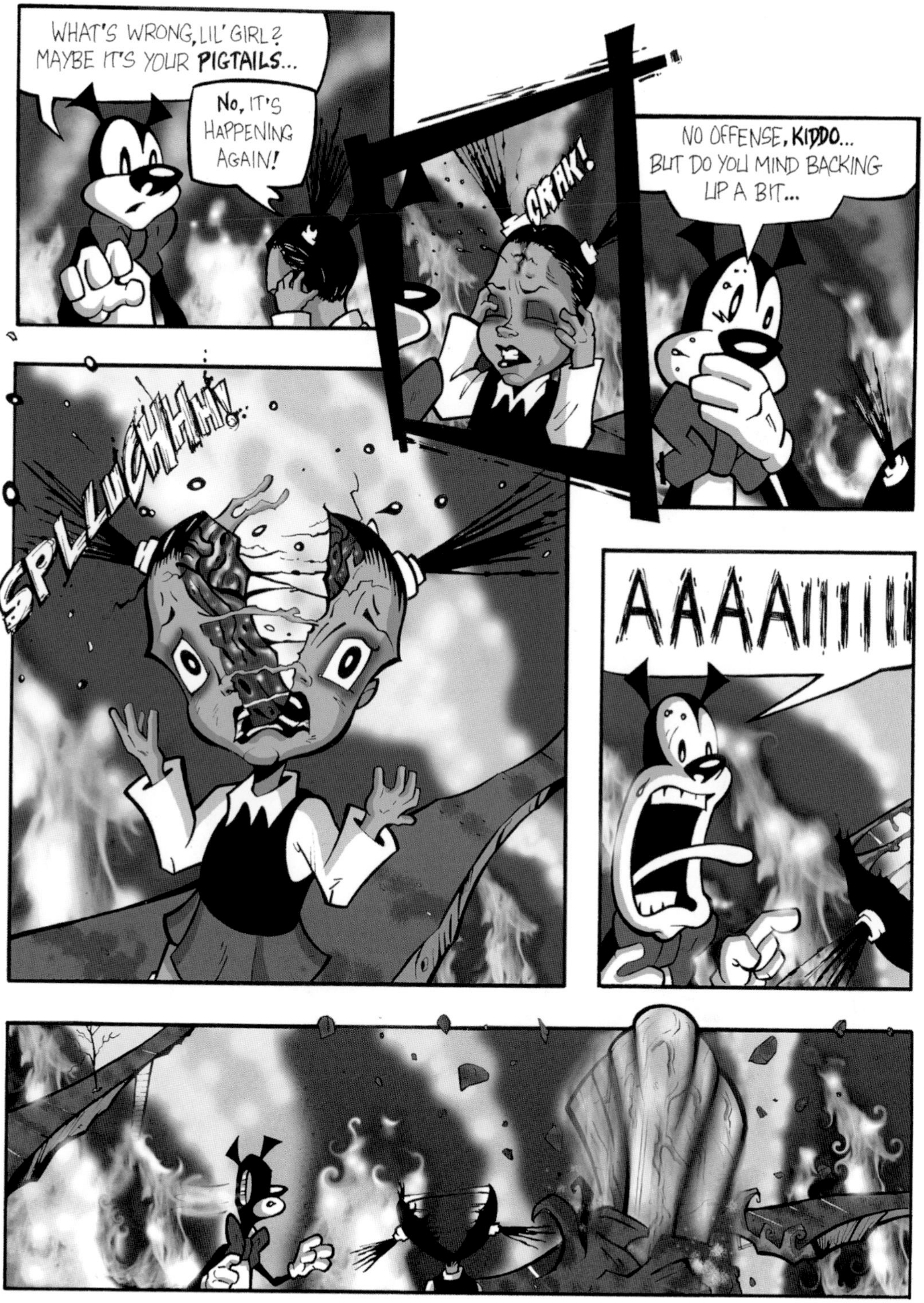

WHAT'S WRONG, LIL' GIRL? MAYBE IT'S YOUR **PIGTAILS**...
No, IT'S HAPPENING AGAIN!
CRAK!
NO OFFENSE, **KIDDO**... BUT DO YOU MIND BACKING UP A BIT...
SPLLUCHHHH!
AAAAIIIIII

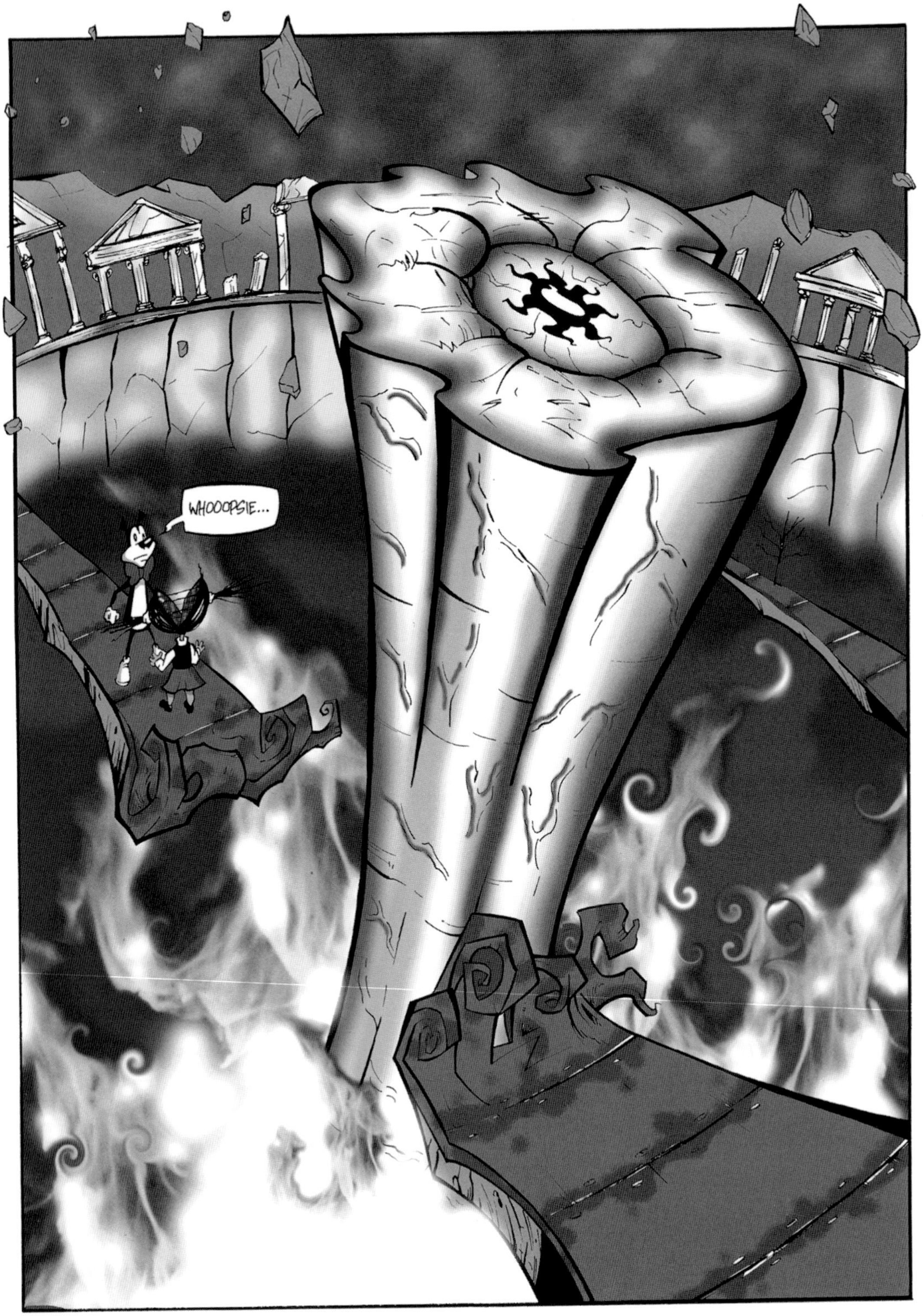
WHOOOPSIE...

THAT'S THE UGLIEST, VEINIEST CANDY CANE I'VE EVER SEEN~

KER' SPLOOK!

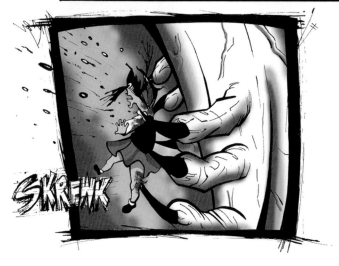

SKREWK

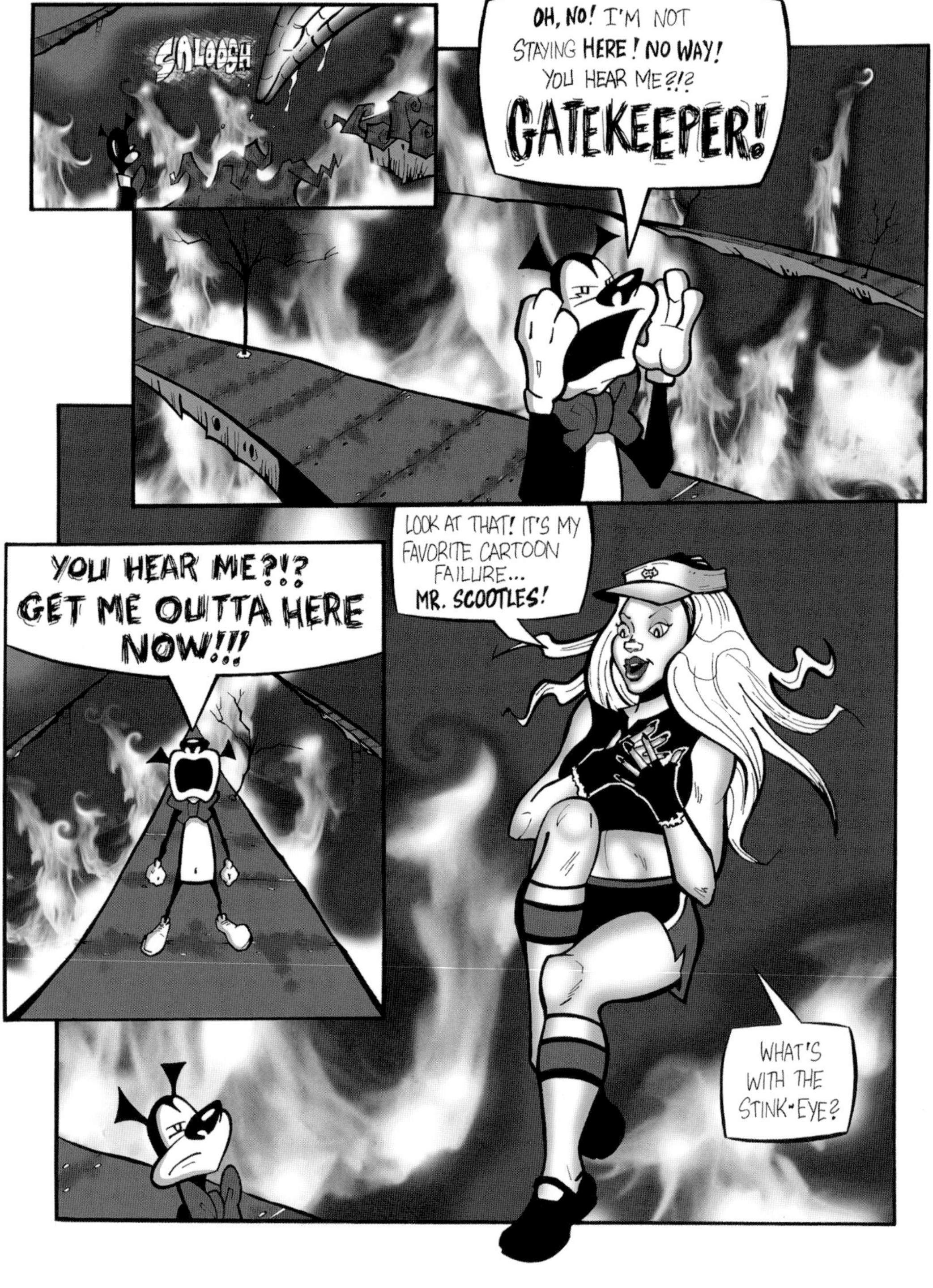
SPLOOSH
OH, NO! I'M NOT STAYING HERE! NO WAY! YOU HEAR ME?!?
GATEKEEPER!
YOU HEAR ME?!? GET ME OUTTA HERE NOW!!!
LOOK AT THAT! IT'S MY FAVORITE CARTOON FAILURE... MR. SCOOTLES!
WHAT'S WITH THE STINK-EYE?

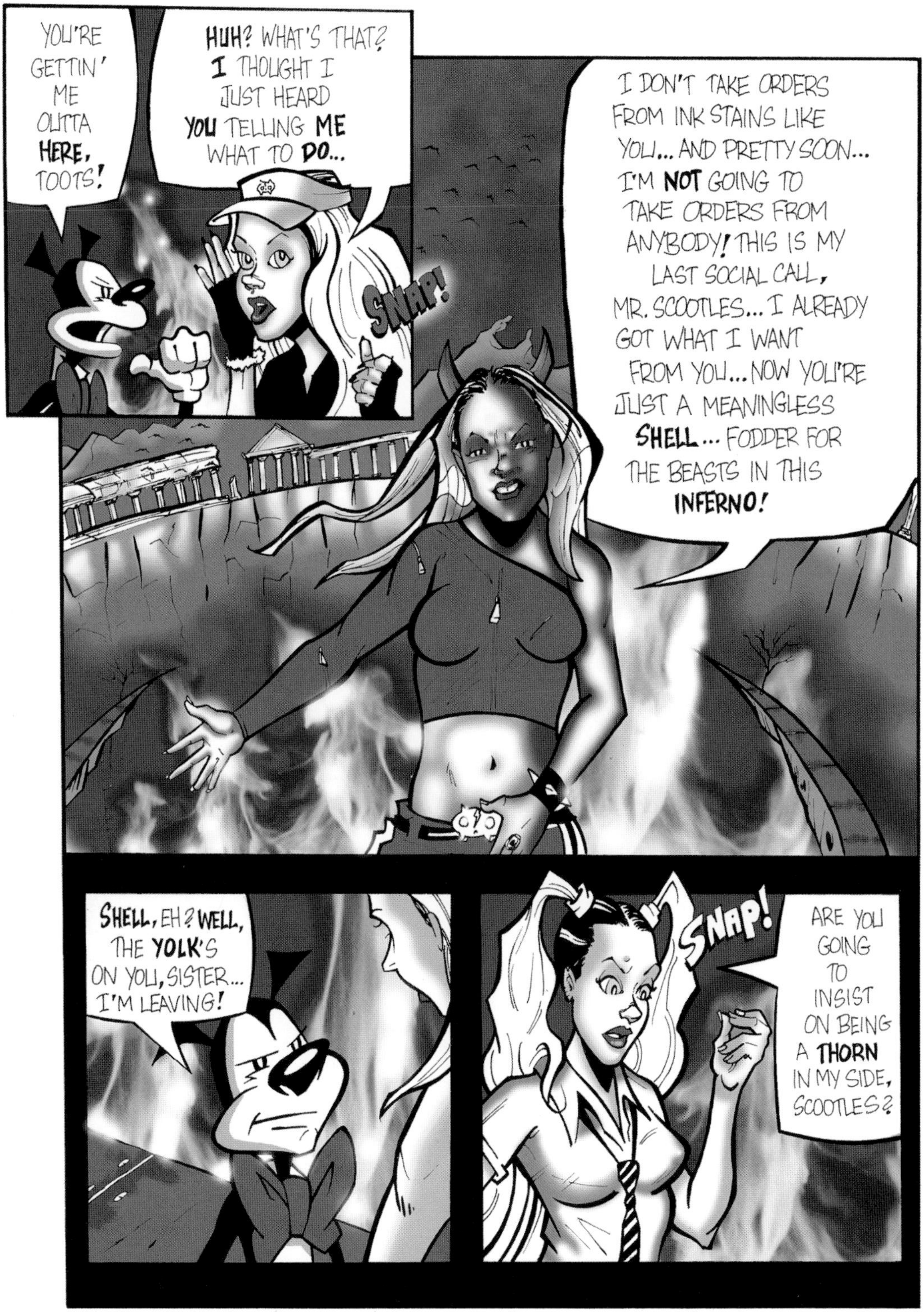
YOU'RE GETTIN' ME OUTTA HERE, TOOTS!
HUH? WHAT'S THAT? I THOUGHT I JUST HEARD YOU TELLING ME WHAT TO DO...
SNAP!
I DON'T TAKE ORDERS FROM INK STAINS LIKE YOU... AND PRETTY SOON... I'M NOT GOING TO TAKE ORDERS FROM ANYBODY! THIS IS MY LAST SOCIAL CALL, MR. SCOOTLES... I ALREADY GOT WHAT I WANT FROM YOU... NOW YOU'RE JUST A MEANINGLESS SHELL... FODDER FOR THE BEASTS IN THIS INFERNO!
SHELL, EH? WELL, THE YOLK'S ON YOU, SISTER... I'M LEAVING!
SNAP!
ARE YOU GOING TO INSIST ON BEING A THORN IN MY SIDE, SCOOTLES?

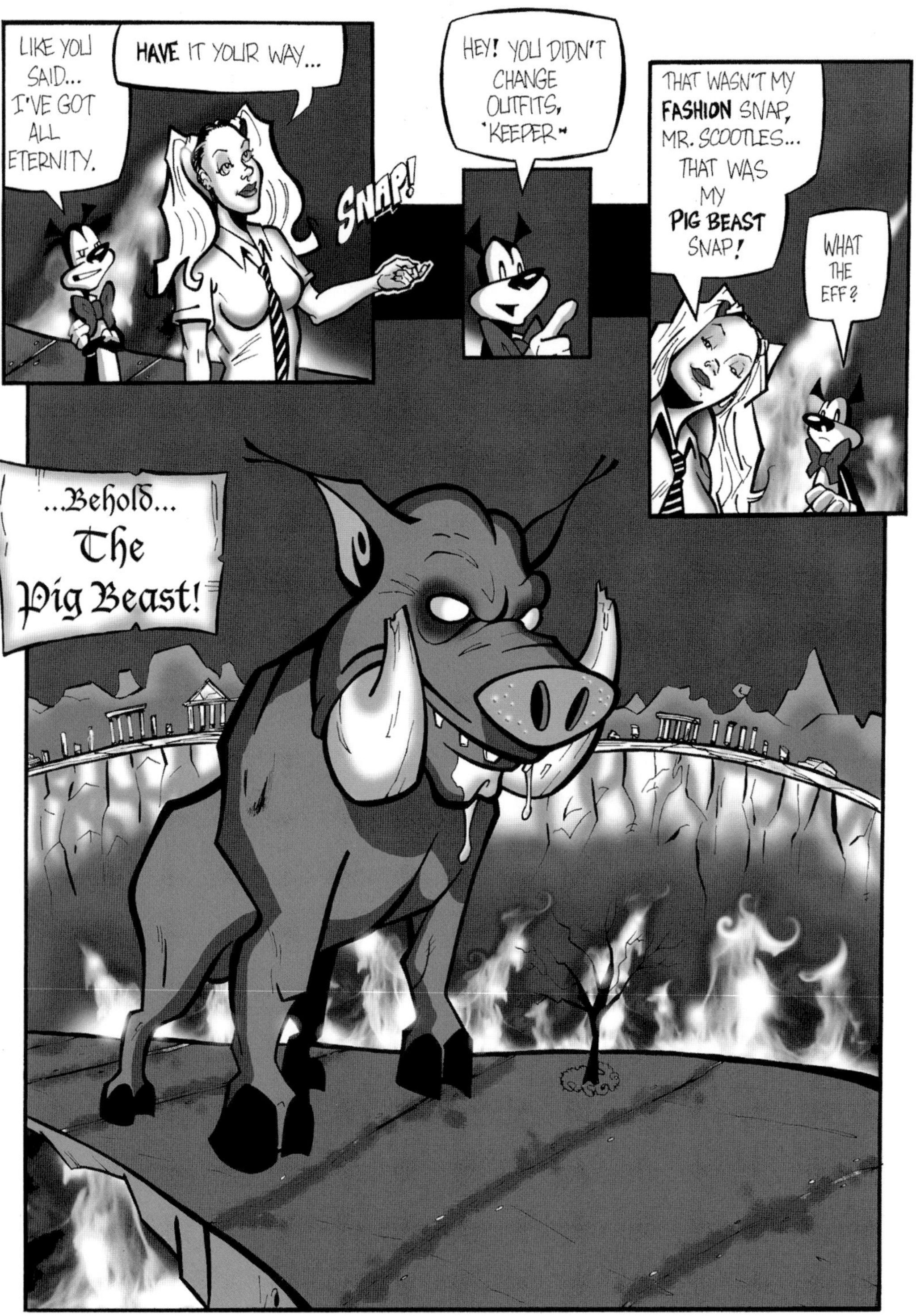
LIKE YOU SAID... I'VE GOT ALL ETERNITY.
HAVE IT YOUR WAY...
SNAP!
HEY! YOU DIDN'T CHANGE OUTFITS, "KEEPER"
THAT WASN'T MY FASHION SNAP, MR. SCOOTLES... THAT WAS MY PIG BEAST SNAP!
WHAT THE EFF?
...Behold... The Pig Beast!

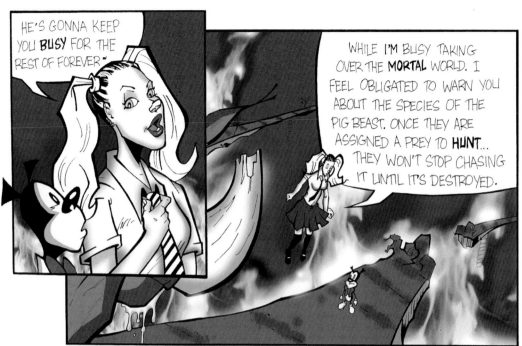

HE'S GONNA KEEP YOU **BUSY** FOR THE REST OF FOREVER~

WHILE I'M BUSY TAKING OVER THE **MORTAL** WORLD. I FEEL OBLIGATED TO WARN YOU ABOUT THE SPECIES OF THE PIG BEAST. ONCE THEY ARE ASSIGNED A PREY TO **HUNT**... THEY WON'T STOP CHASING IT UNTIL IT'S DESTROYED.

YOU'RE **LOONY** TUNES, LADY!

FUNNY... I THOUGHT **YOU** WERE THE CARTOON!

TA-TA, MR. SCOOTLES! THANKS FOR THE PORTAL~

COME AGAIN?

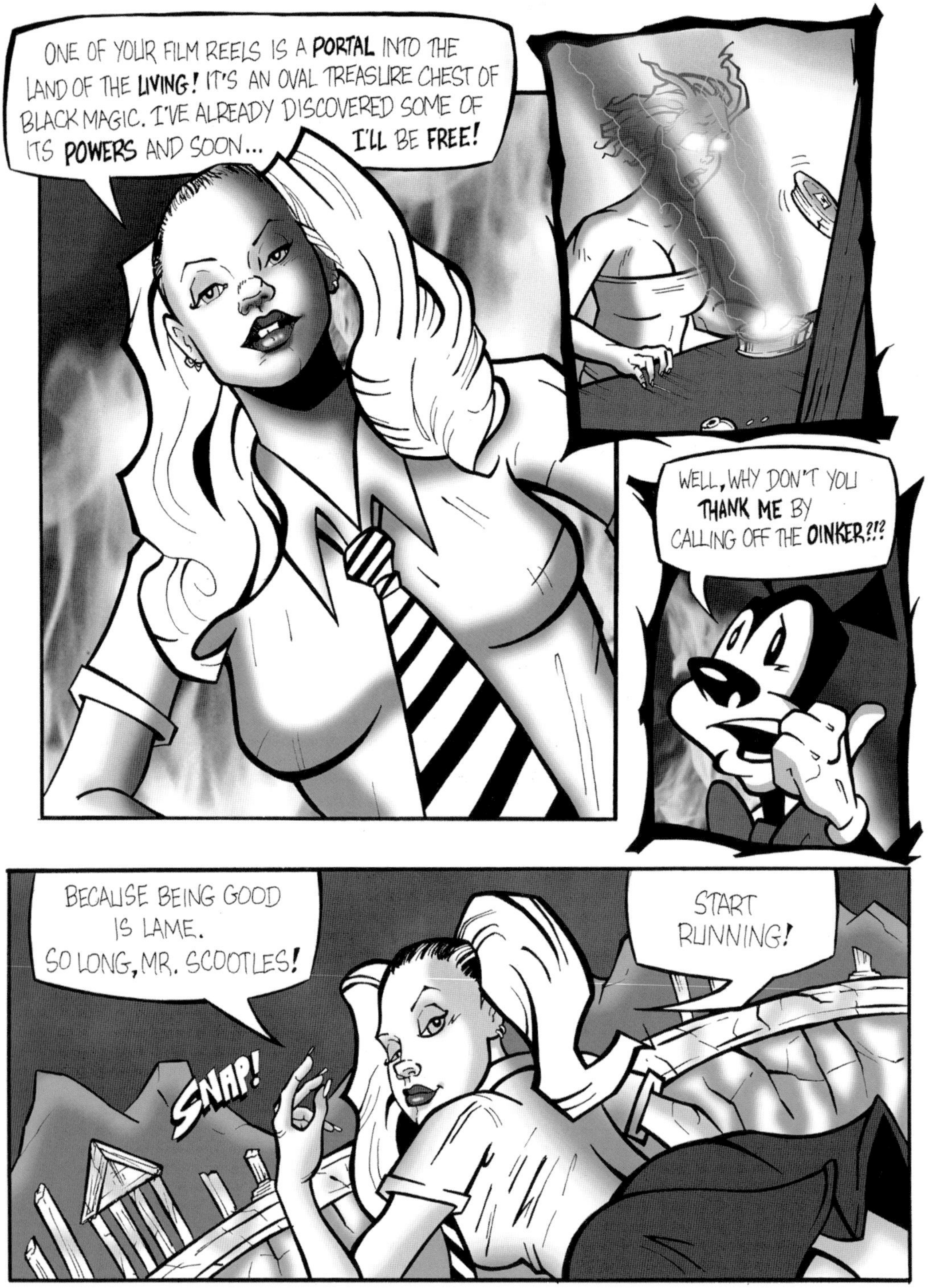
ONE OF YOUR FILM REELS IS A **PORTAL** INTO THE LAND OF THE **LIVING!** IT'S AN OVAL TREASURE CHEST OF BLACK MAGIC. I'VE ALREADY DISCOVERED SOME OF ITS **POWERS** AND SOON... **I'LL BE FREE!**
WELL, WHY DON'T YOU **THANK ME** BY CALLING OFF THE **OINKER?!?**
BECAUSE BEING GOOD IS LAME. SO LONG, MR. SCOOTLES!
START RUNNING!
SNAP!

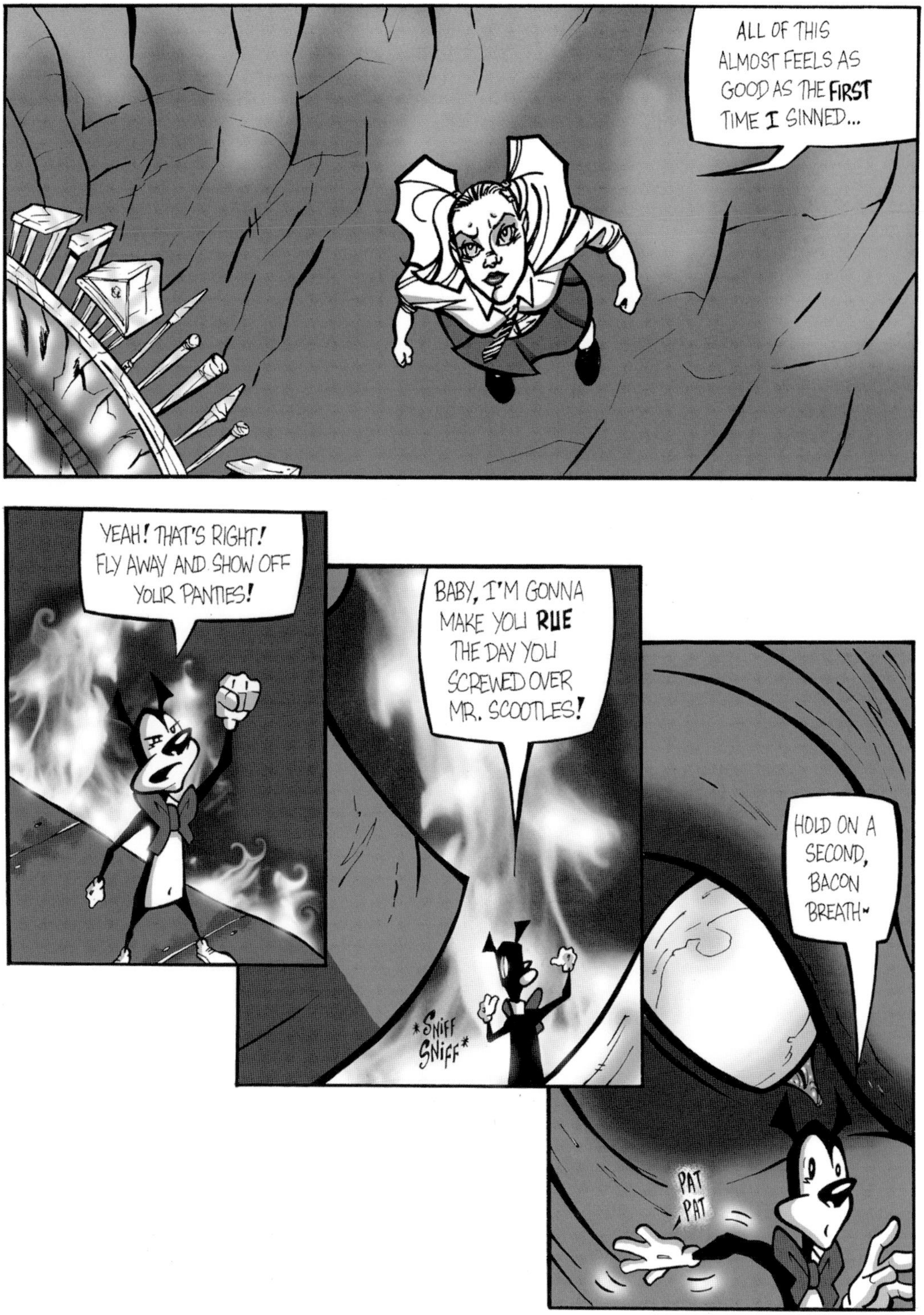
ALL OF THIS ALMOST FEELS AS GOOD AS THE FIRST TIME I SINNED...
YEAH! THAT'S RIGHT! FLY AWAY AND SHOW OFF YOUR PANTIES!
BABY, I'M GONNA MAKE YOU RUE THE DAY YOU SCREWED OVER MR. SCOOTLES!
SNIFF SNIFF
HOLD ON A SECOND, BACON BREATH~
PAT PAT

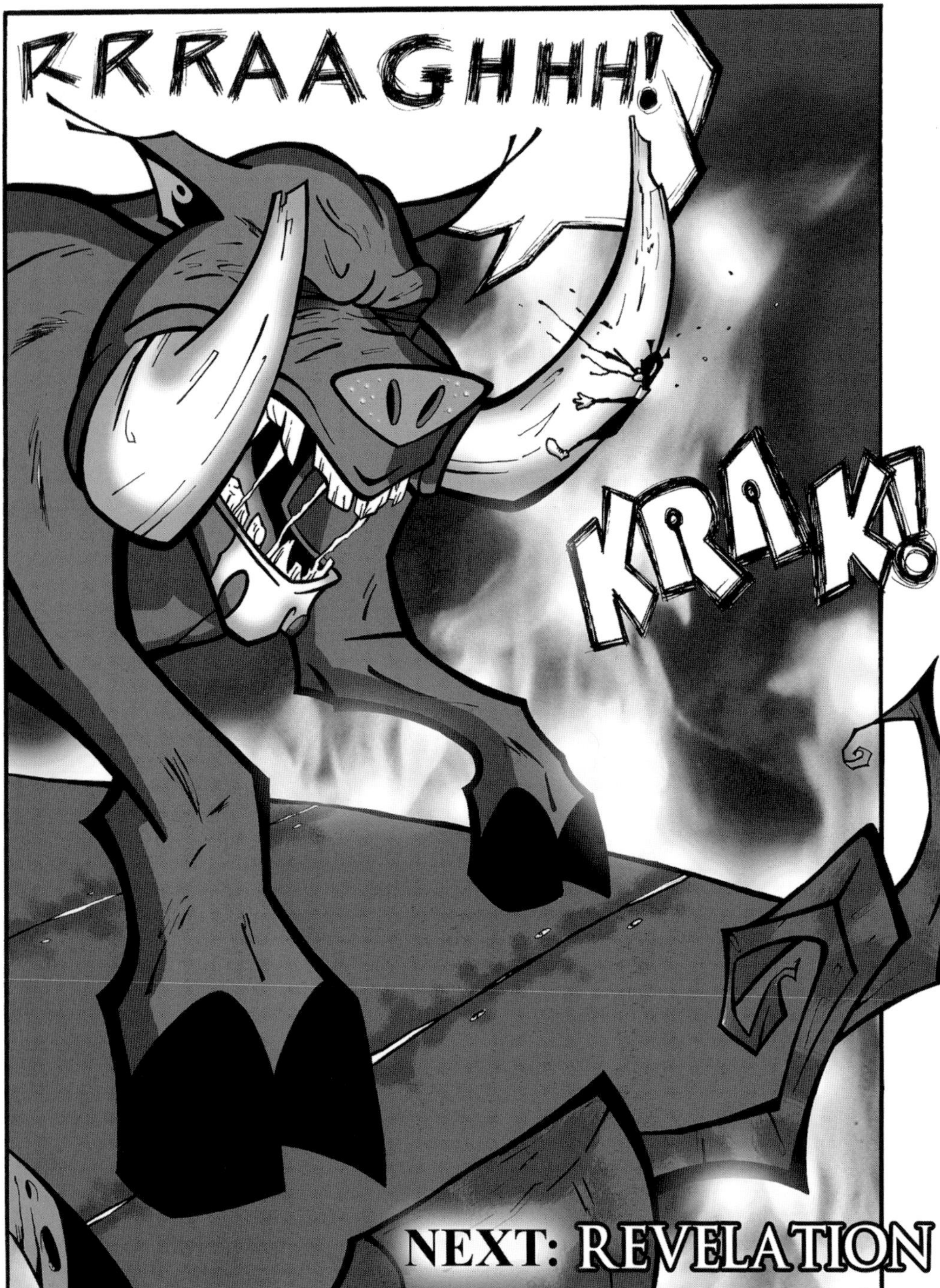
RRRAAGHHH!
KRAK!
NEXT: REVELATION

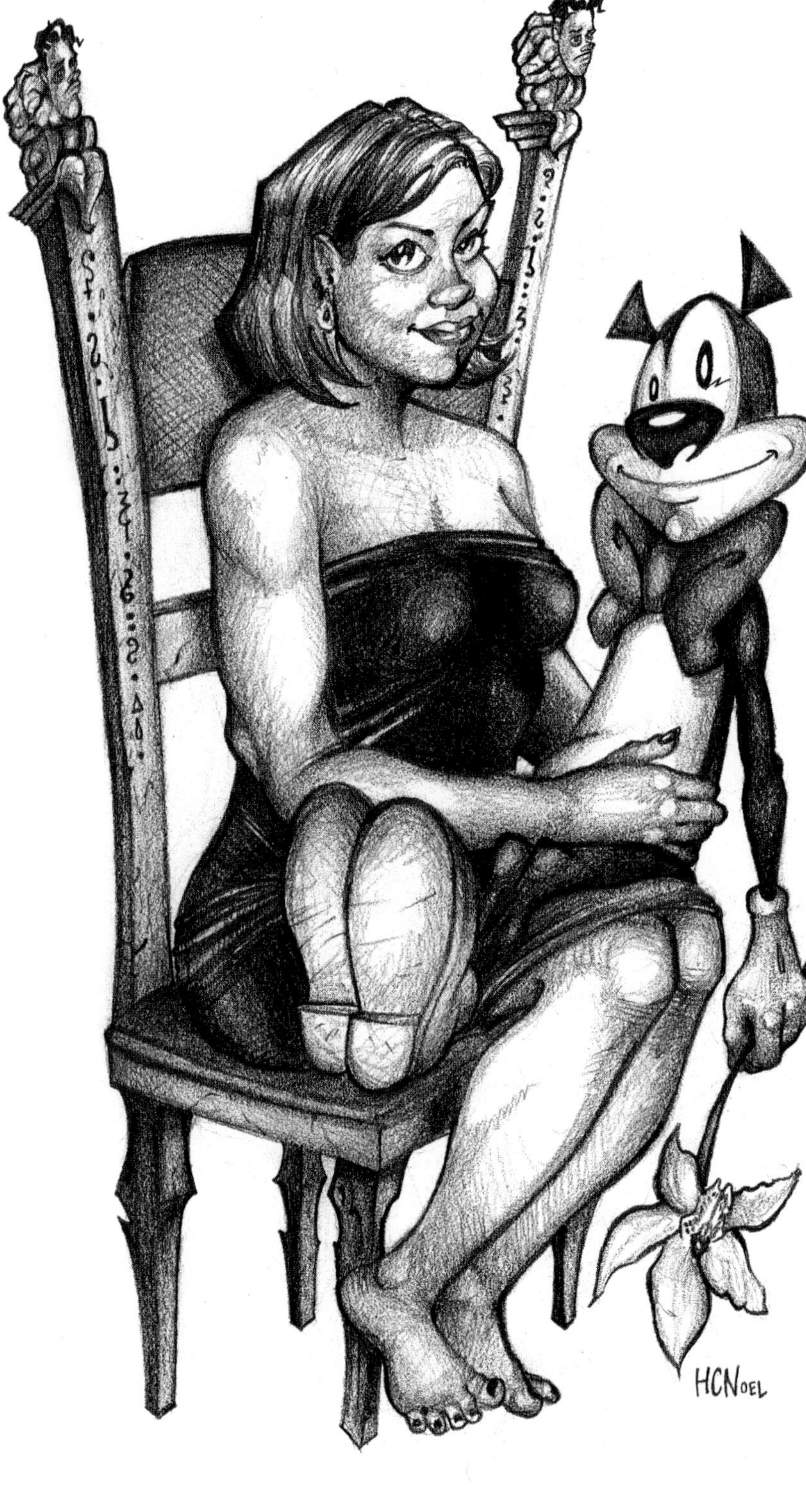
HCNoel

BOOK FOUR ✚ REVELATION

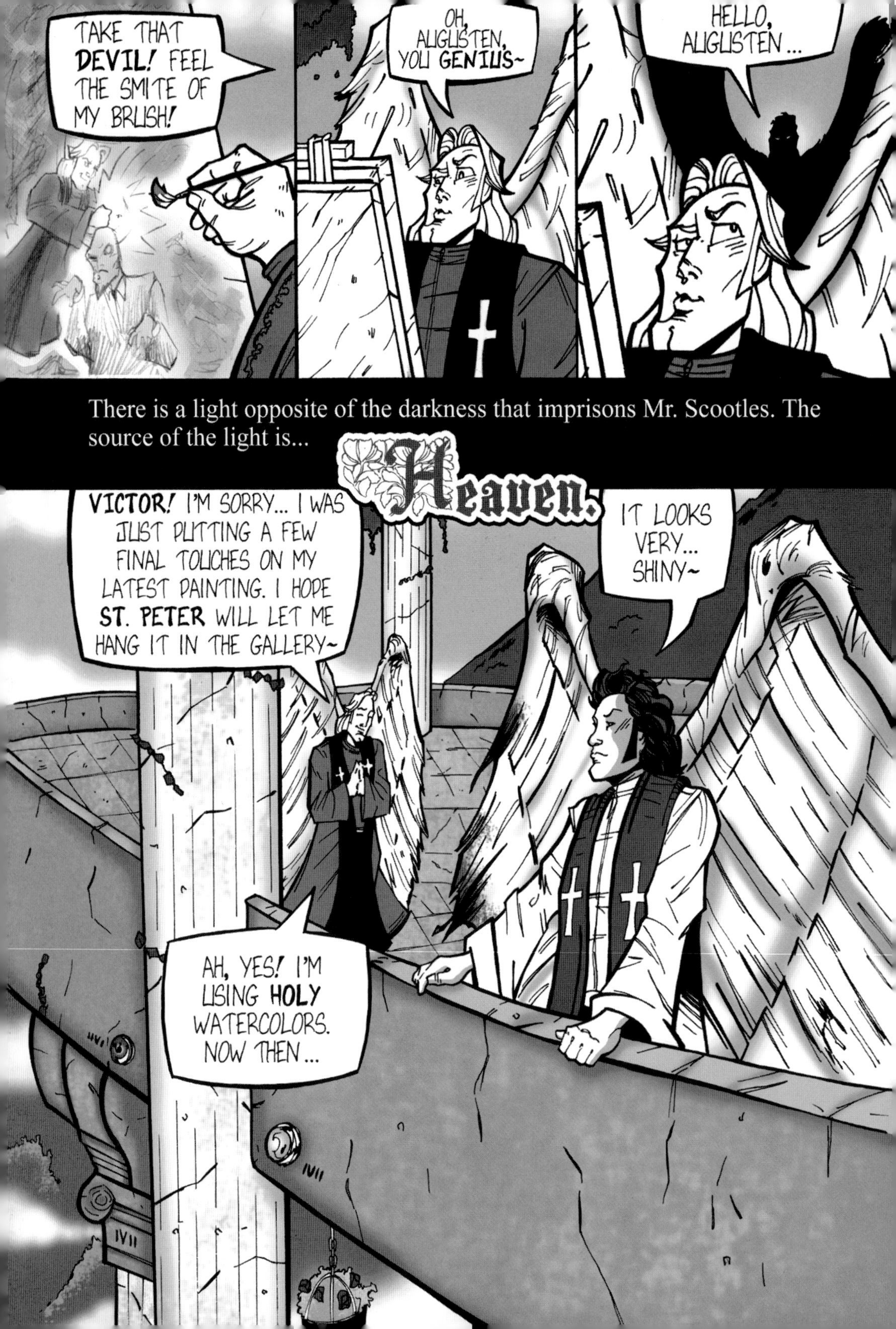
TAKE THAT DEVIL! FEEL THE SMITE OF MY BRUSH!
OH, AUGUSTEN, YOU GENIUS~
HELLO, AUGUSTEN...
There is a light opposite of the darkness that imprisons Mr. Scootles. The source of the light is...
Heaven.
VICTOR! I'M SORRY... I WAS JUST PUTTING A FEW FINAL TOUCHES ON MY LATEST PAINTING. I HOPE ST. PETER WILL LET ME HANG IT IN THE GALLERY~
IT LOOKS VERY... SHINY~
AH, YES! I'M USING HOLY WATERCOLORS. NOW THEN...

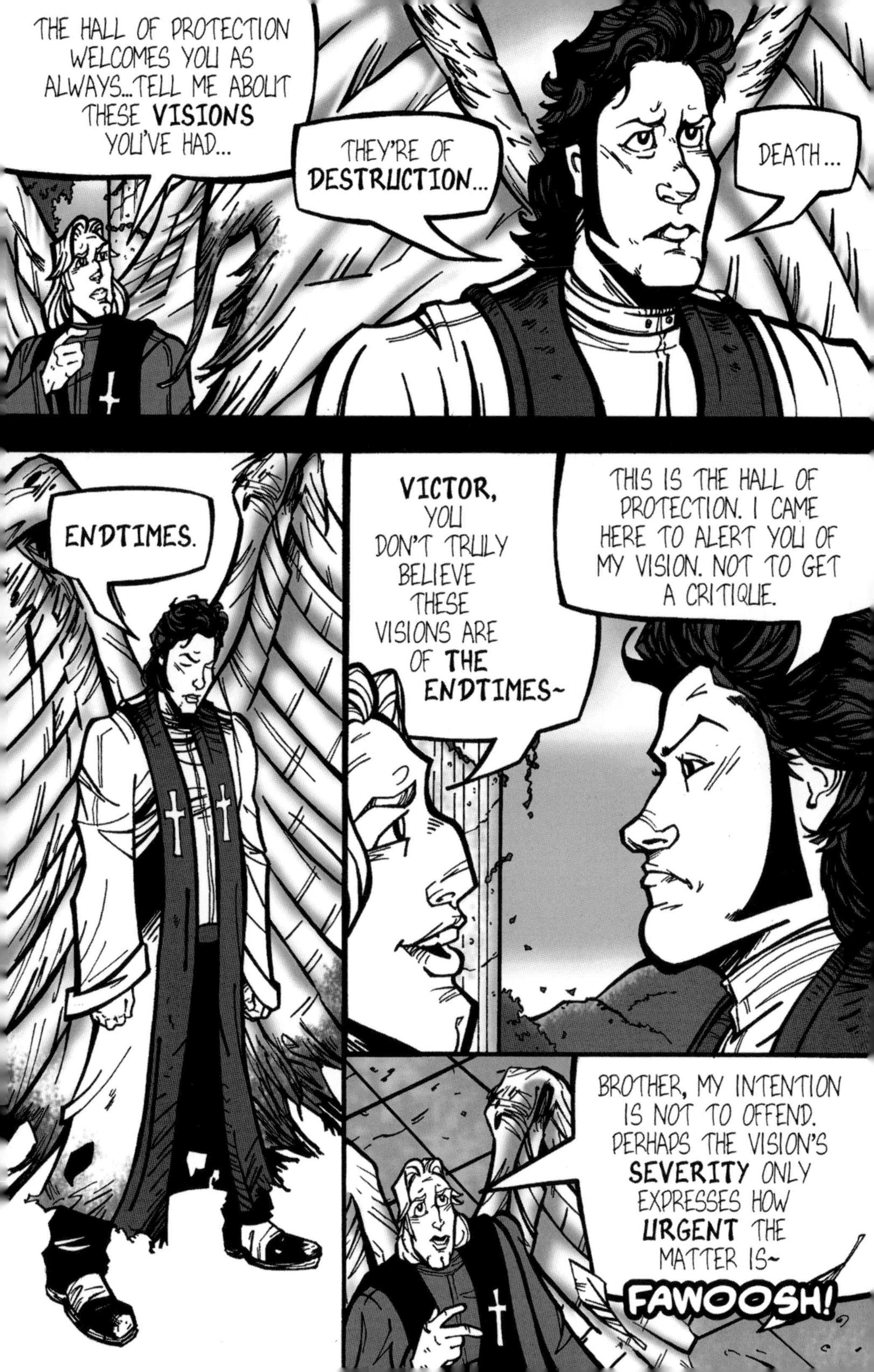
THE HALL OF PROTECTION WELCOMES YOU AS ALWAYS...TELL ME ABOUT THESE **VISIONS** YOU'VE HAD...
THEY'RE OF **DESTRUCTION**...
DEATH...
ENDTIMES.
VICTOR, YOU DON'T TRULY BELIEVE THESE VISIONS ARE OF **THE ENDTIMES**~
THIS IS THE HALL OF PROTECTION. I CAME HERE TO ALERT YOU OF MY VISION. NOT TO GET A CRITIQUE.
BROTHER, MY INTENTION IS NOT TO OFFEND. PERHAPS THE VISION'S **SEVERITY** ONLY EXPRESSES HOW **URGENT** THE MATTER IS~
FAWOOSH!

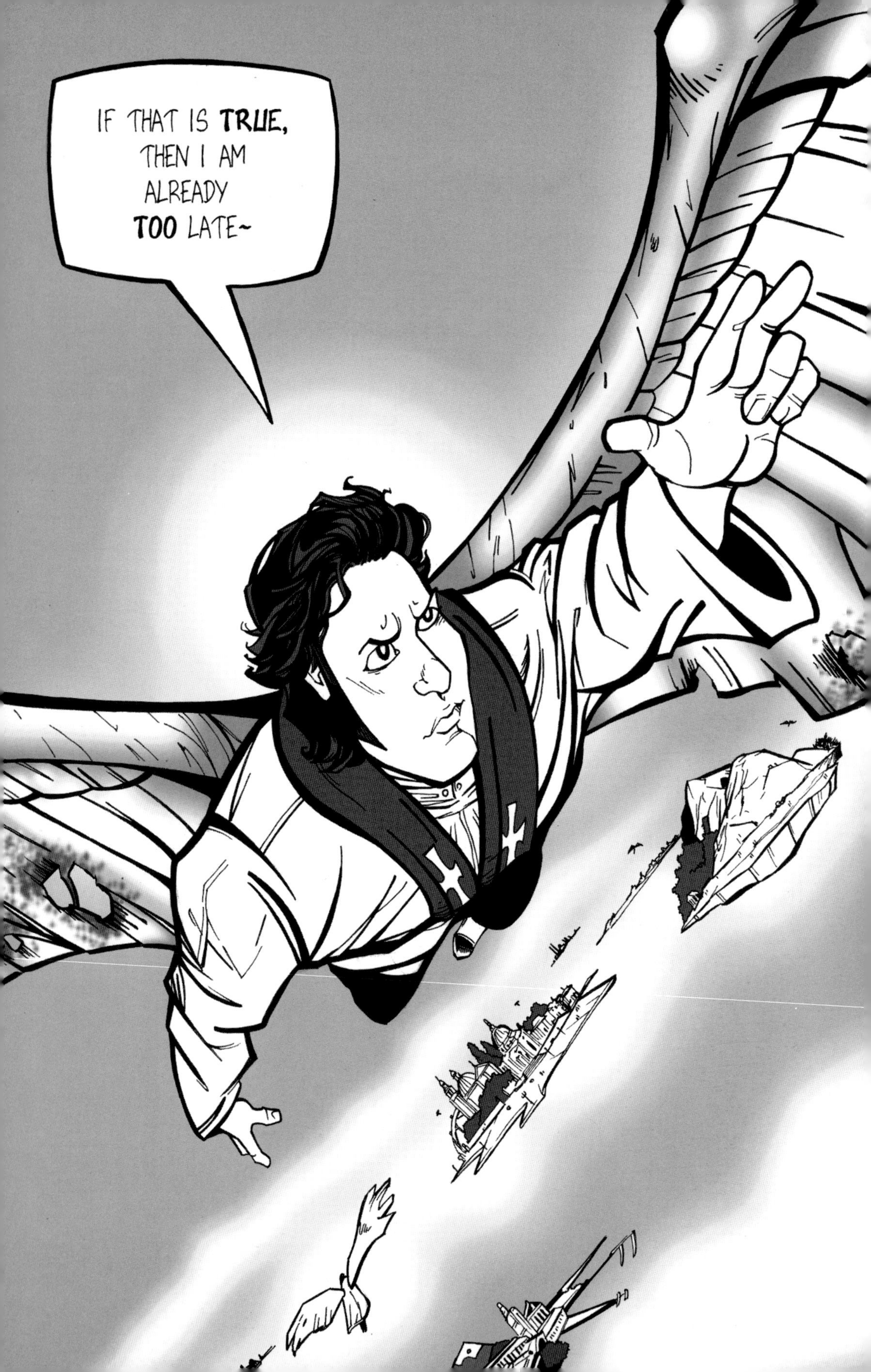
IF THAT IS TRUE, THEN I AM ALREADY TOO LATE~

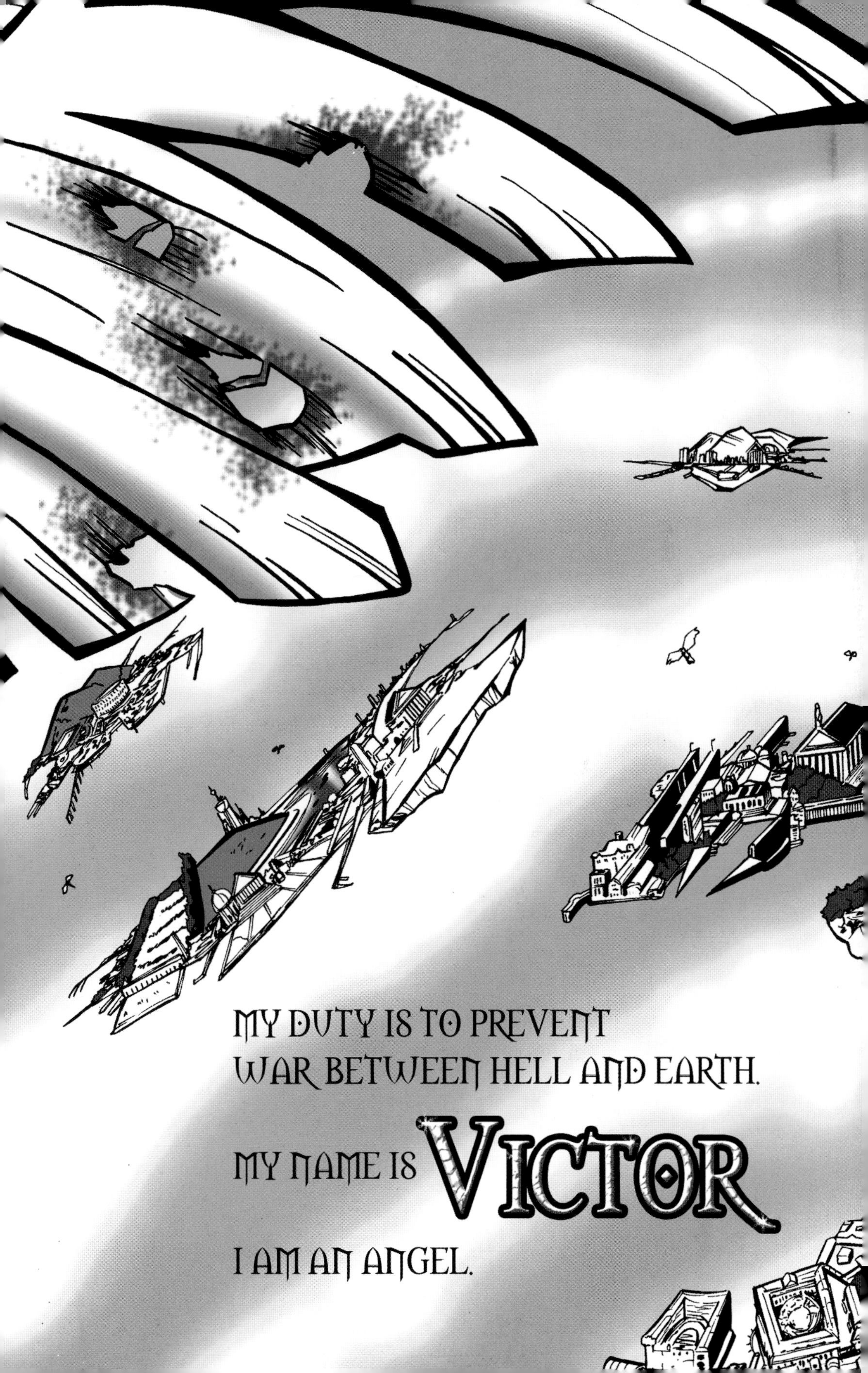
MY DUTY IS TO PREVENT
WAR BETWEEN HELL AND EARTH.
MY NAME IS VICTOR
I AM AN ANGEL.

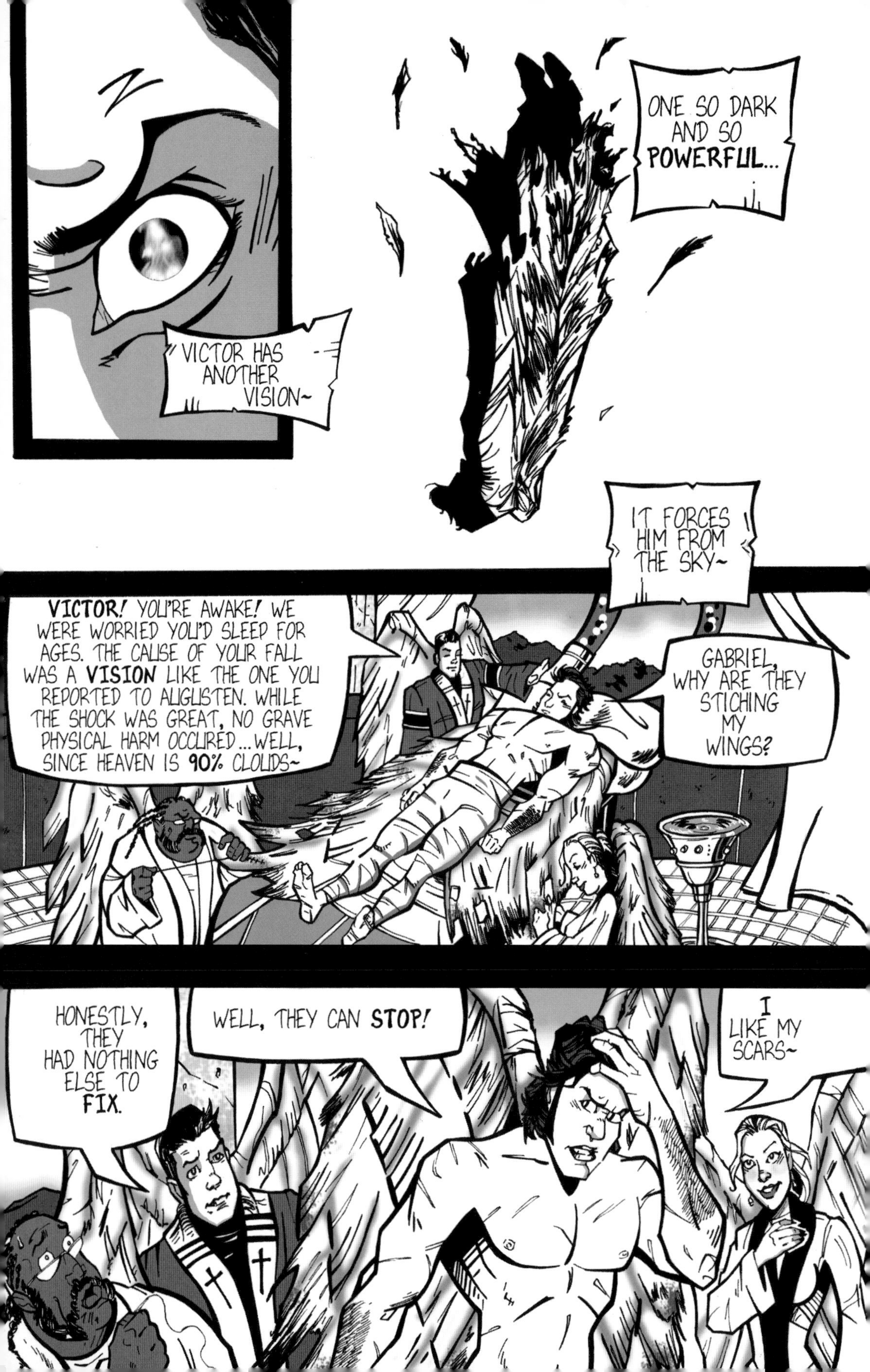
ONE SO DARK AND SO POWERFUL...
VICTOR HAS ANOTHER VISION~
IT FORCES HIM FROM THE SKY~
VICTOR! YOU'RE AWAKE! WE WERE WORRIED YOU'D SLEEP FOR AGES. THE CAUSE OF YOUR FALL WAS A VISION LIKE THE ONE YOU REPORTED TO AUGUSTEN. WHILE THE SHOCK WAS GREAT, NO GRAVE PHYSICAL HARM OCCURED... WELL, SINCE HEAVEN IS 90% CLOUDS~
GABRIEL, WHY ARE THEY STICHING MY WINGS?
HONESTLY, THEY HAD NOTHING ELSE TO FIX.
WELL, THEY CAN STOP!
I LIKE MY SCARS~

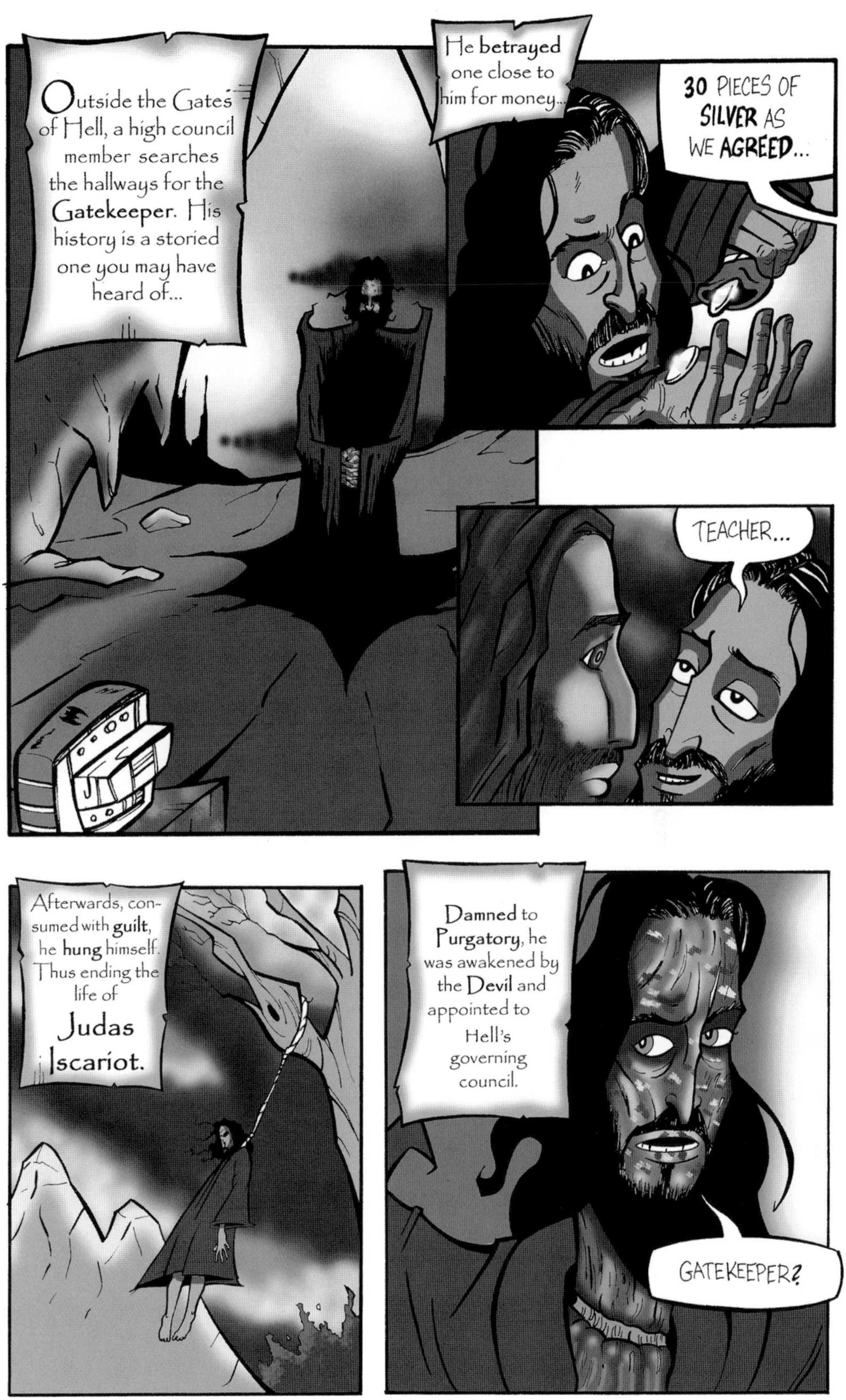
Outside the Gates of Hell, a high council member searches the hallways for the Gatekeeper. His history is a storied one you may have heard of...
He betrayed one close to him for money...
30 PIECES OF SILVER AS WE AGREED...
TEACHER...
Afterwards, consumed with guilt, he hung himself. Thus ending the life of
Judas Iscariot.
Damned to Purgatory, he was awakened by the Devil and appointed to Hell's governing council.
GATEKEEPER?

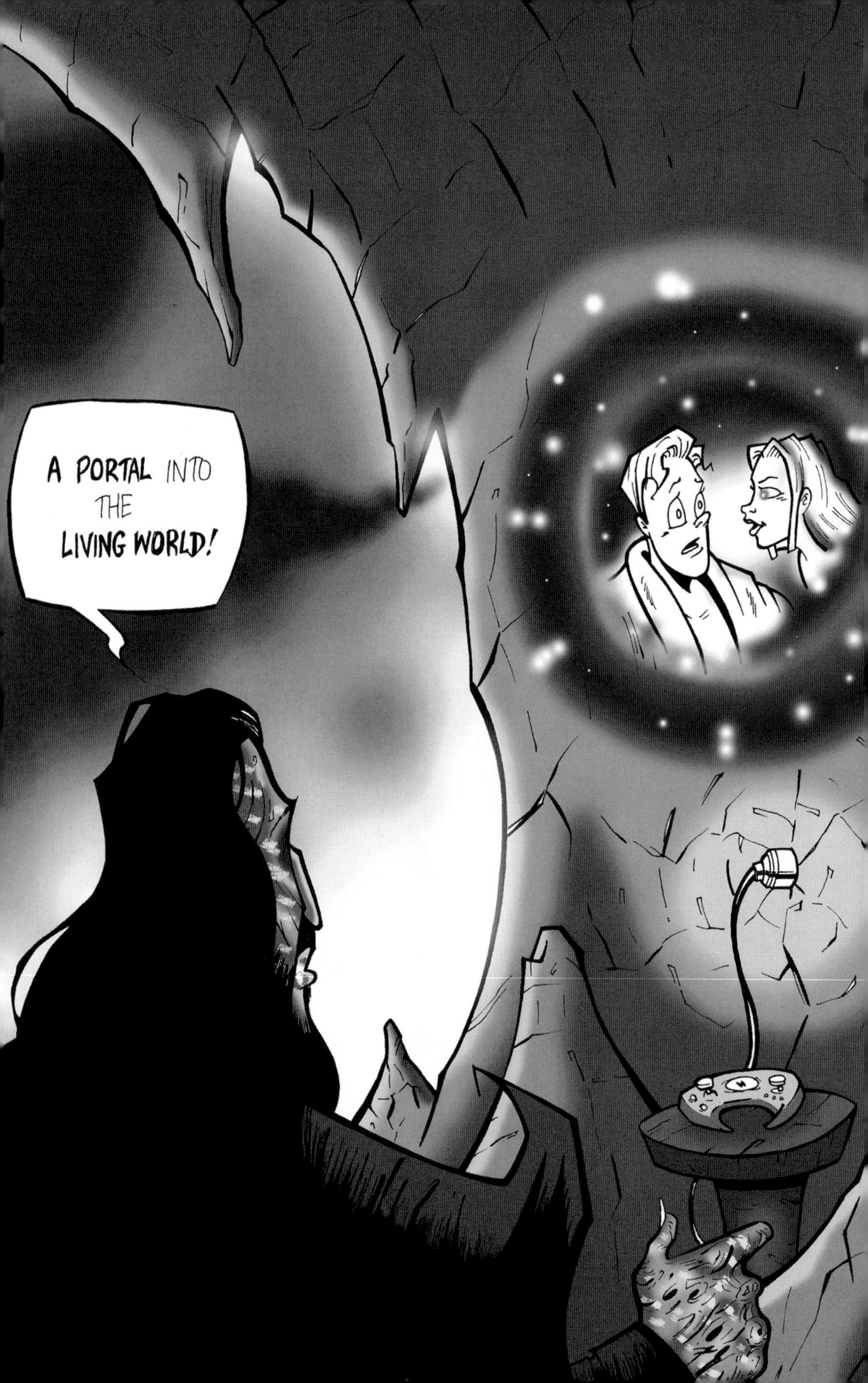
A PORTAL INTO THE LIVING WORLD!

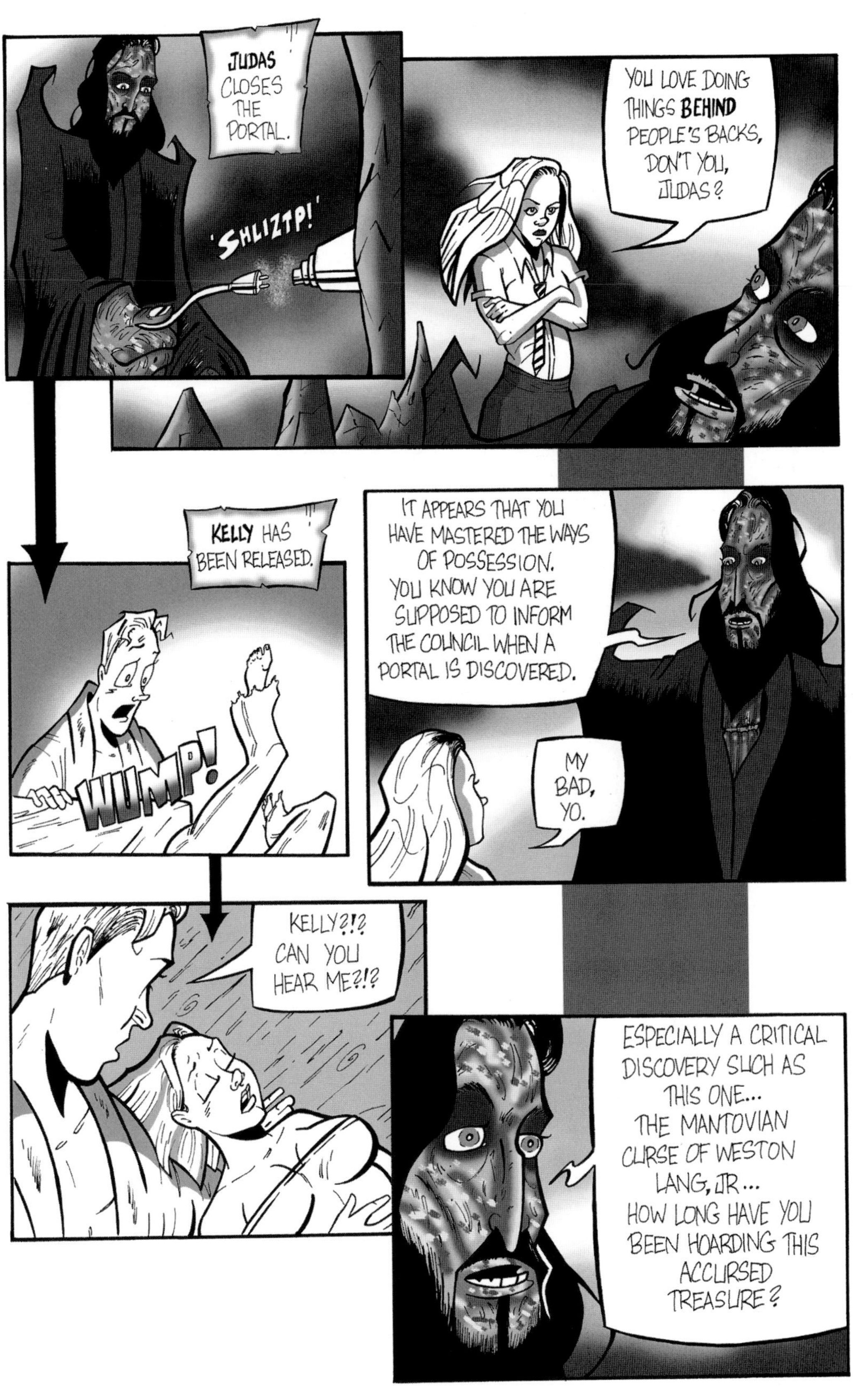
JUDAS CLOSES THE PORTAL.
'SHLIZTP!'
YOU LOVE DOING THINGS BEHIND PEOPLE'S BACKS, DON'T YOU, JUDAS?
KELLY HAS BEEN RELEASED.
WUMP!
IT APPEARS THAT YOU HAVE MASTERED THE WAYS OF POSSESSION. YOU KNOW YOU ARE SUPPOSED TO INFORM THE COUNCIL WHEN A PORTAL IS DISCOVERED.
MY BAD, YO.
KELLY?!? CAN YOU HEAR ME?!?
ESPECIALLY A CRITICAL DISCOVERY SUCH AS THIS ONE... THE MANTOVIAN CURSE OF WESTON LANG, JR... HOW LONG HAVE YOU BEEN HOARDING THIS ACCURSED TREASURE?

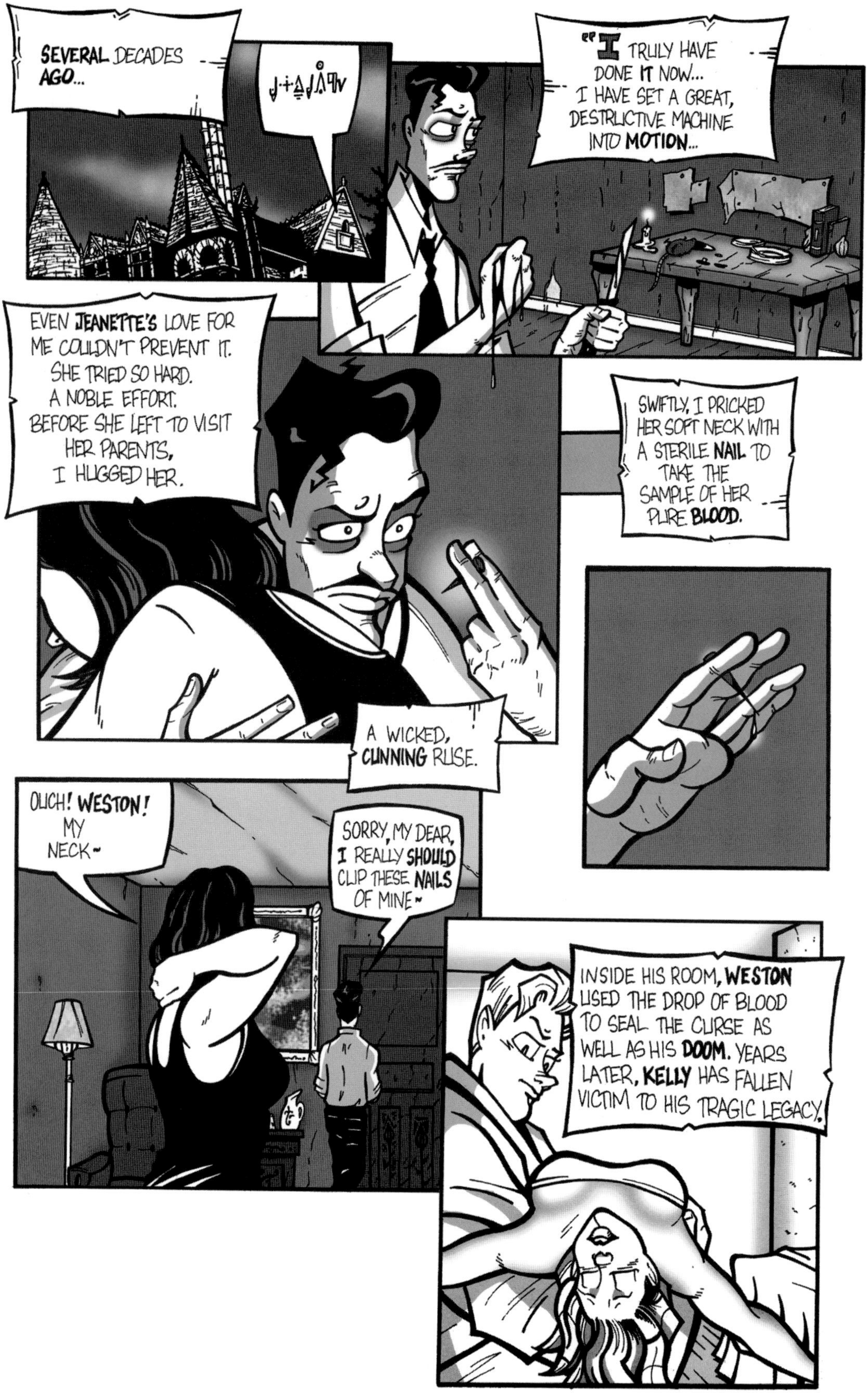
SEVERAL DECADES AGO...
"I TRULY HAVE DONE IT NOW... I HAVE SET A GREAT, DESTRUCTIVE MACHINE INTO MOTION...
EVEN JEANETTE'S LOVE FOR ME COULDN'T PREVENT IT. SHE TRIED SO HARD. A NOBLE EFFORT. BEFORE SHE LEFT TO VISIT HER PARENTS, I HUGGED HER.
SWIFTLY, I PRICKED HER SOFT NECK WITH A STERILE NAIL TO TAKE THE SAMPLE OF HER PURE BLOOD.
A WICKED, CUNNING RUSE.
OUCH! WESTON! MY NECK~
SORRY, MY DEAR, I REALLY SHOULD CLIP THESE NAILS OF MINE~
INSIDE HIS ROOM, WESTON USED THE DROP OF BLOOD TO SEAL THE CURSE AS WELL AS HIS DOOM. YEARS LATER, KELLY HAS FALLEN VICTIM TO HIS TRAGIC LEGACY.

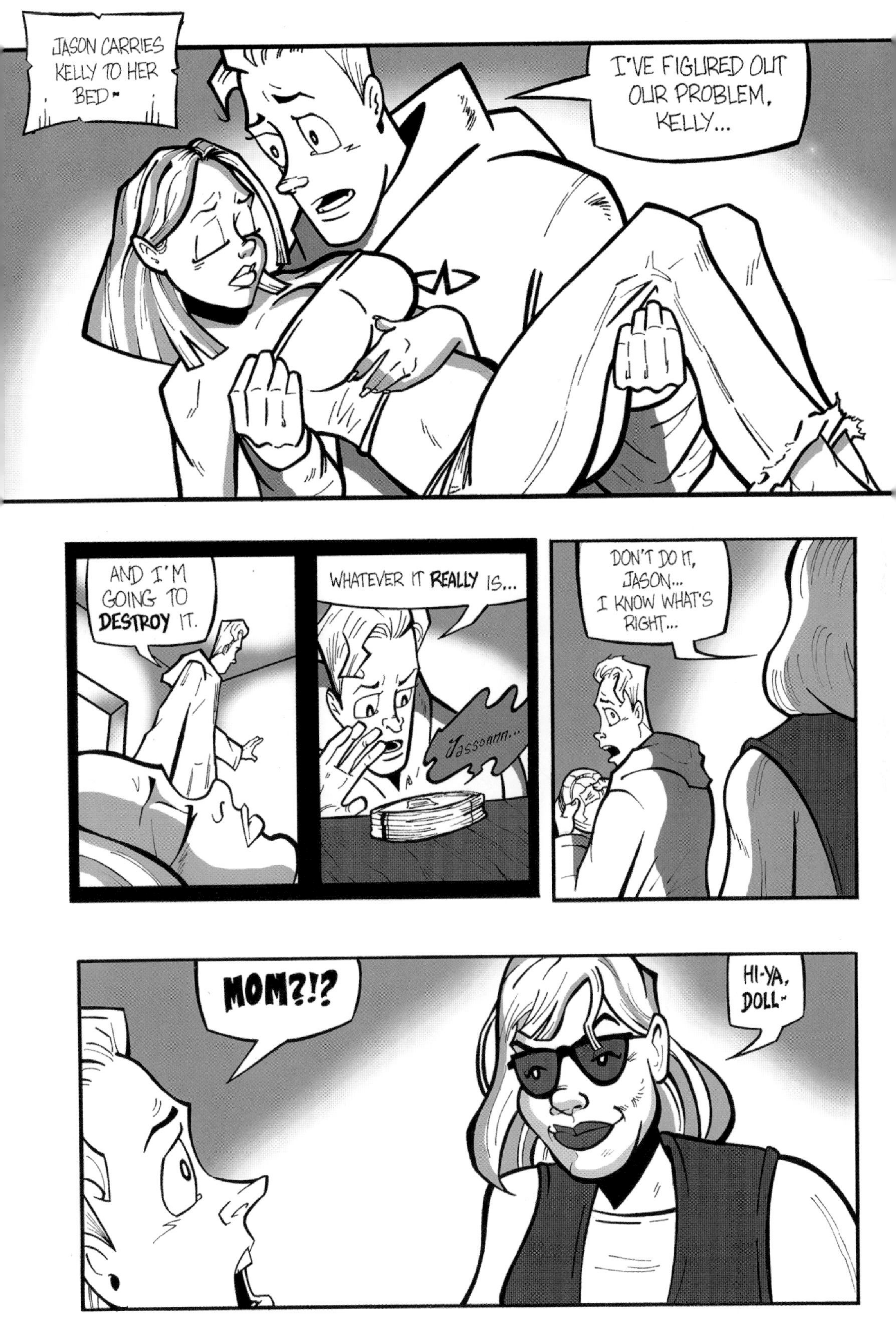
JASON CARRIES KELLY TO HER BED~
I'VE FIGURED OUT OUR PROBLEM, KELLY...
AND I'M GOING TO DESTROY IT.
WHATEVER IT REALLY IS...
Jassonnn...
DON'T DO IT, JASON... I KNOW WHAT'S RIGHT...
MOM?!?
HI-YA, DOLL~

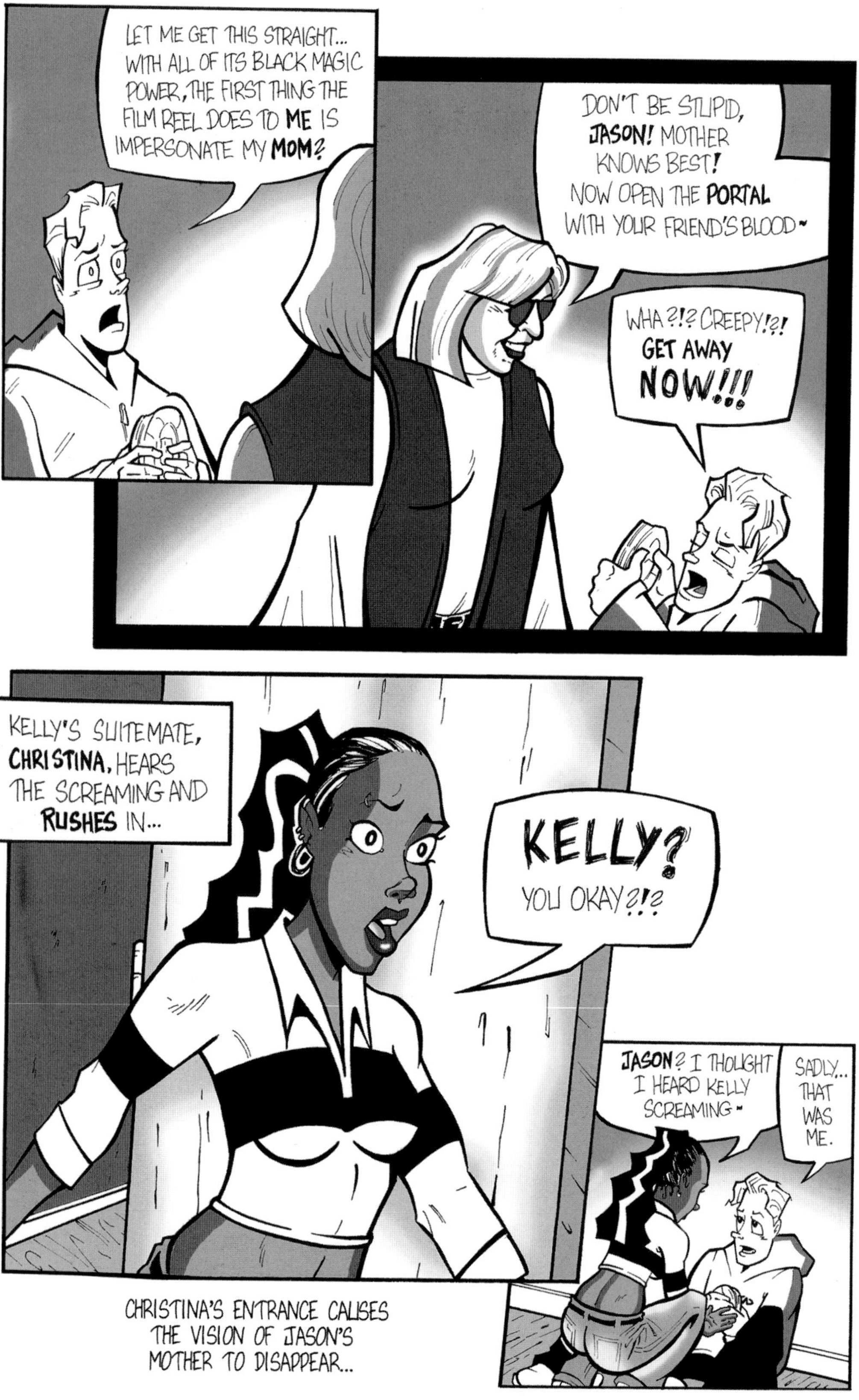
LET ME GET THIS STRAIGHT... WITH ALL OF ITS BLACK MAGIC POWER, THE FIRST THING THE FILM REEL DOES TO ME IS IMPERSONATE MY MOM?
DON'T BE STUPID, JASON! MOTHER KNOWS BEST! NOW OPEN THE PORTAL WITH YOUR FRIEND'S BLOOD~
WHA?!? CREEPY!?! GET AWAY NOW!!!
KELLY'S SUITEMATE, CHRISTINA, HEARS THE SCREAMING AND RUSHES IN...
KELLY? YOU OKAY?!?
JASON? I THOUGHT I HEARD KELLY SCREAMING~
SADLY... THAT WAS ME.
CHRISTINA'S ENTRANCE CAUSES THE VISION OF JASON'S MOTHER TO DISAPPEAR...

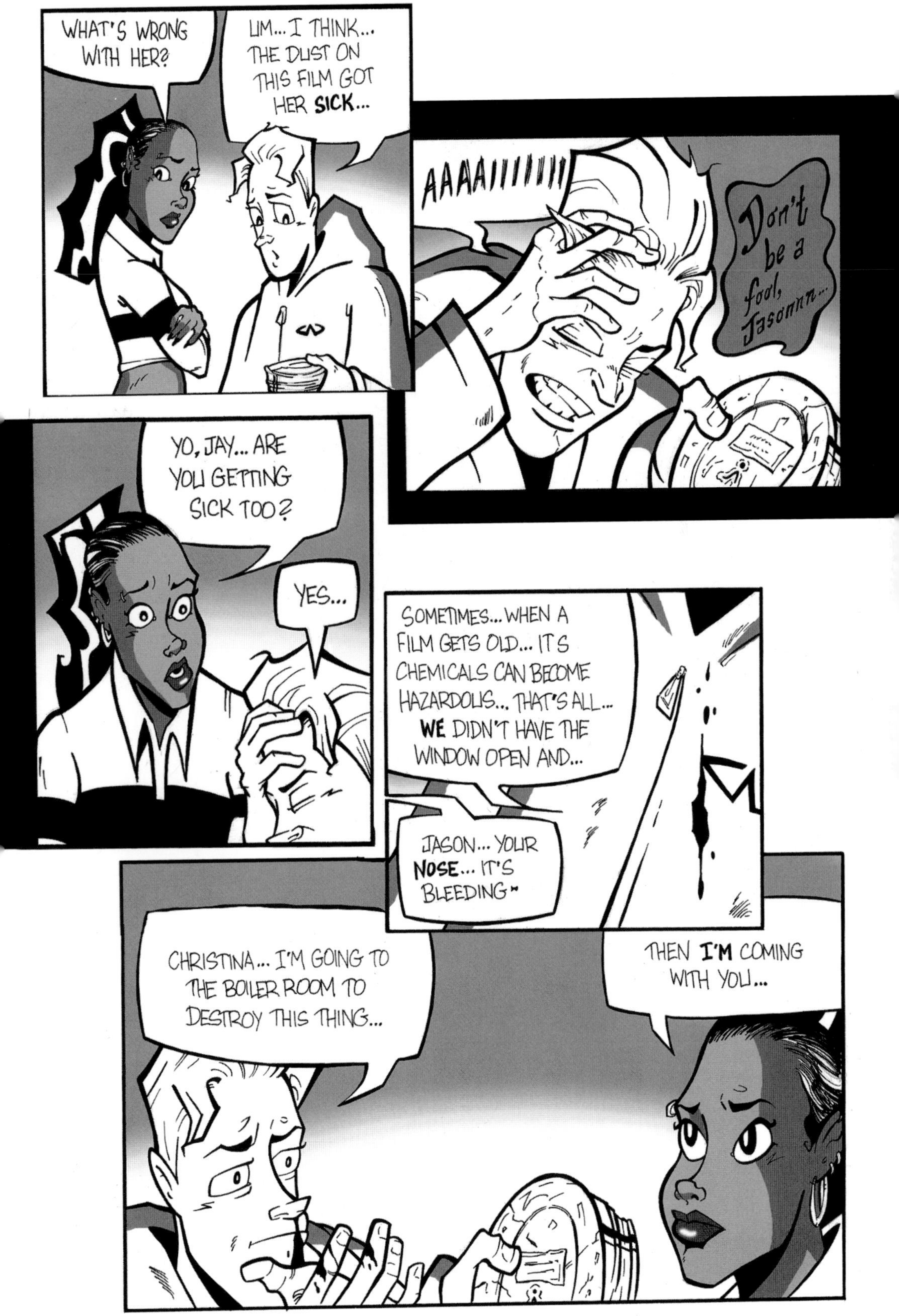
WHAT'S WRONG WITH HER?
UM... I THINK... THE DUST ON THIS FILM GOT HER **SICK**...
AAAAIIIIIIII
Don't be a fool, Jasonnn...
YO, JAY... ARE YOU GETTING SICK TOO?
YES...
SOMETIMES... WHEN A FILM GETS OLD... IT'S CHEMICALS CAN BECOME HAZARDOUS... THAT'S ALL... **WE** DIDN'T HAVE THE WINDOW OPEN AND...
JASON... YOUR **NOSE**... IT'S BLEEDING...
CHRISTINA... I'M GOING TO THE BOILER ROOM TO DESTROY THIS THING...
THEN **I'M** COMING WITH YOU...

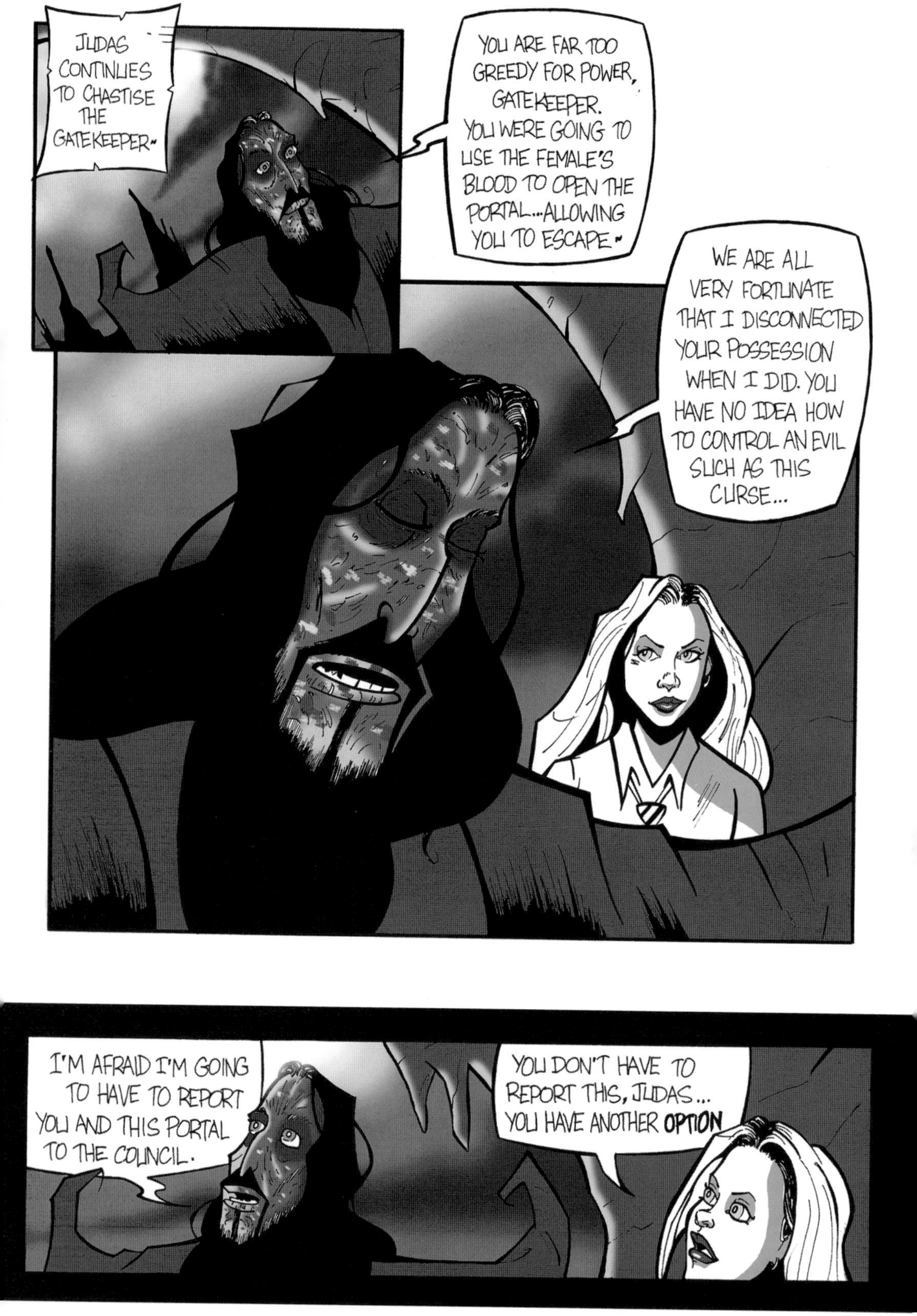
JUDAS CONTINUES TO CHASTISE THE GATEKEEPER…
YOU ARE FAR TOO GREEDY FOR POWER, GATEKEEPER. YOU WERE GOING TO USE THE FEMALE'S BLOOD TO OPEN THE PORTAL…ALLOWING YOU TO ESCAPE…
WE ARE ALL VERY FORTUNATE THAT I DISCONNECTED YOUR POSSESSION WHEN I DID. YOU HAVE NO IDEA HOW TO CONTROL AN EVIL SUCH AS THIS CURSE…
I'M AFRAID I'M GOING TO HAVE TO REPORT YOU AND THIS PORTAL TO THE COUNCIL.
YOU DON'T HAVE TO REPORT THIS, JUDAS… YOU HAVE ANOTHER **OPTION**

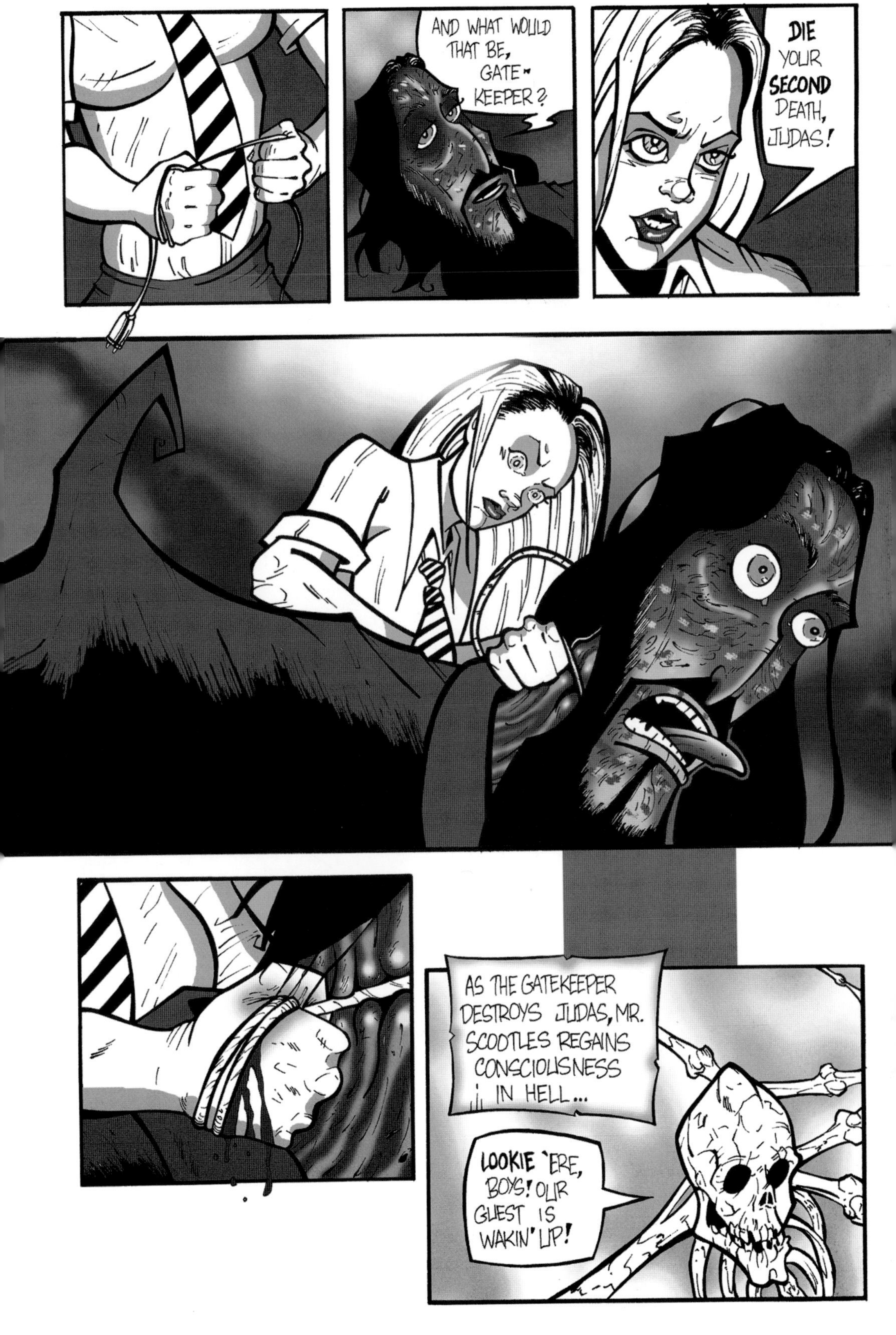
AND WHAT WOULD THAT BE, GATE-KEEPER?
DIE YOUR SECOND DEATH, JUDAS!
AS THE GATEKEEPER DESTROYS JUDAS, MR. SCOOTLES REGAINS CONSCIOUSNESS IN HELL...
LOOKIE 'ERE, BOYS! OUR GUEST IS WAKIN' UP!

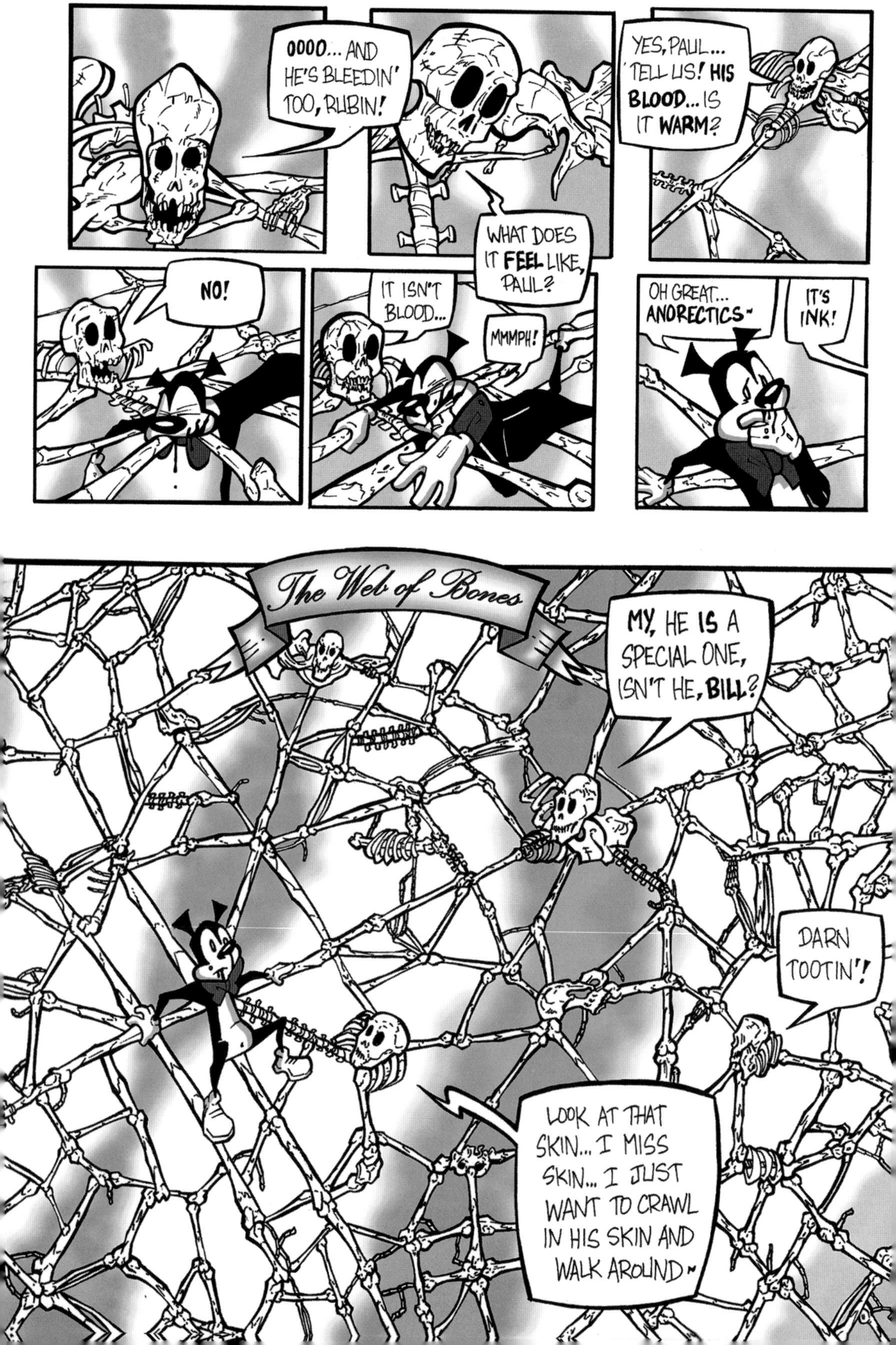
OOOO... AND HE'S BLEEDIN' TOO, RUBIN!
YES, PAUL... TELL US! HIS BLOOD... IS IT WARM?
WHAT DOES IT FEEL LIKE, PAUL?
NO!
IT ISN'T BLOOD...
MMMPH!
OH GREAT... ANORECTICS~
IT'S INK!
The Web of Bones
MY, HE IS A SPECIAL ONE, ISN'T HE, BILL?
DARN TOOTIN'!
LOOK AT THAT SKIN... I MISS SKIN... I JUST WANT TO CRAWL IN HIS SKIN AND WALK AROUND~

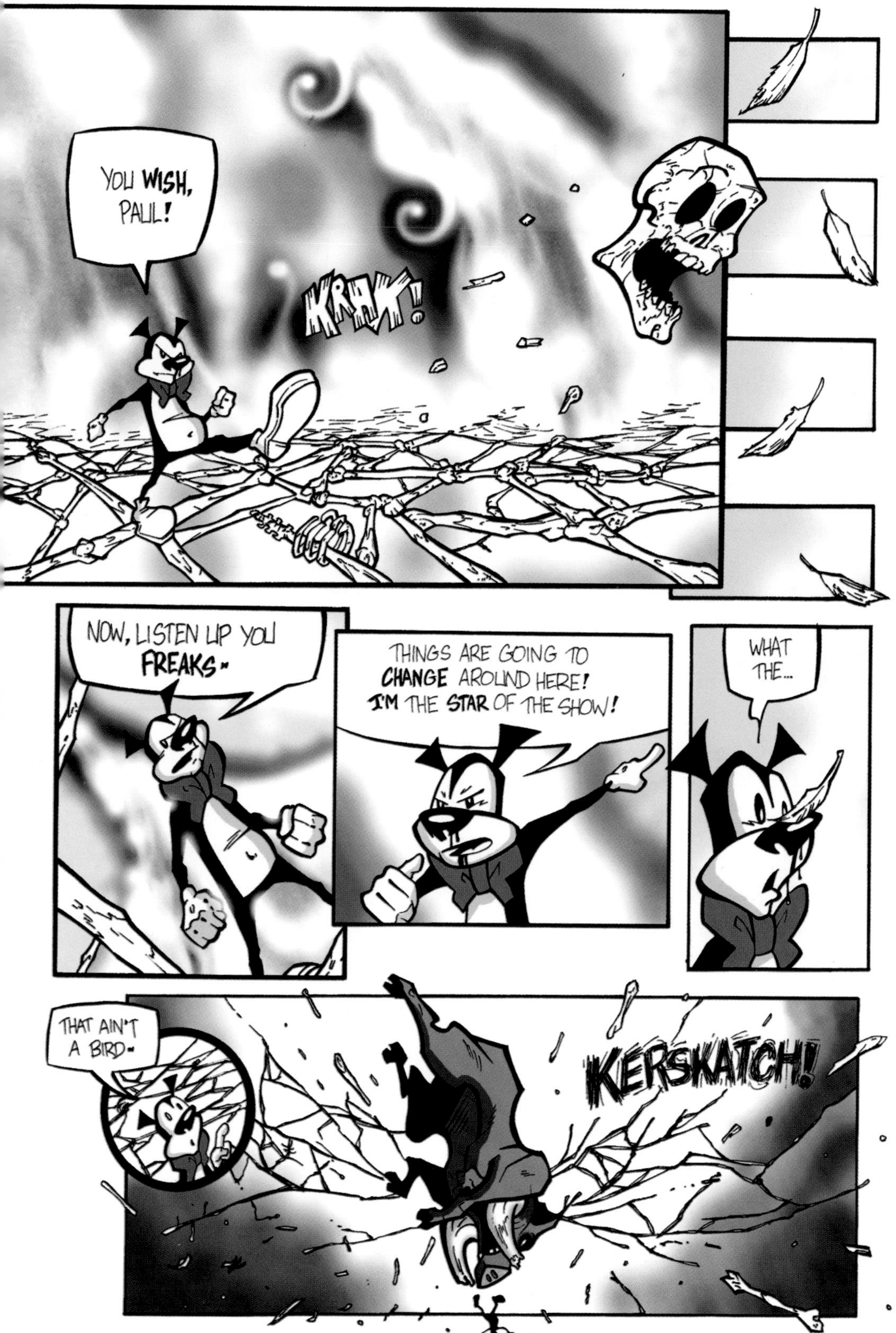
YOU WISH, PAUL!
KRAK!
NOW, LISTEN UP YOU FREAKS..
THINGS ARE GOING TO CHANGE AROUND HERE! I'M THE STAR OF THE SHOW!
WHAT THE...
THAT AIN'T A BIRD..
KERSKATCH!

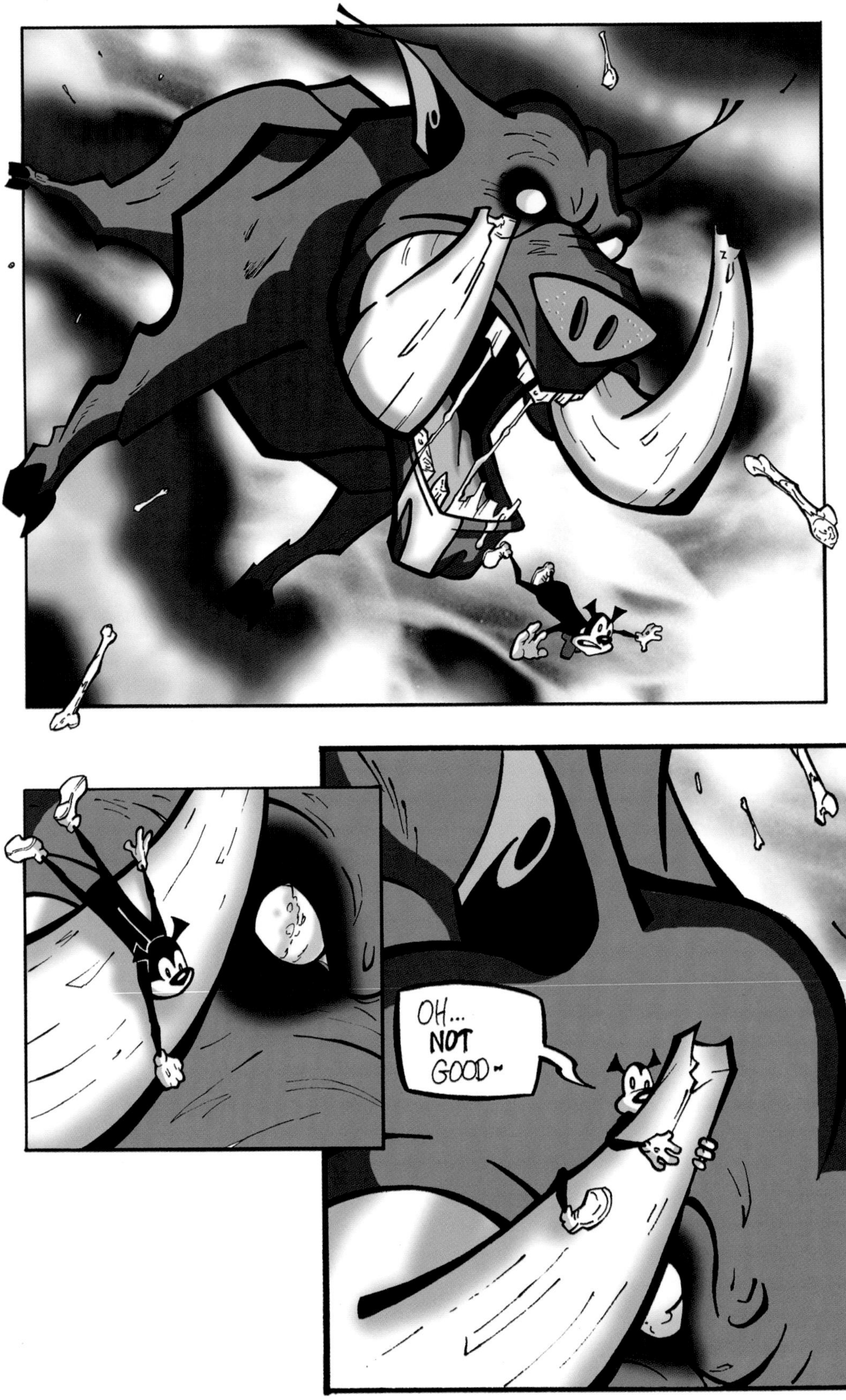
OH... NOT GOOD--

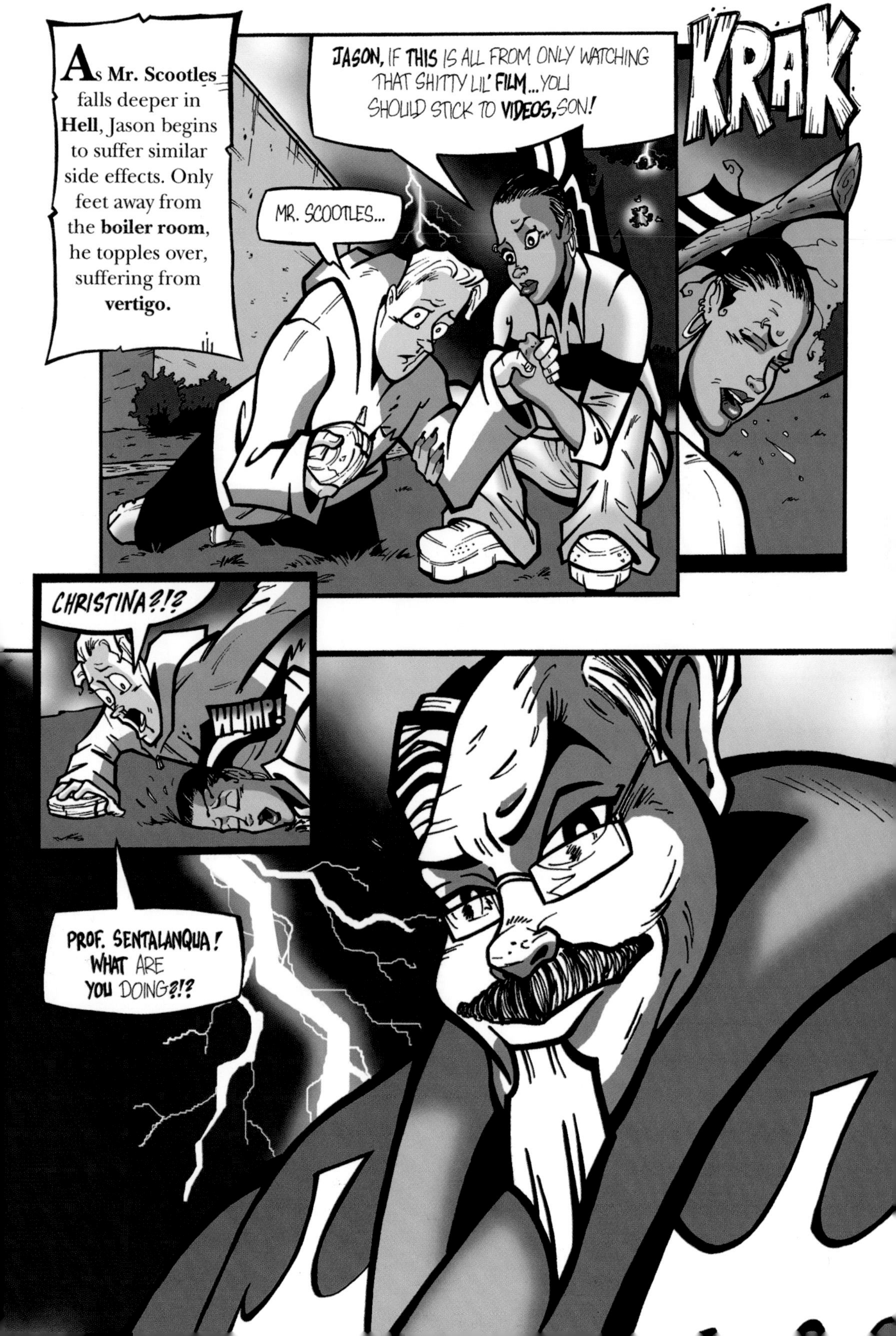
As Mr. Scootles falls deeper in Hell, Jason begins to suffer similar side effects. Only feet away from the boiler room, he topples over, suffering from vertigo.
JASON, IF THIS IS ALL FROM ONLY WATCHING THAT SHITTY LIL' FILM... YOU SHOULD STICK TO VIDEOS, SON!
MR. SCOOTLES...
KRAK
CHRISTINA?!?
WUMP!
PROF. SENTALANQUA! WHAT ARE YOU DOING?!?

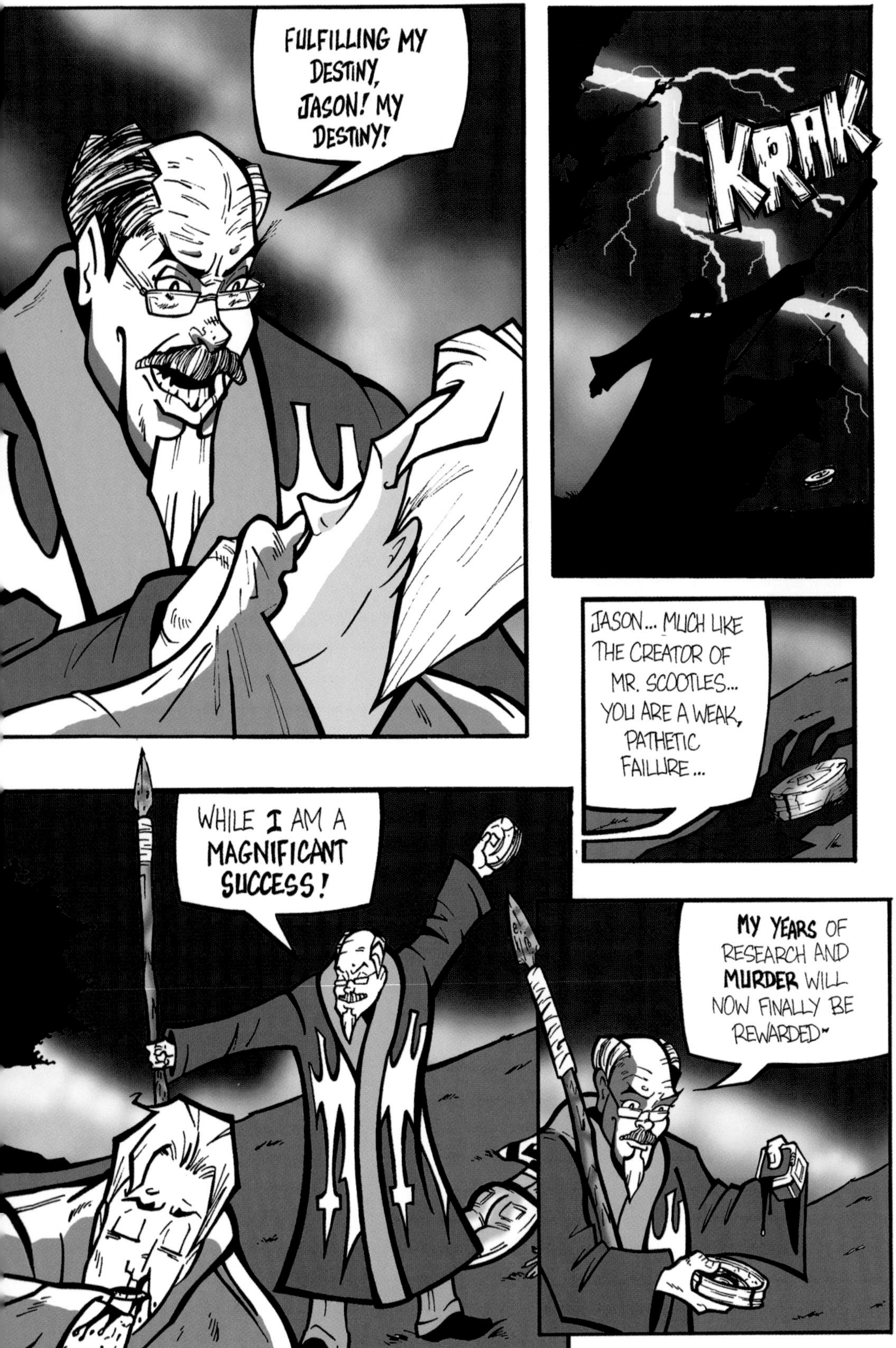
FULFILLING MY DESTINY, JASON! MY DESTINY!
KRAK
JASON... MUCH LIKE THE CREATOR OF MR. SCOOTLES... YOU ARE A WEAK, PATHETIC FAILURE...
WHILE I AM A MAGNIFICANT SUCCESS!
MY YEARS OF RESEARCH AND MURDER WILL NOW FINALLY BE REWARDED

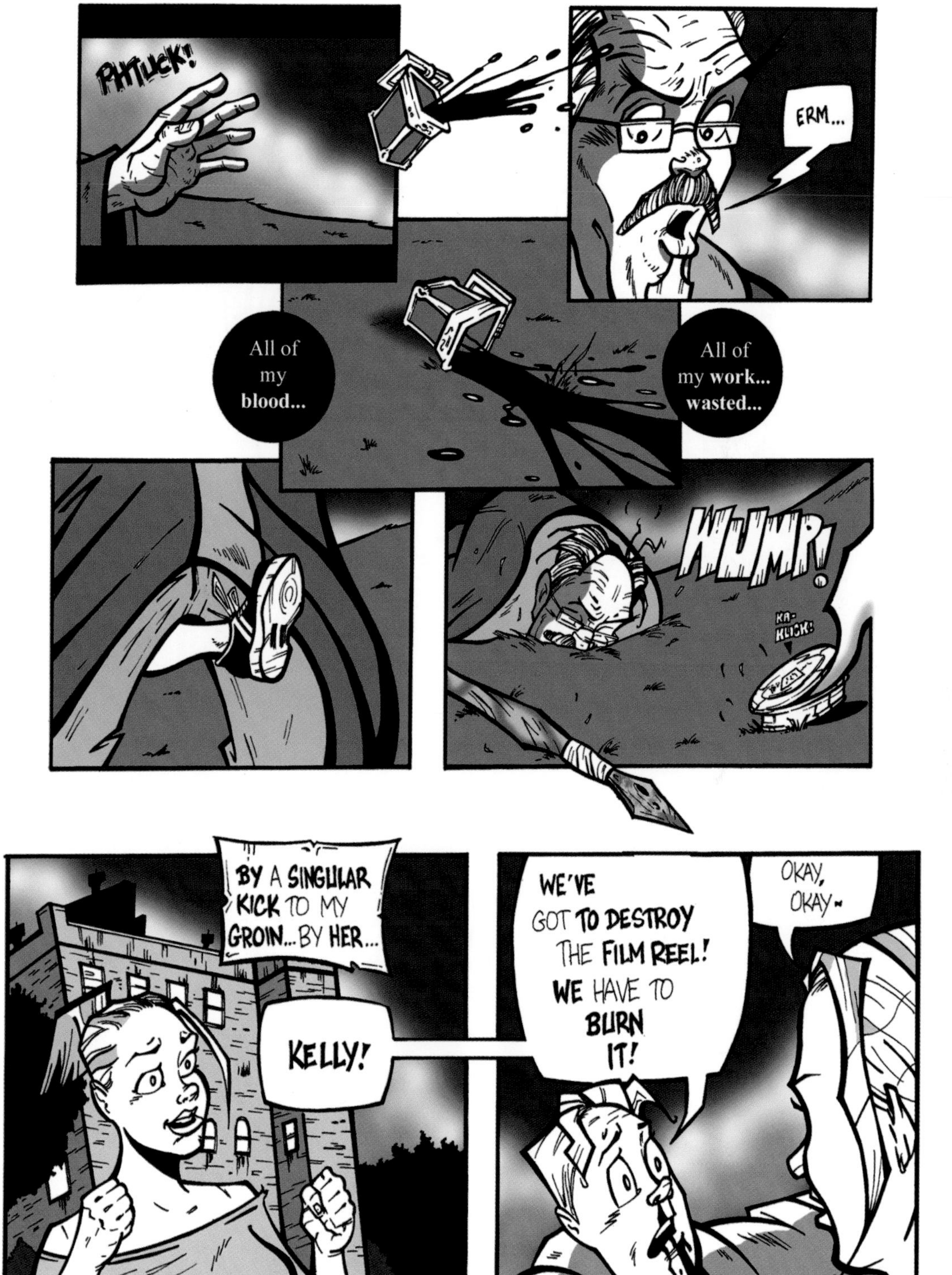
PHTUCK!
ERM...
All of my blood...
All of my work... wasted...
WUMP!
KA-KLICK!
BY A SINGULAR KICK TO MY GROIN... BY HER...
KELLY!
WE'VE GOT TO DESTROY THE FILM REEL! WE HAVE TO BURN IT!
OKAY, OKAY.

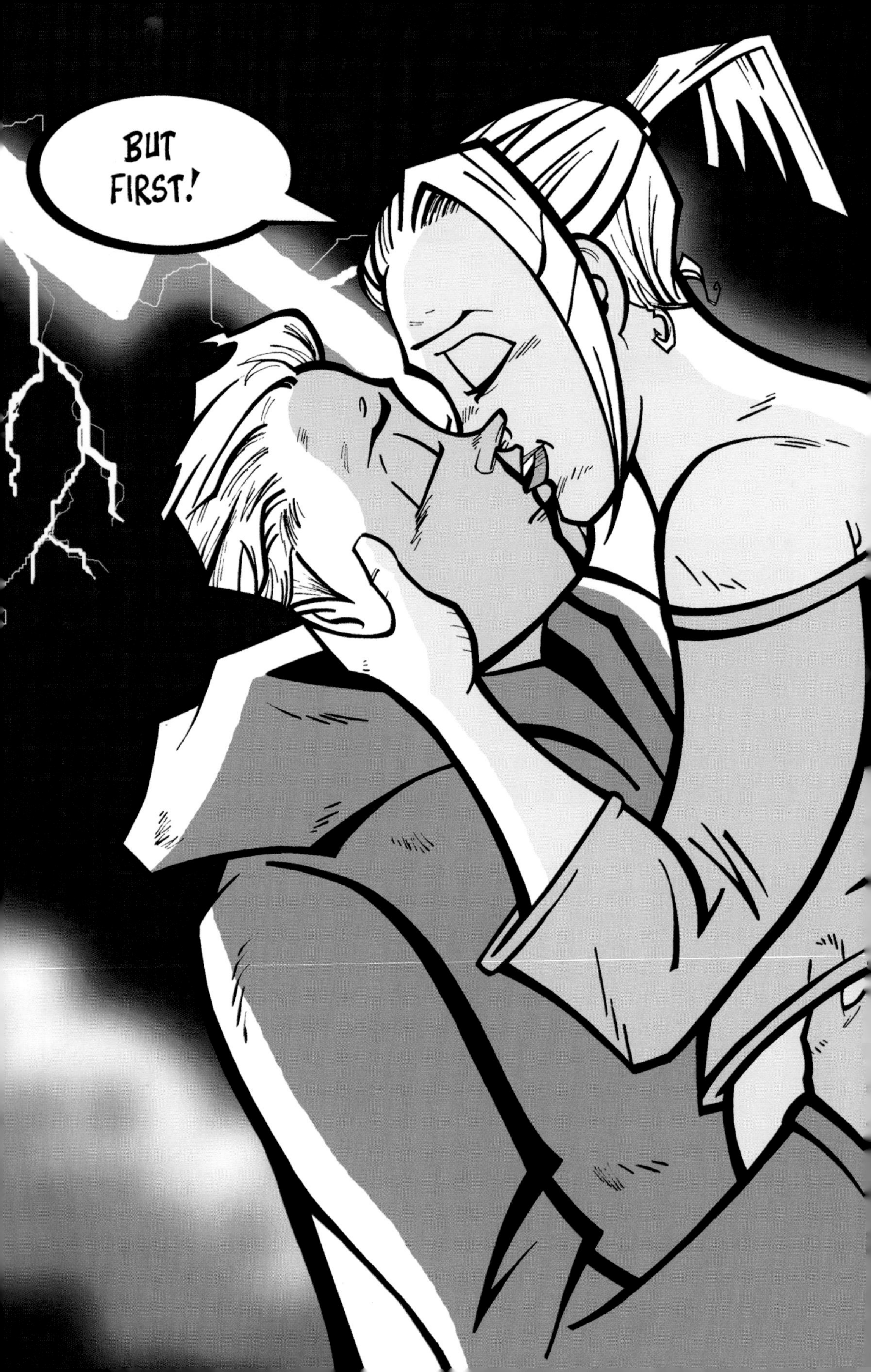
BUT FIRST!

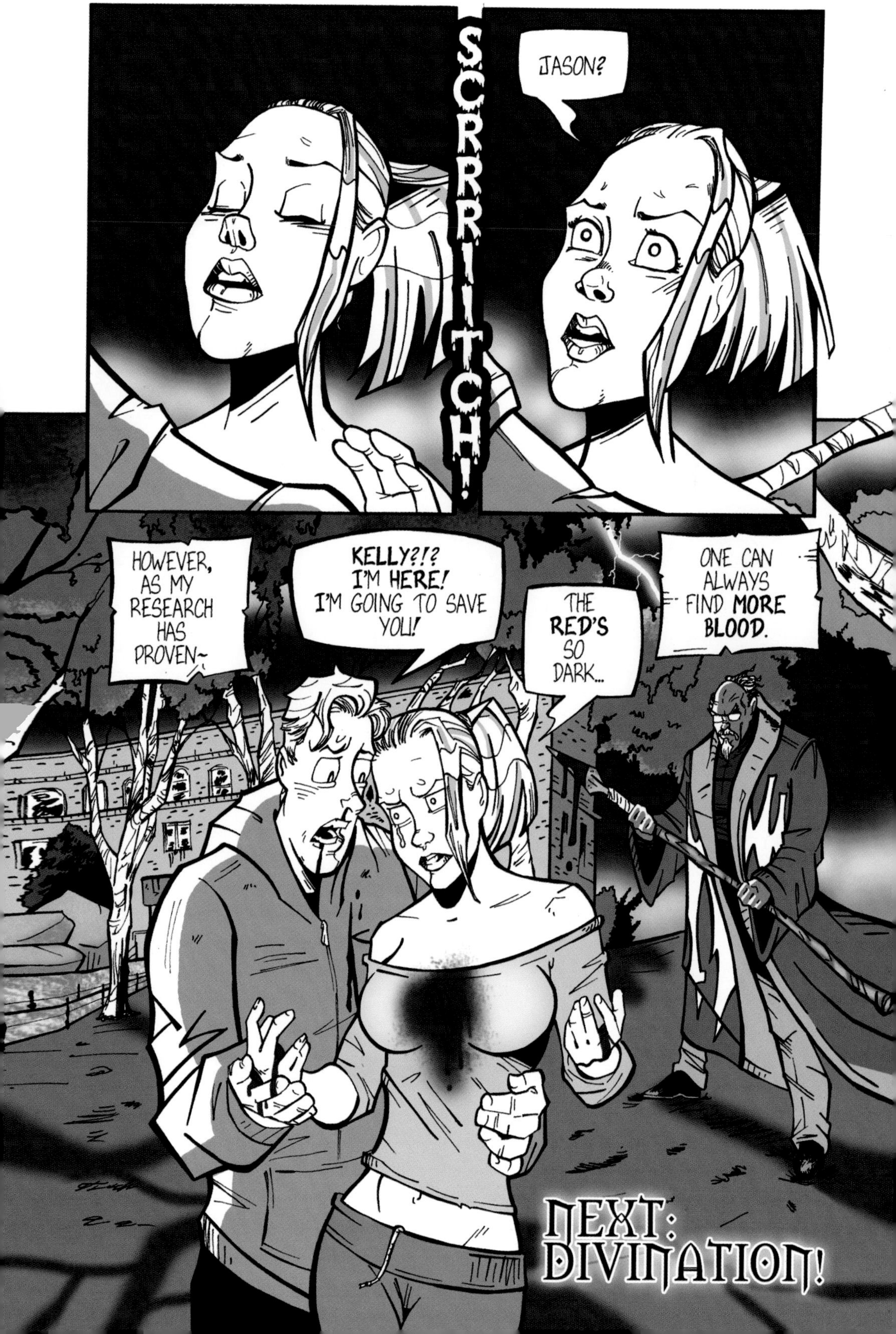
SCRRRIITCH!
JASON?
HOWEVER, AS MY RESEARCH HAS PROVEN~
KELLY?!? I'M HERE! I'M GOING TO SAVE YOU!
THE RED'S SO DARK...
ONE CAN ALWAYS FIND MORE BLOOD.
NEXT: DIVINATION!

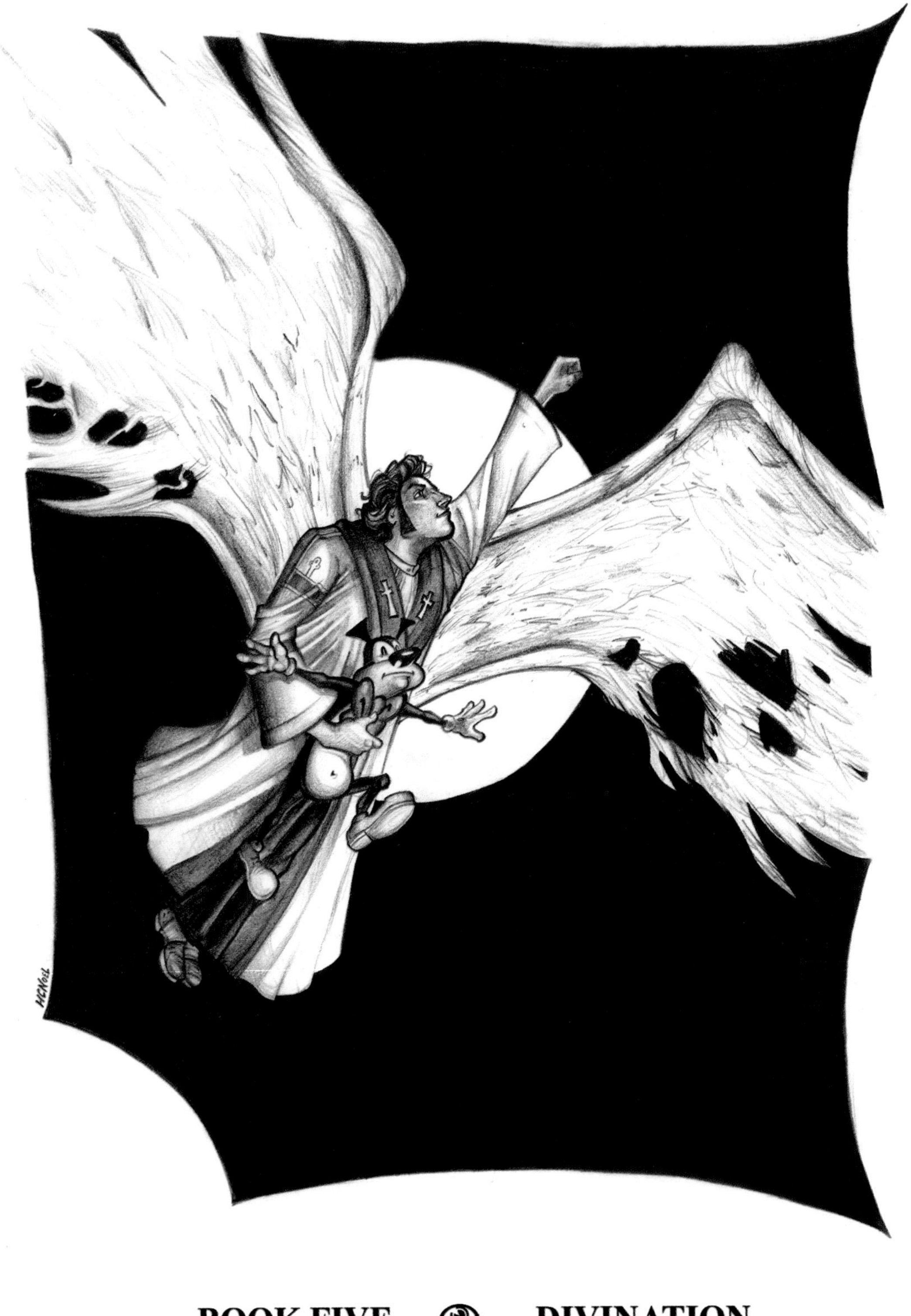

BOOK FIVE DIVINATION

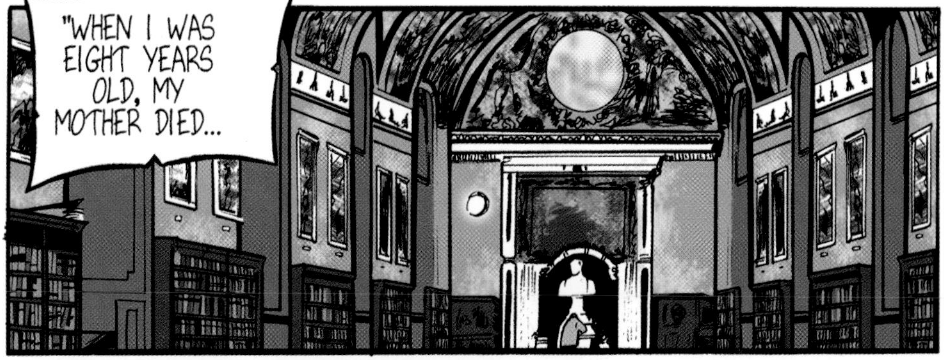
"WHEN I WAS EIGHT YEARS OLD, MY MOTHER DIED...

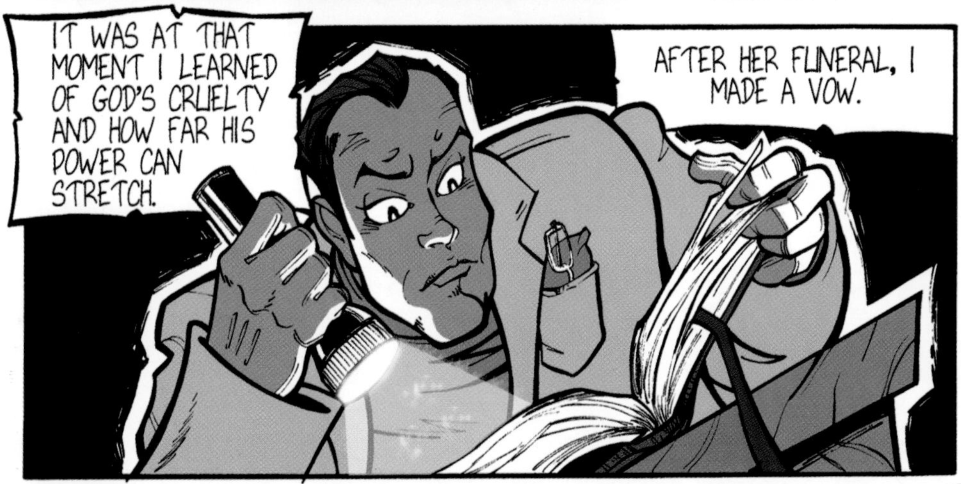
IT WAS AT THAT MOMENT I LEARNED OF GOD'S CRUELTY AND HOW FAR HIS POWER CAN STRETCH.
AFTER HER FUNERAL, I MADE A VOW.

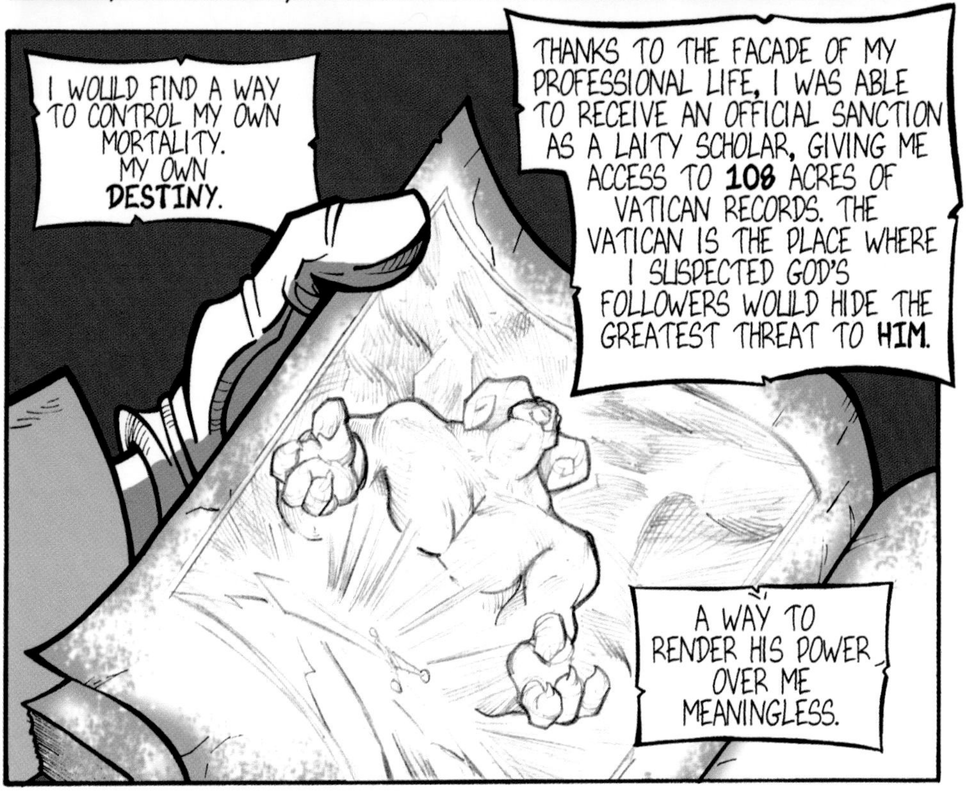
I WOULD FIND A WAY TO CONTROL MY OWN MORTALITY. MY OWN DESTINY.
THANKS TO THE FACADE OF MY PROFESSIONAL LIFE, I WAS ABLE TO RECEIVE AN OFFICIAL SANCTION AS A LAITY SCHOLAR, GIVING ME ACCESS TO 108 ACRES OF VATICAN RECORDS. THE VATICAN IS THE PLACE WHERE I SUSPECTED GOD'S FOLLOWERS WOULD HIDE THE GREATEST THREAT TO HIM.
A WAY TO RENDER HIS POWER OVER ME MEANINGLESS.

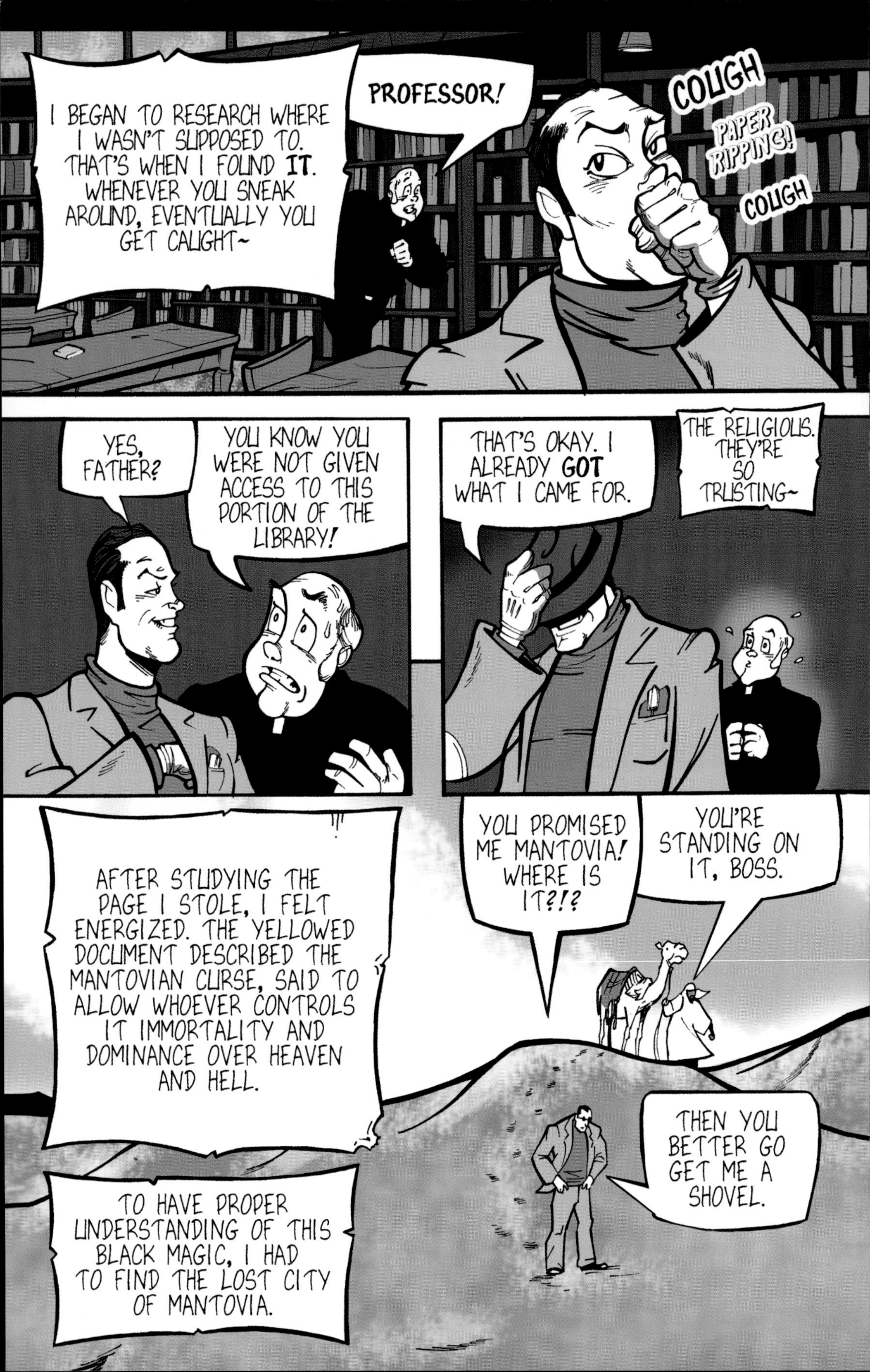
I BEGAN TO RESEARCH WHERE I WASN'T SUPPOSED TO. THAT'S WHEN I FOUND **IT**. WHENEVER YOU SNEAK AROUND, EVENTUALLY YOU GET CAUGHT~
PROFESSOR!
COUGH
PAPER RIPPING!
COUGH
YES, FATHER?
YOU KNOW YOU WERE NOT GIVEN ACCESS TO THIS PORTION OF THE LIBRARY!
THAT'S OKAY. I ALREADY **GOT** WHAT I CAME FOR.
THE RELIGIOUS. THEY'RE SO TRUSTING~
AFTER STUDYING THE PAGE I STOLE, I FELT ENERGIZED. THE YELLOWED DOCUMENT DESCRIBED THE MANTOVIAN CURSE, SAID TO ALLOW WHOEVER CONTROLS IT IMMORTALITY AND DOMINANCE OVER HEAVEN AND HELL.
YOU PROMISED ME MANTOVIA! WHERE IS IT?!?
YOU'RE STANDING ON IT, BOSS.
THEN YOU BETTER GO GET ME A SHOVEL.
TO HAVE PROPER UNDERSTANDING OF THIS BLACK MAGIC, I HAD TO FIND THE LOST CITY OF MANTOVIA.

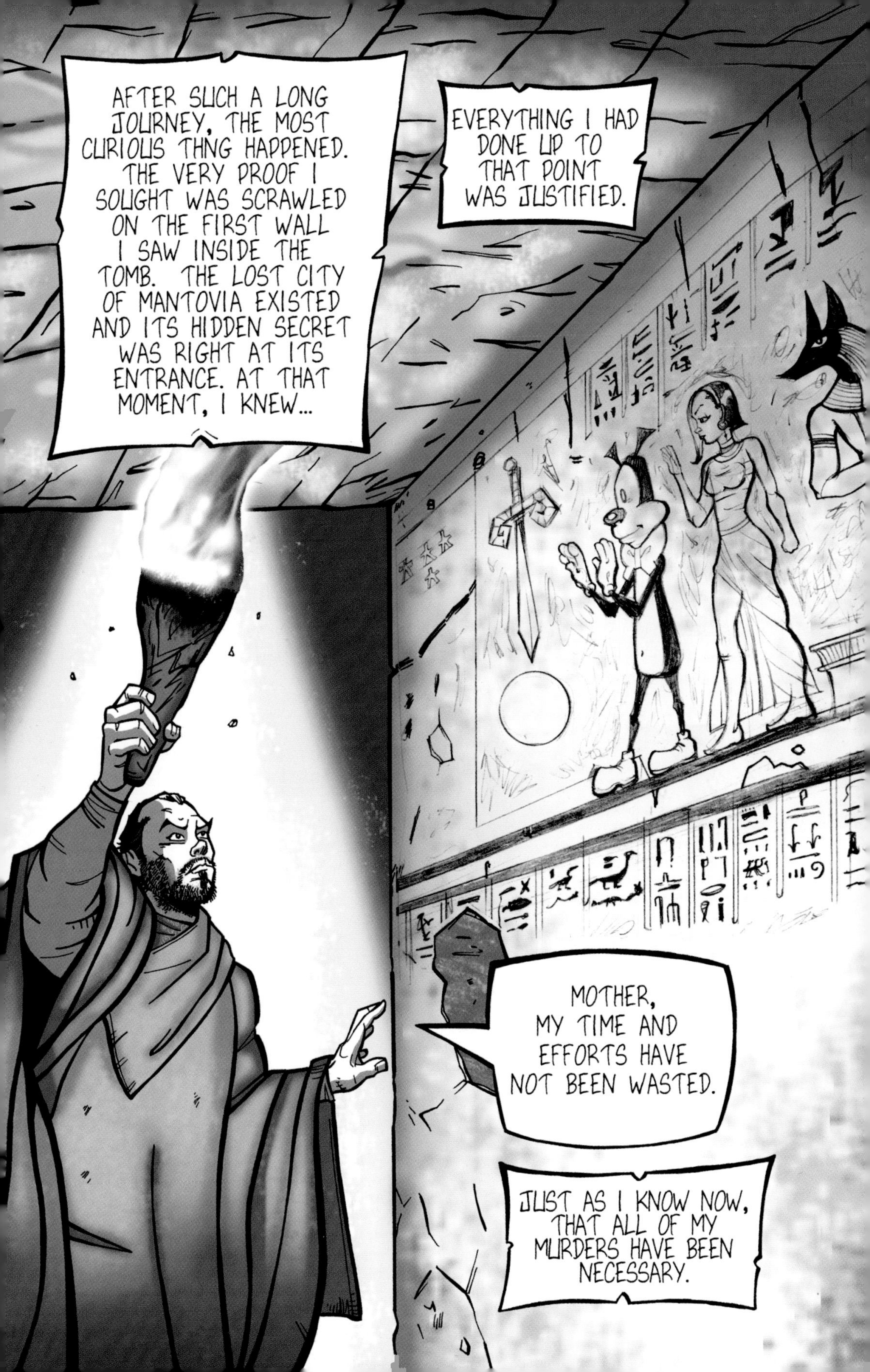
AFTER SUCH A LONG JOURNEY, THE MOST CURIOUS THNG HAPPENED. THE VERY PROOF I SOUGHT WAS SCRAWLED ON THE FIRST WALL I SAW INSIDE THE TOMB. THE LOST CITY OF MANTOVIA EXISTED AND ITS HIDDEN SECRET WAS RIGHT AT ITS ENTRANCE. AT THAT MOMENT, I KNEW...
EVERYTHING I HAD DONE UP TO THAT POINT WAS JUSTIFIED.
MOTHER, MY TIME AND EFFORTS HAVE NOT BEEN WASTED.
JUST AS I KNOW NOW, THAT ALL OF MY MURDERS HAVE BEEN NECESSARY.

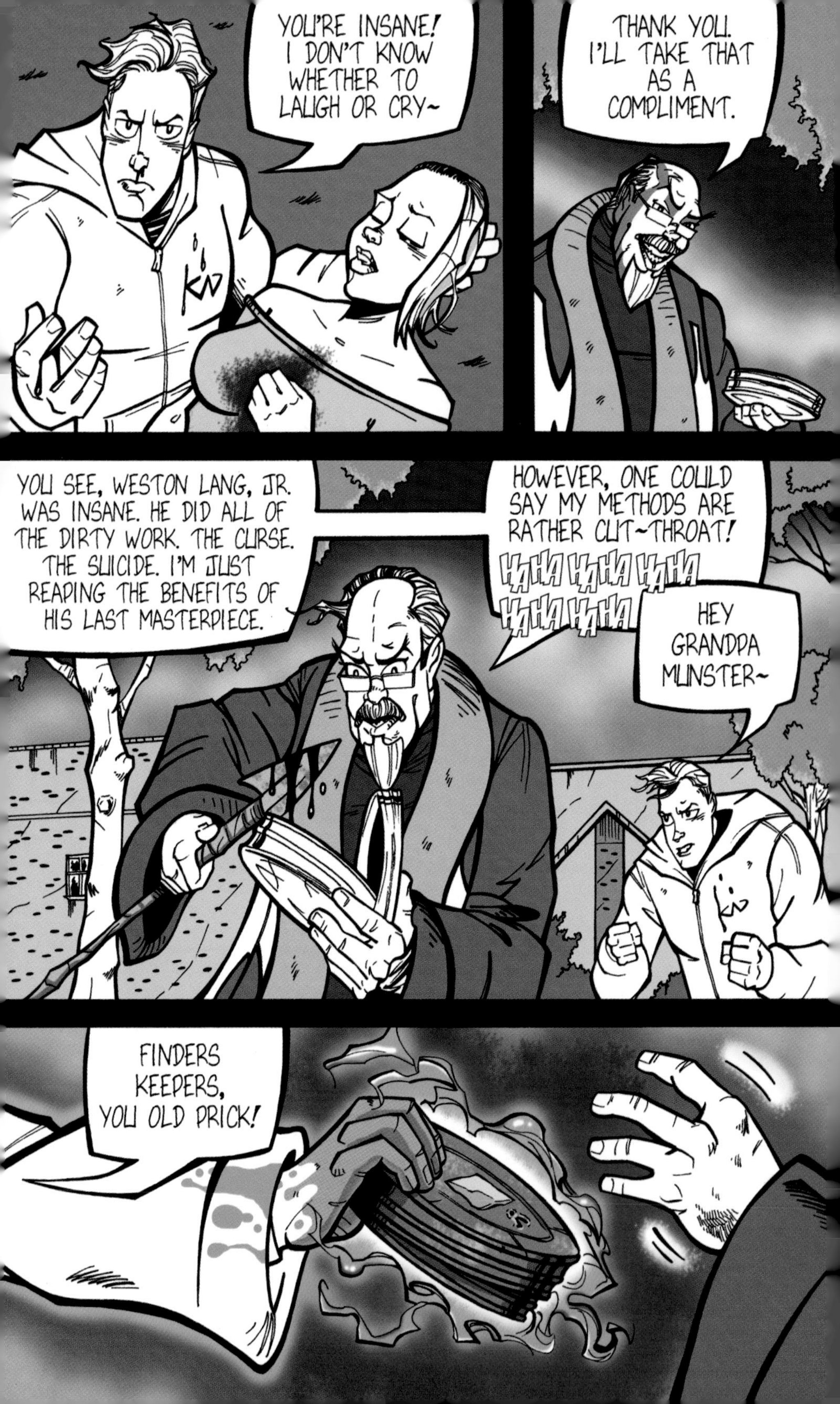
YOU'RE INSANE! I DON'T KNOW WHETHER TO LAUGH OR CRY~
THANK YOU. I'LL TAKE THAT AS A COMPLIMENT.
YOU SEE, WESTON LANG, JR. WAS INSANE. HE DID ALL OF THE DIRTY WORK. THE CURSE. THE SUICIDE. I'M JUST REAPING THE BENEFITS OF HIS LAST MASTERPIECE.
HOWEVER, ONE COULD SAY MY METHODS ARE RATHER CUT~THROAT!
HAHA HAHA HAHA HAHA HAHA
HEY GRANDPA MUNSTER~
FINDERS KEEPERS, YOU OLD PRICK!

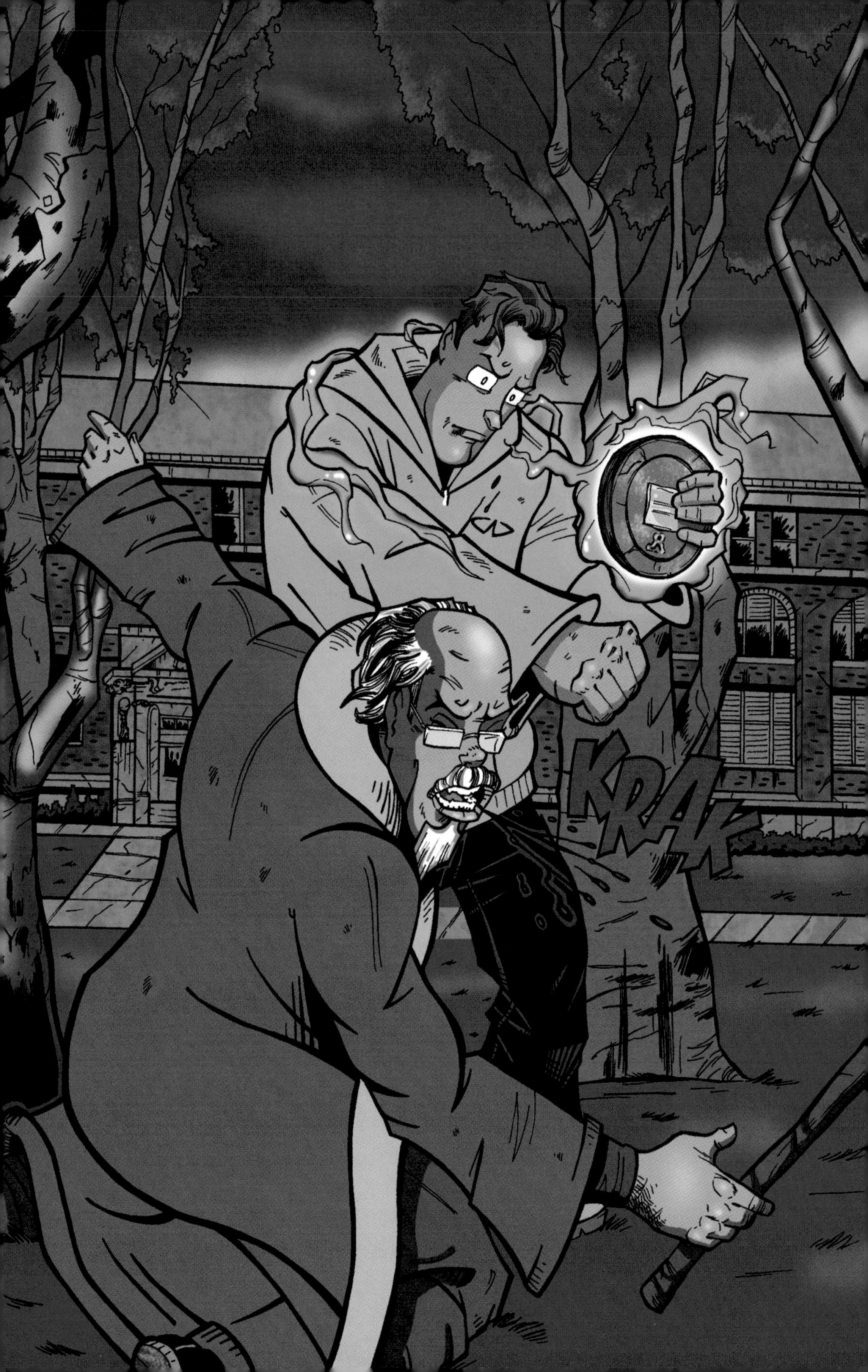
KRAK

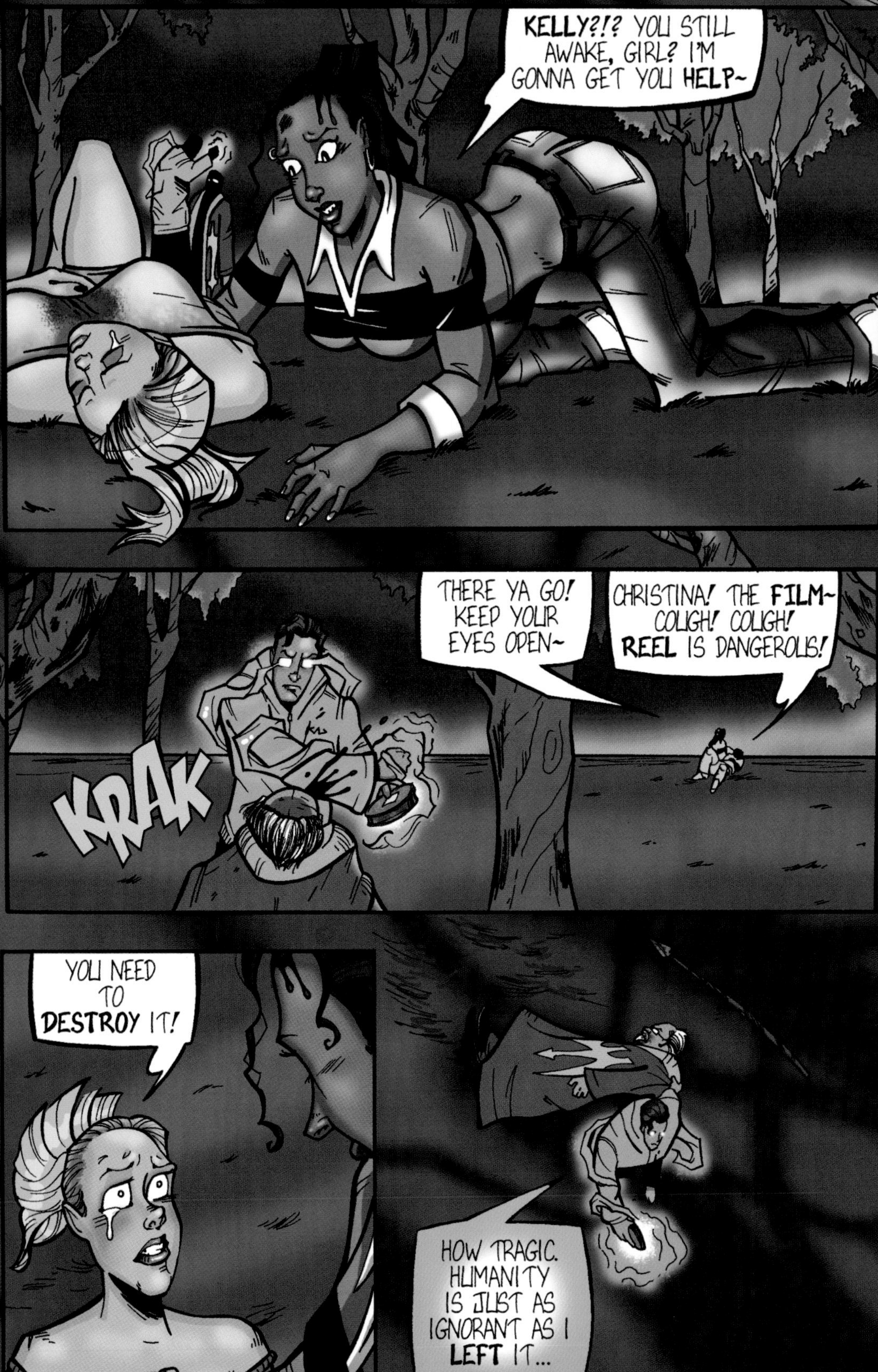
KELLY?!? YOU STILL AWAKE, GIRL? I'M GONNA GET YOU HELP~
THERE YA GO! KEEP YOUR EYES OPEN~
CHRISTINA! THE FILM~ COUGH! COUGH! REEL IS DANGEROUS!
KRAK
YOU NEED TO DESTROY IT!
HOW TRAGIC. HUMANITY IS JUST AS IGNORANT AS I LEFT IT...

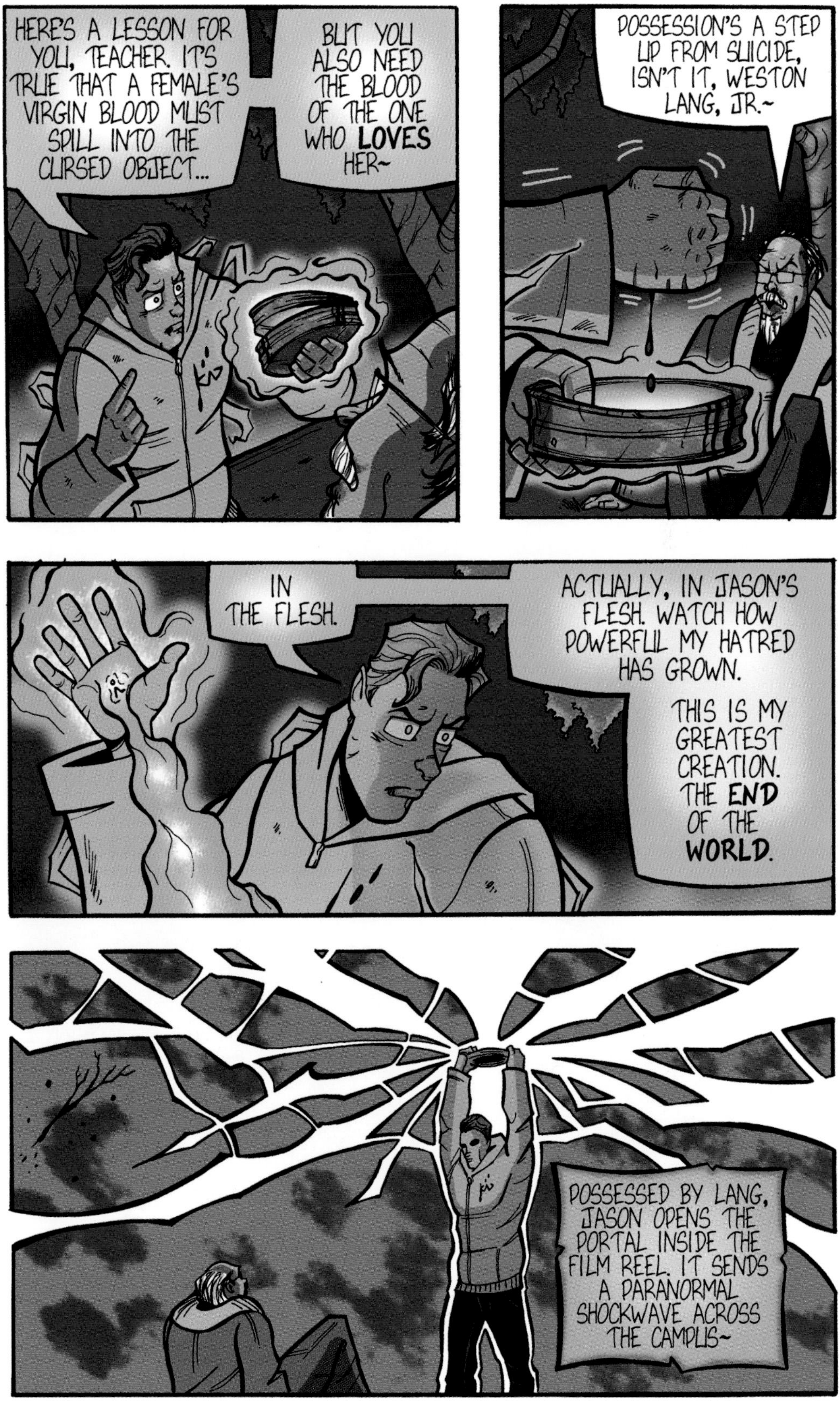
HERE'S A LESSON FOR YOU, TEACHER. IT'S TRUE THAT A FEMALE'S VIRGIN BLOOD MUST SPILL INTO THE CURSED OBJECT...
BUT YOU ALSO NEED THE BLOOD OF THE ONE WHO **LOVES** HER~
POSSESSION'S A STEP UP FROM SUICIDE, ISN'T IT, WESTON LANG, JR.~
IN THE FLESH.
ACTUALLY, IN JASON'S FLESH. WATCH HOW POWERFUL MY HATRED HAS GROWN.
THIS IS MY GREATEST CREATION. THE **END** OF THE **WORLD**.
POSSESSED BY LANG, JASON OPENS THE PORTAL INSIDE THE FILM REEL. IT SENDS A PARANORMAL SHOCKWAVE ACROSS THE CAMPUS~

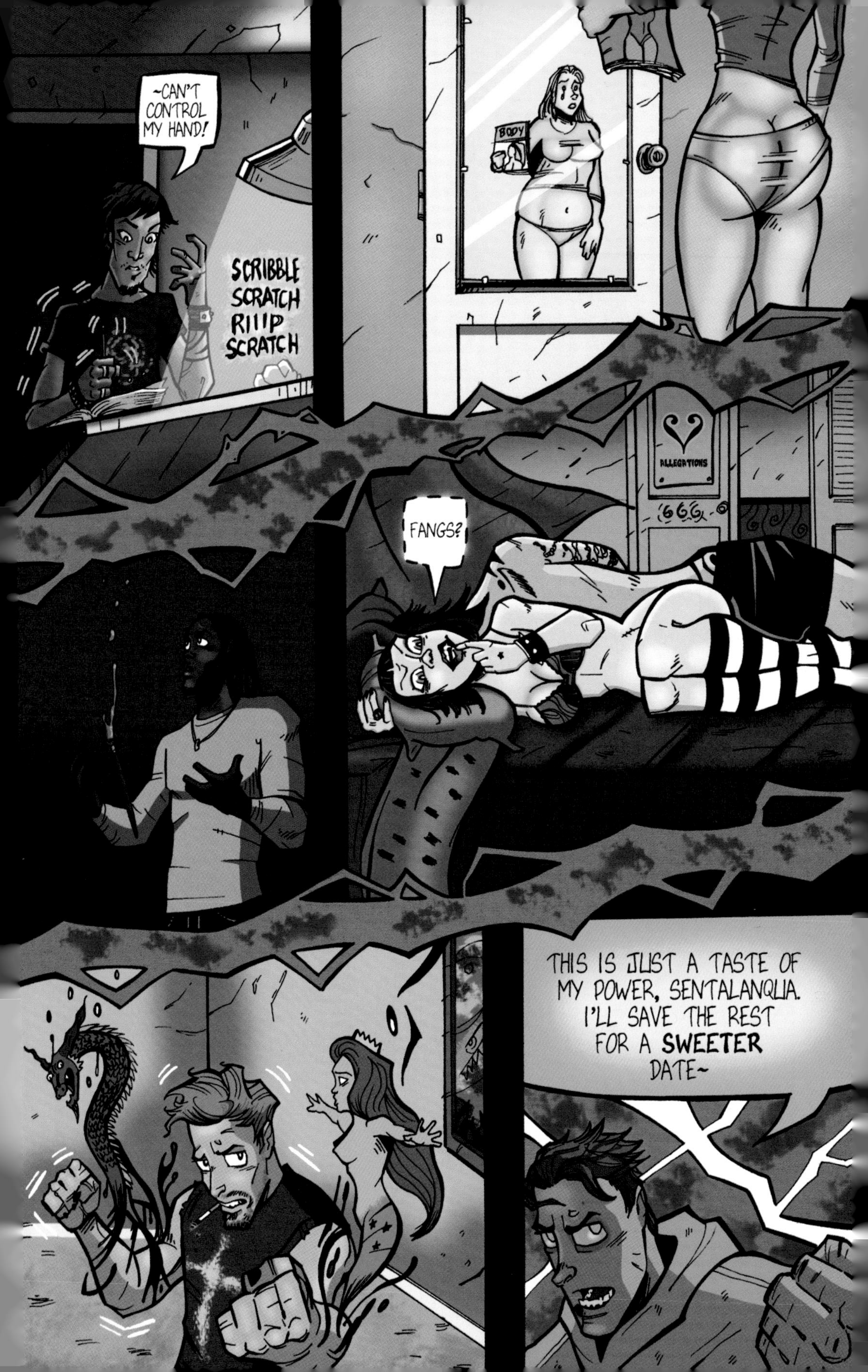
~CAN'T CONTROL MY HAND!
SCRIBBLE SCRATCH RIIIP SCRATCH
BODY
ALLEGATIONS
666
FANGS?
THIS IS JUST A TASTE OF MY POWER, SENTALANQUIA. I'LL SAVE THE REST FOR A **SWEETER** DATE~

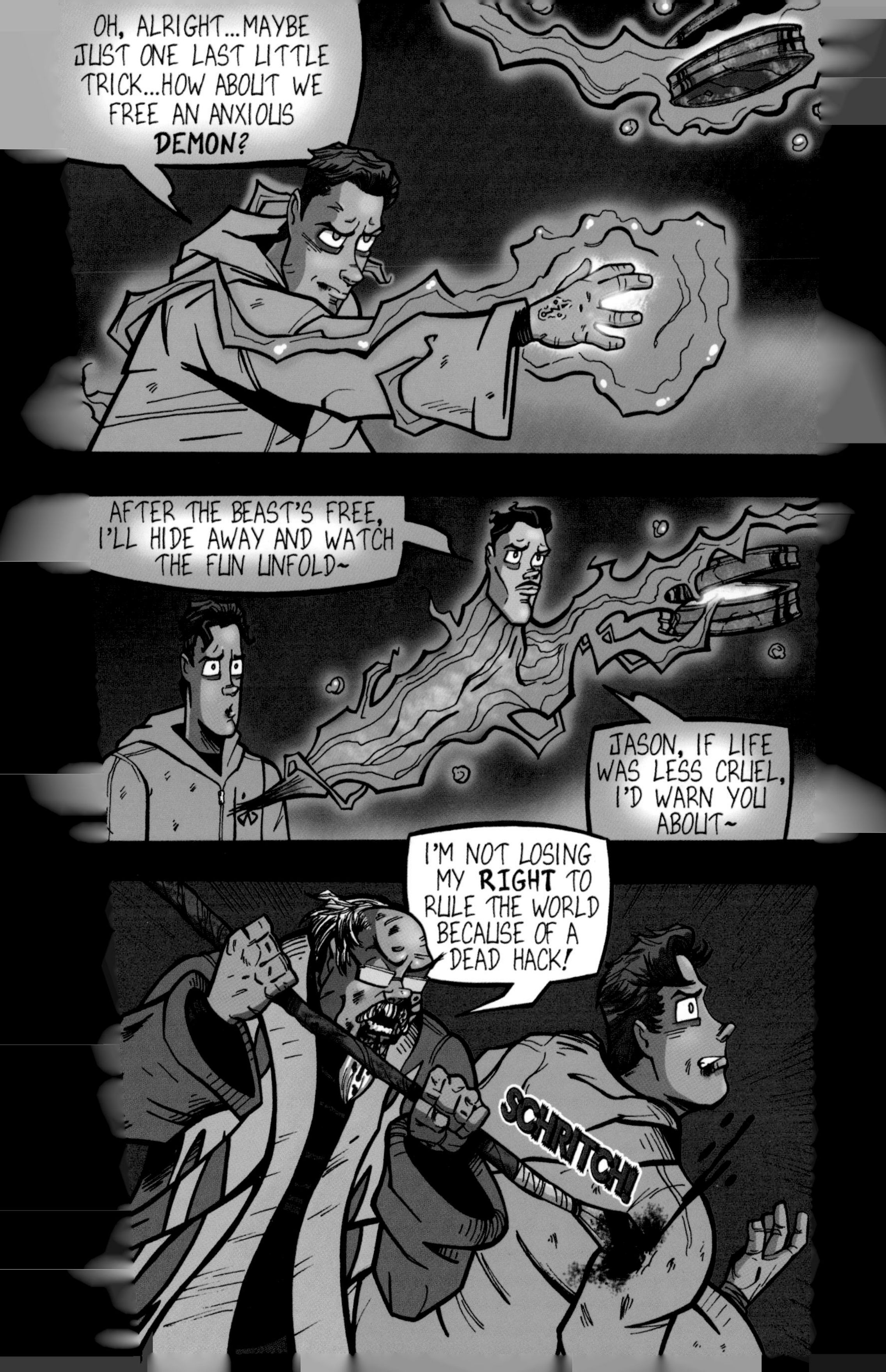
OH, ALRIGHT...MAYBE JUST ONE LAST LITTLE TRICK...HOW ABOUT WE FREE AN ANXIOUS **DEMON**?
AFTER THE BEAST'S FREE, I'LL HIDE AWAY AND WATCH THE FUN UNFOLD~
JASON, IF LIFE WAS LESS CRUEL, I'D WARN YOU ABOUT~
I'M NOT LOSING MY **RIGHT** TO RULE THE WORLD BECAUSE OF A DEAD HACK!
SCHRITCH!

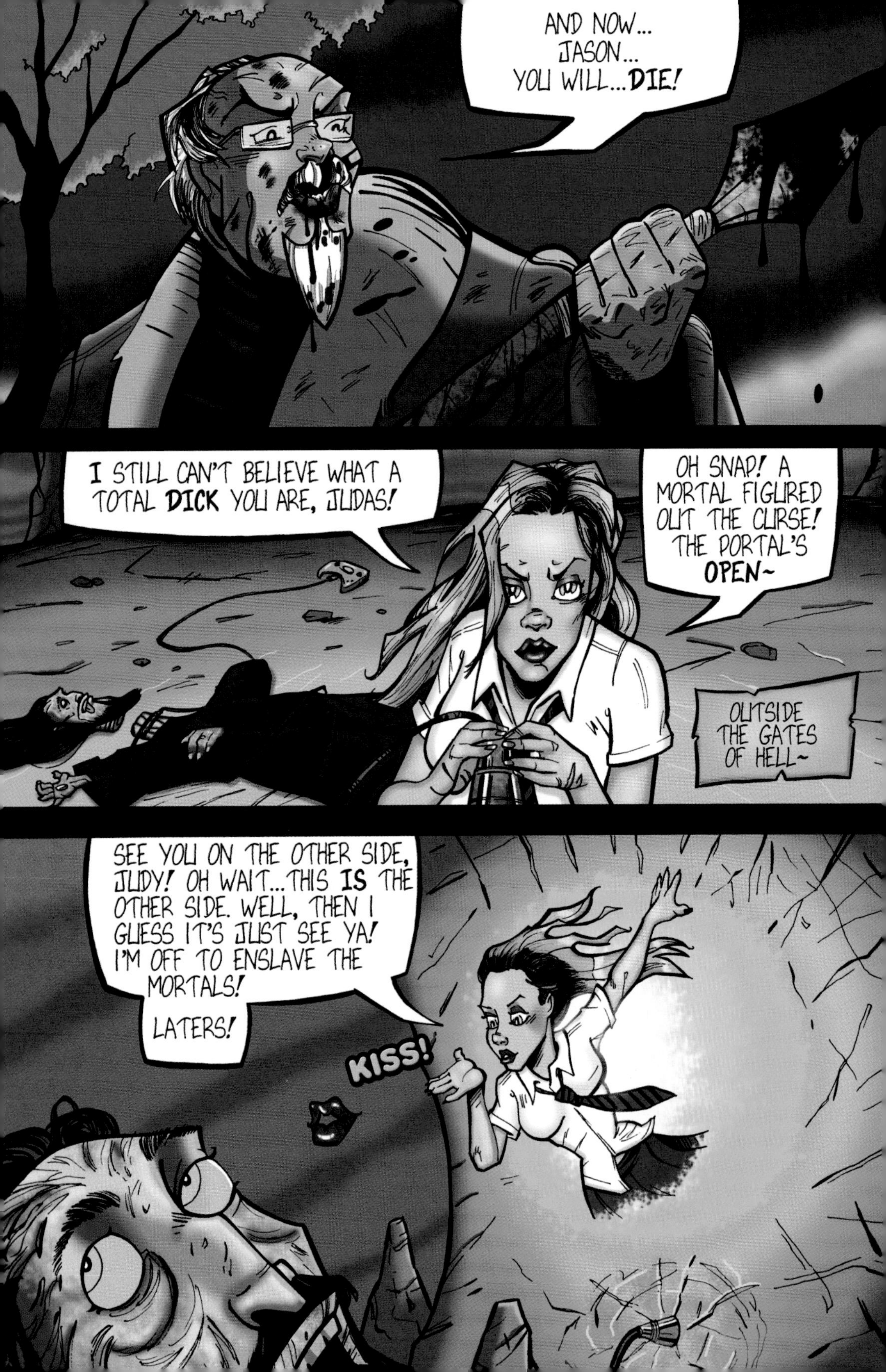
AND NOW... JASON... YOU WILL...DIE!
I STILL CAN'T BELIEVE WHAT A TOTAL DICK YOU ARE, JUDAS!
OH SNAP! A MORTAL FIGURED OUT THE CURSE! THE PORTAL'S OPEN~
OUTSIDE THE GATES OF HELL~
SEE YOU ON THE OTHER SIDE, JUDY! OH WAIT...THIS IS THE OTHER SIDE. WELL, THEN I GUESS IT'S JUST SEE YA! I'M OFF TO ENSLAVE THE MORTALS!
LATERS!
KISS!

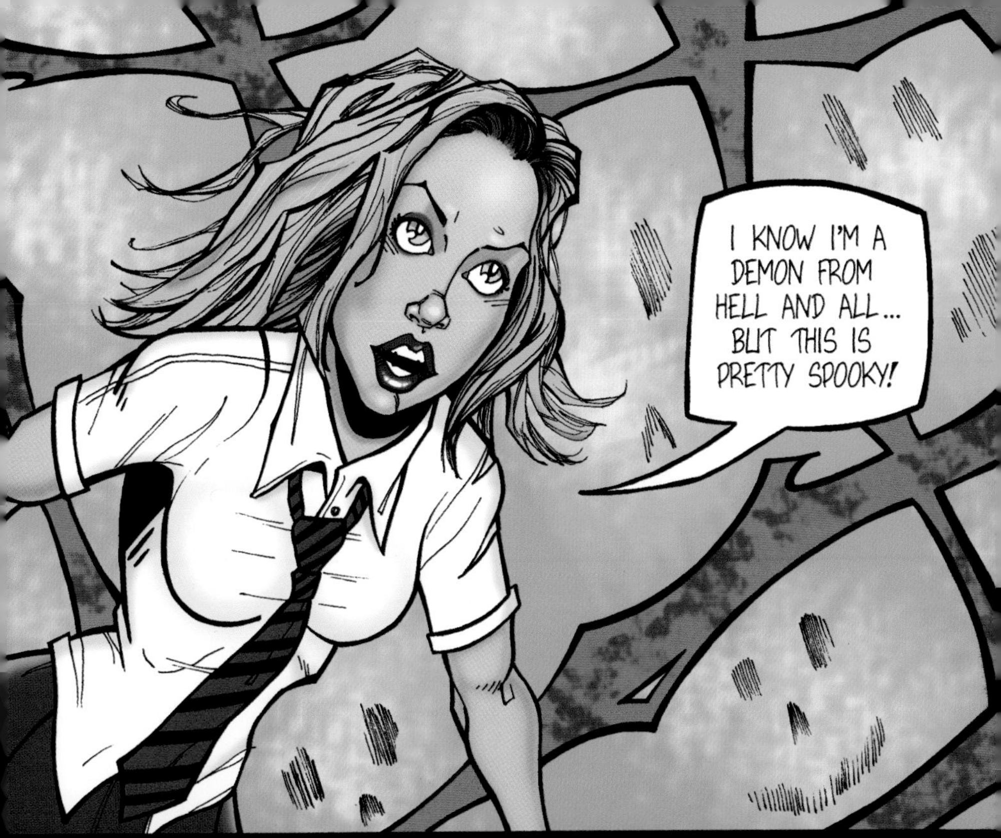
I KNOW I'M A DEMON FROM HELL AND ALL... BUT THIS IS PRETTY SPOOKY!

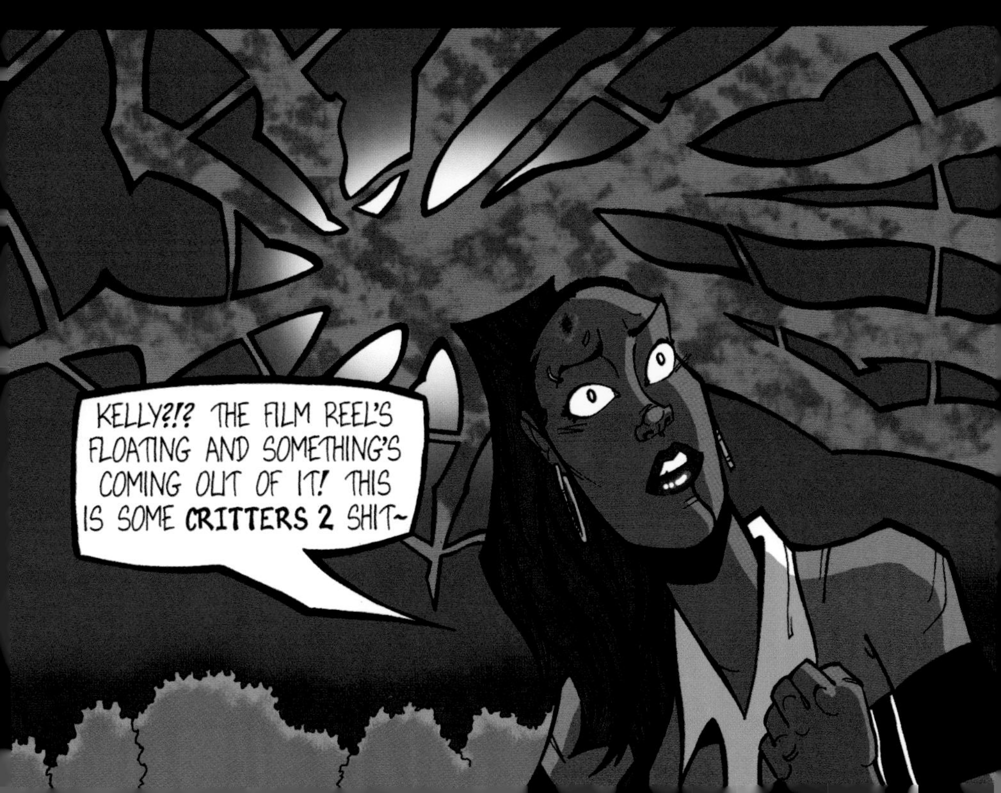
KELLY?!? THE FILM REEL'S FLOATING AND SOMETHING'S COMING OUT OF IT! THIS IS SOME **CRITTERS 2** SHIT~

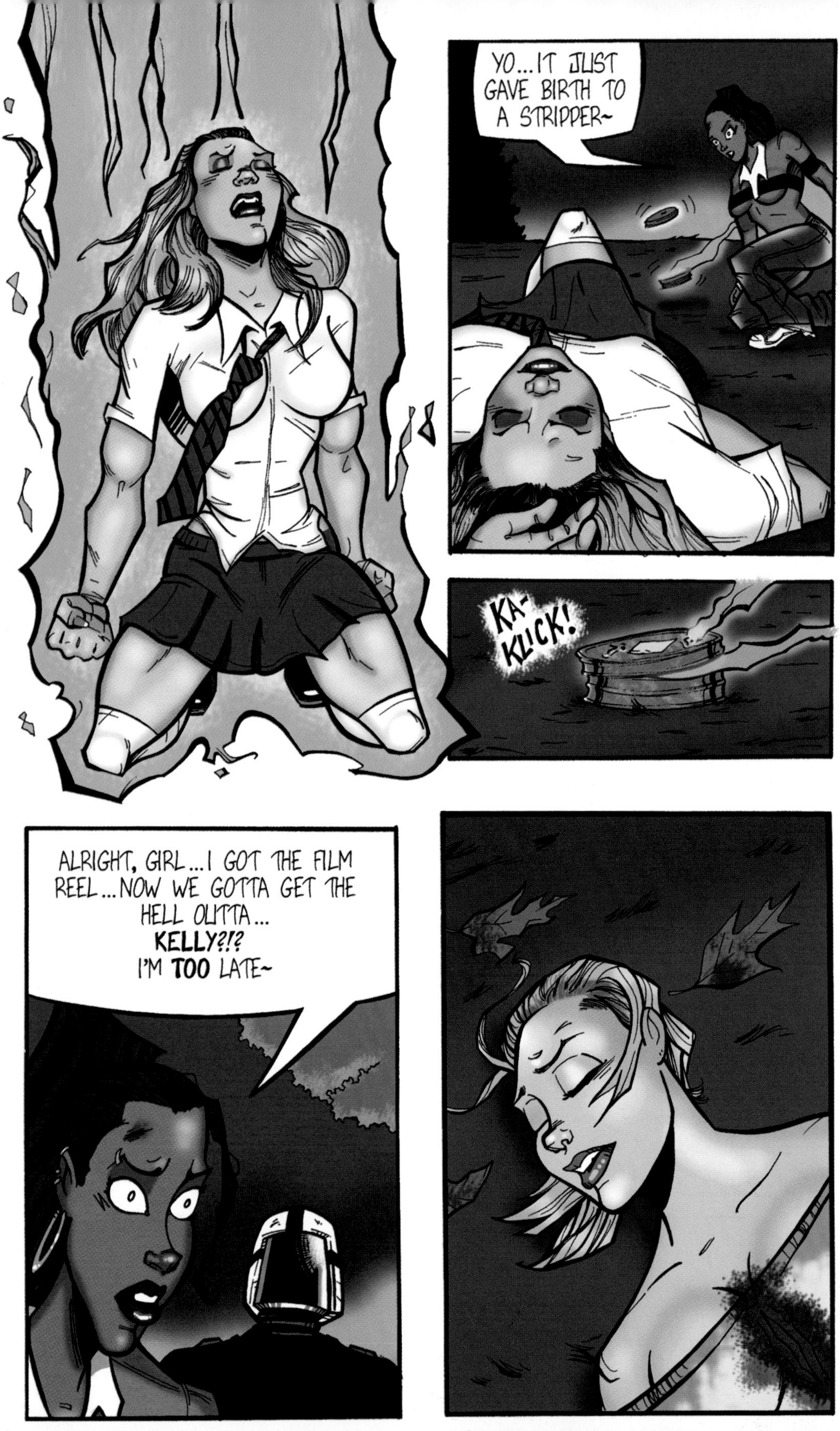
YO...IT JUST GAVE BIRTH TO A STRIPPER~
KA-KLICK!
ALRIGHT, GIRL...I GOT THE FILM REEL...NOW WE GOTTA GET THE HELL OUTTA... **KELLY?!?** I'M **TOO** LATE~

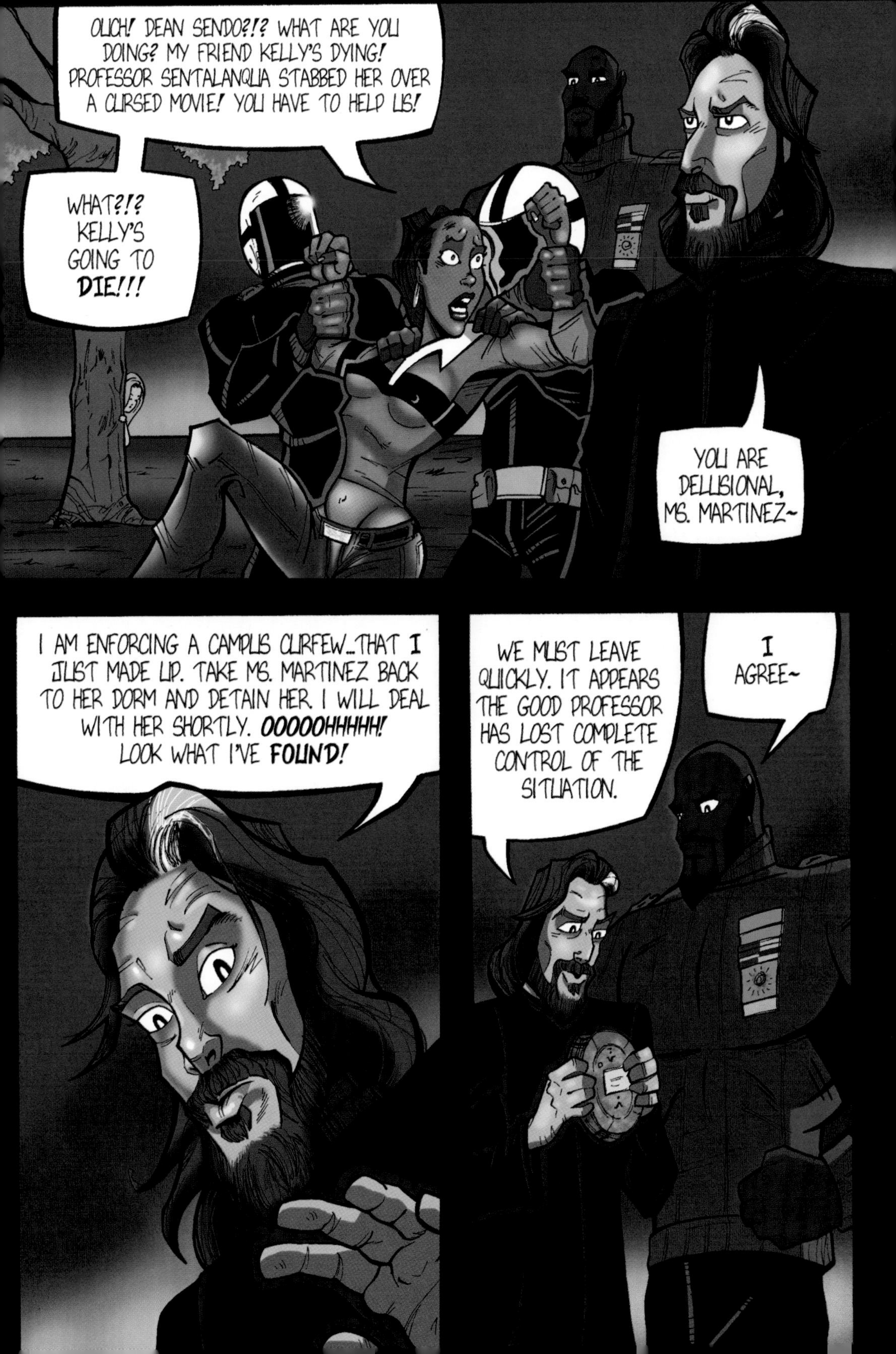
OUCH! DEAN SENDO?!? WHAT ARE YOU DOING? MY FRIEND KELLY'S DYING! PROFESSOR SENTALANQUA STABBED HER OVER A CURSED MOVIE! YOU HAVE TO HELP US!
WHAT?!? KELLY'S GOING TO DIE!!!
YOU ARE DELUSIONAL, MS. MARTINEZ~
I AM ENFORCING A CAMPUS CURFEW...THAT I JUST MADE UP. TAKE MS. MARTINEZ BACK TO HER DORM AND DETAIN HER. I WILL DEAL WITH HER SHORTLY. OOOOOHHHHH! LOOK WHAT I'VE FOUND!
WE MUST LEAVE QUICKLY. IT APPEARS THE GOOD PROFESSOR HAS LOST COMPLETE CONTROL OF THE SITUATION.
I AGREE~

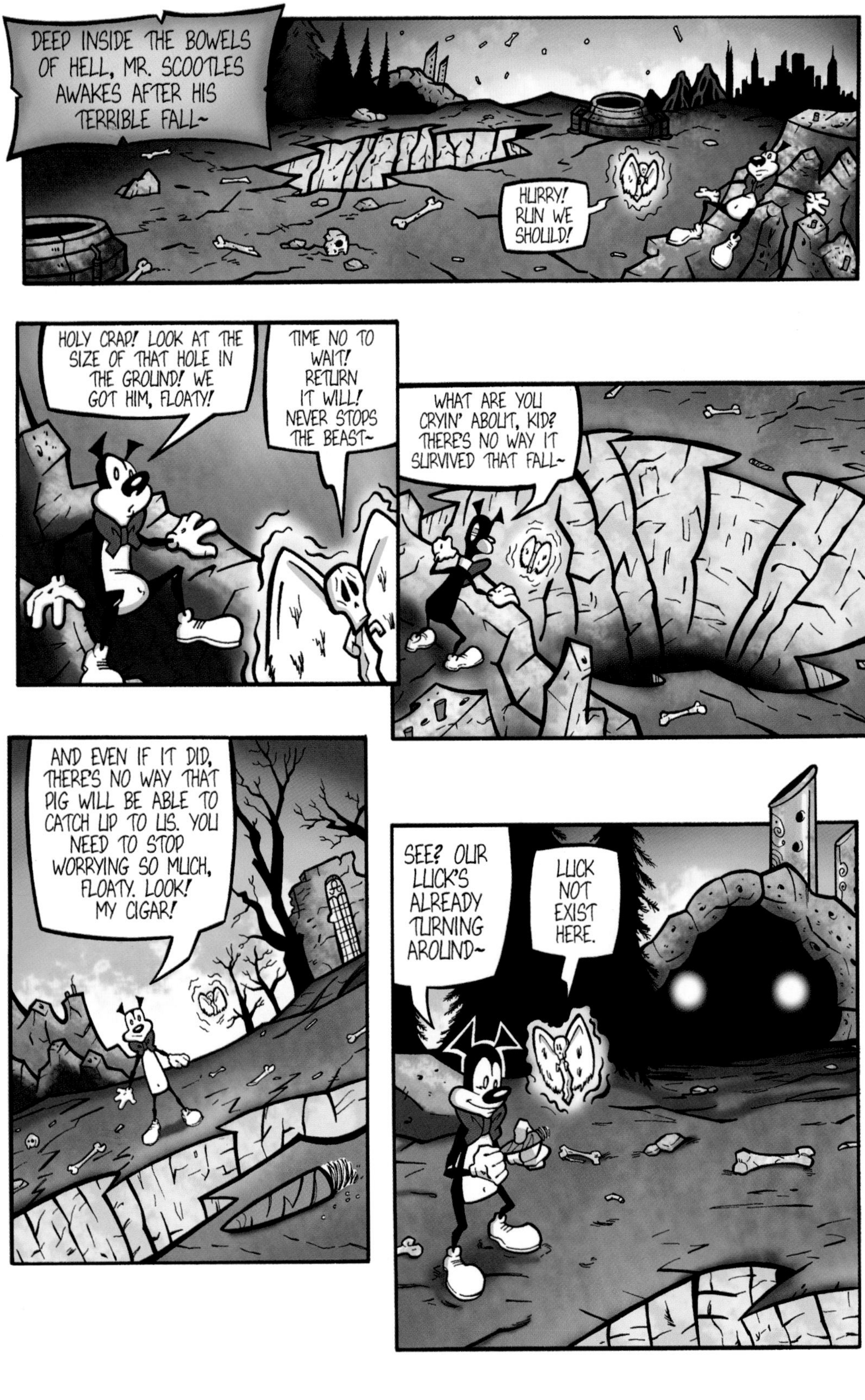
DEEP INSIDE THE BOWELS OF HELL, MR. SCOOTLES AWAKES AFTER HIS TERRIBLE FALL~
HURRY! RUN WE SHOULD!
HOLY CRAP! LOOK AT THE SIZE OF THAT HOLE IN THE GROUND! WE GOT HIM, FLOATY!
TIME NO TO WAIT! RETURN IT WILL! NEVER STOPS THE BEAST~
WHAT ARE YOU CRYIN' ABOUT, KID? THERE'S NO WAY IT SURVIVED THAT FALL~
AND EVEN IF IT DID, THERE'S NO WAY THAT PIG WILL BE ABLE TO CATCH UP TO US. YOU NEED TO STOP WORRYING SO MUCH, FLOATY. LOOK! MY CIGAR!
SEE? OUR LUCK'S ALREADY TURNING AROUND~
LUCK NOT EXIST HERE.

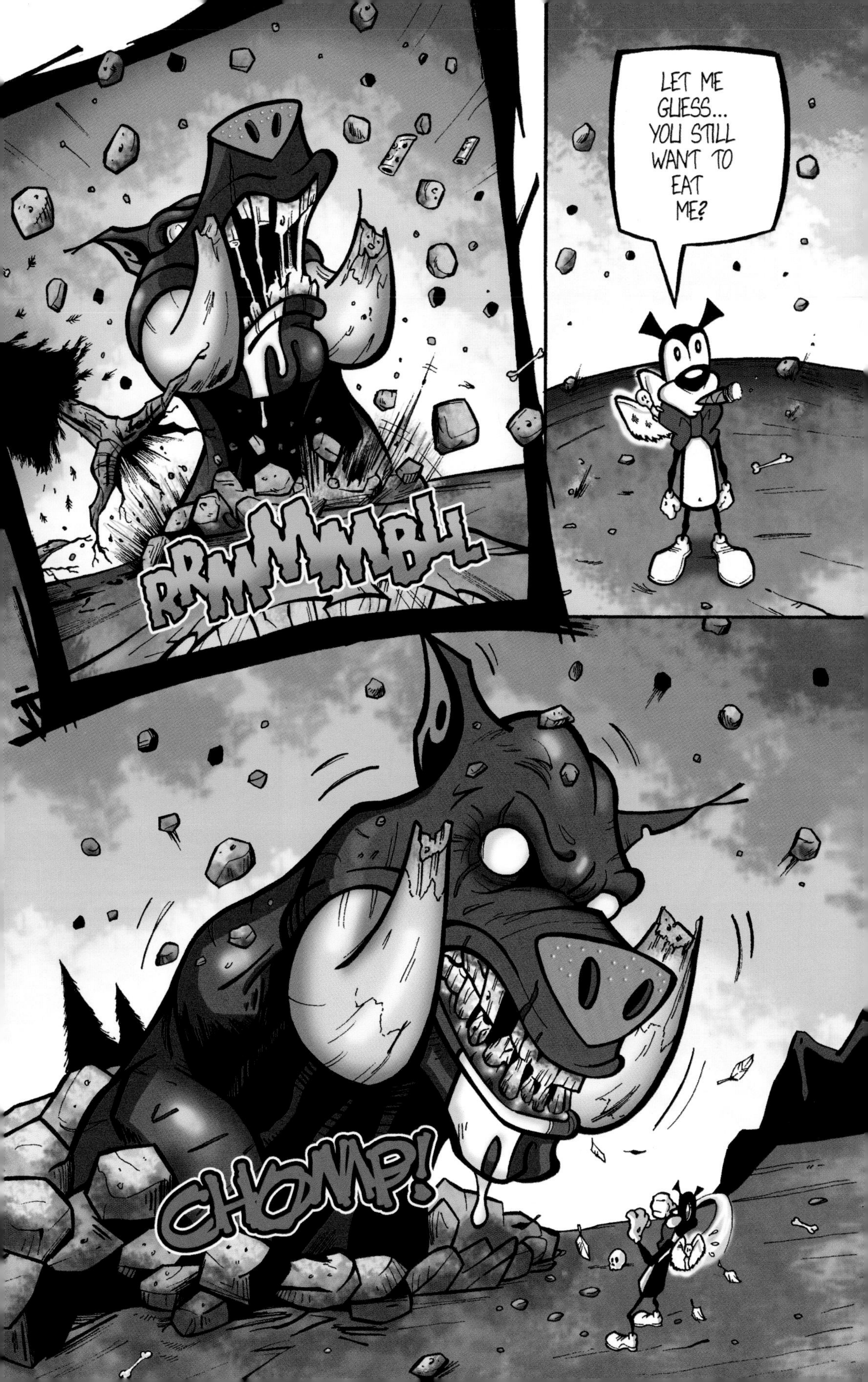
RRMMMMBLL
LET ME GUESS... YOU STILL WANT TO EAT ME?
CHOMP!

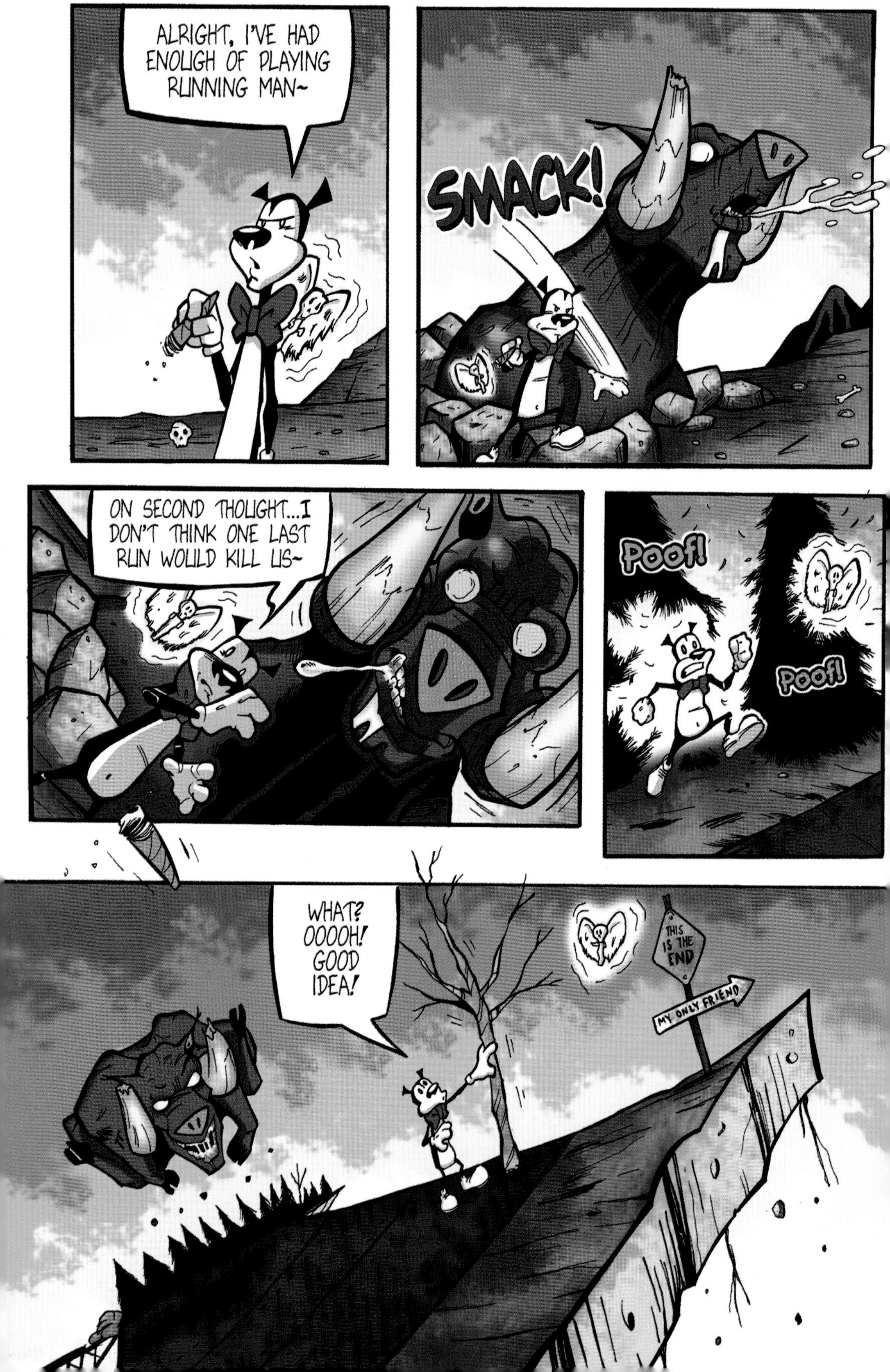
ALRIGHT, I'VE HAD ENOUGH OF PLAYING RUNNING MAN~
SMACK!
ON SECOND THOUGHT...I DON'T THINK ONE LAST RUN WOULD KILL US~
Poof!
Poof!
WHAT? OOOOH! GOOD IDEA!
THIS IS THE END
MY ONLY FRIEND

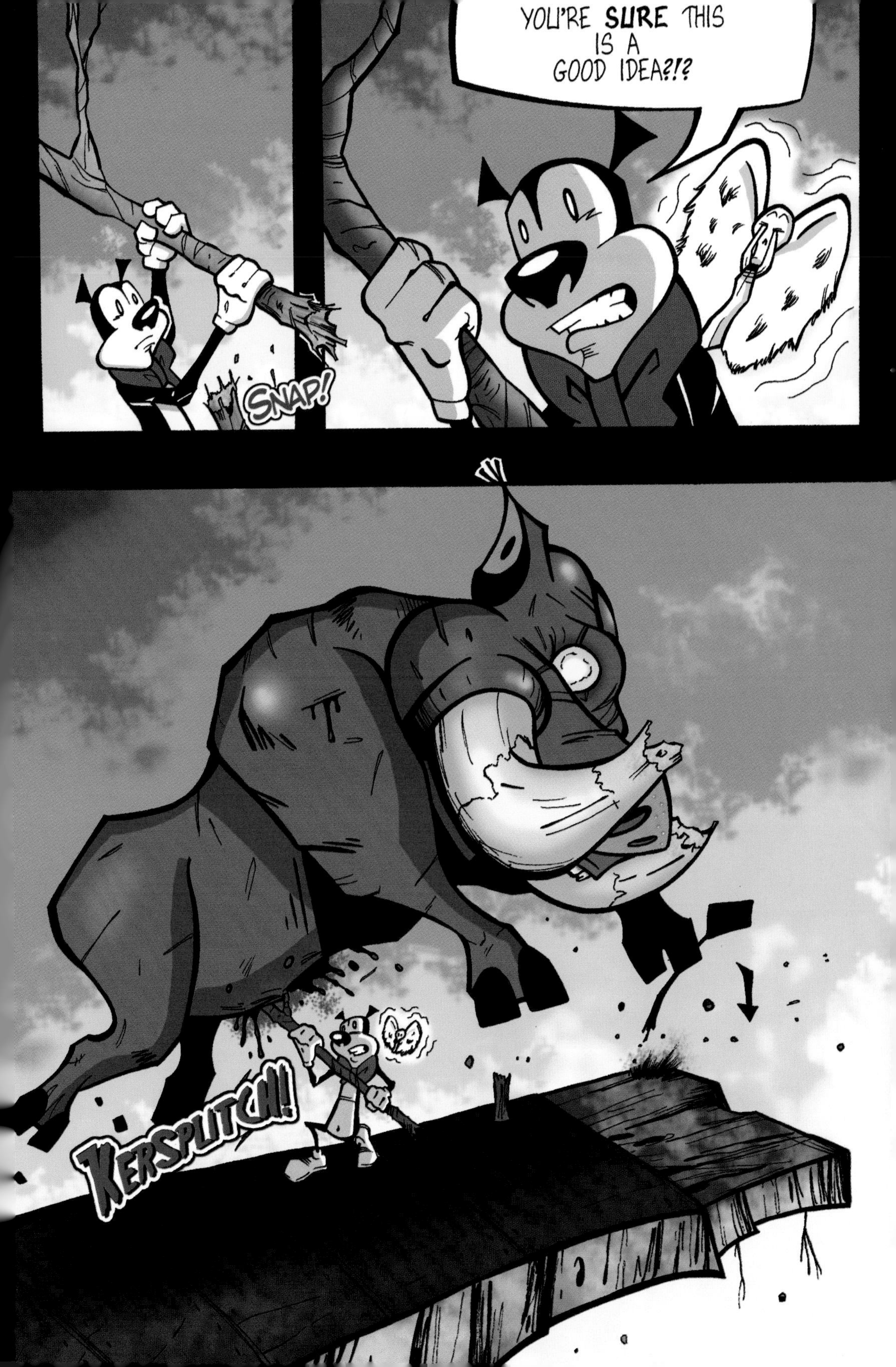

SNAP!
YOU'RE SURE THIS IS A GOOD IDEA?!?
KERSPLITCH!

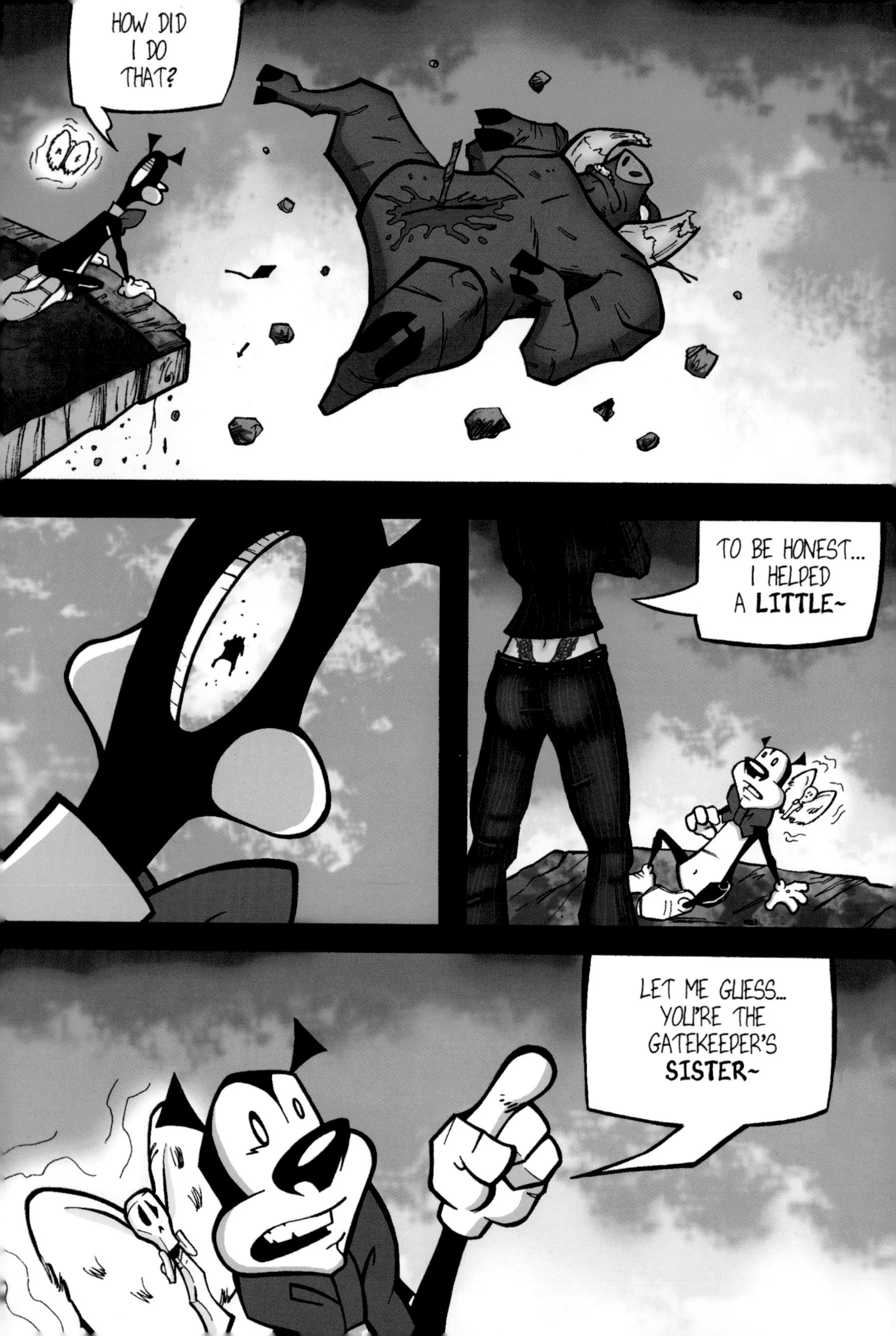

HOW DID I DO THAT?
TO BE HONEST... I HELPED A LITTLE~
LET ME GUESS... YOU'RE THE GATEKEEPER'S SISTER~

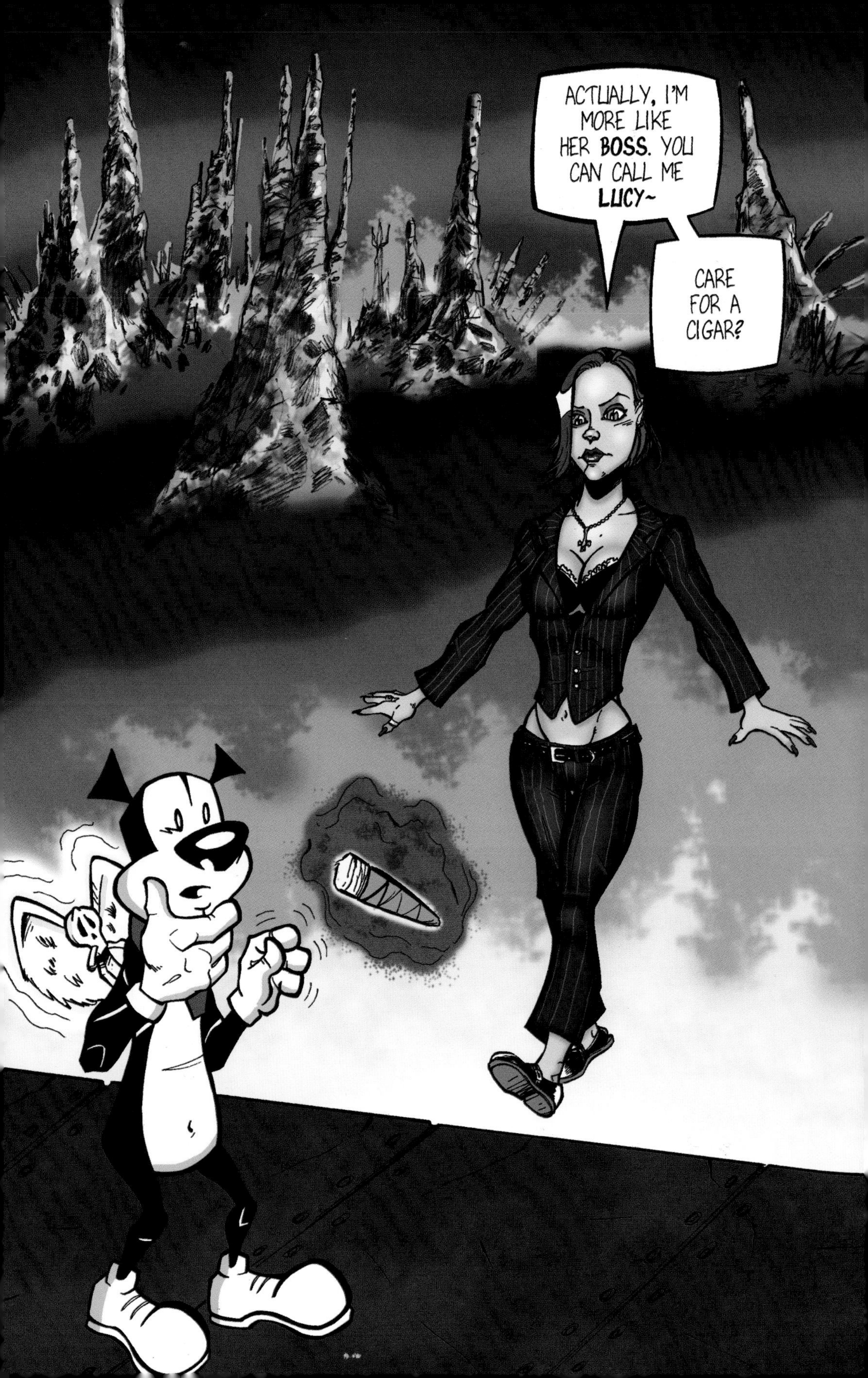
ACTUALLY, I'M MORE LIKE HER **BOSS**. YOU CAN CALL ME **LUCY**~
CARE FOR A CIGAR?

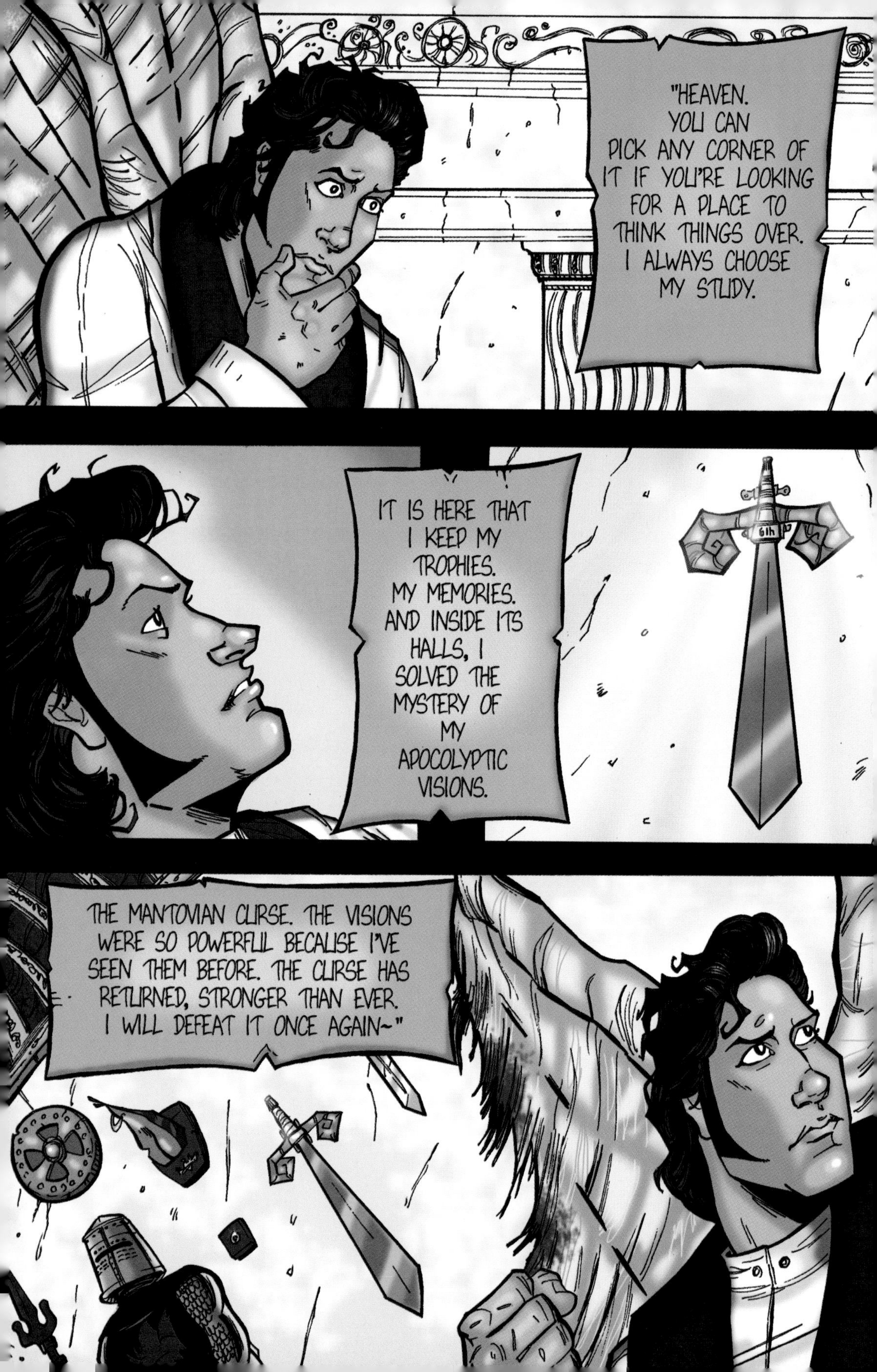
"HEAVEN. YOU CAN PICK ANY CORNER OF IT IF YOU'RE LOOKING FOR A PLACE TO THINK THINGS OVER. I ALWAYS CHOOSE MY STUDY.
IT IS HERE THAT I KEEP MY TROPHIES. MY MEMORIES. AND INSIDE ITS HALLS, I SOLVED THE MYSTERY OF MY APOCOLYPTIC VISIONS.
THE MANTOVIAN CURSE. THE VISIONS WERE SO POWERFUL BECAUSE I'VE SEEN THEM BEFORE. THE CURSE HAS RETURNED, STRONGER THAN EVER. I WILL DEFEAT IT ONCE AGAIN~"

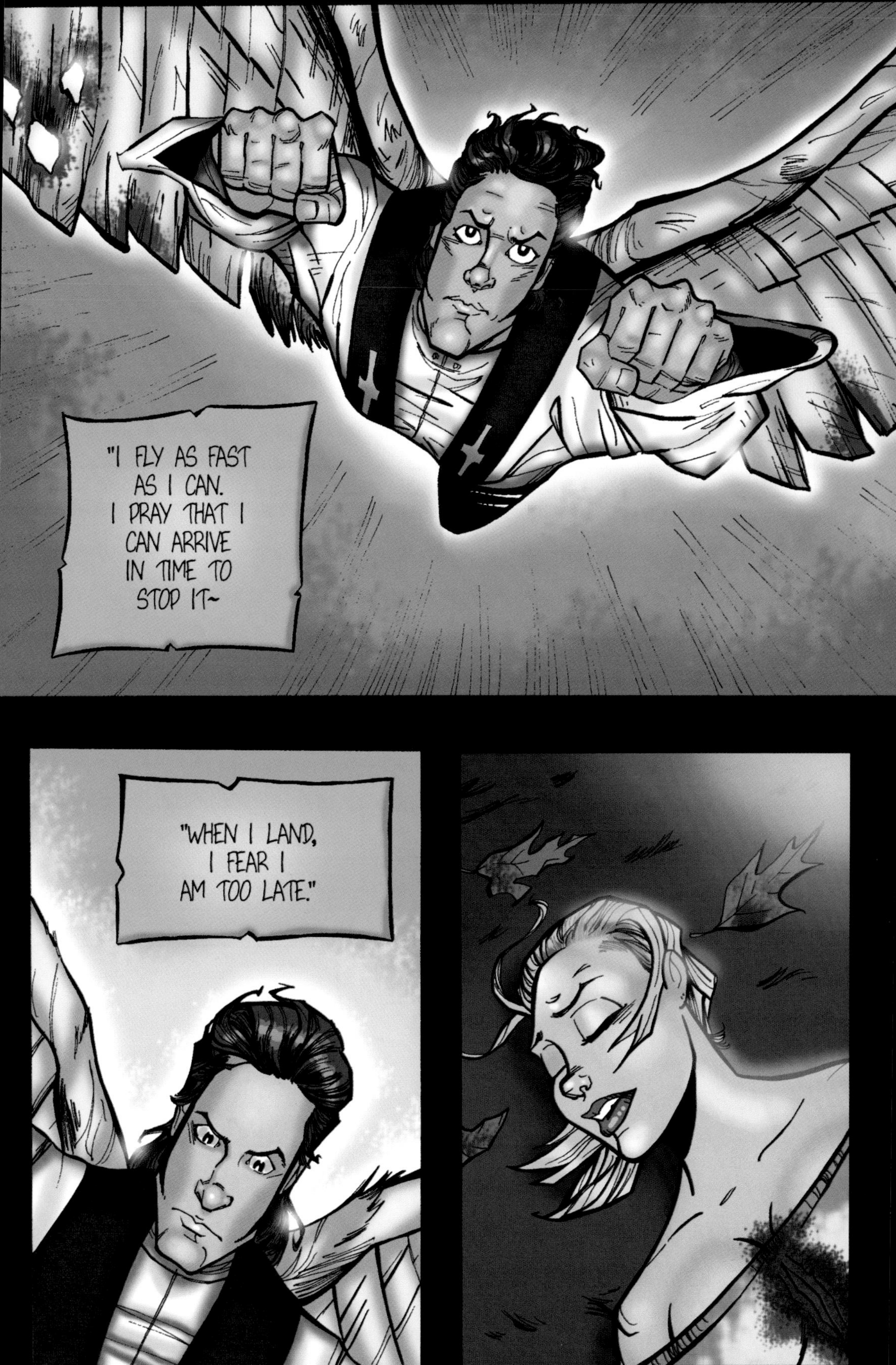
"I FLY AS FAST AS I CAN. I PRAY THAT I CAN ARRIVE IN TIME TO STOP IT~
"WHEN I LAND, I FEAR I AM TOO LATE."

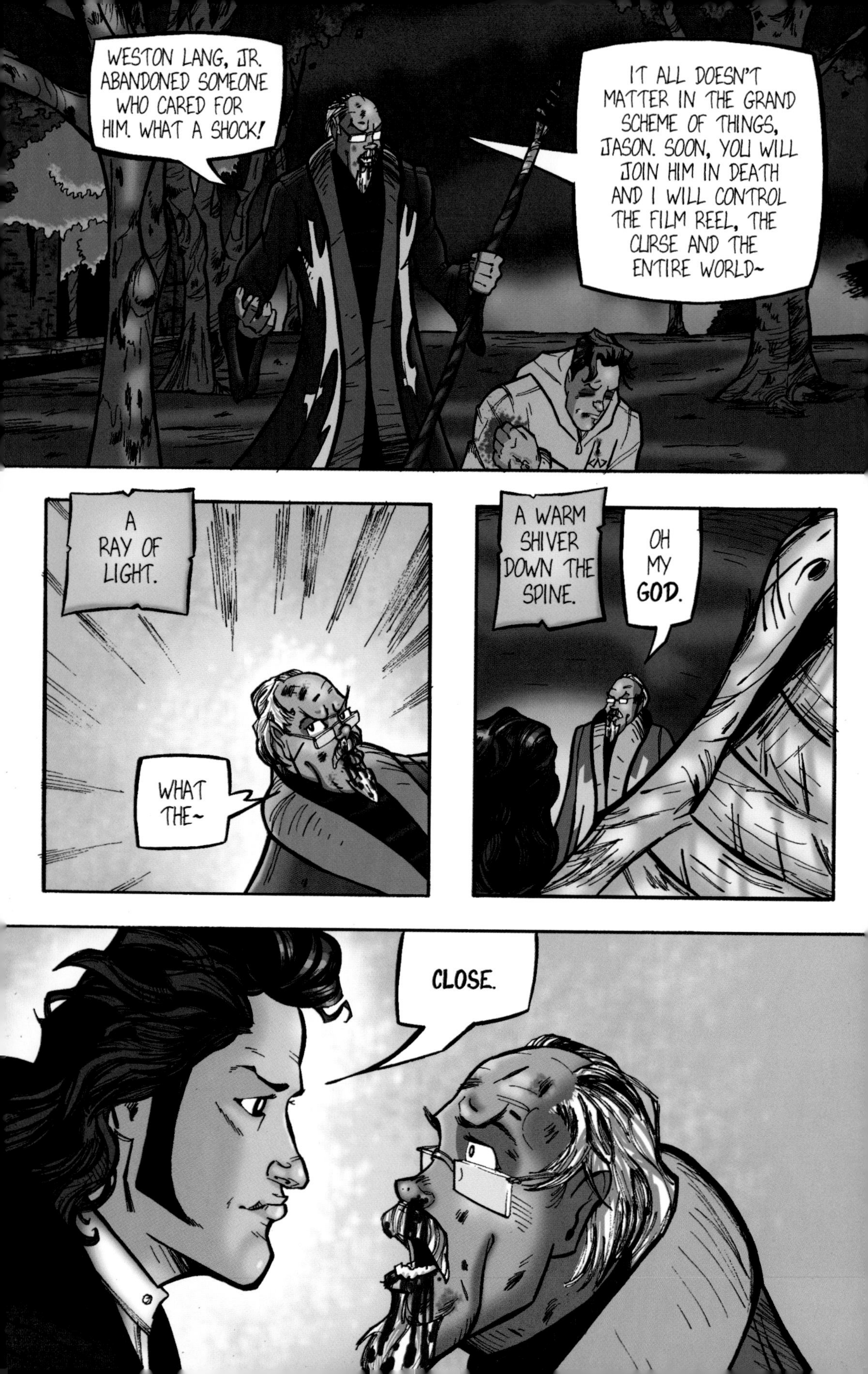
WESTON LANG, JR. ABANDONED SOMEONE WHO CARED FOR HIM. WHAT A SHOCK!
IT ALL DOESN'T MATTER IN THE GRAND SCHEME OF THINGS, JASON. SOON, YOU WILL JOIN HIM IN DEATH AND I WILL CONTROL THE FILM REEL, THE CURSE AND THE ENTIRE WORLD~
A RAY OF LIGHT.
WHAT THE~
A WARM SHIVER DOWN THE SPINE.
OH MY **GOD**.
CLOSE.

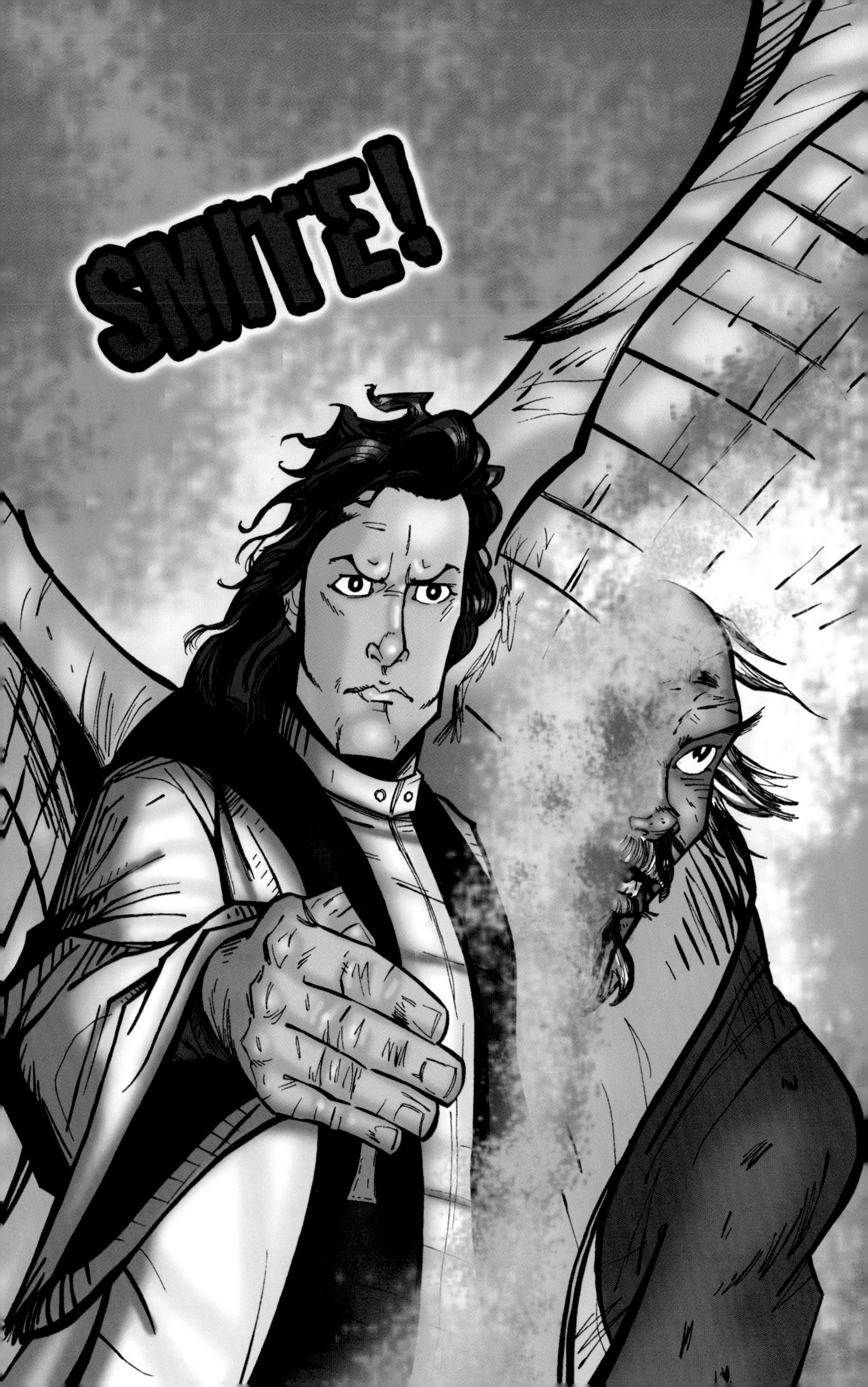
SMITE!

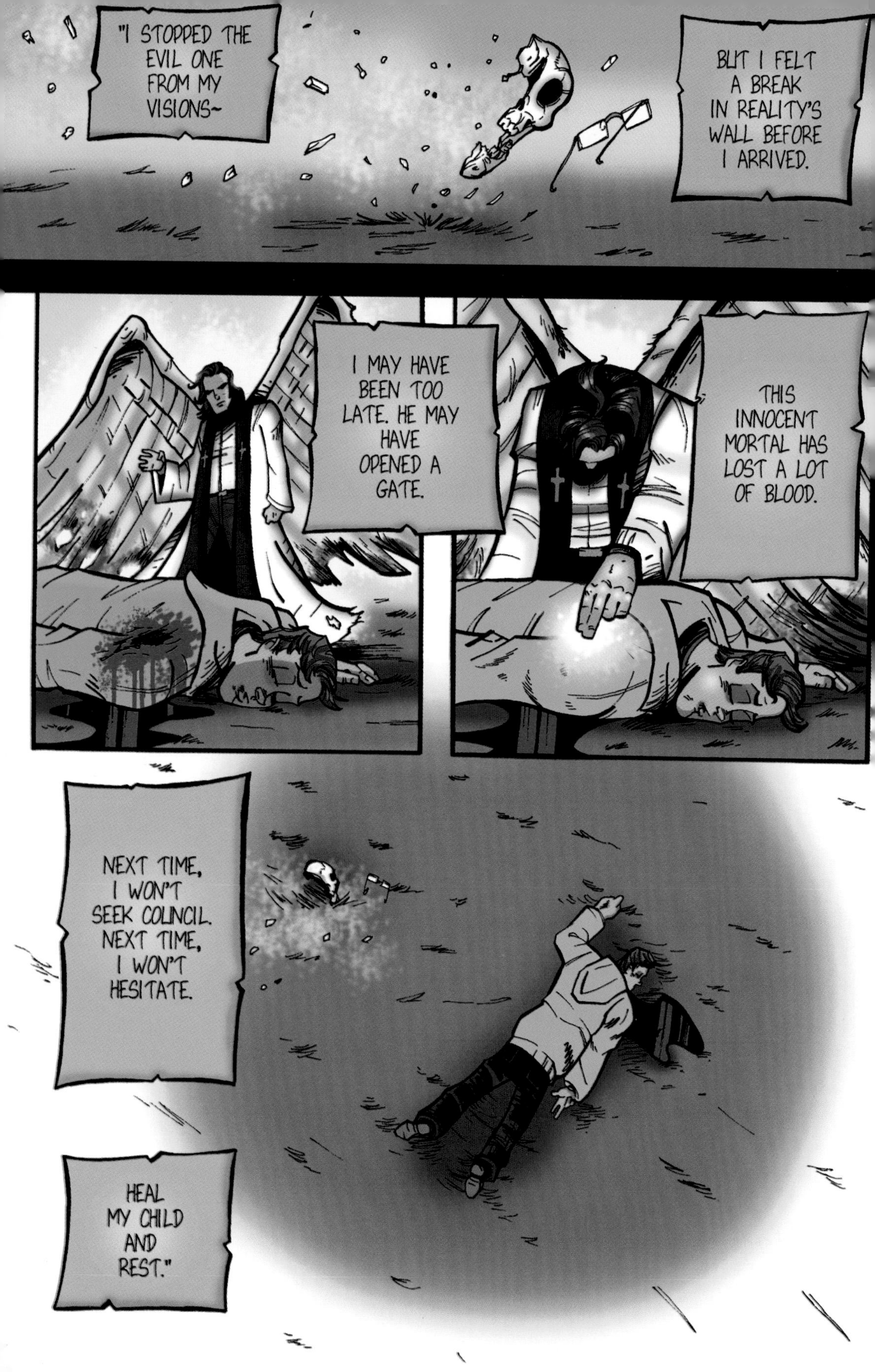
"I STOPPED THE EVIL ONE FROM MY VISIONS~
BUT I FELT A BREAK IN REALITY'S WALL BEFORE I ARRIVED.
I MAY HAVE BEEN TOO LATE. HE MAY HAVE OPENED A GATE.
THIS INNOCENT MORTAL HAS LOST A LOT OF BLOOD.
NEXT TIME, I WON'T SEEK COUNCIL. NEXT TIME, I WON'T HESITATE.
HEAL MY CHILD AND REST."

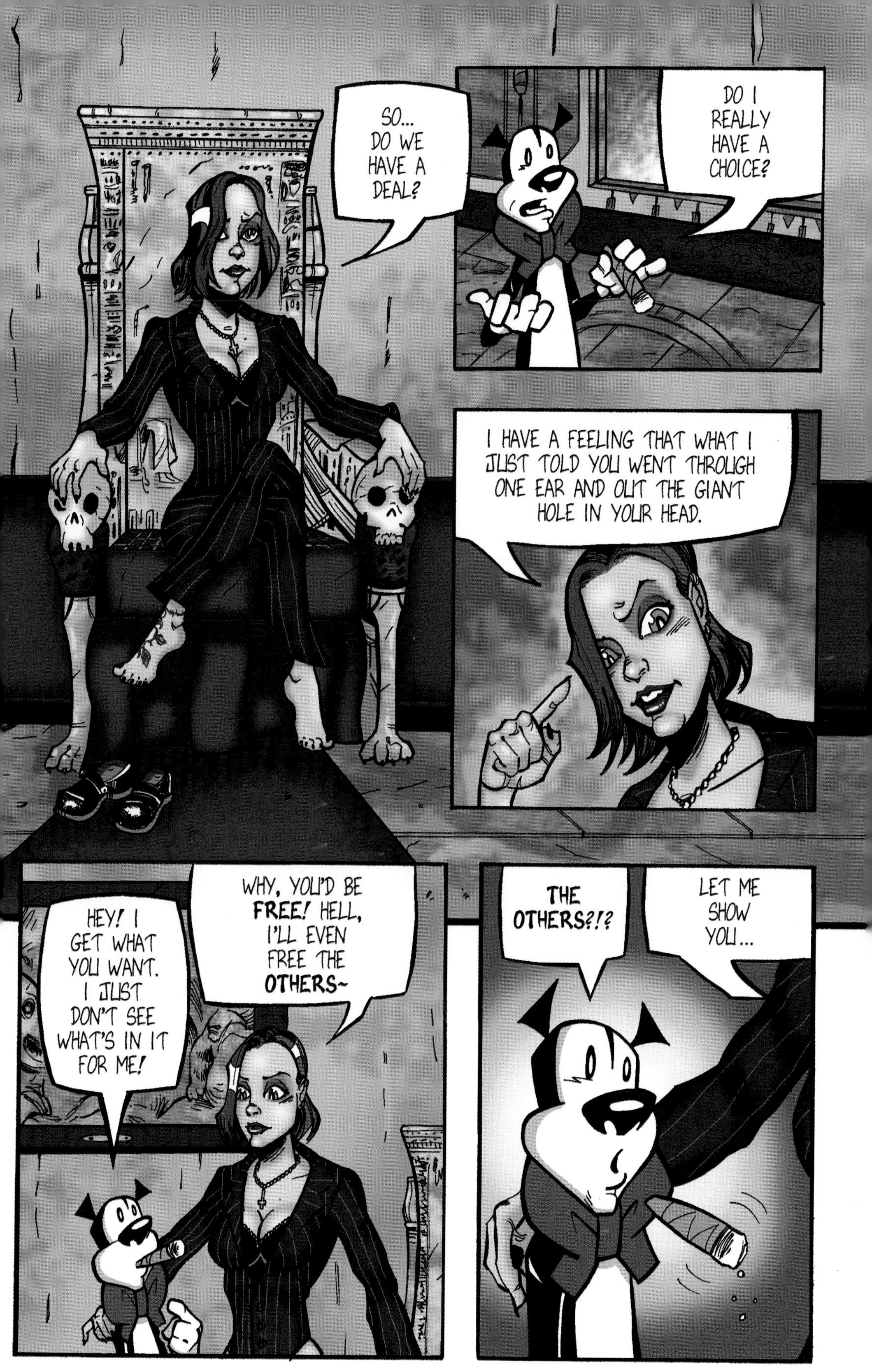
SO... DO WE HAVE A DEAL?
DO I REALLY HAVE A CHOICE?
I HAVE A FEELING THAT WHAT I JUST TOLD YOU WENT THROUGH ONE EAR AND OUT THE GIANT HOLE IN YOUR HEAD.
HEY! I GET WHAT YOU WANT. I JUST DON'T SEE WHAT'S IN IT FOR ME!
WHY, YOU'D BE **FREE!** HELL, I'LL EVEN FREE THE **OTHERS~**
THE OTHERS?!?
LET ME SHOW YOU...

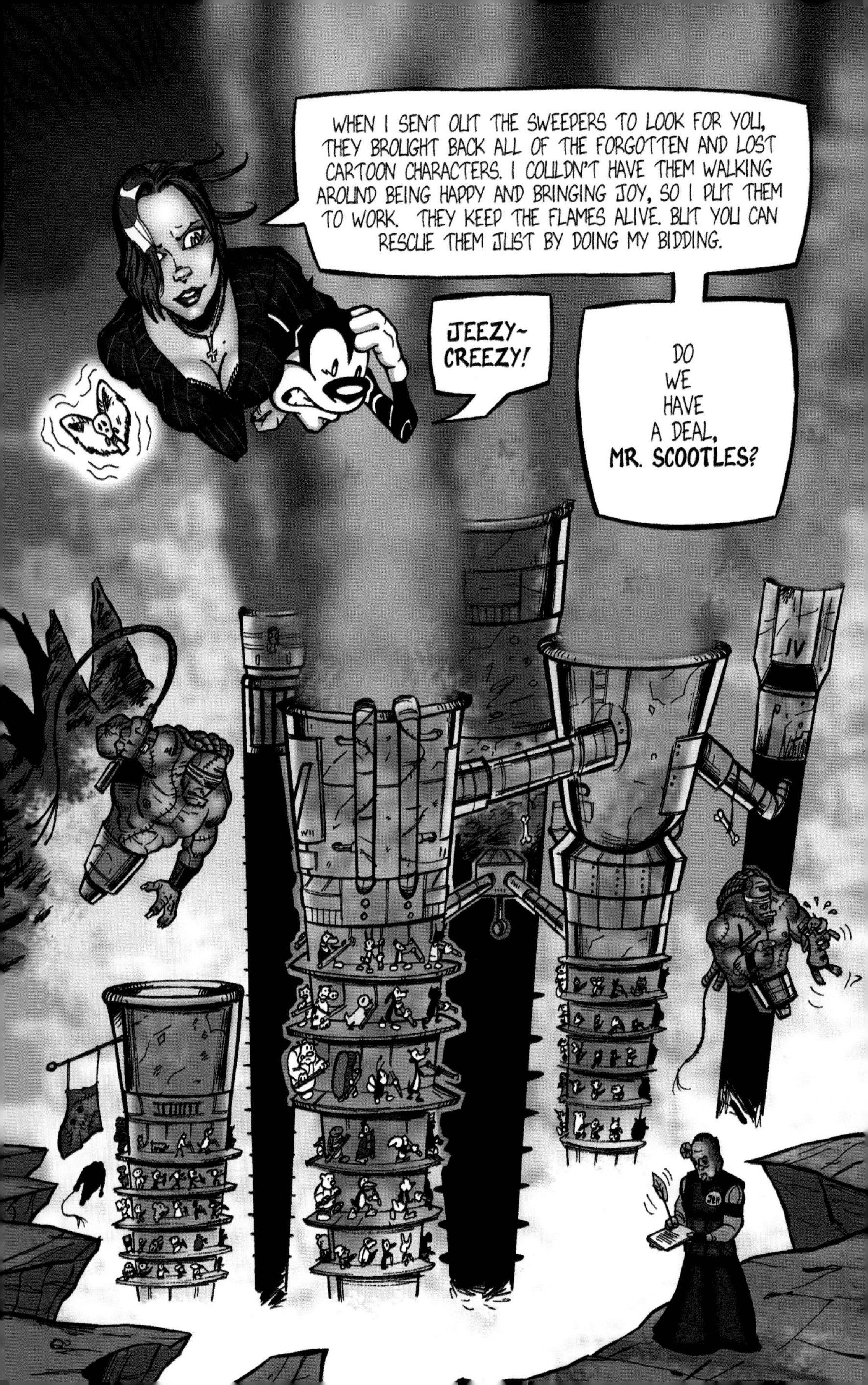
WHEN I SENT OUT THE SWEEPERS TO LOOK FOR YOU, THEY BROUGHT BACK ALL OF THE FORGOTTEN AND LOST CARTOON CHARACTERS. I COULDN'T HAVE THEM WALKING AROUND BEING HAPPY AND BRINGING JOY, SO I PUT THEM TO WORK. THEY KEEP THE FLAMES ALIVE. BUT YOU CAN RESCUE THEM JUST BY DOING MY BIDDING.
JEEZY-CREEZY!
DO WE HAVE A DEAL, MR. SCOOTLES?
IV

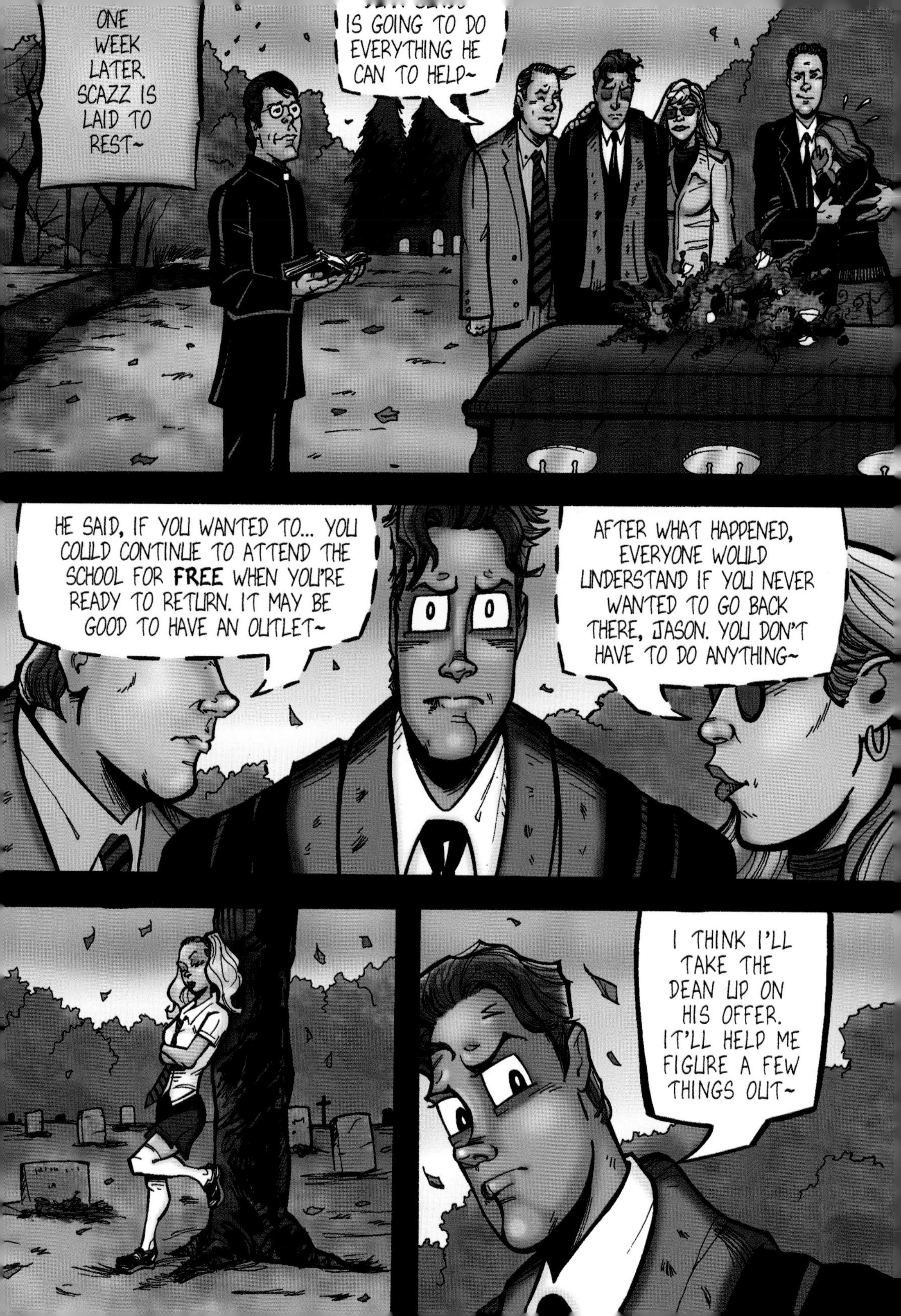
ONE WEEK LATER. SCAZZ IS LAID TO REST~
IS GOING TO DO EVERYTHING HE CAN TO HELP~
HE SAID, IF YOU WANTED TO... YOU COULD CONTINUE TO ATTEND THE SCHOOL FOR **FREE** WHEN YOU'RE READY TO RETURN. IT MAY BE GOOD TO HAVE AN OUTLET~
AFTER WHAT HAPPENED, EVERYONE WOULD UNDERSTAND IF YOU NEVER WANTED TO GO BACK THERE, JASON. YOU DON'T HAVE TO DO ANYTHING~
I THINK I'LL TAKE THE DEAN UP ON HIS OFFER. IT'LL HELP ME FIGURE A FEW THINGS OUT~

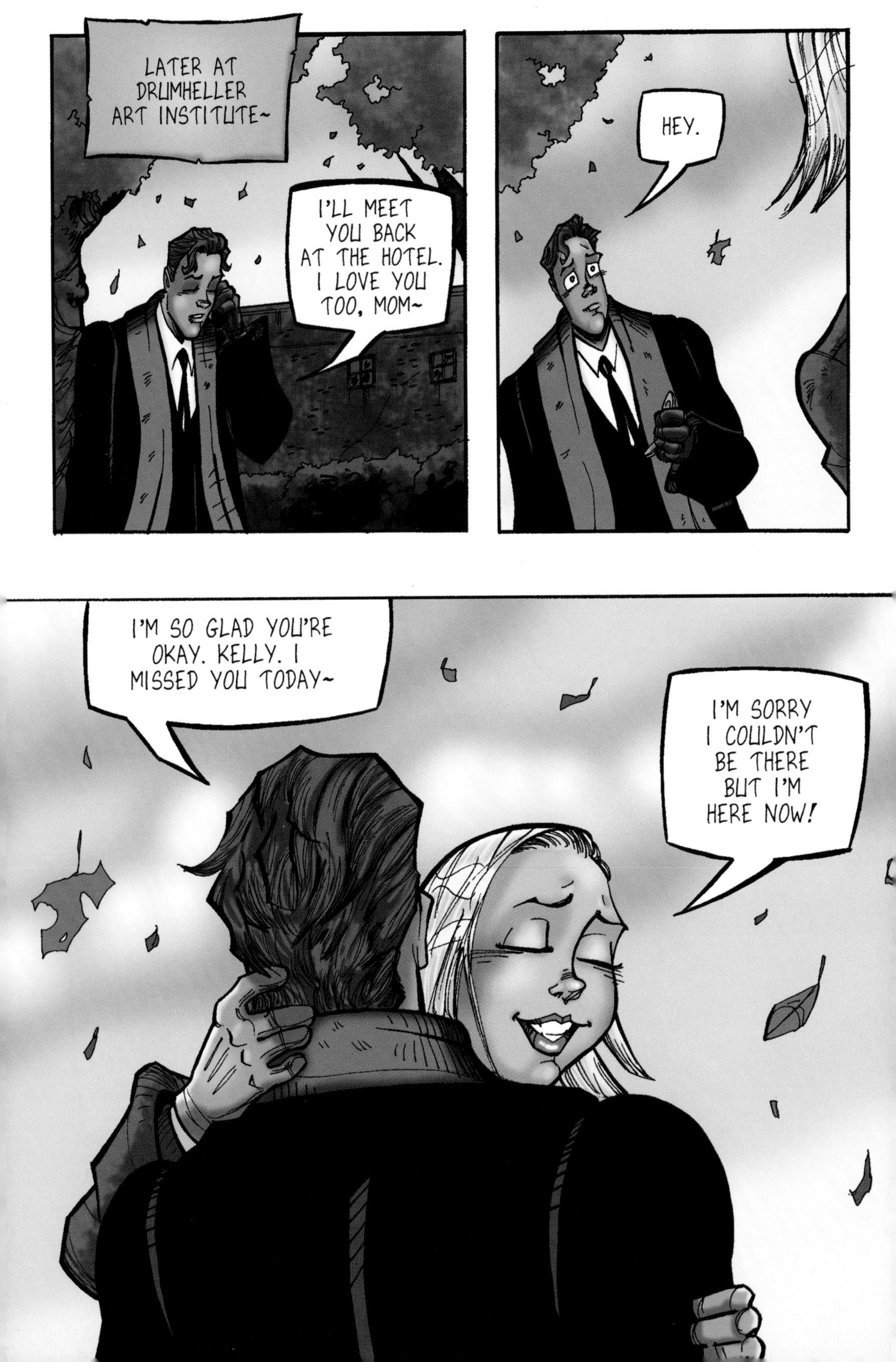
LATER AT DRUMHELLER ART INSTITUTE~
I'LL MEET YOU BACK AT THE HOTEL. I LOVE YOU TOO, MOM~
HEY.
I'M SO GLAD YOU'RE OKAY. KELLY. I MISSED YOU TODAY~
I'M SORRY I COULDN'T BE THERE BUT I'M HERE NOW!

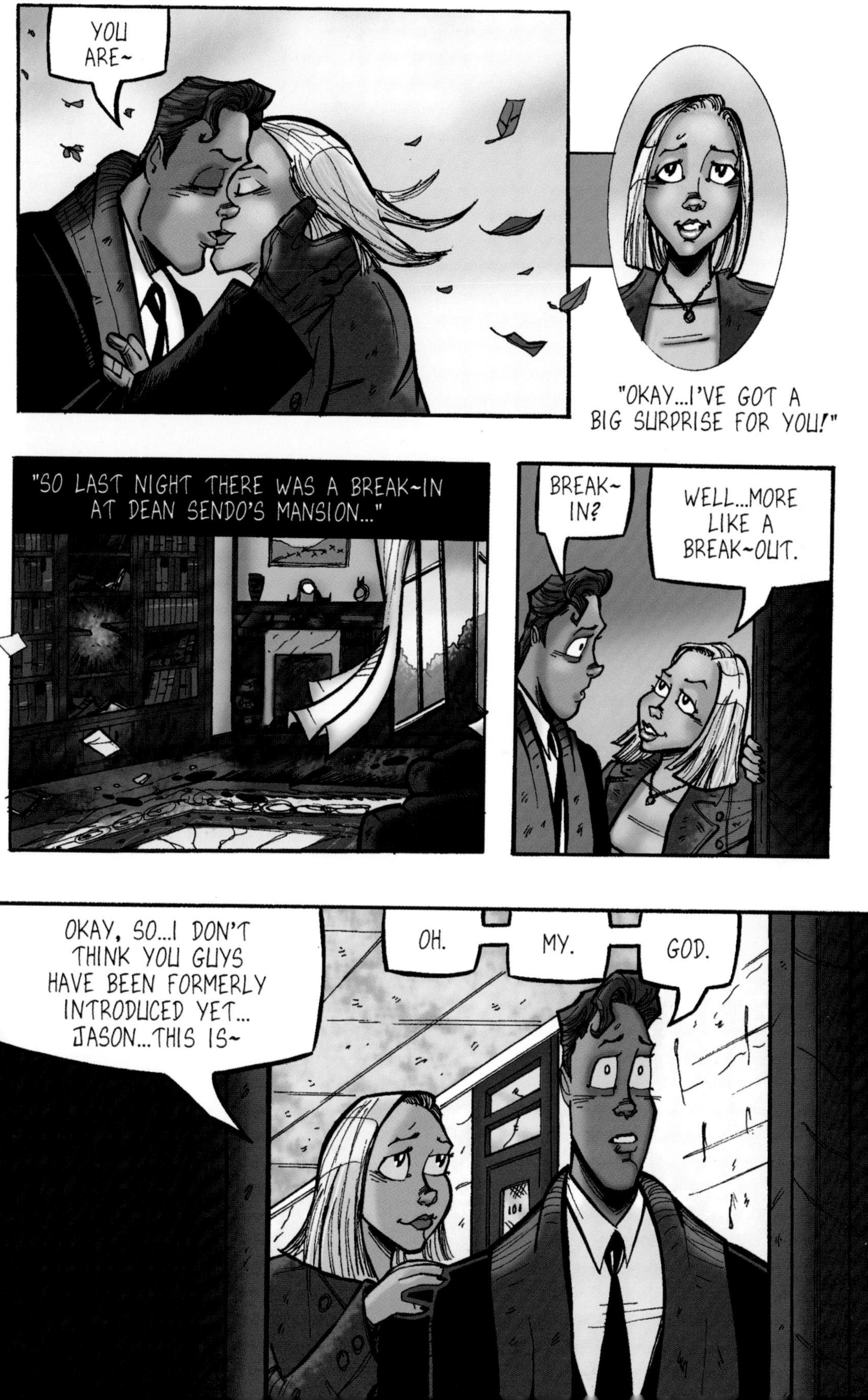
YOU ARE~
"OKAY...I'VE GOT A BIG SURPRISE FOR YOU!"
"SO LAST NIGHT THERE WAS A BREAK~IN AT DEAN SENDO'S MANSION..."
BREAK~IN?
WELL...MORE LIKE A BREAK~OUT.
OKAY, SO...I DON'T THINK YOU GUYS HAVE BEEN FORMERLY INTRODUCED YET... JASON...THIS IS~
OH.
MY.
GOD.

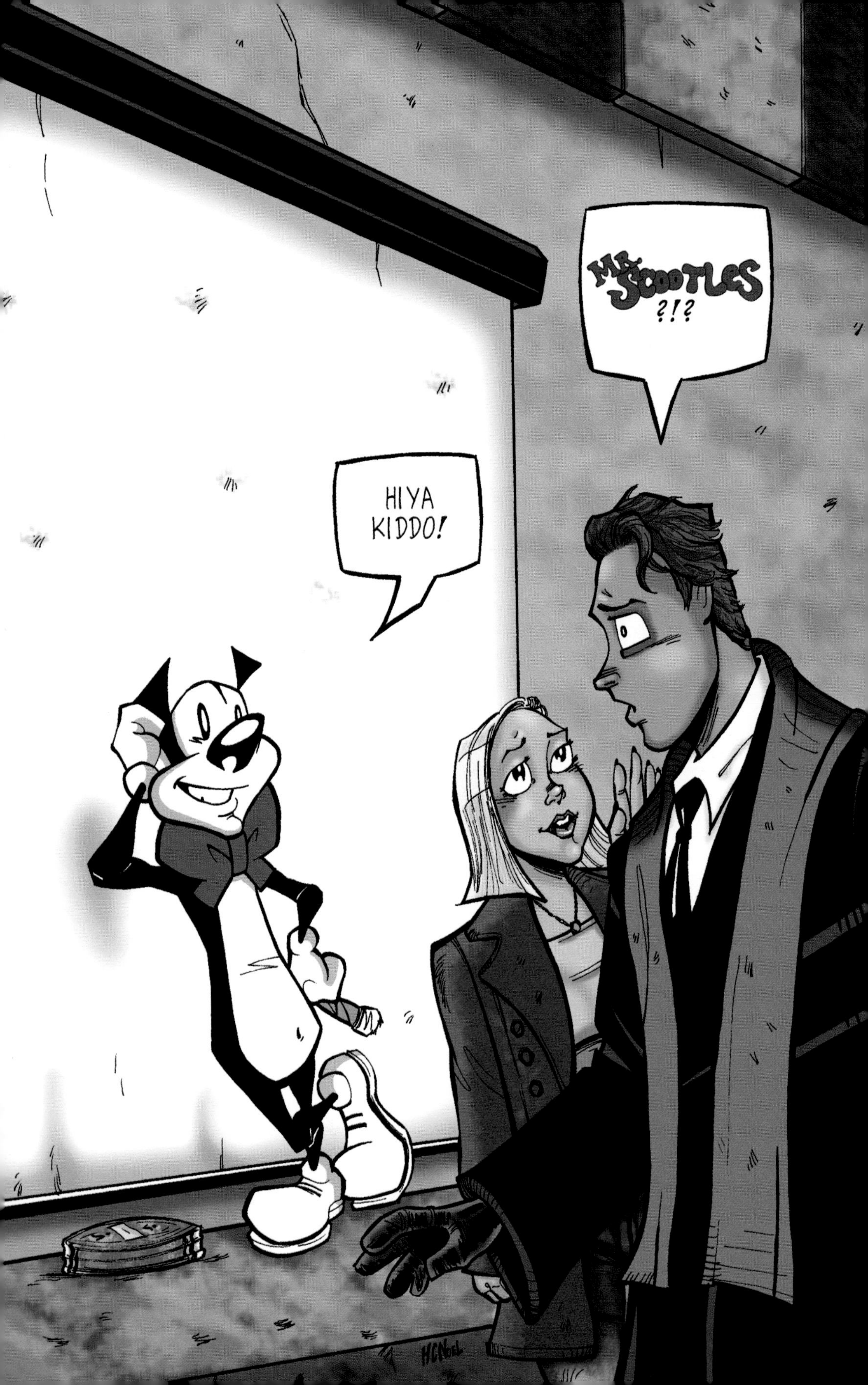
MR. SCOOTLES ?!?
HIYA KIDDO!
HCNoel

THE END...

IS THE BEGINNING...

OF THE
END.

SAVES THE WORLD

COMING SOON

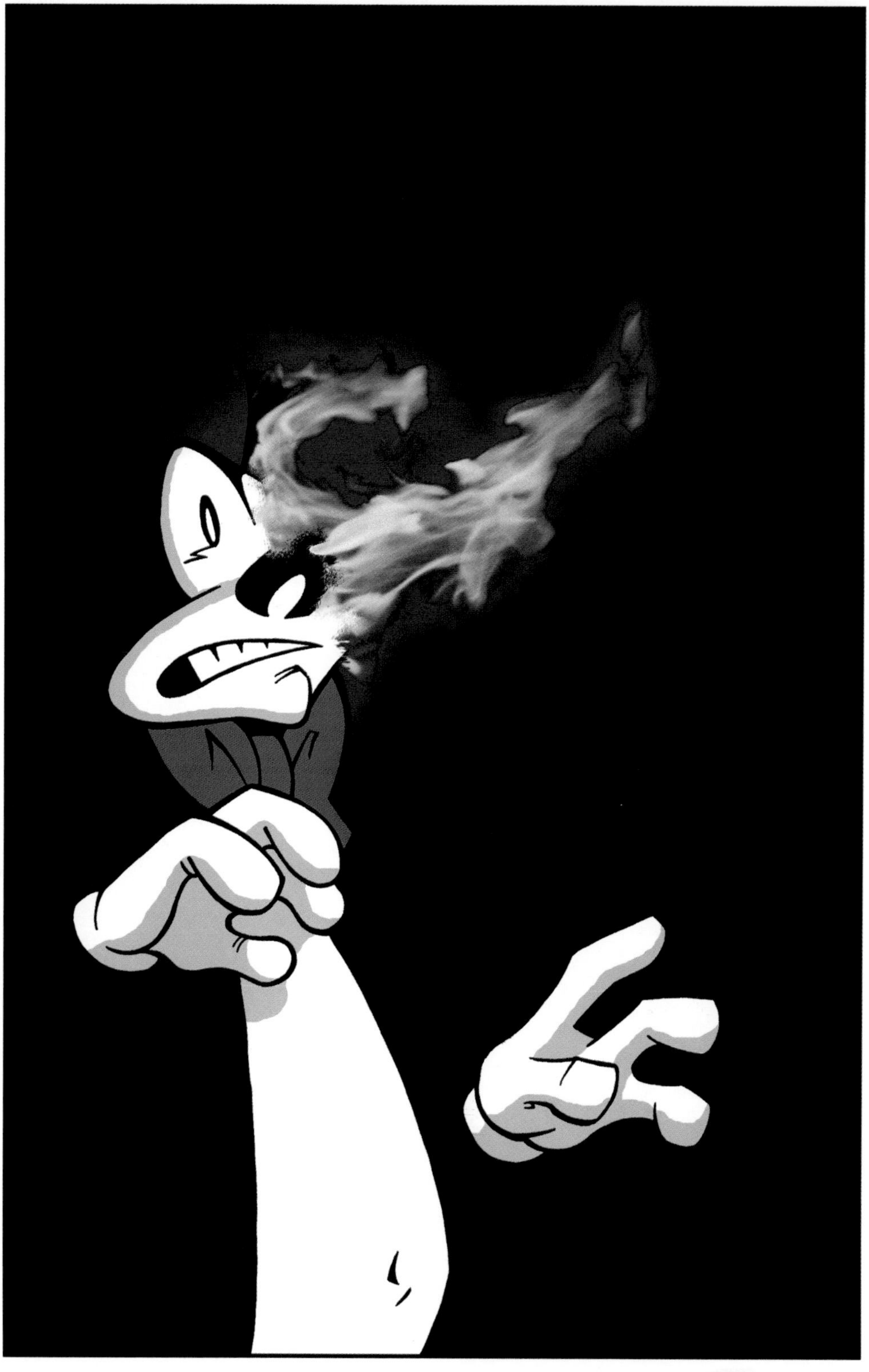

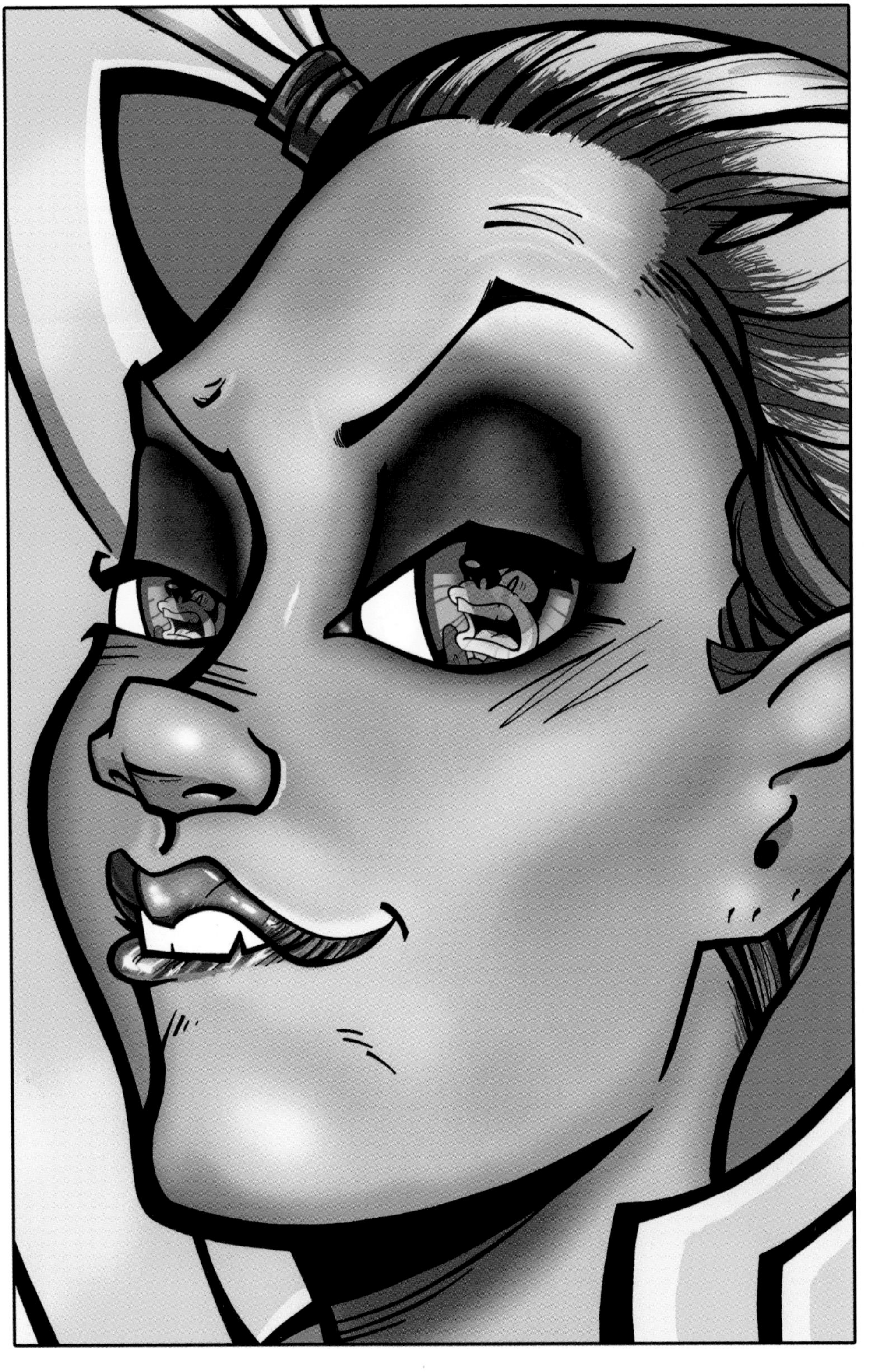

MR. SCOOTLES #2

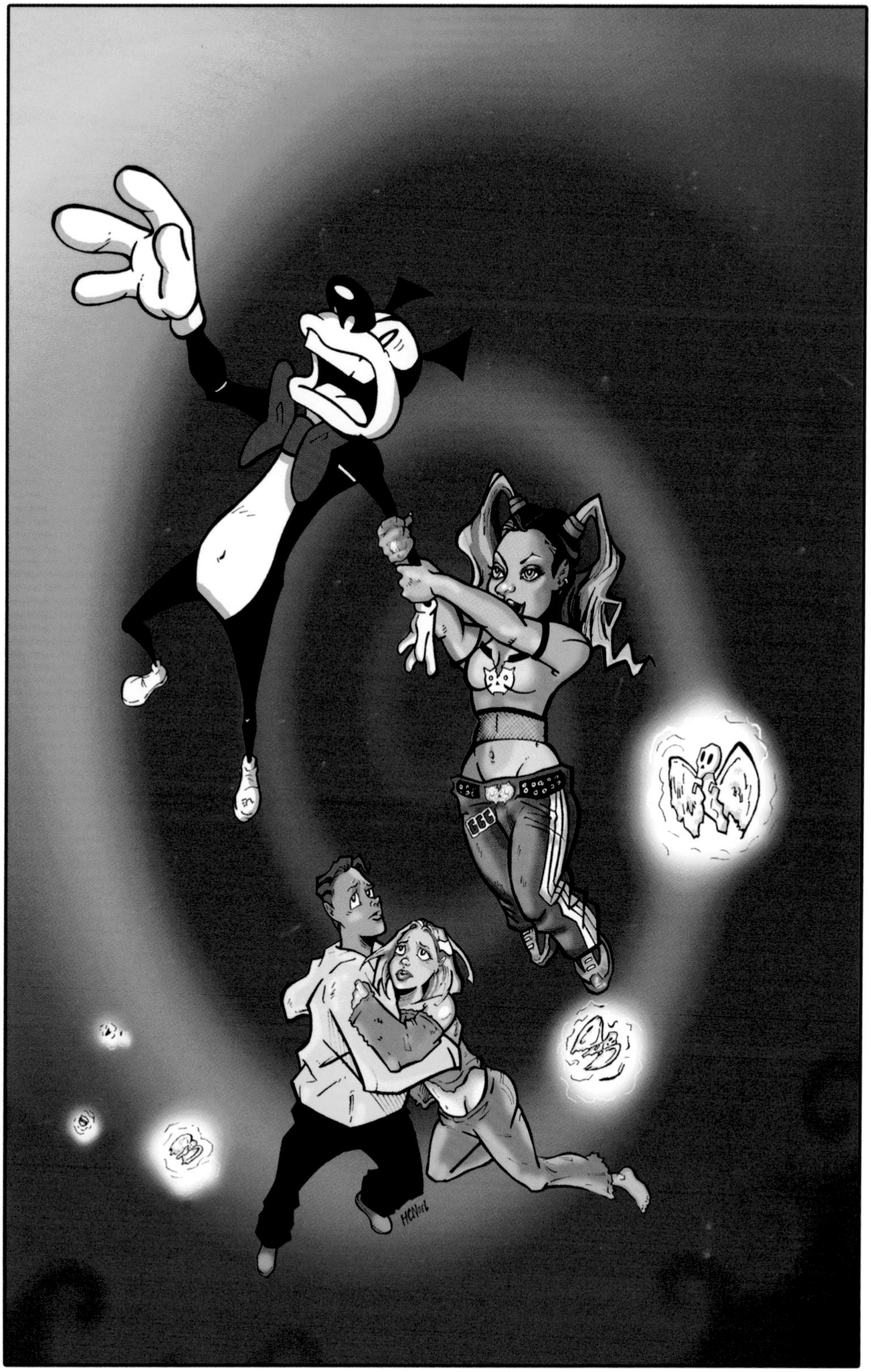

MR. SCOOTLES #2 (ORIGINAL COVER)

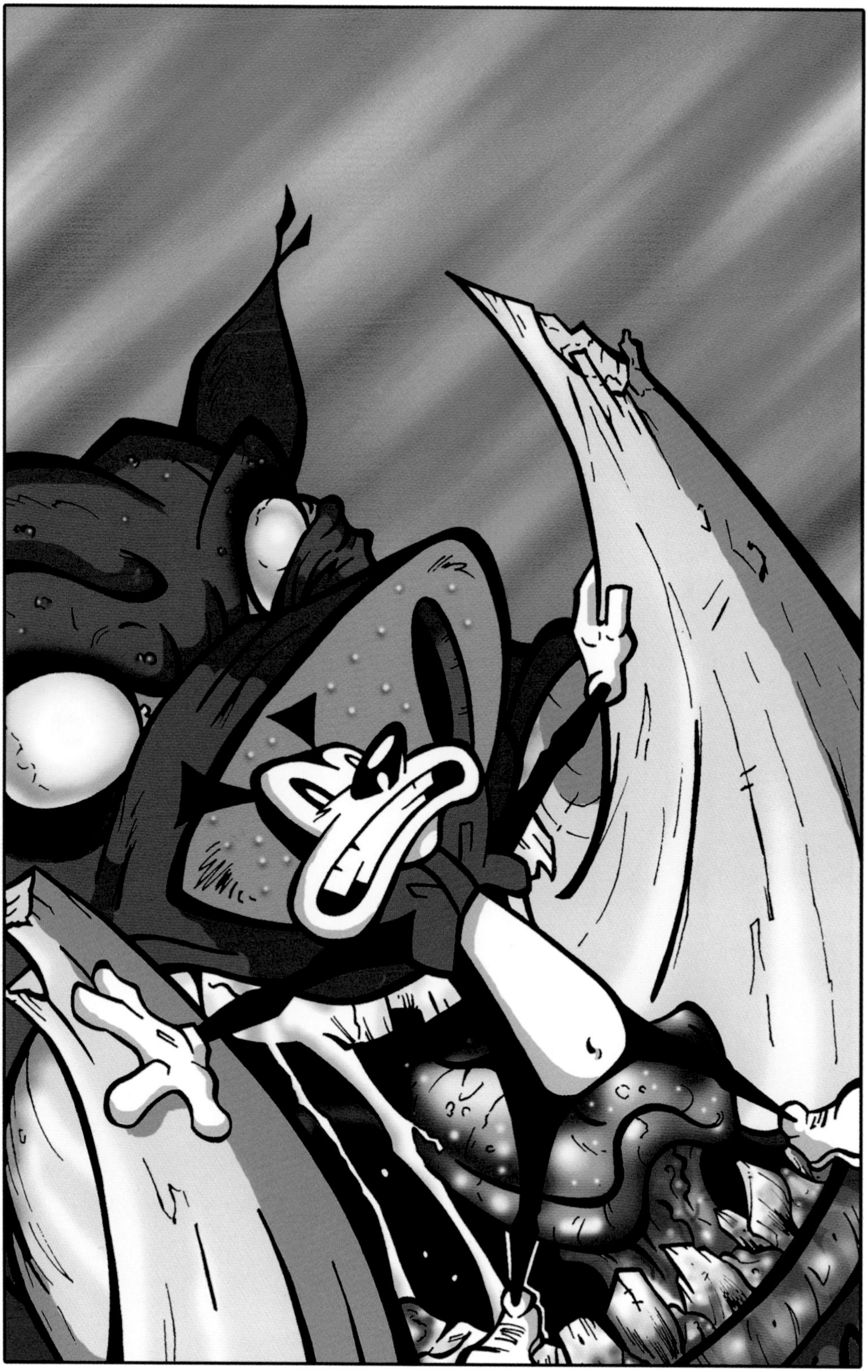

MR. SCOOTLES #3

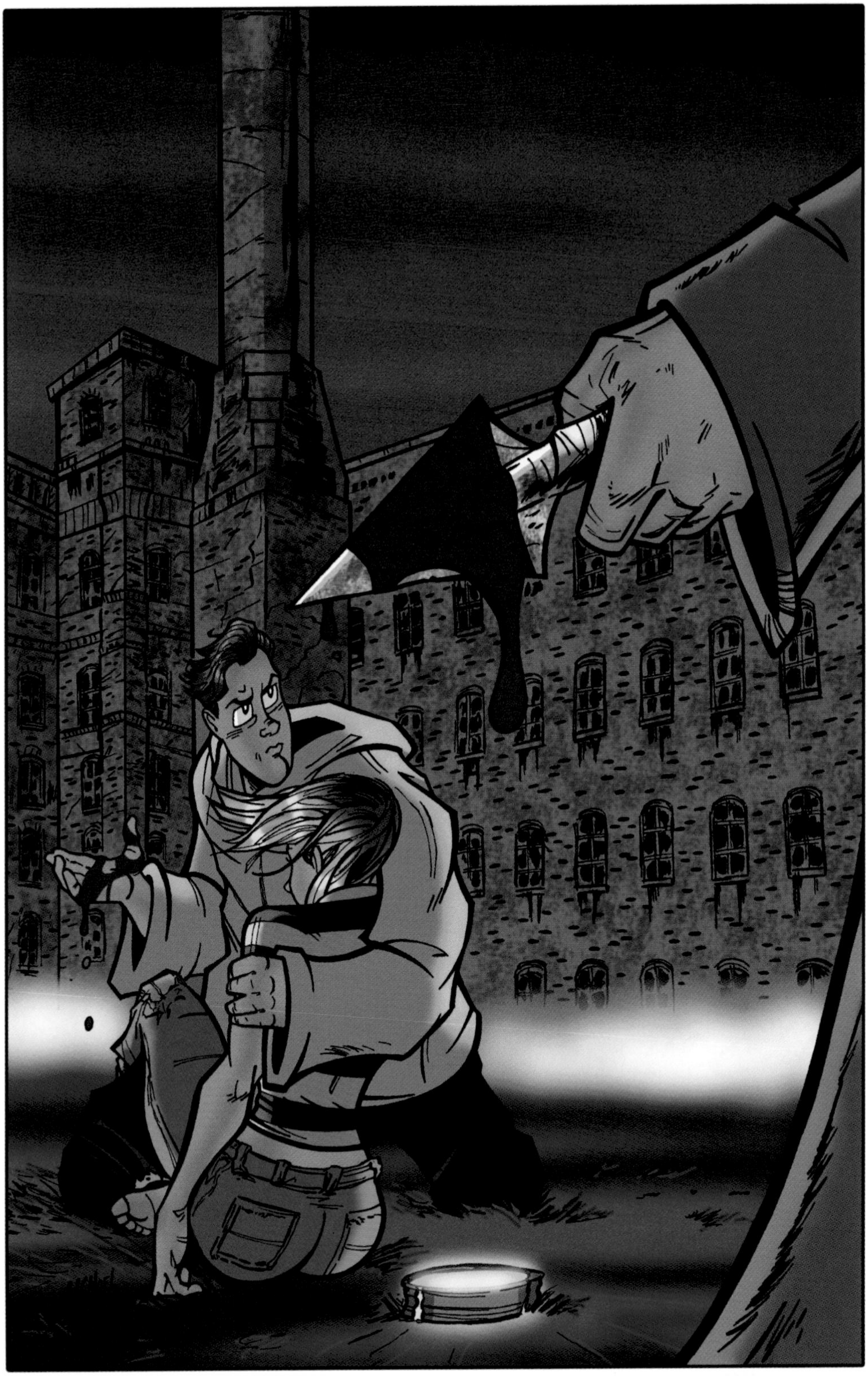

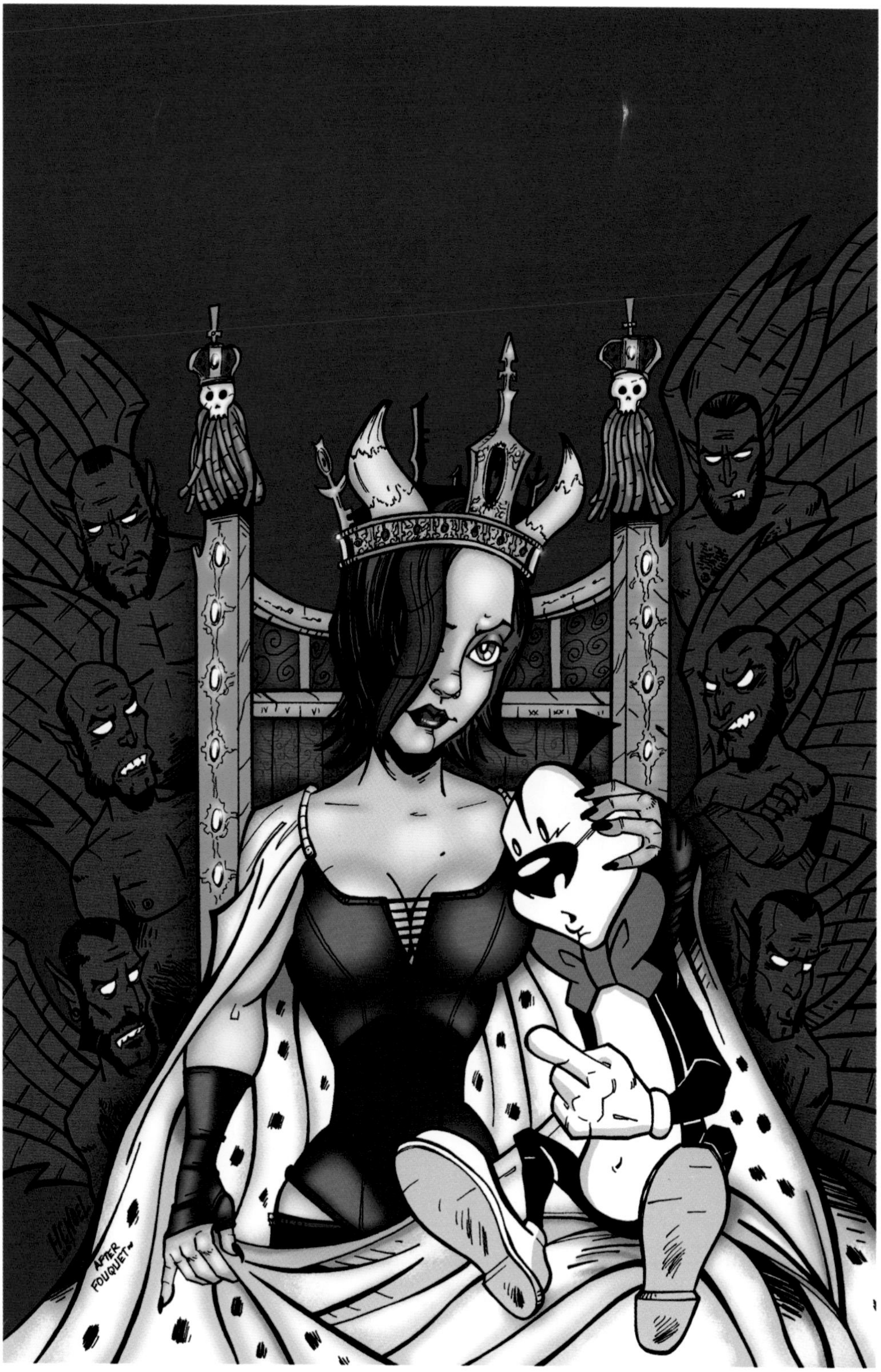
AFTER FOUQUET

MR. SCOOTLES #5

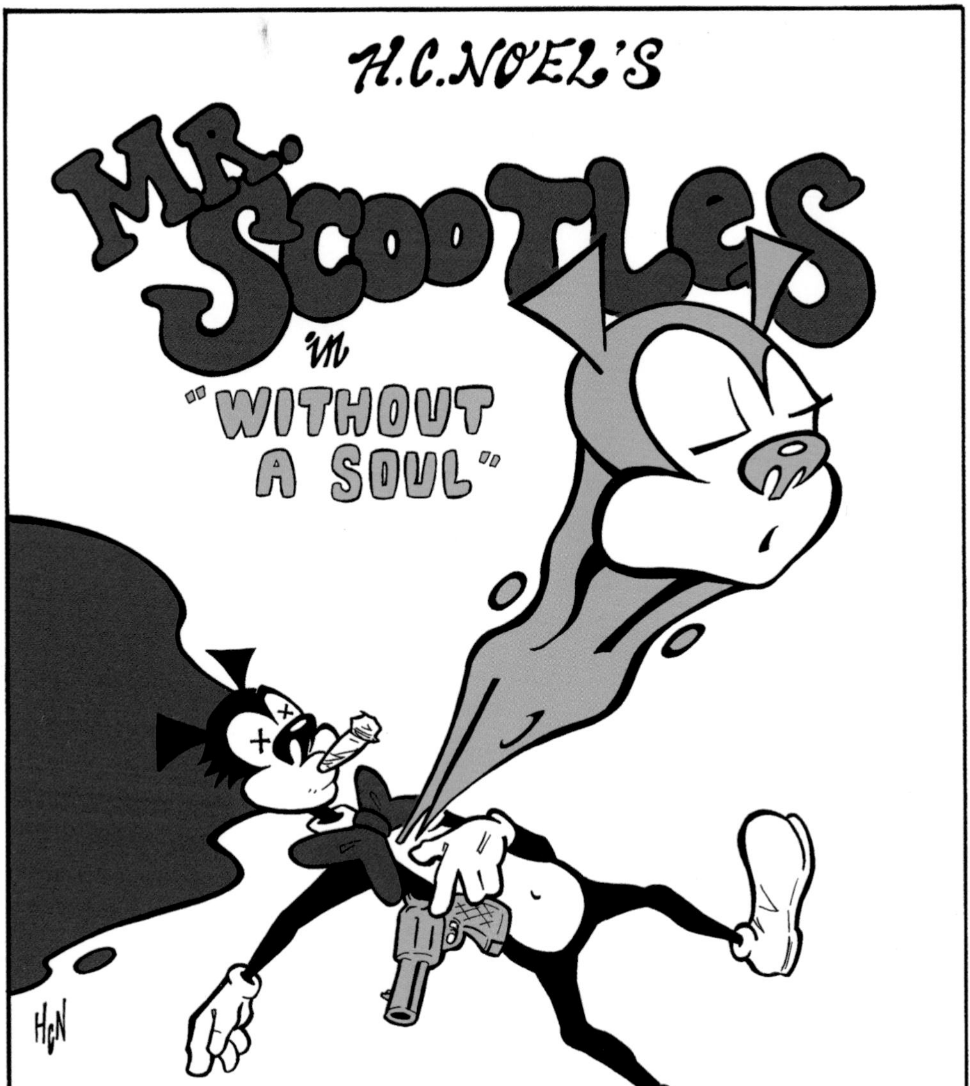
H.C.NOEL'S
MR. SCOOTLES
in
"WITHOUT A SOUL"
HCN
ELEMENTARY FILM IDEAS, INC.

MR. SCOOTLES ANIMATION MOVIE POSTER

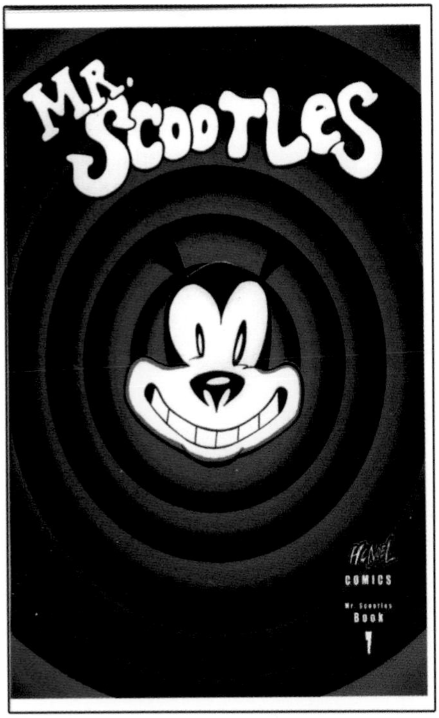
MR. SCOOTLES
HCNOEL
COMICS
Mr Scootles
Book
1

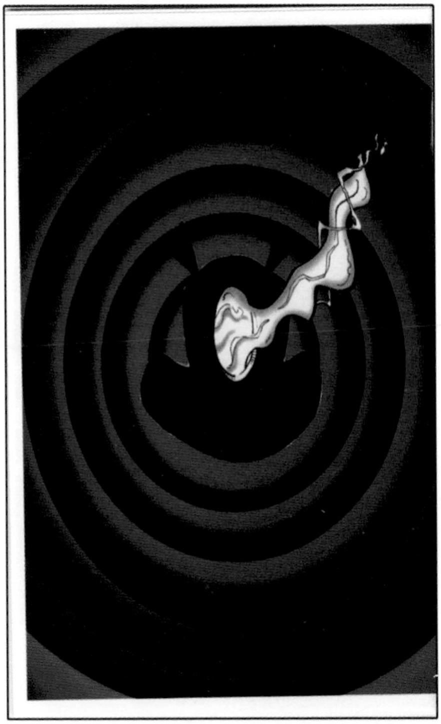

ABOVE: Front and back covers for the ashcan release of Mr. Scootles #1.
BELOW: Covers for Drumbeat ashcan and the "limited editon" stickers from the ashcan editons.

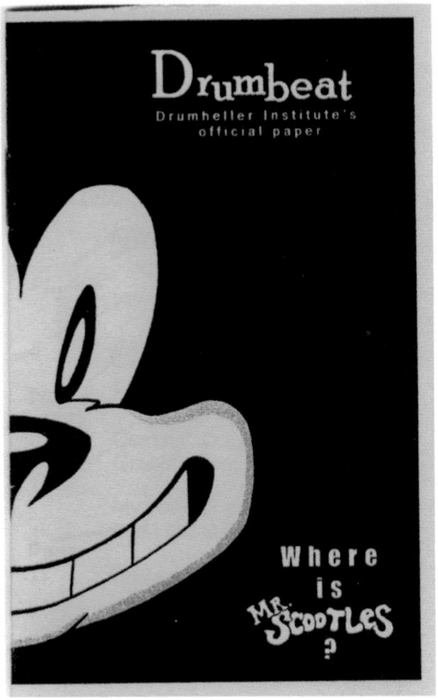
Drumbeat
Drumheller Institute's
official paper
Where
is
MR. SCOOTLES
?

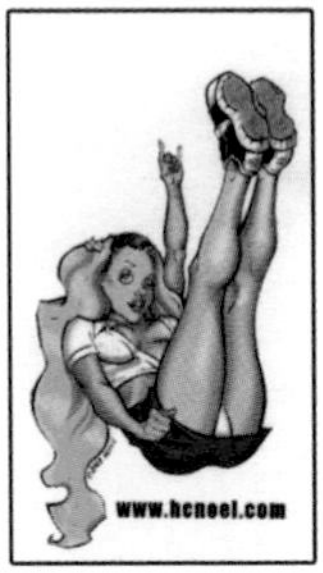
www.hcnoel.com

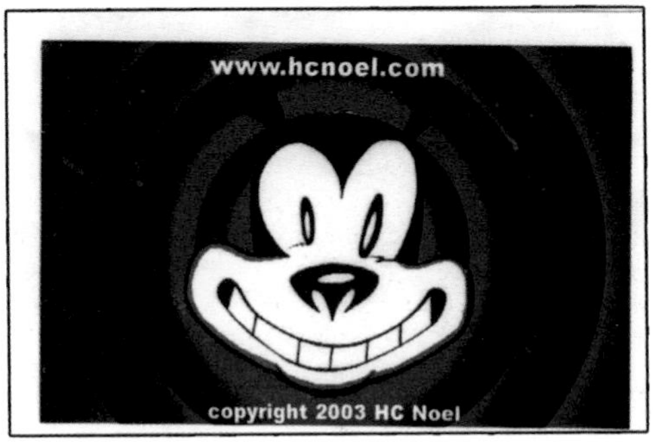
www.hcnoel.com
copyright 2003 HC Noel

MR. SCOOTLES ASHCAN GALLERY

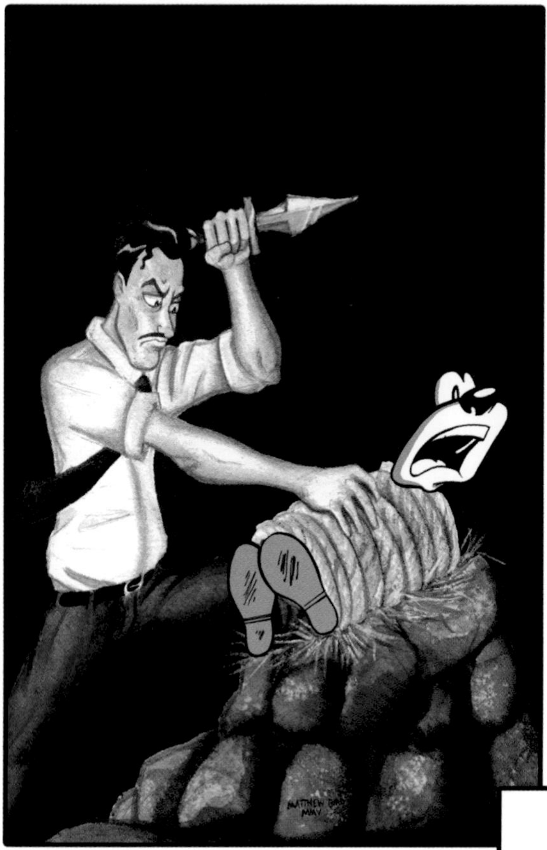

LEFT: Illustrator Matthew Bird and H.C.Noel joined forces to create this pin-up of Weston Lang, Jr. and his creation, Mr. Scootles. Matthew painted over Noel's pencils. Noel also provided the "pen and ink" illustration of Mr. Scootles.

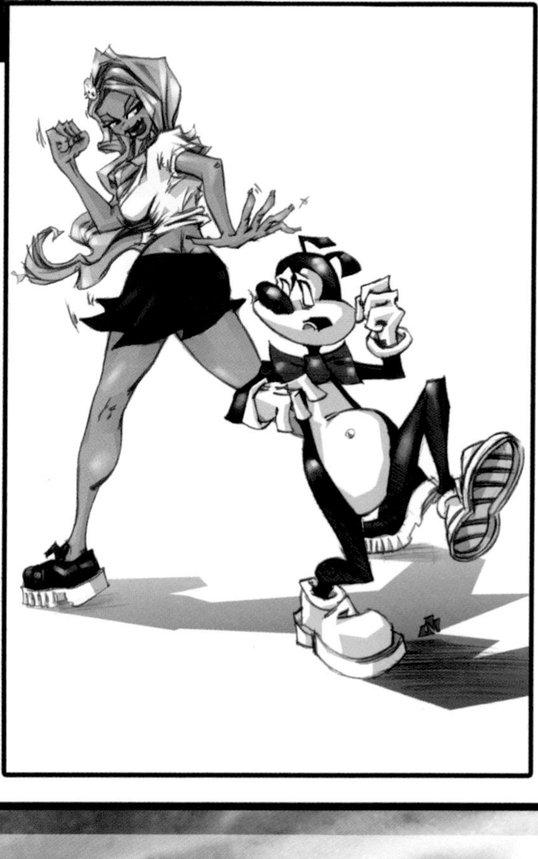

RIGHT: Jason Martin, creator of Super Real, produced this amazing pin-up of the Gatekeeper and Mr. Scootles.

MR. SCOOTLES PIN-UPS

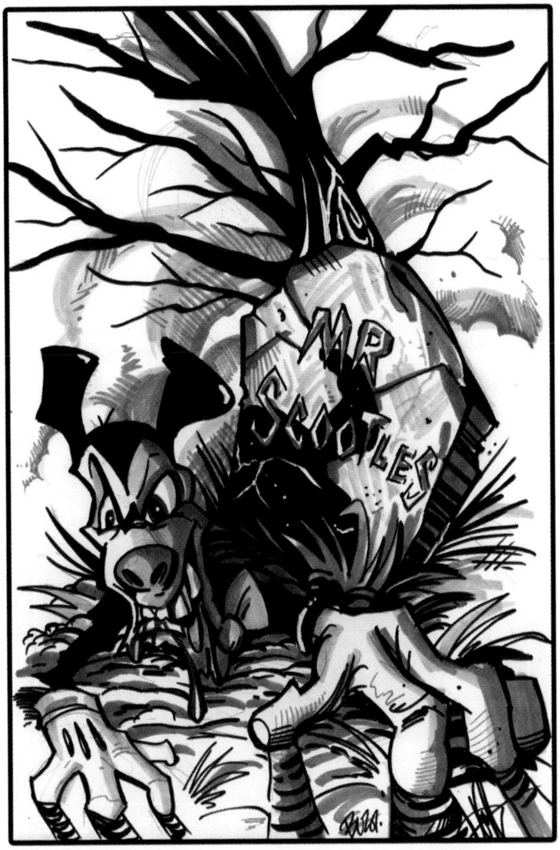
MR
SCOOTLES

LEFT: Ken Haeser and Buz Hasson, creators of The Living Corpse, gave life to this pin-up of Zombie Mr. Scootles.

BOTTOM LEFT: Travis Kenealy created this pin-up of a vampire Mr. Scootles and Fetus Ghosts.

BOTTOM RIGHT: Charles Dowd illustrated this animated pin-up of Mr. Scootles and Fetus Ghosts.

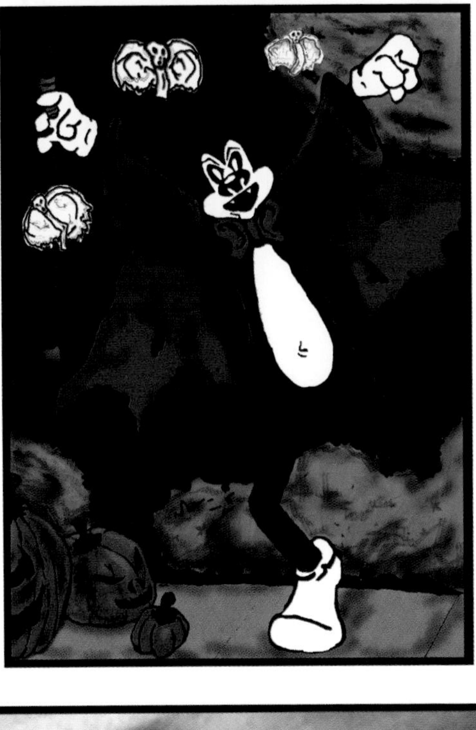

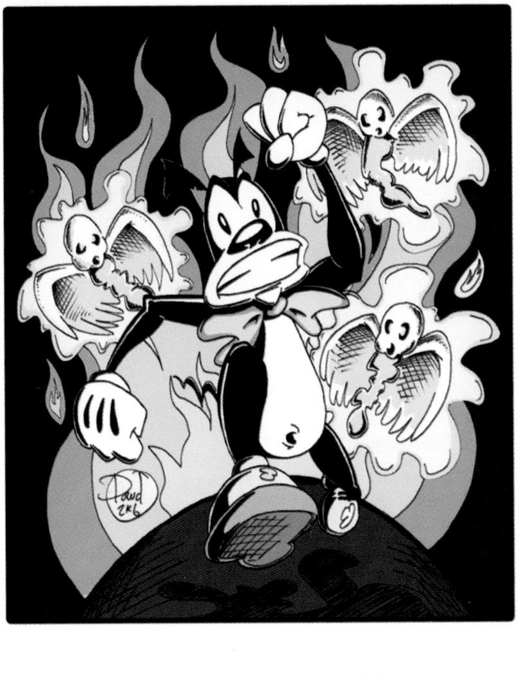

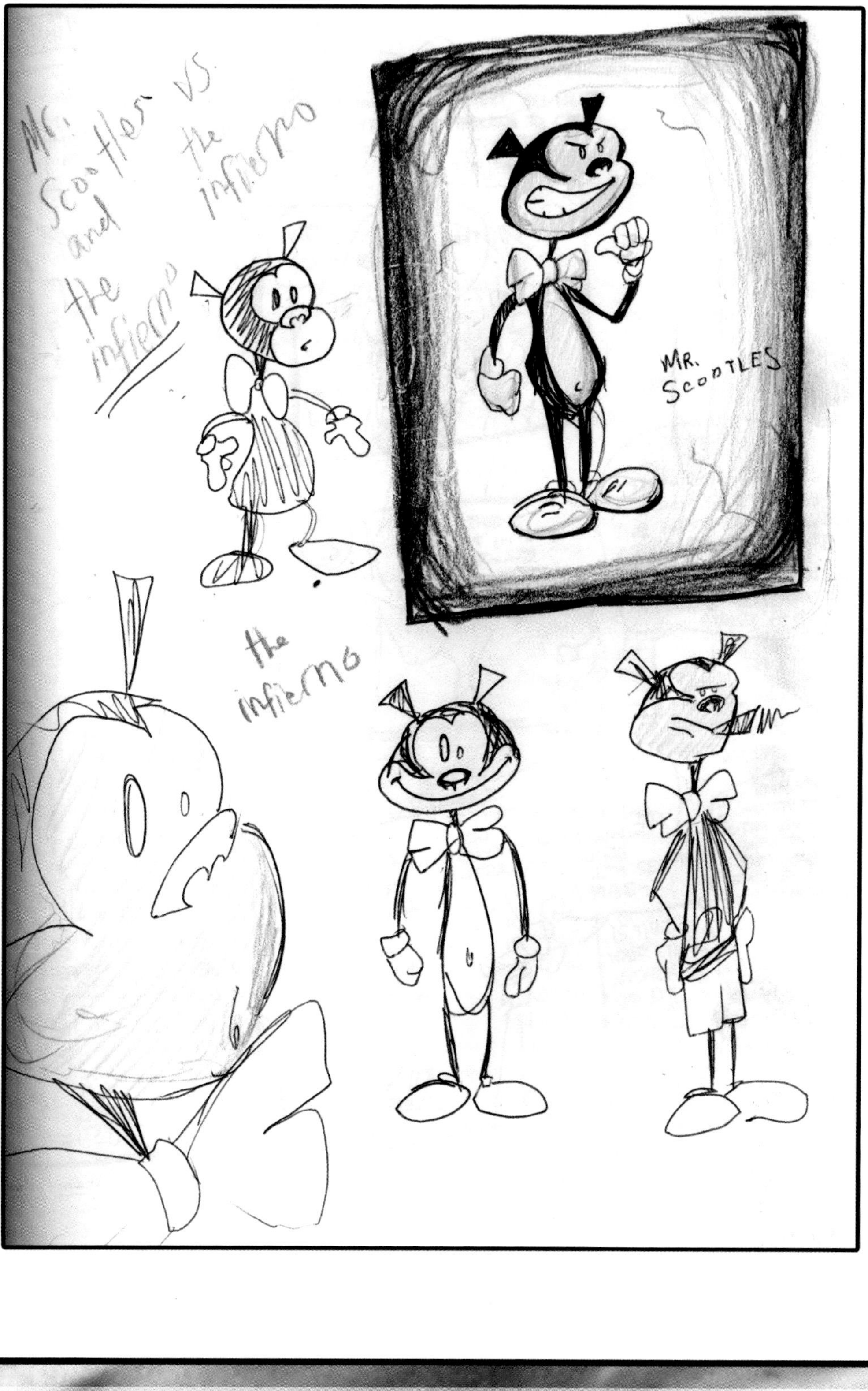
Mr. Scootles vs the infierno and the infierno
MR. SCOOTLES
the infierno

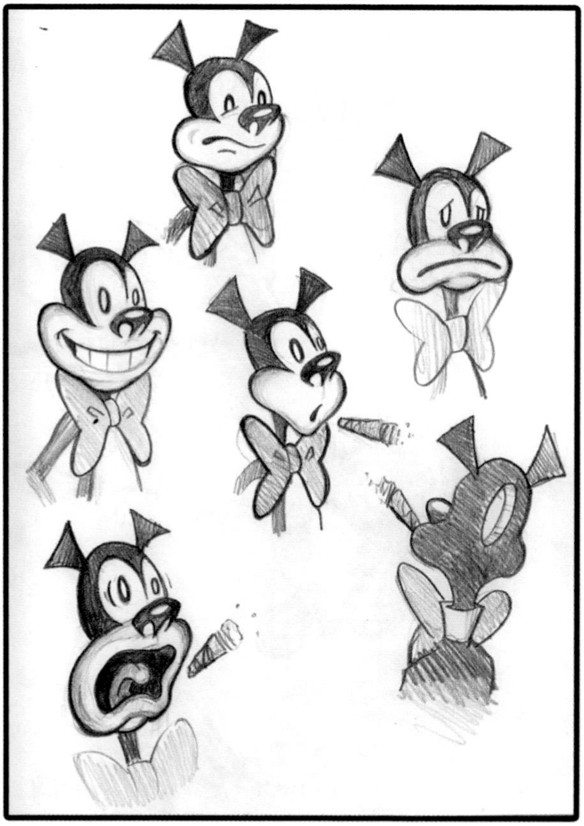

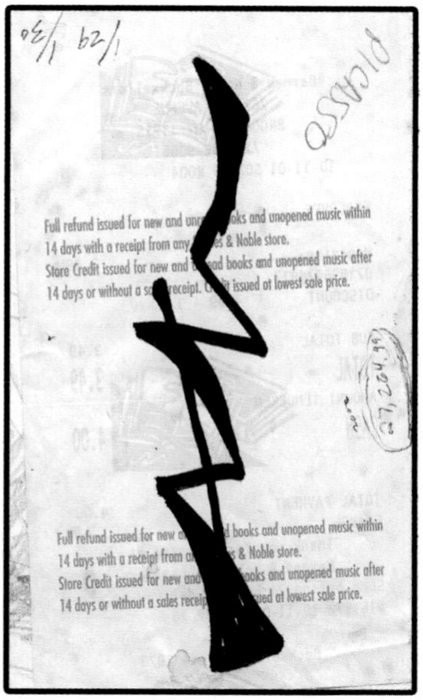

ABOVE: First sketch of Picasso.

Below:
(Left) Sketch of Victor.
(Right) Sketch of
Pig Beast chasing Mr. Scootles.

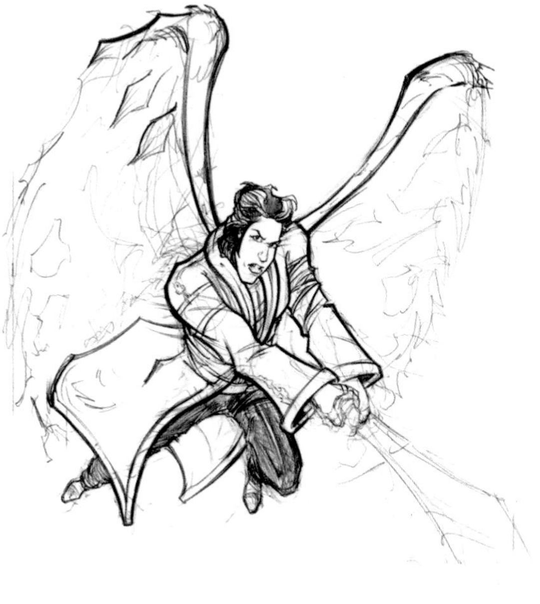

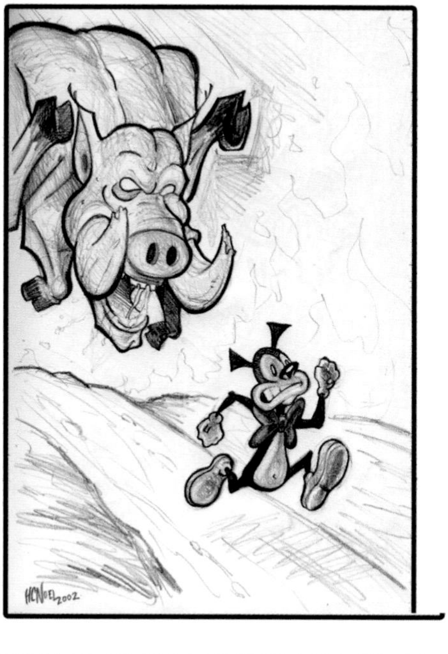
HCNOEL 2002

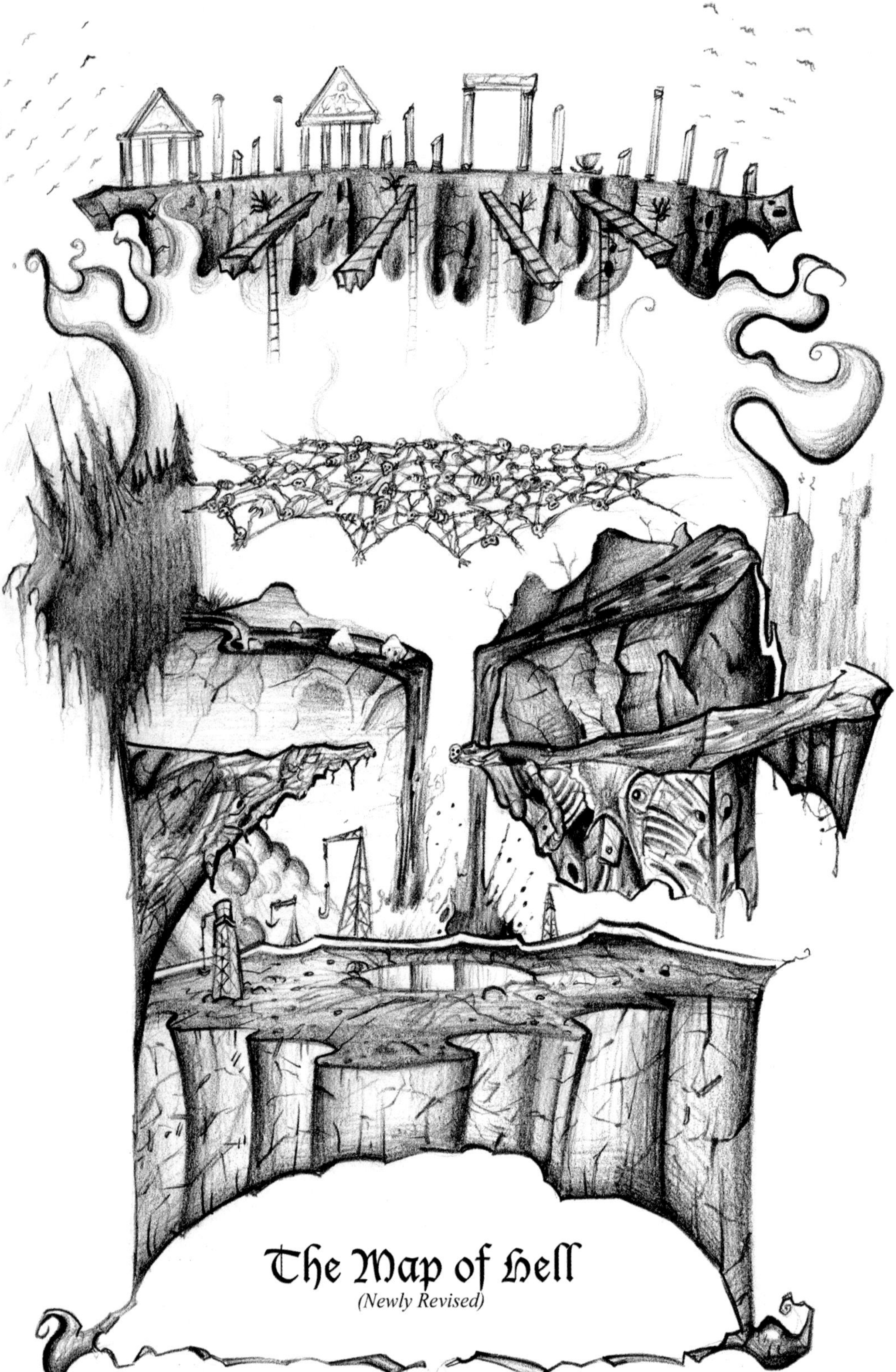

The Map of Hell
(Newly Revised)

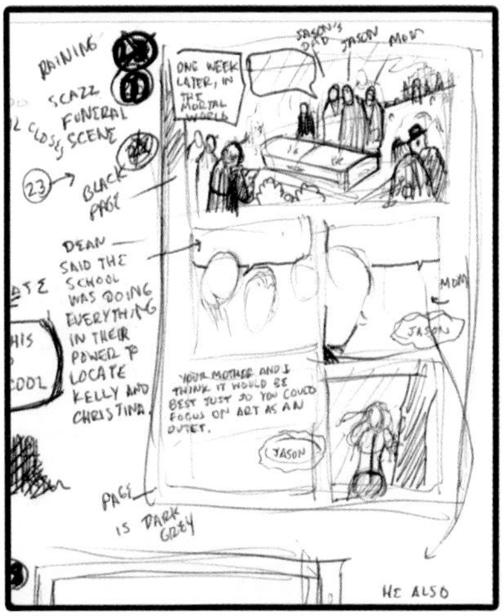
RAINING
SCAZZ FUNERAL SCENE
BLACK PAGE
ONE WEEK LATER, IN THE MORTAL WORLD
JASON'S DAD
JASON
MOM
DEAN SAID THE SCHOOL WAS DOING EVERYTHING IN THEIR POWER TO LOCATE KELLY AND CHRISTINA.
JASON
YOUR MOTHER AND I THINK IT WOULD BE BEST JUST SO YOU COULD FOCUS ON ART AS AN OUTLET.
JASON
PAGE IS DARK GREY
HE ALSO

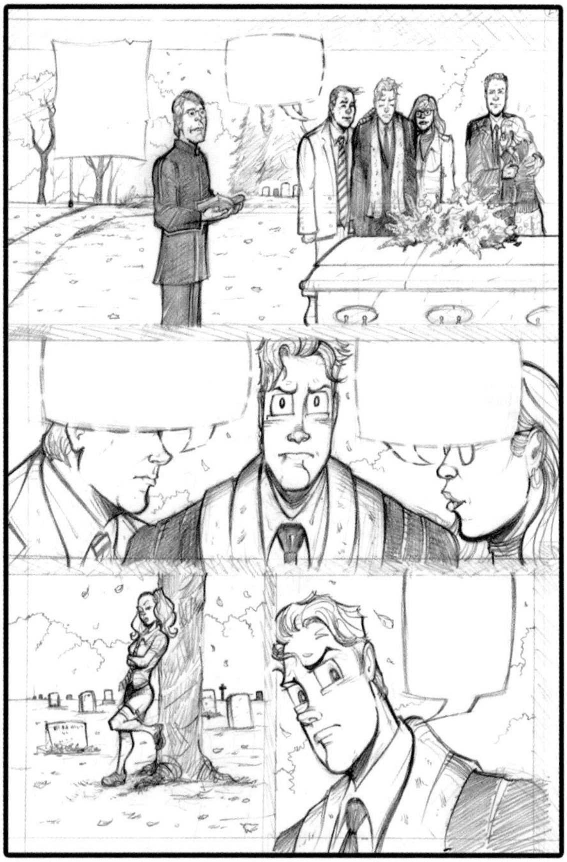

ABOVE: The first step is scripting the page which is usually done through a series of rough thumbnails.

RIGHT: Pencils are next, and unlike many of today's comics, the word balloons and text boxes are hand drawn. Also, H.C.Noel's parents star in this page as Jason's parents.

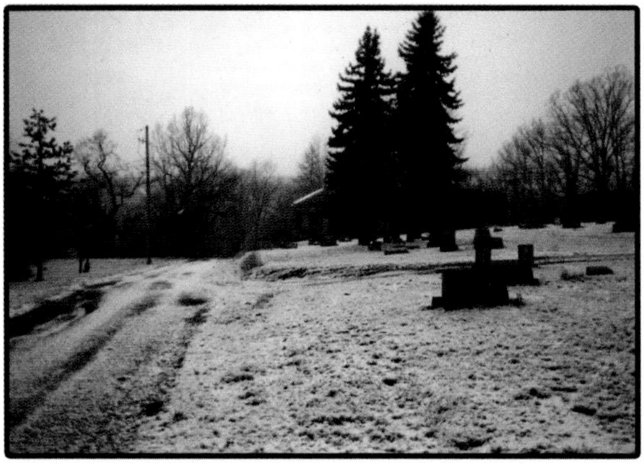

RIGHT: Reference is a great tool for an artist to use, and when I had the chance to visit the same cemetery where "Night of the Living Dead" was filmed I made sure to bring my camera. Sadly, there were no zombies present that day.

Once the final pencils are completed, I ink the artwork and then scan it. All coloring is done in Photoshop and then I hold a black magic ceremony with a one toothed rat, two quarters from the Denver mint, one female virgin and a medium pizza to transform the computerized artwork into a comic book.

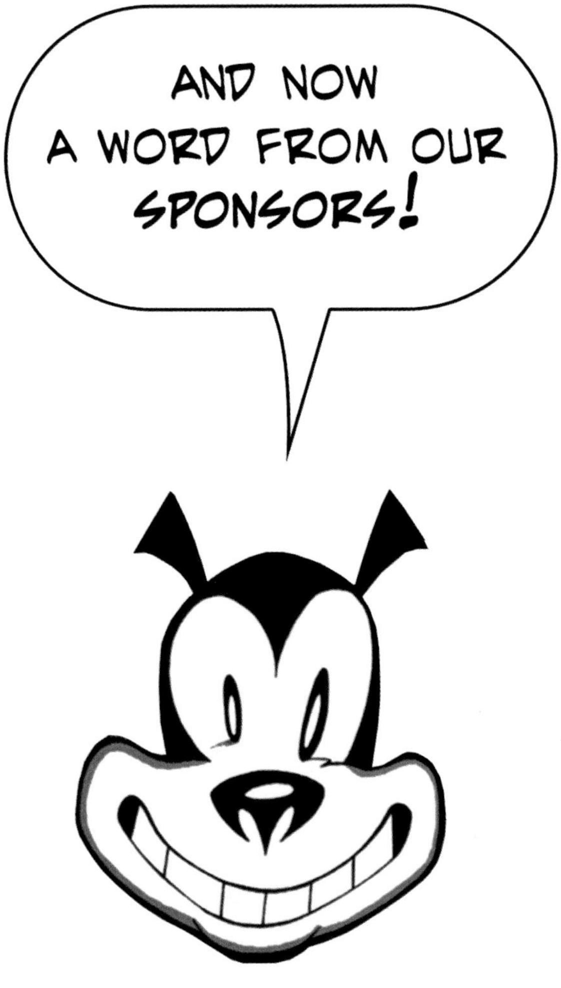
AND NOW A WORD FROM OUR SPONSORS!

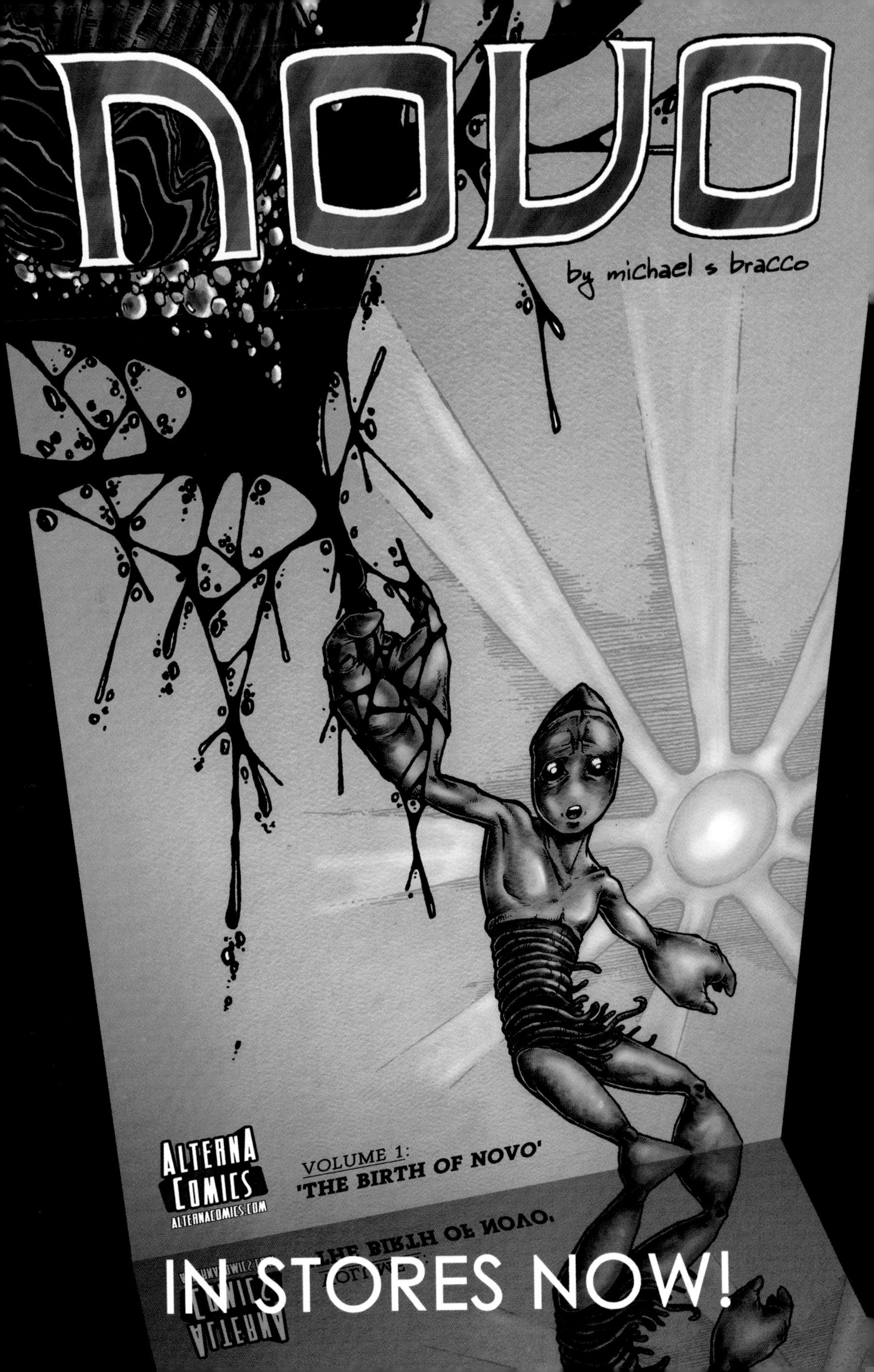
NOVO
by michael s bracco
ALTERNA COMICS
ALTERNACOMICS.COM
VOLUME 1:
'THE BIRTH OF NOVO'
IN STORES NOW!

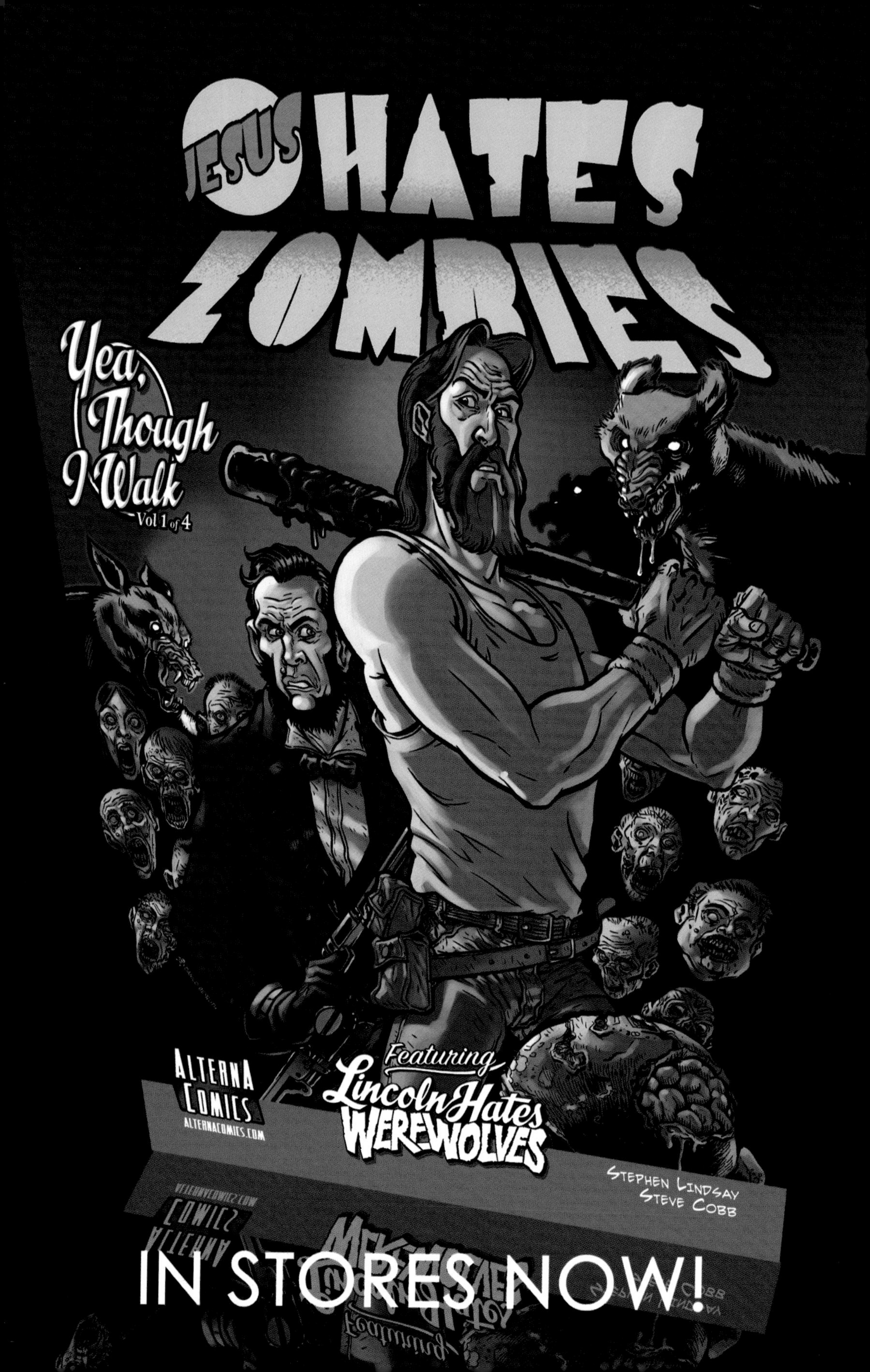
JESUS HATES ZOMBIES
Yea, Though I Walk
Vol 1 of 4
ALTERNA COMICS
ALTERNACOMICS.COM
Featuring
Lincoln Hates WEREWOLVES
Stephen Lindsay
Steve Cobb
IN STORES NOW!

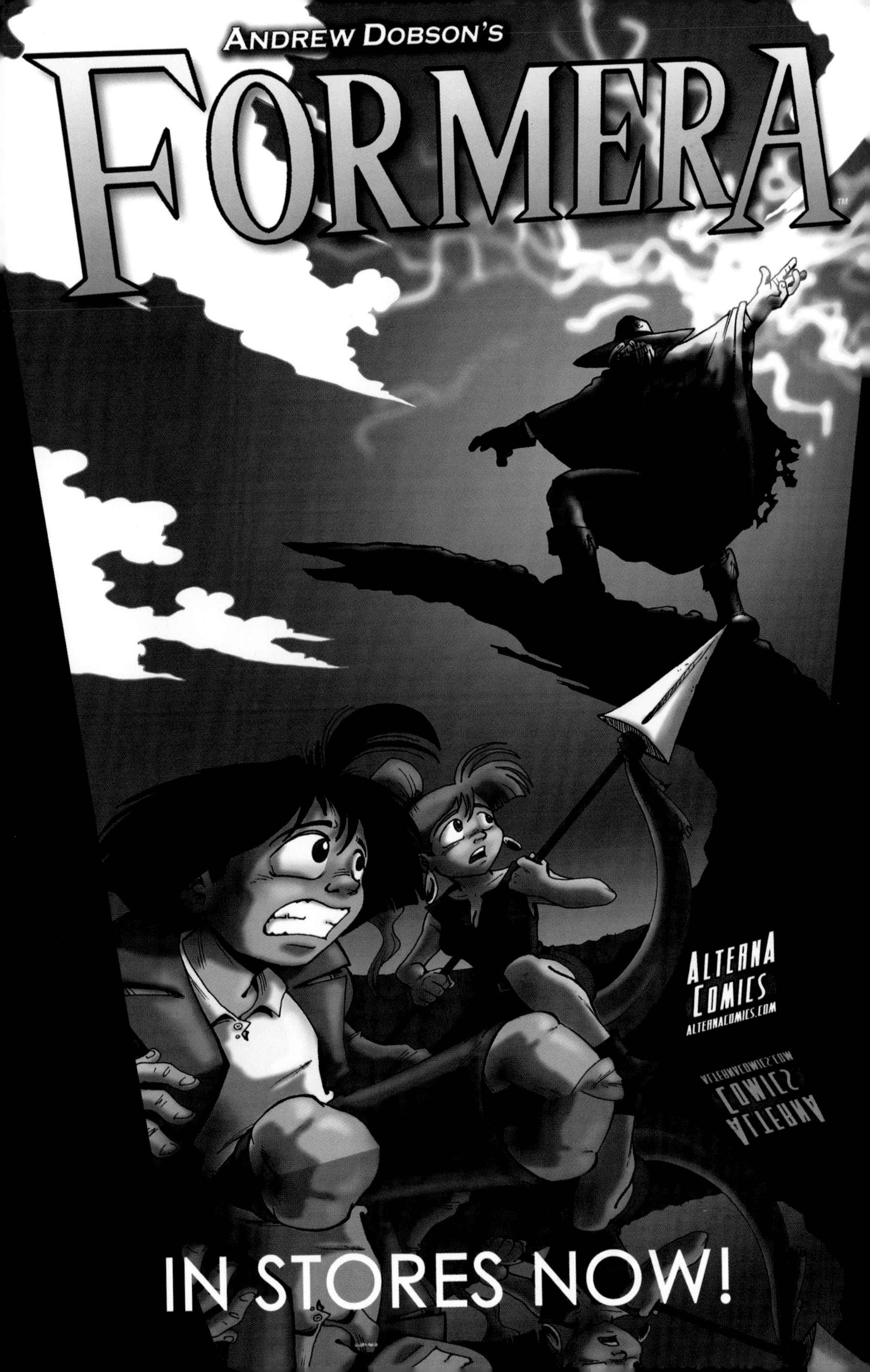

ANDREW DOBSON'S
FORMERA™
ALTERNA COMICS
ALTERNACOMICS.COM
IN STORES NOW!

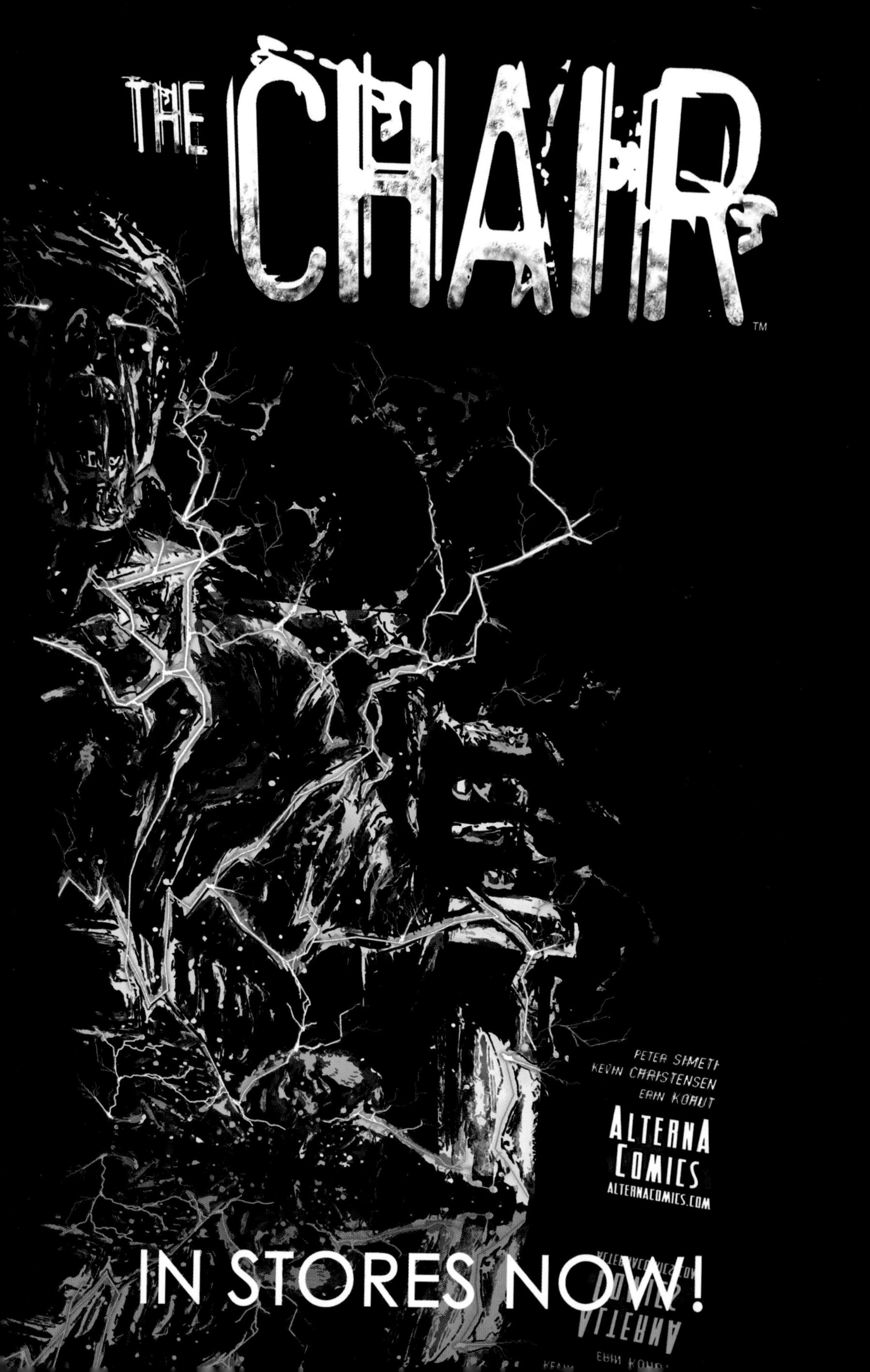

THE CHAIR™
PETER SIMETI
KEVIN CHRISTENSEN
ERIN KOHUT
ALTERNA COMICS
ALTERNACOMICS.COM
IN STORES NOW!

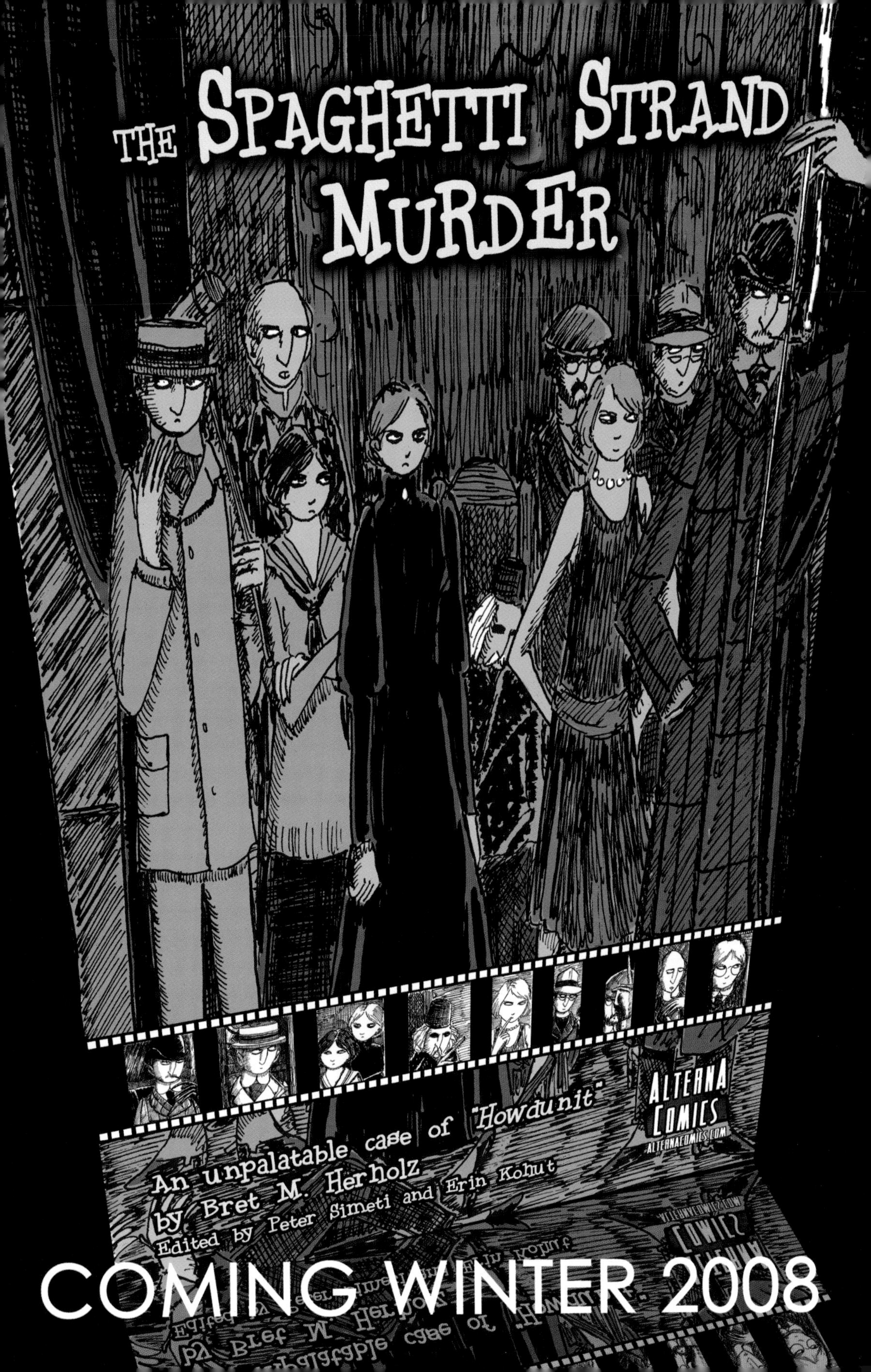

THE SPAGHETTI STRAND MURDER
An unpalatable case of "Howdunit"
by Bret M. Herholz
Edited by Peter Simeti and Erin Kohut
ALTERNA COMICS
ALTERNACOMICS.COM
COMING WINTER 2008

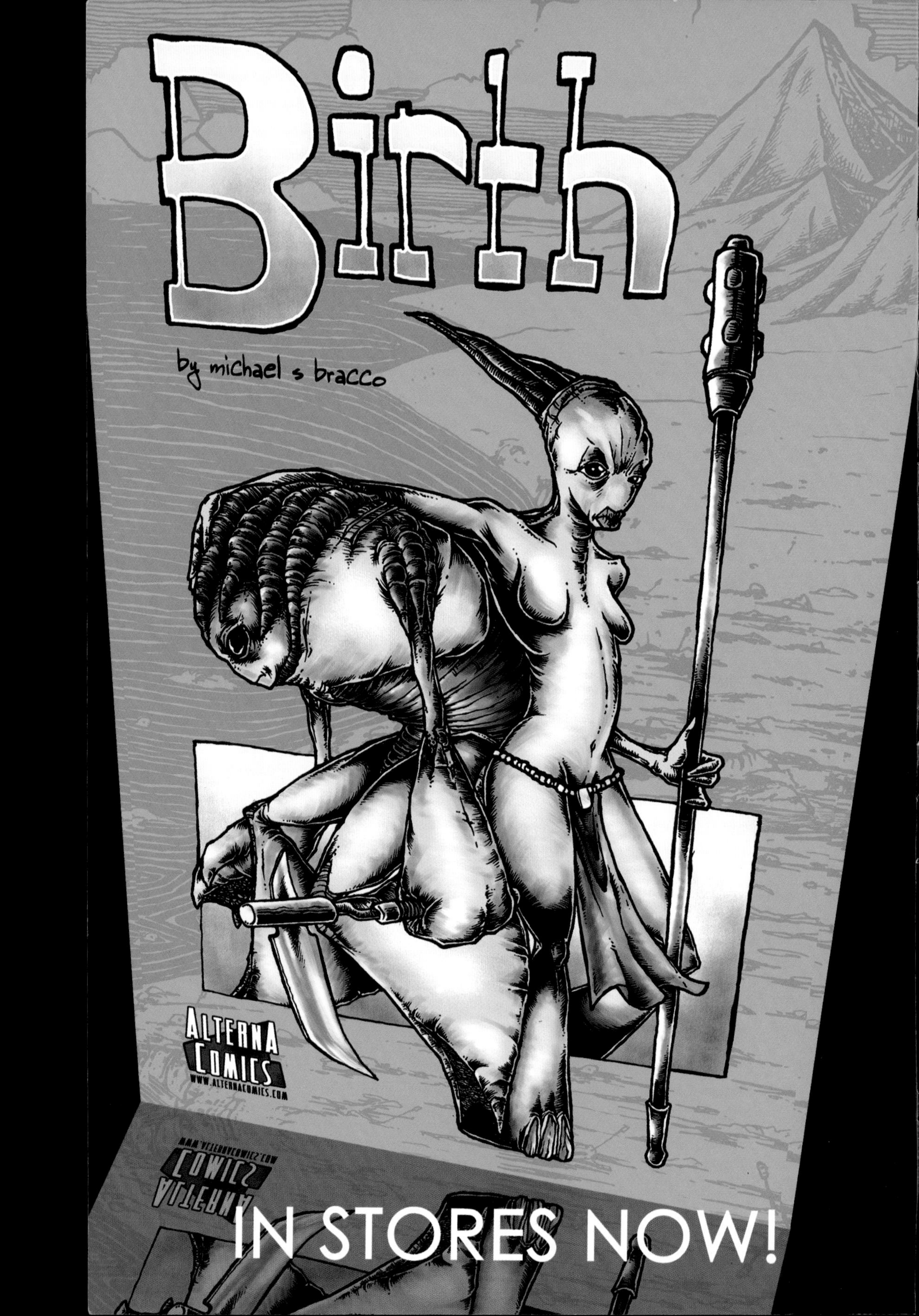

Birth
by michael s bracco
ALTERNA COMICS
WWW.ALTERNACOMICS.COM
IN STORES NOW!

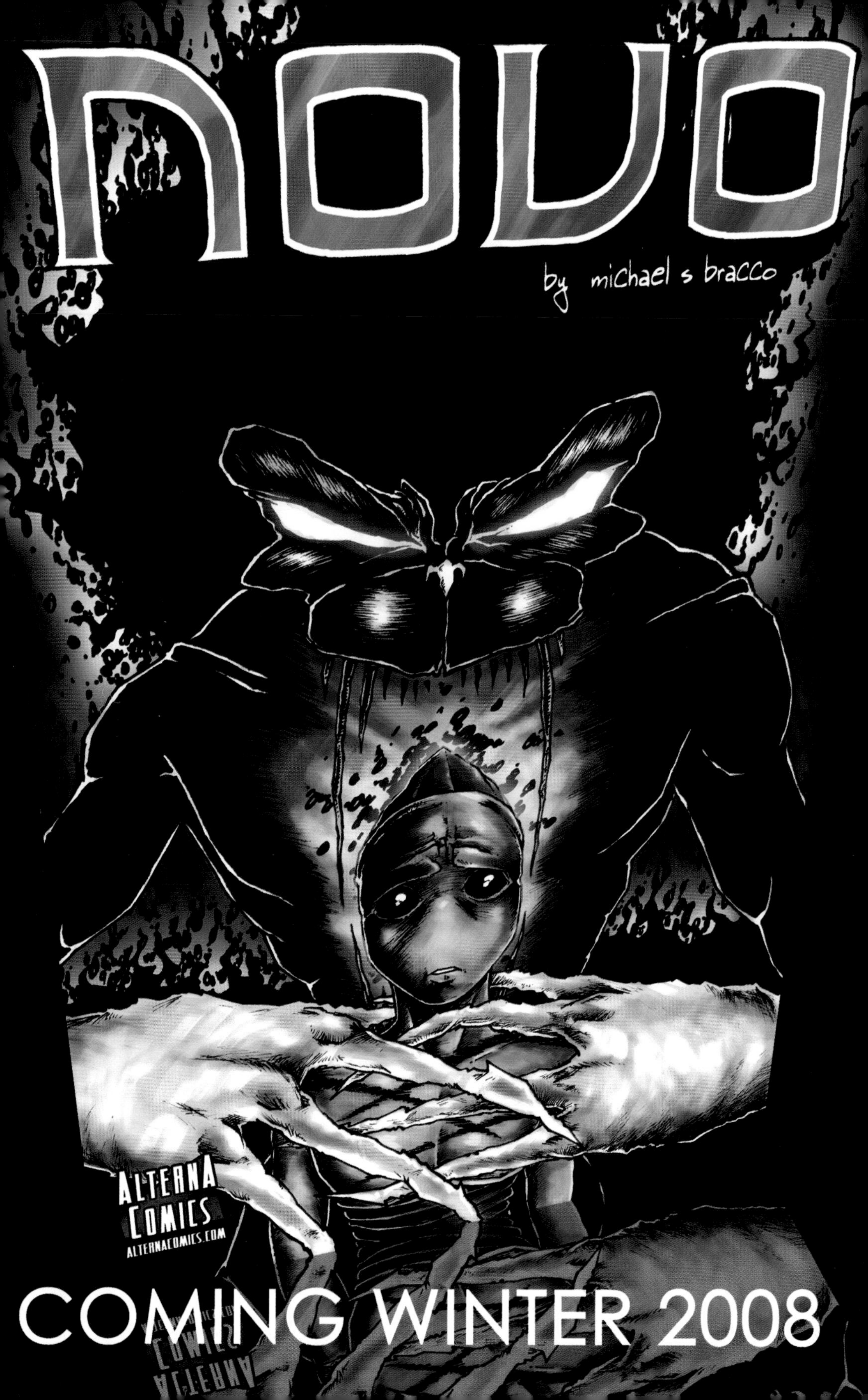
NOVO
by michael s bracco
ALTERNA COMICS
ALTERNACOMICS.COM
COMING WINTER 2008

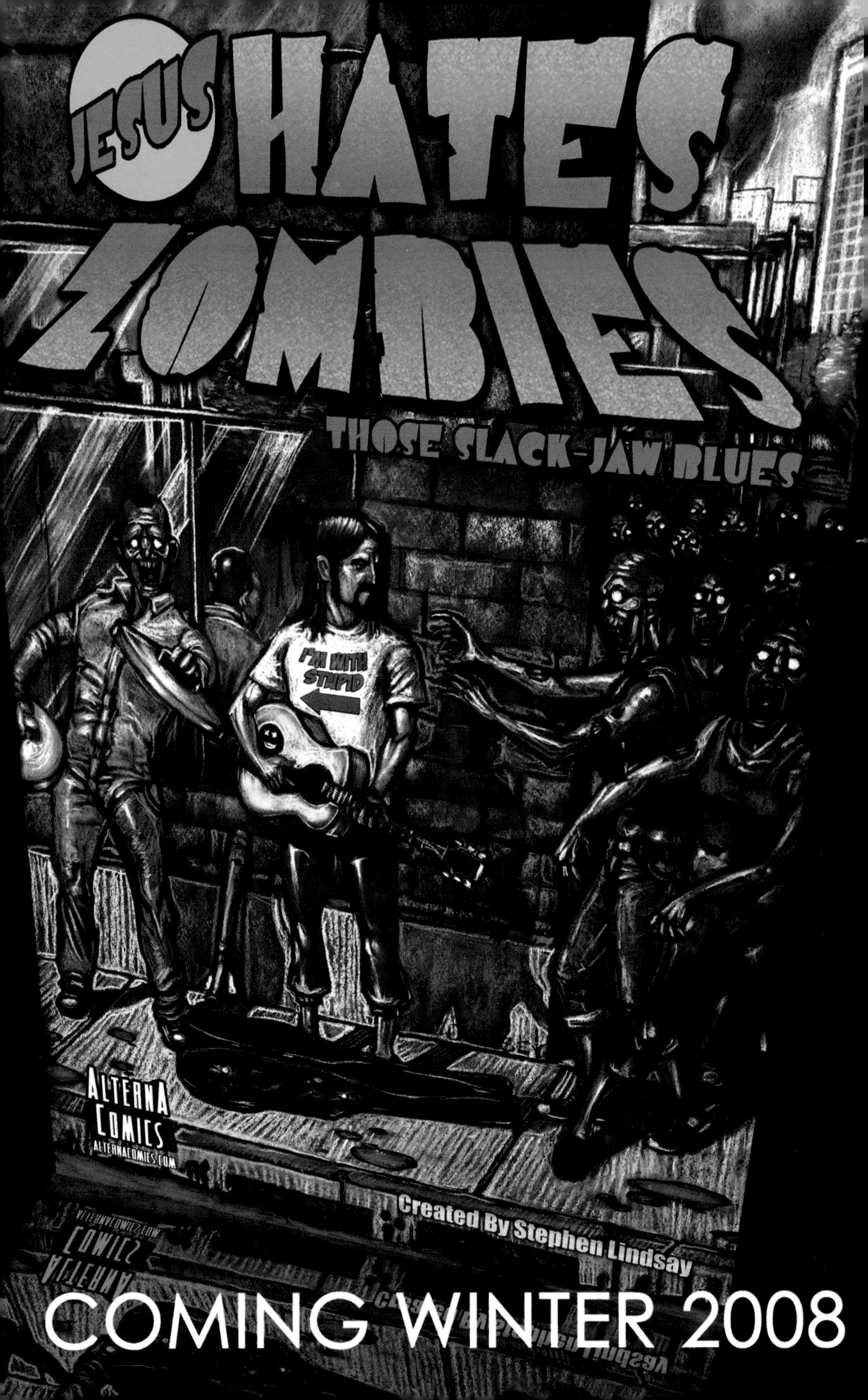
JESUS HATES ZOMBIES
THOSE SLACK-JAW BLUES
I'M WITH STUPID
ALTERNA COMICS
ALTERNACOMICS.COM
Created By Stephen Lindsay
COMING WINTER 2008